AQUAPONICS

PLANS AND INSTRUCTIONS

MEDIA-BED (FLOOD-AND-DRAIN) SYSTEM

2nd Edition

David H Dudley, PMP, PE

Aquaponics Plans and Instructions
Media-Bed (Flood-and-Drain) Systems
2nd Edition

Paperback ISBN: 978-1-68489-048-4
ePub ISBN: 978-1-68489-049-1
Also available for Kindle.

Published by:
Primedia eLaunch LLC

CONTENTS

Dedication. 5

NOTES TO READER 7

INTRODUCTION. 9

PART I   **Aquaponic Fundamentals** **13**
  CHAPTER 1   Aquaponics Overview 15
  CHAPTER 2   Benefits of Aquaponics 19
  CHAPTER 3   History of Aquaponics 23
  CHAPTER 4   Aquaponics Globally and the Big Picture 25
  CHAPTER 5   Toxic Food vs. Healthy Organic Aquaponic Food 47
  CHAPTER 6   The Best Locations for Aquaponics 75
  CHAPTER 7   Nitrogen Cycle 81
  CHAPTER 8   The Different Types of Aquaponic Systems. 89

PART II   **Plants and Fish** **93**
  CHAPTER 9   Plants and Crops — Keys to Success 95
  CHAPTER 10   Fish — Everything You Need to Know 113
  CHAPTER 11   Fish Feed 133

PART III **Components Used in Aquaponics** **153**
  CHAPTER 12   Equipment & Component Overview 155
  CHAPTER 13   Fish Tanks and Ponds 163
  CHAPTER 14   Liner Material. 175
  CHAPTER 15   Plumbing 179
  CHAPTER 16   Making a Water Tight Container 193
  CHAPTER 17   Pumps & Choosing the Right Pump. 197
  CHAPTER 18   Filtration (Mechanical, Biofiltration, Natural) 201
  CHAPTER 19   Growing Media for Plants (Flood-and-Drain System) 211
  CHAPTER 20   Greenhouses 217

Contents Continued Next Page

PART IV   **Flood and Drain System Design and Layout** **231**

     CHAPTER 21   Flood-and-Drain System Instructions & Procedures 233

     CHAPTER 22   Media Grow Bed Drain Options, Drawings, and Information 257

     CHAPTER 23   How to Make a Auto Siphon (Bell Siphon) 265

     CHAPTER 24   Design Plans and Construction Details DIY Flood-and-Drain System 273

     CHAPTER 25   Design Plans and Construction Details
                   Using IBC Containers Flood-and-Drain System. 287

PART V   **Operation and Maintenance** **309**

     CHAPTER 26   Starting, Operating, and Troubleshooting Your Aquaponic System 311

     CHAPTER 27   Water Quality 327

     CHAPTER 28   Fish Breeding, Fish Reproduction, and Raising Your Own Crop of Fish 347

PART VI   **Appendix** **357**

     APPENDIX 1   Helpful Resources 359

     APPENDIX 2   FarmYourSpace.com *Website Topics* 359

     APPENDIX 3   www.CountryBreezeFarm.org 377

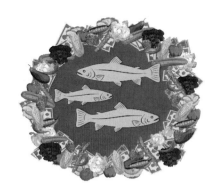

DEDICATION

This book is dedicated to my son, Nathan, and my daughter, Hannah, both of whom I love and cherish more than words could ever describe. Thanks be to God for the blessings you are to me.

This book is created for every person, young and old, employed and unemployed, educated and those with little schooling, who desire to eat truly healthy food, dream of becoming better off financially, who genuinely care about the environment, and aspire to build a happy, successful, and rewarding life. It doesn't matter where you live — in the city, suburbs, or country — this book was written with the hope and intention of enabling you to bring your dreams to fruition, directly where you are in life and location.

If you benefit from this book, would you please leave me a positive review on Amazon? It only takes a moment. Reviews from readers like you tremendously help independent authors, such as me.

Thank you SO much!

NOTES TO READER

Note #1: I appreciate the fact that for some the main objective for acquiring this book was to access the user-friendly, aquaponic system design plans included within and immediately get started on building an aquaponic system. Although I applaud your enthusiasm, I would like to encourage all readers to obtain a good understanding of aquaponics before taking on the construction process. Such will ensure optimum success, prevent much aggravation, and save you money and time.

Great advice on any project is to "start with the end in mind." Staying focused on that goal, and understanding what is involved in achieving that goal, enables us to have greater success. Immediately jumping into a "build" project without a solid foundation of the fundamentals, not knowing what is involved, and with unrealistic expectations is not a prudent strategy, regardless of the undertaking.

With that said, I hope you will invest some time better educating yourself on the material provided within this book before constructing your aquaponic system. Although this book addresses everything one could possibly need to be successful in aquaponics, I want to assure you that it is not necessary to memorize the material in this book. A good engineer, attorney, or physician doesn't have everything memorized, but they are good at finding information fast. This book is laid out in a way that will enable you to find reliable and thorough information you need very quickly, whether it be a question about fish stocking density, water quality, pumps, growing media, troubleshooting, etc.

Furthermore, please allow me to assure you that aquaponics really is not that difficult. With a basic understanding of the fundamentals, anyone can be successful.

Keep in mind, however, that success means different things to different people. For some, success in aquaponics is having a cool hobby and a fun conversation topic to discuss at social gatherings. For others, it means lowering food costs and supplementing their food supply with year-round organically grown healthy produce and fish. For others, it means growing enough extra food to sell, barter, and give to friends/family. For some, having a profitable aquaponic business is the meaning of success.

They are all possible, and I am confident this book will provide you with everything you need to know in order to achieve and enjoy your definition of success in aquaponics.

Note #2: Please understand that aquaponics really is not that difficult. With a basic understanding of the fundamentals, anyone can be successful. Keep in mind, however, that success means different things to different people. For some, success in aquaponics is having a cool hobby and a fun conversation topic to discuss at social gatherings. For others, it means lowering food costs and supplementing their food supply with year-round organically grown healthy produce and fish. For others, it means growing enough extra food to sell, barter, and give to friends/family. For some, having a profitable aquaponic business is the definition of success. Regardless, rest assured that they are all possible with some basic knowledge about aquaponics and application of what you learn.

Note #3: My next project is a series of 'how to' videos showing and explaining every aspect of aquaponics (e.g., building a system, expanding an existing system, build and operational costs, greenhouse options, best plants for the highest profit margin, fish stocking density, fish breeding, maintaining and monitoring your system, achieving and maintaining optimal water quality, troubleshooting and addressing problems, automation, grow lights, pros and cons of media materials, fish ponds and tanks, NFT systems, DWC systems, Flood-and-Drain systems, bartering your harvest, and profiting from aquaponics, etc.). Although these topics are covered extensively within the aquaponic books I have published to date, I realize that some people learn better through videos, and so I want to address these topics in a video format.

Please check the website www. FarmYourSpace.com periodically for these forthcoming videos.

Note #4: I chose not to provide references for every statement made within this book for several reasons. First of all, I have discovered that it is extremely rare for readers to search out a reference. Therefore, I did not want to interrupt the flow of text with references which would seldom be used.

Secondly, all statements and facts made within this book are easily verifiable. One simply needs to do quick Internet search if they want to verify anything stated within this book.

Lastly, references would increase the page count and book cost, which are unfavorable options.

Note #5: I greatly appreciate that you are checking out this book. I have invested several years of my life, made tremendous sacrifices, and invested a lot of money creating this book. It is rewarding to know that all of that hard work and time will benefit others, our environment, local communities, and produce much needed healthy food. If benefited from this book, as I trust you will, I would GREATLY appreciate it very much if you would please give this book a positive review. Positive reviews greatly help small independent self-publishing authors such as me. Self-publishing authors don't have a large publishing company, so marketing options are limited. A positive review goes a long way in helping to promote a book, which in turn spreads the word out about all of the benefits that aquaponics provides to others, local communities, and the environment. Thank you SO much!

INTRODUCTION

While aquaponics has been around for thousands of years, only during the past century, and especially the past decade, has it really taken off. There are good reasons as to why aquaponics is on the rise worldwide. The noble benefits associated with it being a sustainable farming practice, requiring very little water, and having the multitude of other environmentally friendly advantages makes it an extremely appealing agricultural method. Although these are persuasive forces, when it comes right down to it, most people get into aquaponics for more personal reasons, such as the attraction of having a constantly available supply of healthy, organic food; to lower their food costs; the ability to produce much higher yields compared to those of traditional farming; having a known food supply with a much higher nutrient density content than mass-produced crops; and/or the benefits of being able to convert a small part of their property into a viable revenue-generating space.

During the past century, and even more so over the last two decades, the appeal of aquaponics has become increasingly more popular because of the readily available assimilation of information from the internet; increasing media attention; the advancement of new technologies (i.e., plastics, fiberglass, electric pumps); and the relatively low cost of materials.

Additionally, as people become more concerned about the high cost of food and more educated about our toxic food system and the detrimental impact it has upon their family's health, they seek better ways to meet their dietary requirements. Aquaponics offers the perfect solution to all of these concerns.

Indeed, raising your own healthy food is an extremely rewarding process. Saving big money while consuming your own homegrown, organic healthy food at much higher nutrient density content than conventional grocery store food is priceless; and aquaponics in of itself is really an interesting process. An aquaponics setup can be as small as a 20-gallon aquarium or as big as several acres.

Furthermore, you will find that aquaponics is a stimulating conversation topic for people from all walks of life, and most everyone is eager to learn more about it. You will also get many requests from people wanting to see your system in operation. This social element adds even more joy beyond the satisfaction derived from growing your own healthy food.

I have also thoroughly enjoyed bringing my family into aquaponics and teaching my children many of the valuable lessons associated with the operation (i.e. plants, fish, water dynamics, harvest, work ethic, responsibilities, business lessons, etc.). Aquaponics can be a fun family affair and a wonderful way to connect with your spouse and children. Aquaponics truly is a win-win enterprise all the way around for many reasons.

I fell in love with aquaponics for all of the above reasons. As a professionally licensed civil engineer, with a strong background in nutrition/dietetics, decades of experience in aquaculture, a passion for vegetable gardening, hydroponics and vertical gardening, I spent years studying aquaponics from all these perspectives.

I discovered many ways to set up and operate an aquaponics system. I researched every aquaponic method and system out there while on my own journey to discover the best way to raise healthy, organic, nutrient-rich food at maximum yields. After successfully achieving those goals I began searching for the best way to transfer those methods into a commercial operation that would produce a respectable profit margin. During the process, and while pursuing a parallel career path serving as the Construction Manager on the Oklahoma Aquarium project, designing a $5M aquaculture farm for white sturgeon, serving as the Engineering Manager overseeing four large aquaculture farms for the largest caviar producer in the United States, and designing a large fishing clinic facility for the U.S. Dept. of Wildlife, I have been blessed to become not only an expert in aquaponics, but a consultant in the industry. I have helped many people not only get into aquaponics but turn their operations into a profitable business. I trust this book will help you achieve success in aquaponics, as well. The more wholesome, organic healthy food we can make available, the better for all.

Over the years it has become quite apparent that most people desiring to get into aquaponics are of the Do-It-Yourself camp. Yes, some do purchase package units, but the vast majority of aquaponic enthusiasts build their own systems, either because they cannot afford an expensive packaged system or because they see the simplicity of it. The problem—and why there are so many different types of aquaponic setups out there—is that a lot of information on how to develop and maintain an aquaponics operation is either too expensive for most people to acquire, requires a substantial sacrifice of time to learn (university courses or weeks at an onsite training course), or is found to be based upon information that is not reliable, thorough, or user-friendly.

Seeing the need for a one-stop source for "everything you need to know," laid out in one efficient, easy-to-understand resource is what inspired me to prepare this book (a "how-to" instructional guide). I have made every attempt to cover all aspects of aquaponics and present the information in a way that everyone can understand. The magnitude of all that is involved can seem somewhat mind boggling at first, but you should not get discouraged or feel over- whelmed by it all. Quite frankly, it really is a simple process once you learn the fundamentals. This book not only addresses the fundamentals but shows you how to do aquaponics using the most efficient and effective means possible, whether you are doing it just to supplement your dietary needs, feed your family, or to make it a profitable business.

In addition to being a licensed professional engineer who loves farming, as mentioned above, I was also working in the aquaculture/aquaponics industry which provided me the opportunity to gain much experience about critical life support systems and very unique aquatic construction methods. Overseeing four large aquaculture farms that were providing 80 percent of the caviar consumed in the U.S., as well as shipping fish meat and caviar all over the world, I have been directly responsible for overseeing all infrastructure and equipment needed to provide optimal conditions for rearing fish.

I obtained a bachelor's degree in nutrition/dietetics in the 1980s after which I worked as a professional nutritionist for several years before returning to school to study engineering. However, my interest in nutrition has remained high over the years. I have always enjoyed researching and reading about nutrition, and over the past two decades I have invested much time acquiring additional nutrition and health-related certificates. As a result, as you read this book you will find I could not resist the temptation to provide additional information regarding the health benefits of aquaponics and to call attention to some of the problems associated with our current food industry.

My hope and intention is for this book to provide you with the knowledge and confidence needed to achieve success in the most efficient cost effective way possible. I believe that you will find that I have covered all issues associated with aquaponics in an easy to understand user-friendly approach so as to meet that objective.

On one final note, I am in the process of creating a website at www.FarmYourSpace.com which will have additional valuable information posted such as photos and videos related to aquaponics, vertical gardening techniques, and other beneficial ideas which will further help you efficiently achieve optimal success growing food within the space you have available, and how to get the most out of your space, regardless of size. I would encourage you to visit the website.

Thank you for checking out this book. I welcome your feedback and comments. My desire as an aquaponics consultant is to continue improving the resources I have made available, and to create additional aquaponic resources, so as to best assist everyone who has an interest in aquaponics. Aquaponics is, by all accounts, most certainly a worthwhile endeavor. It is also made up of a special community of people who typically are better able to see the 'big picture' in regards to the problems associated with our current food supply, appreciate good health, care about the environmental health of our planet, and desire to improve their economic situation. I truly hope this book is the catalyst that brings your dreams to fruition. I wish you the very best of success.

If you benefit from this book, would you please leave me a positive review on Amazon? It only takes a moment. Reviews from readers like you tremendously help small independent authors, such as me.

Thank you SO much!

PART 1

Aquaponic Fundamentals

CHAPTER 1

Aquaponics Overview

Overview

Aquaponics is essentially the combination of Aquaculture and Hydroponics. Aquaculture, also known as aquafarming, is the farming of marine or freshwater food fish or shellfish—such as oysters, clams, salmon, and trout—under controlled conditions. Hydroponics is a method of growing plants using mineral nutrient solutions, in water, without soil. Terrestrial plants may be grown with their roots either in the mineral nutrient solution only or in an inert medium, such as perlite, gravel, mineral wool, expanded clay pebbles or coconut husk.

Both aquaculture and hydroponics have some operational downsides. Hydroponics requires expensive nutrients to feed the plants and also requires periodic flushing of the systems—a process that can lead to waste disposal issues. Re-circulating aquaculture needs to have excess nutrients removed from the system; normally, this means that a percentage of the water is removed, generally on a daily basis. This nutrient rich water then needs to be disposed of and replaced with clean fresh water.

While re-circulating aquaculture (raising fish) and hydroponics (growing plants) are both efficient methods of producing food, when we look at combining the two, their individual negative aspects are turned into positives. The positive aspects of both aquaculture and hydroponics are retained, and the negative aspects no longer exist. Aquaponics can be either a simple or a very complex operation. The plants extract the water and nutrients they need to grow, thus cleaning the water for the fish. There are bacteria that live on the surface of the growbed media. These bacteria convert ammonia wastes from the fish into nitrates that can be used by the plants. The conversion of ammonia into nitrates is often termed "the nitrogen cycle." There are three distinct types of aquaponic systems. They are Nutrient Film Technique (NFT),

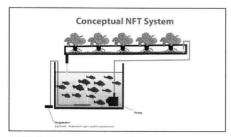

FIGURE 1. Nutrient Film Technique (NFT)

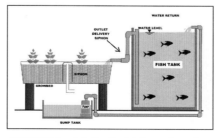

FIGURE 2. Media Bed (also referred to as Flood-and-Drain)

FIGURE 3. Deep-Water Culture (DWC)

Media Bed (also referred to as Flood-and-Drain), and Deep-Water Culture (DWC). See Figures 1, 2, 3. Although these are not the only three designs, they are the most common.

Additionally, some systems integrate more than one type of aquaponic system. For instance, a fish tank used for a media bed system may have a floating raft with plants being grow on it, making it also a DWC system. See Figure 4

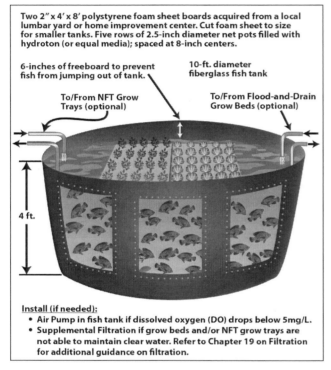

Two 2" x 4' x 8' polystyrene foam sheet boards acquired from a local lumbar yard or home improvement center. Cut foam sheet to size for smaller tanks. Five rows of 2.5-inch diameter net pots filled with hydroton (or equal media); spaced at 8-inch centers.

6-inches of freeboard to prevent fish from jumping out of tank.

10-ft. diameter fiberglass fish tank

To/From NFT Grow Trays (optional)

To/From Flood-and-Drain Grow Beds (optional)

4 ft.

Install (if needed):
- Air Pump in fish tank if dissolved oxygen (DO) drops below 5mg/L.
- Supplemental Filtration if grow beds and/or NFT grow trays are not able to maintain clear water. Refer to Chapter 19 on Filtration for additional guidance on filtration.

FIGURE 4.

Nutrient Film Technique

Best Use:

NFT systems are popular in the commercial industry because of their space efficiency and lower labor costs. Because crops can also be grown on a vertical plane (or shelf), they are easily accessible and harvestable. Most popular with hydroponic production, this method is best suited for leafy greens. This design is not suited for large plants as their root masses may clog the channel and their top-heavy weight may

not be supported, as the roots are unable to anchor the plant.

Pros

- Continuous supply of water, oxygen, and nutrients.
- Space efficient.
- Easy to access.
- Lower labor inputs.

Cons

- Susceptible to clogging.
- Higher possibility of water temperature fluctuation.
- Plant diversity is limited (mostly used for lettuce type plants).

Media Beds (Flood-and-Drain)

The media bed form of aquaponics uses containers filled with some type of media material such as gravel or clay pebbles to support the plants by via the roots establishing an anchor in the media. The bed is flooded and drained of nutrient rich water from the fish tank to give the plants the nutrients and oxygen they need. The media enables the plants to establish support, so they don't fall over. The media also serves as a biofilter, whereby with the help of beneficial bacteria, waste from the fish tank (which would otherwise by harmful to the fish) is broken down and provides nutrients for the plants.

Best Use

This technique is the most widely used method for aquaponics. It is inexpensive, simple to put together, can be used to grow a wide variety of fish and plants, and can produce a great deal of product (fish and plants) in a small area.

Pros

- Grows larger crops well.
- Good biofiltration.

- Simple and inexpensive to implement.
- Media acts as filtration.
- Great for small to mid-size aquaponic operations.

Cons

- Not the best method for large operations.
- Requires more cleaning.
- Higher maintenance and labor.

Deep Water Culture (DWC)

Also known as raft or float systems, this method uses floating rafts to suspend plant roots into nutrient rich and aerated water. The plant roots grow directly into a pool of water. Since there is no media to capture and process the solid wastes, filtration techniques must be built into the design. This necessitates more advanced aquaculture techniques and system requirements, leading to higher upfront costs.

Best Use

This design is common with commercial production of green leafy vegetables (e.g., lettuce, chard, kale, etc.). Because there is much more water in the system, drastic nutrient and temperature fluctuations are much less likely to occur. It is best suited for warmer climates because although it would resist daily temperature swings, heating the water in colder climates is costly. In addition, larger root zone plants can be used and removing plants is much easier than in media beds. Since plants do not have a way to anchor themselves, taller plants cannot be grown in the system without providing support.

Pros:

- Commercial scalability.
- Productive.
- Good for warmer tropical climates.
- Inexpensive.
- Not as susceptible to large temperature and nutrient fluctuations.

Cons:

- Filtration demands.
- Labor demand and cost.
- Space efficiency.
- Taller plants cannot be grown without providing support.

Growbeds, filled with a media such as gravel or expanded clay pebbles, are a common method of growing plants in a media bed aquaponic system, but there are many different methods that can be used. In fact, any method of hydroponic growing can be adapted to aquaponics. Plants can be grown in floating foam rafts that sit on the water surface. Vegetables can also be grown using N.F.T. (Nutrient Film Technique), or through various other methods using a "run to waste" style of growing. This is done by circulating the fish tank water through the media where vegetables are grown.

Many different species of fish can be grown in an aquaponic system, and your species selection will depend on a number of factors that include your local government regulations. Quite high stocking densities of fish can be grown in an aquaponic system, and, because of the recirculating nature of the systems, very little water is used. Research has shown that an aquaponic system uses about 1/10 of the water used to grow vegetables in the ground. An aquaponic system can be incredibly productive. For instance, 125 lbs. (approx. 57kg) of fish and hundreds of kilograms of vegetables can be produced within 6 months in an area the size of an average carport, 13-ft x 26-ft (approx. 4 m x 8 m). Best of all, a typical small aquaponics system as was just described requires no bending, weeding or fertilizers, and uses only about the same power it takes to operate two household light bulbs.

Summary

Aquaponics consists of two main parts, with the aquaculture part for raising aquatic animals and the hydroponics part for growing plants. Aquatic effluents, resulting from uneaten feed and waste from raising aquatic animals such as fish, accumulate in most aquaculture systems. In high concentrations, without proper filtration, the effluent-rich water becomes toxic to the aquatic animals, but these effluents, in controlled aquaponic operations, provide nutrients essential for plant growth. The plants (along with beneficial bacteria in the grow bed) clean the water for return to the fish tank.

It is important to have a clear understanding of your purpose for getting into aquaponics. Consider the pros and cons of each type of system, when evaluating which type of aquaponic method is most suitable to your goals.

CHAPTER 2

Benefits of Aquaponics

Sustainability Benefits of Aquaponics Farming

There are many benefits to aquaponics. As a matter of fact, the advantages of aquaponic farming have been clearly demonstrated to have substantial environmental, social, economic, community, and personal health benefits. This chapter addresses those benefits.

- Tremendous conservation of water is achieved through water reuse and recycling. Aquaponics preserves our fresh water resources and can produce food in water scarce environments. Aquaponics uses up to 90 percent less water than does traditional soil-based farming.
- Organic fertilization of plants is accomplished with natural fish emulsion.
- The elimination of solid waste is accomplished efficiently and naturally, as compared to most other types of farming.
- The reduction of needed cropland to produce crops. Aquaponic farming methods yield larger harvest per square foot of grow space compared to soil based farming yield. In soil, plants compete for limited nutrients.
- Healthier plants with a much higher nutrient density. In aquaponics, nutrients are constantly produced throughout the system. These nutrients

are delivered to the plant roots via the water column. Since there is no competition for nutrients, plants can be grown very close together with no nutrient loss.

- The overall reduction of the environmental footprint of crop production. Aquaponics uses less land and can even be applied indoors in urban settings to produce fresh fish and organic produce.
- Aquaponically grown produce is fresh, guaranteed organic, and has minimal impact on the environment.
- Aquaponics systems are pure and healthy. If we used chemical pesticides, herbicides, or fertilizers, our fish would die. Not only do you know for certain your produce is chemical free but you know that your fish are fresh and clean as well! No mercury or heavy metals are present in your food supply.
- Greenhouses, when integrated into aquaponics, ensure optimal dependable food production, food security against possible contamination, and vast reduction of travel time, distribution and fuel costs.
- Building small efficient commercial installations near markets reduces food transportation miles,

which means less pollution and a reduction in the consumption of natural resources.

- Reduction of pathogens that often plague aquaculture production systems.
- Reduction of erosion by eliminating the need to plough the soil.

Feed Conversion Ratios

Animals must be fed. Raising animals and growing the feed to sustain them takes land and tremendous amounts of energy resources. Obviously, minimizing these requirements is best for our planet as a whole. With such in mind, it is encouraging to see how raising fish has the lowest negative footprint over that of other animal products. Following is a list of the average pounds of feed needed to produce 1 lb. of product for various animal groups:

- Fish = 1.7 lbs
- Chicken = 2.4 lbs
- Turkey = 5.2 lbs
- Pork = 4.9 lbs
- Lamb = 8.0 lbs
- Beef = 9.0 lbs

Summary of Benefits

- Healthy food (100 percent organic food).
- Saves money.
- Helps the environment.+
- Grow a tremendous amount of food in a relatively small area.
- Uses very little energy and can even be solar- or wind-powered should the "grid" become unusable or undesirable.
- Grow your own food year-round for your own needs, to use for bartering, or sell to others. This option could be criticallyimportant should there be a disruption in commerce or should you desire to become more self-reliant.

Benefits of Aquaponics— Itemized

Aquaponics is a high efficiency food-production method for growing food year round, in any climate. Following is an itemized list of aquaponic benefits:

- Aquaponics is the most energy efficient farming method in the world.
- Most aquaponic systems can be modularized for ease of construction and operation.
- It is relatively easy to replace mechanical components.
- Automated water circulation—plants never need watering.
- Waist high work area for efficiency and reduced injury potential.
- No weeding necessary.
- No need to clean medium/gravel.
- No need to clean fish tanks.
- No need for pesticides, herbicides, or fungicides.
- No hormones, harsh chemicals or antibiotics used.
- Ability to grow a wide variety of plants based on preference or demand.
- Entire system can be automated and remotely monitored to notify you if any needs arise.
- Waste produced is nontoxic and is a very efficient fertilizer for plants growing in ground.
- Solar or alternative-energy power can be utilized.
- Uses 90 percent less water than does traditional in-ground growing methods.
- Precious topsoil is not needed.
- Utilizes locally available inexpensive materials for construction.
- Can be installed in almost any location.
- Food can be harvested quickly and often.
- Does not require a higher education or skilled labor to operate.
- Time demands and labor needs are small once operational.
- Can be installed indoors in warehouses, basements, etc., with the use of grow lights.
- Excellent Return on Investment—three to five years depending on markets and varieties of vegetables grown.
- Systems are expandable and scalable.

- Can be used as an educational tool. The educational component, teaching others about aquaponics, can also be an additional source of income.
- It is a fast growing food system that provides the freshest produce.
- Transportation costs are negligible.
- Produce plantings can be seasonally adjusted to maximize their value in the marketplace
- Additional enhanced methods for aquaponics, including revolutionary greenhouse cover and specialized induction lighting, speeds production by its ideal growing conditions.
- Aquaponics growing produces healthy food at the maximum possible growth rate.
- Healthy organic food is in high demand. This food will save your family money and enhance your family's health. Extra food can be sold, or used to barter a good value on a variety of goods and services provided by others.

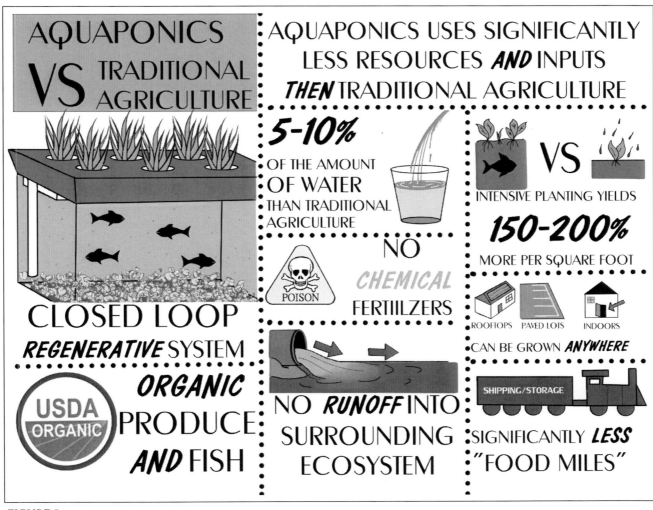

FIGURE 5.

FOOD MILES

WHAT ARE THEY AND HOW DO THEY AFFECT OUR WORLD?

TIME + DISTANCE FROM THE POINT & TIME WHERE FOOD IS **GROWN** TO WHERE IT IS **CONSUMED**. THE SMALLER, THE BETTER!!

AMERICAN FOOD TRAVELS AN **AVERAGE** OF 1,500 TO 2,500 MILES FROM FARM TO TABLE

GROWING FOOD CLOSER TO **HOME** ALLOWS US TO HAVE FRESHER FOODS AND MORE VARIETIES OF FOODS

60-70% OF THE COST OF YOUR FOOD GOES TO THE **PRODUCTION INPUTS**

(FERTILIZER, OIL/GAS, WATER, ETC.), TRANSPORTATION AND STORAGE THAT USE **LIMITED** RESOURCES, PETROCHEMICALS, & GENERATE HARMFUL POLLUTANTS.

FOOD MILES ARE AMONG THE FASTEST-GROWING SOURCES OF AIR POLLUTION **WORLDWIDE**

FRUITS AND VEGETABLES ALLOWED TO **GROW TO FULL RIPENESS** HAVE MORE NUTRITIONAL VALUE THAN CONVENTIONAL PRODUCE HARVESTED EARLY AND RIPENED WITH CHEMICAL GASSES IN TRANSPORT AND STORAGE

FIGURE 6.

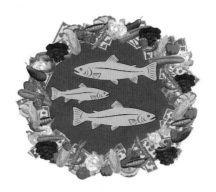

CHAPTER 3

History of Aquaponics

Beginnings of Aquaponics

Aquaponics has ancient roots, although there is some debate concerning its first use in history. However, the confirmed history of aquaponics goes back over 1,500 years.

Most scholars and anthropologists believe that the notion of using fish waste to fertilize plants has its roots in early Asian and South American civilizations. For instance, in early Asia, the existence of cultivated rice in fields, in combination with fish, is an example of early aquaponics. These farming systems employed a system of integrated aquaculture in which finfish, catfish, ducks and plants co-existed.

The ducks were housed in cages over the finfish ponds, and then the finfish processed the uneaten food and waste from the ducks. In a lower pond, the catfish lived on the wastes that had flowed from the finfish pond. The water from the catfish ponds was used to irrigate rice and vegetable crops.

The Inca's of Peru also practiced a form of aquaponics. They dug oval ponds near their mountain dwellings, leaving an island in the center. After the ponds filled, they added fish. Migratory geese would fly in to forage from the water surrounding while roosting on the island. Fish were readily at hand, natural fertilizer was left behind by the geese This

FIGURE 7. *The Tomb of Nakht, 1500 BC, contains a tilapia hieroglyph just above the head of the central figure.*

system supplied food to more people in the Peruvian highlands than had any other method of farming.

Another reference explains it this way: Early Aztecs cultivated agricultural islands known as *chinampa* for agricultural use. In this system, plants were raised on stationary islands in lake shallows formed by waste materials dredged from the chinampa canals and surrounding cities. The canals and lake shallows irrigated the plants.

Aquaponics Today

In recent years, aquaponics has gained in popularity due to ecological benefits and easy methods for establishing a sustainable farming system that provides higher yields than do traditional farming methods. The purpose is to preserve water and to reduce pollution in waterways that receive chemicals and fertilizers from traditional methods. Current methods help reduce water pollution by recycling water and wastes, thus making recycled water available for other uses.

Aquaponics is one of the fastest growing segments of agriculture and is becoming more popular at an astonishing rate. Aquaponic growers range from those with small garage and backyard operations to commercial endeavors employing large tank systems for culturing fish combined with greenhouse and open-environment systems for plant production. Aquaponics' current popularity stems from people's interest in participating in sustainable and urban applications of agriculture, and from the advantages provided when you "grow your own healthy more affordable organic food."

CHAPTER 4

Aquaponics Globally and the Big Picture

Worldwide Aquaponics

U.S. sales of organic food and beverages grew from $1 billion in 1990 to $26.7 billion in 2010. The demand for organic food is expected to increase by 16% a year to an estimated 323.56 billion by 2024 according to Market Research.

Consumers are demanding more from organic food products; they are increasingly looking at ethical sourcing, traceability, the carbon footprint, sustainability, and corporate social responsibility when making their food buying decisions.

Aquaponics offers an ideal solution. In a nutshell, aquaponics is a sustainable healthy food production alternative that aims to conserve and reduce the amount of unnecessary resources. It allows virtually anyone to produce his/her own organic food while maintaining a sustainable way of life, at a low cost. This method of food production combines aquaculture and agriculture without the use of soil. Plants, fish, herbs, fruits, and vegetables to thrive in this system. Aquaponics uses only 10 percent of the water of that used for traditional food production systems. Furthermore, aquaponics uses no unhealthy chemicals. Chemicals used in traditional agricultural methods have proven to be harmful to people and the environment.

One of the most beneficial aspects of aquaponics is that virtually anyone set up an aquaponics system. Aquaponics mimics the ecosystems found in nature, to create a 'perfect' balance for plants and animals. Combining fish and plant production, this system allows for optimum growth by providing each species the nutrients that it needs. The plants provide the fish with clean, purified water while waste from the fish tank provides the plants the nutrients they need to thrive. Although aquaponics may seem quite complicated at first, it is basically a simple cycle between the plants and the fish.

This method of sustainable food production does not stop at a reduction in water usage. Recycled materials, such as plastic drums, containers, and pipes are often used as equipment for these systems. Wood, a renewable resource, is often used to construct other components of the aquaponic system. This strategy or reducing water usage, using renewable and recyclable material, and provides a more sustainable way to produce healthy food at its finest.

Seriously disturbing weather and rain patterns happen globally. Massive crop failures, due to drought, are quite common.

Even the so-called 'drought resistant' genetically modified crops are not immune to the major droughts that ravage our planet. Conventional agriculture, whether it be organic, GMO or something in between, depends on reservoirs with increasing use demands and rapidly depleting underground water supplies. The vast majority of fertilizer used in agriculture today is made from natural gas and oil dependent feedstock. All of these ingredients are finite; meaning they are limited and will keep going up in price until they are eventually depleted. The cost is always passed on to the consumer.

In many parts of the world, the cost for basic staple foods already exceeds personal incomes. As a result, hunger has become a normal daily experience for many people because food grown conventionally is becoming too expensive, and conventional agriculture is vulnerable to unpredictable weather. Food insecurity and hunger is becoming a reality for everyone.

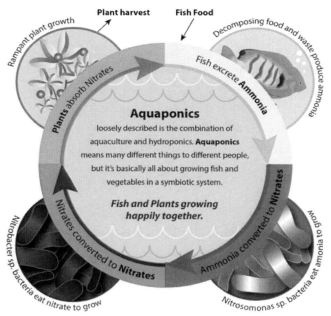

FIGURE 8. *Aquaponics Life Cycle*

Furthermore, billion-dollar corporations are buying, or have already purchased food companies, farms (large and small) huge tracts of land, food distribution companies, and water resources. This practice has been, and is, taking place all over the world—in both developing countries and in rich countries such as the United States.

How, then, are we going to eat? While debates rage and conventional agriculture goes on with business as usual -- crops are often being bombarded with droughts and destructive storms, toxic pesticides are being applied on our food, massive amounts of pollution is being generated via of our modern food production practices, Natural wildlife habitat is being destroyed at an alarming rate to make room for more crops, and crop-devastating diseases immune to modern controls become more proficient – hunger and increased food costs are increasing their grip on growing human populations across the globe. Conventional agriculture is proving totally unsustain- able, if not downright unworkable in current and forthcoming global conditions. Global food prices are rising annually validates these statements.

The answer has already been invented and is catching on. It is totally sustainable. It does not use soil, toxic pesticides, herbicides, artificial fertilizers, harmful chemicals, genetically modified crops or fish, or antibiotics. It wastes 90 percent less water than conventional agriculture methods. It does not need expensive, unhealthy genetically modified seeds or plants. It promises to end food insecurity for millions of people. The answer is aquaponics. Aquaponics farms both the fish and the vegetables in an environmental friendly sustainable way. Aquaponic systems growing fish and vegetables together is also the real certified Organic and sustainable way to produce food.

Furthermore, water evaporation is greatly reduced (especially when the fish tank is shaded or housed indoors), so at least 90 percent less water wastage occurs than in conventional agriculture. Water is constantly recycled between the fish and the vegetables.

Aquaponics is a proven technology that has been used commercially since the 1970s. It uses around

17 percent of the energy used by conventional farming, since no trucks, tractors, or other machinery is necessary. As a meager user of energy, it is very well suitable for alternative energy sources such as wind power or solar panels. Working with the plants and harvesting is quick and easy, since everything is done at a comfortable ergonomically correct waist-high level. In addition, a much higher yield of product (fish and plants), can be grown in the same amount of space compared to other agricultural methods. Lastly, aquaponics produces extremely nutrient dense vegetables in comparison to vegetables grown through other modern day large scale commercial agricultural methods. In summary, aquaponics is an efficient way to grow highly productive, environmentally friendly, sustainable, organic, and healthy food. It is the true definition of agriculture being 'green'.

Foreign Owned/Controlled Farmland and Food Supply

Another disturbing practice, occurring at an exponential rate over the last decade, is the purchase of real estate by foreign countries and companies. A slew of foreigners—primarily Chinese state corporations and Gulf sheiks— are buying up farmland through- out the world at an accelerated pace to acquire as much precious soil, farmland, and water as possible. This phenomenon is known as "land grabbing," This practice displaces family farms and drives up food costs. Large companies and foreign countries are rap- idly obtaining the ability to control food supply and distribution. Other countries regularly farm USA land and then ship the harvest back to their country. The economic outlook of forthcoming higher food prices in the near future, because of this practice, is alarming. Data shows that this troubling trend, of foreign governments with trillion-dollar budgets and large foreign corporate companies with million-dollar budgets, purchasing enormous amounts of precious limited farmland. Although this has been occurring since the 70's it has been increasing at an exponential

rate over the past couple of decades. According to a May 2019 NPR report, "nearly 30 million acres of U.S. farmland are held by foreign investors. That number has doubled in the past two decades.

Foreign entities are also buying up critical farmland and water source acreage in enormous quantities in Mexico, Central America, South America, Caribbean, Asia, and Africa. Again, the pace and amount of land being grabbed is astonishing and truly disturbing. As of 2013 "water grabbing" by corporations amounted to 454 billion cubic meters peryear globally. Cooperate and foreign investors from around developed countries are purchasing water rights in some of the most agricultural and environmentally sensitive regions in the world, as well as in arid places where water is already scare for the region's populations. India, United Kingdom, Egypt, China and Israel—accounted for 60 percent of the water acquired under these deals.

Between 2000 and 2012 nearly two-thirds of the land being purchased was in Eastern Africa and Southeast Asia. During this period over 205 million acres of land have been purchased by foreigners and large corporations. About 62 percent of these deals were in Africa. More than one economist has stated that China is buying Africa to feed its rapidly growing population.

These large land grabs push out small farmers and destabilizes the local economy. In Sudan, for instance, the local population is becoming increasingly dependent on food aid and international food subsidies because the land grabbers are pushing out small farmers, and the produce being harvested is shipped to markets in other parts of the world. Evidence also shows that these large land grabs lead to lost natural ecosystems, as a result of farming at such a large commercial scale. Another problem resulting from these land grabs is the large-scale displacement of local peoples without adequate compensation. These displacements often result in resettlement in marginal lands, loss of livelihoods especially in the case of pastoralists, and the erosion of social networks. Lastly, the reduction of available land drives up land prices and is going to make it all the more difficult for the average person to afford real estate.

Some examples for foreign corporate land purchases include the company Cargill purchased 775,000 acres of Brazil's valuable soybean farmland. Nile Trading and Development purchase of 1,482,632 acres of east Africa's rich farmland. BHP Billiton, a large mining company, purchase of 877,000 acres in Indonesia. Ted Turner of AOL and CNN fame, purchased of 111,000 acres in Argentina. The South Korean corporation Daewoo purchased of 1.3 million hectares, half of all Madagascar's agricultural land, to produce corn and palm oil. This is just a small fraction of some of the land grab transactions.

Economics: Food Demand Increases

"The two root causes of our environmental crisis— exploding population growth and wasteful consumption of irre- placeable resources. Over- consumption and overpopulation underlie every environmental problem we face today"
–Jacques Cousteau

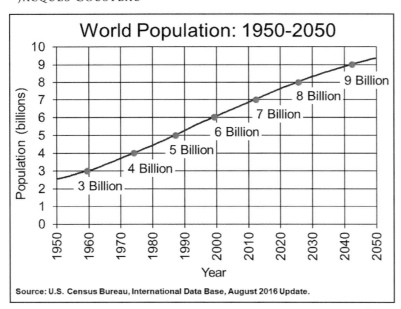

FIGURE 9.

Economics and how human behavior could be synthesized down to lines on a graph is fascinating. Take the famous graph of the law of supply and demand. It says that if demand rises and supply stays constant, prices will go up. There are more dollars "chasing" the same number of goods.

There are several main drivers of the projected increase in global demand for food in the next forty years: global population growth, increasing standards of living for developing nations, and depletion of resources.

Population Growth

First, demographers' project the world- wide population will grow from the current seven billion to over nine billion by 2050. The dilemma lies in the fact that we are rapidly approaching our planet's ability to support even the life we have now. We are now consuming planetary resources faster than they are being regenerated, including the planet's ability to process waste.

Increasing Standards of Living for Developing Nations

The second big impact on world food demand is globalization. Rising standards of living, especially in China and India where the populations are the highest, will increase demand for a more American lifestyle, especially regarding meat consumption. The technological revolution that is connecting us all is leveling the playing field and opening up a world of possibilities to everyone, no matter what the development status of the country. This opens the eyes of millions across the globe to what a better life looks like, but it brings with it significant change.

Plastic pollution has increased tenfold since 1980, 300-400 million tons of heavy metals, solvents, toxic sludge and other wastes from industrial facilities are dumped annually into the world's waters, and fertilizers entering coastal ecosystems have produced more than 400 ocean 'dead zones', totaling more than 245,000 km2 (591-595) – a combined area greater than that of the United Kingdom. Urban areas have more than doubled since 1992.

This eye opening is driving ever-increasing demand. Consumption is the primary source of strain on the earth's resources. This problem multiplies when we try to equally elevate the standards of the developing world. What if other countries were able to increase their standard of living to match that of North America? The Associated Press revealed that each American presently consumes as much as 13 Chinese or 31 Indians. If the Chinese consumed the way we do, we would roughly double world consumption rates. If India and China were to catch up, world consumption rates would triple. If the whole developing world were suddenly to catch up, world rates would increase at least eleven-fold. It is certainly fair that the citizens of the developing world have the right to improve their circumstances, but can the world really afford to have the entire population at the same consumption rate? Imagine if the entire planet suddenly achieved a much higher standard of living.

FIGURE 10. *Earths needed to sustain population at the current growth rate.*

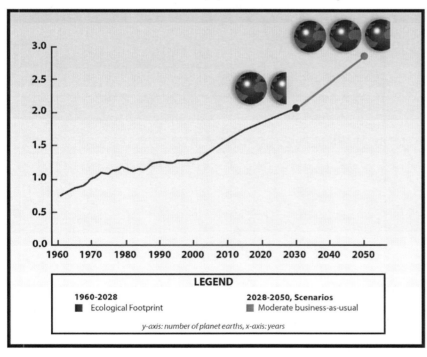

FIGURE 11.

Economics: Food Supply Decreases

As discussed above there are two reasons global food demand will increase over the next forty years: population growth and increasing standards of living. Based on supply and demand, let's now examine why supply—our ability to grow food at the same rate we have been growing it—is destined to decline.

Our current model of industrial agriculture depends on three factors that are uncertain: inexpensive fossil fuels, political stability, and unlimited water. Following, we will look at how these inputs affects our food supply and show why we should be concerned about our future.

FIGURE 12. Train in India

FIGURE 13. Beach in China

Petroleum Use in Agriculture

As farmers know well, every step in the agricultural process utilizes fossil fuel. From planting (tractors, fertilizers, weed and pest control) to harvesting, factory processing and delivering, all the products and all the steps are dependent upon petroleum. Currently, we use ten calories of energy for every one calorie of food we produce worldwide. This is only sustainable if there is an unlimited supply of cheap, renewable energy. Petroleum, the energy engine of agriculture, is not a renewable resource. While scientists, researchers and activists are debating the exact date of "peak oil," no one disagrees that our supplies are limited. If the supply of something is limited and the demand increases, then the price will rise. Because oil is so intricately woven into every aspect of our current food-production system, increasing oil prices have a direct impact upon the price of food.

All the really easy (and therefore cheap) oil has already been pumped out of the ground. To keep production levels high, energy companies are turning to highly disruptive exploration techniques like fracking which use a cocktail of toxic chemicals, and mining oil sand beds, which causes major environ- mental damage to large geographical areas. Now the energy industry is spending more and more money and resources for every barrel of oil they can recover. When cheap oil collapses, cheap food will no longer be available. The planting, harvesting, storage and transportation of food requires enormous quantities of fossil fuels under our current agricultural system. Other alternative power sources such as wind and wave energy are simply not capable of replacing our current fossil fuel economy—not by a long shot. Solar power is often talked about as a replacement for fossil fuels, but such delusions are mere pipe dreams. For starters, solar panels require rare earth minerals from China in order to be manufactured. Energy derived from solar panels cannot be easily stored or transported, and there are no electric farm tractors because the energy expenditure of tractors is very high and requires high-density fuels.

Technology is a long way from developing an electric vehicle motor and battery bank that can replace the petroleum-powered tractor engines that run our agricultural system today. Many of today's tractors have engines which produce over 200 horsepower.

FIGURE 14.

Petroleum Use in Aquaponics vs. Traditional Agriculture

In aquaponics, energy needs are small and can generally come from renewable sources. There is no soil to till, so there is no longer a need to use tractors and gas-powered farm equipment. Most large-scale commercial aquaponics operations typically employ either a raft method, where the plants float in water until they are harvested, or a nutrient flow technique, where nutrient rich water flows along plant grow channels. Most small and mid-size aquaponic systems are a flood-and-drain operation, where plants are grown in a media filled grow bed. These systems will be discussed extensively in the chapters ahead, but for now it is enough to know that none of the aquaponic systems used requires the energy commitment found in soil-based farming. Since there are no weeds in aquaponics, there is no need to mechanically remove them or spray herbicides. The plant nutrients and water are both integral to an aquaponics system, so there is no need for petroleum-based fertilizers or truck-mounted irrigators. Additionally, aquaponically grown plants are either growing in waist-high grow beds or in rafts floating in water, which makes them easier to harvest than soil-grown plants.

Aquaponics is very well adapted to providing food to local communities that may not have fertile soil available for growing. It is especially important that food-growing facilities be established closer to the people rather than trucking food in from distant locations, since over half of the population now lives in cities. Currently, most of our produce is shipped hundreds, if not thousands of miles. Growing food within population centers would save a tremendous amount of fuel.

Water Use in Agriculture

Over 70 percent of our Earth's surface is covered by water. Of all that water on earth 97.5 percent is salt water. Only 2.5 percent of the earth's water is freshwater. Of that, less than one percent of the earth's water is actually available for human use.

Unfortunately, people are using that one percent at an increasing rate. In a speech on February 5, 2009, United Nations Deputy Secretary-General Asha-Rose Migiro warned that two-thirds of the world's population will face a lack of water in less than twenty years if current trends in population growth, population growth, rural-to-urban migration and consumption continue. Also, interesting to note is that agriculture consumes roughly three-quarters of the world's fresh water. The proportion is higher in Africa and the United States, with as much as 90 percent of our water use being for agricultural purposes, according to both the United Nations and the USDA.

When the earth had six billion inhabitants, in year 2000, we used nearly 30 percent of the world's accessible, renewable water supply. Projections for 2025 indicate we will be using 70 percent of the world's accessible, renewable water supply, and like other natural resources, water use will not be evenly distributed. Fresh water is made available to us in three ways: rain, surface water (lakes, reservoirs, streams, etc.) and near surface groundwater aquifers. All three sources are currently being threatened by overuse and pollution. If the groundwater is not recharged at the same rate that it is being withdrawn, it becomes depleted and eventually disappears.

About one third of the world is completely dependent upon groundwater. As the global population increases, and our need for water rises accordingly, our groundwater supplies will decrease. Already evident in China, groundwater levels in some areas have dropped at the rate of 5-feet (1.5 meters) per year over the past ten years. According to the Ministry of Water Resources, as of 2009, 90 percent of that fresh water was polluted.

In the United States, 40 percent of our fresh water comes from groundwater supplies. The most famous example is the Ogallala Aquifer, the nation's largest aquifer underlying some 250,000 square miles stretching from Texas to South Dakota. More than 90 percent of the groundwater pumped from the Ogallala is used for agricultural irrigation. The Ogallala Aquifer is being depleted at a rate much faster than it is being replenished.

Aquifer depletion has drastic consequences that go well beyond the obvious lack of water. The land above a depleted aquifer can turn into a sinkhole and become dangerous and unusable. If an aquifer is close to an ocean, lowering the water level can destabilize the barriers between the aquifer and the salt water. This results in seepage of ocean water into the aquifer, and the remaining water in the aquifer becomes unusable as a fresh water source.

Worse yet, the water we can use is being polluted through the very agriculture that it nurtures. The National Water Quality Inventory reported that agricultural pollution is the leading source of water quality issues on surveyed rivers and lakes, the second largest source of impairments to wetlands and a major contributor to contamination of surveyed estuaries and ground water. What is this type of pollution? It is pollution that comes from a wide array of sources instead of a single "point" like a factory or a sew- age treatment plant. Agricultural activities that cause this problem include poorly located or managed animal feeding operations; overgrazing; plowing too often or at the wrong time; and improper, excessive or poorly timed application of pesticides, irrigation water and fertilizer. Pollutants that result from farming and ranching include sediment, nutrients, pathogens, pesticides, metals and salts. The consequence is widespread water pollution and degradation of our lakes, streams and groundwater.

FIGURE 15. *Irrigating crop*

FIGURE 16. *Crop irrigation*

FIGURE 17. *Lake water recedes from heavy water use*

FIGURE 18. *Typical crop irrigation method*

Impacts of California Drought and Water Woes Threaten Energy, Agriculture, and Tourism

(News: *August 7, 2021*)

Agriculture is a significant sector in California's economy, producing nearly $50 billion in revenue in 2018. California's 77,500 farms produce more than 400 commodities, and two-thirds of the nation's fruits and nuts. California has 25.5 million acres of farm and ranch land, and the average farm size was 329 acres. California has more certified organic farms than any other state. In 2016, more than a million acres in the state were certified organic. CA grows 90% or more of the U.S. production of Organic almonds, artichokes, avocados, broccoli, cauliflower, celery, dates, figs, grapes, strawberries, lemons, lettuce, plums, and walnuts. California's Salinas Valley is often called the "Salad Bowl of the World." Roughly 70 percent of the nation's lettuce crop is grown there, along with plenty of other produce.

California's agricultural sector saw exports totaling $21.7 billion in 2019, with organic product sales of more $10.4 billion. Now, farmers in the state – one of America's most important agricultural regions – are being told by regulators that they can no longer take water out of major rivers and streams.

California is seeing the effects of the West's historic "megadrought," which has cut off critical water resources in multiple states. As heat waves continue to threaten communities, the state has been forced to scrutinize the way it distributes the water that's still accessible. According to the U.S. Drought Monitor, more than 95% of the region is in "moderate" to "exceptional" drought.

On Thursday, the Golden State was forced to shut down the six-turbine Edward Hyatt Power Plant – one of its largest hydroelectric plants – because there is not enough water to power it. The plant draws from the Oroville Dam reservoir that has sunk to a historic low of fewer than 642 feet above mean sea level.

Low water levels are visible at Lake Oroville, which is the second largest reservoir in California, is near 35% capacity. Officials said that it was the lowest level since the country's tallest dam was finished in 1967 and the first time the hydroelectric plant has been shut due to a lack of water.

The plant can produce enough power for 80,000 homes and businesses. Hydropower provides around 15% of California's electricity.

Reservoirs and other water sources around California are drying up. Residents are being forced to haul in houseboats and the state is transporting millions of impacted salmon to the coast.

Lake Mead, a key reservoir on the Colorado River that supplies 40 million people including Californians, also dipped to its record low last month and is expected to

continue declining until November. The water level there impacts hydropower generation at Hoover Dam.

Lake Oroville, Lake Mead, Utah's Great Salt Lake and Lake Powell — the second-largest reservoir in the U.S. which sits on the Utah-Arizona border and has also seen its water level plummet to a historic low.

Many farmers in one of the country's most important agricultural regions will have to stop taking water out of major rivers and streams because of a severe drought that is rapidly depleting the state's reservoirs and killing endangered species of fish.

With less snowpack and extreme conditions fueled by long-term, speculated to be caused by human-caused climate change, and a 20-year drought, water shortages are expected to worsen over time as warming trends continue. The states' tourism, transportation, agriculture, and energy industries are all expected to be negatively impacted.

California Governor Newsom has asked residents and businesses to voluntarily cut their water use by 15%. Officials warned that much of the state's drinking water supply would be at risk if the drought continues into 2022.

California Farm Bureau senior counsel Chris Scheuring said farmers are "discouraged" and "dismayed." "In general, farmers understand drought and they understand lean rain years. That's the business we're in," he said. "But they don't understand the downward slide in water reliability we are facing in California, sort of on a systemic level."

Water Use in Aquaponics vs. Traditional Agriculture

Modern agricultural methods waste an incredible amount of water. Water is either sprayed or flooded through fields where a huge amount either evaporates into the air or seeps past the plant roots onto the surrounding ground or into the water table, pulling chemical fertilizers, herbicides, and pesticides down with it.

Aquaponics, on the other hand, is a closed, recirculating system. The only water that leaves the system is the small amounts taken up by the plants, transpired through the plant leaves, or that evaporated from the top of the tank. This allows aquaponics to use less than one tenth the amount of water a comparable soil-based garden would use.

Aquaponics is even more water thrifty than its horticultural cousin, hydroponics. With hydroponics being a completely human-managed, chemical-based system, the nutrients regularly become unbalanced. At a particular stage in the process these nutrient chemicals build up to toxic levels. Every two to four weeks, the entire nutrient solution reservoir needs to be pumped out and replaced with fresh chemicals. This nutrient waste is full of chemical mineral salts that need to be carefully disposed of and prevented from running into our sanitary sewer system, streams, or seeping into our groundwater.

Conversely, aquaponics is an organic ecosystem in which the nutrients are balanced naturally, so there is never any toxic nutrient levels. In fact, since the water in an aquaponics system is so full of healthy biological constitutes, it is possible to never discharge the water from your fish tank. Even if a rare problem event occurred requiring a water exchange, the discharge from an aquaponics system is completely organic and would not have any negative pollution impacts.

Pollution and Traditional Agriculture vs. Aquaponics

Aquaponics is a food-growing system that has an inconsequential impact on our planet compared to traditional agricultural practices, especially if the pumps and heaters are powered through renewable energy sources. Except for purely wild food-growing systems, such as the ocean, and most permaculture techniques, no other food system can likely make that claim. Furthermore, aquaponics can be done where development has already occurred, such as in urban areas, the suburbs, and the residential neighborhoods, preserving wildlife habitat and our natural ecosystems.

On the other hand, as previously addressed, traditional agriculture is the single largest contributor of CO_2 emissions, while simultaneously consuming and requiring more natural habitats for growing crops and raising cattle. The main pollutant sources are CO_2 emissions from petroleum operated equipment used in farm production and food transportation, methane from cattle production, and nitrous oxide from over-fertilizing. Aquaponics requires none of these inputs. These pollutants are non-existent or negligible in aquaponics. The need for petroleum is next to nothing in Aquaponics (maybe a backup generator on rare occasions). Furthermore, fish do not produce methane as cattle do, and there is no chance of over-fertilizing an aquaponics system.

Perhaps, most importantly, aquaponic systems can be started anywhere. This alleviates the need to clear jungles and forests and allows the focus to be with urban areas, like old factories or warehouse buildings as the farms of the future. While not necessarily suited to growing vast fields of grain, aquaponics allows growth of any vegetable and many types of fruit crops and does so in a way that is even more productive on a square foot basis, even in an urban setting. Aquaponics can produce 50,000 pounds of tilapia and 100,000 pounds of vegetables per year in a single acre of space. By contrast, one grass-fed cow requires eight acres of grassland. Another way of looking at it is that over the course of a year, aquaponics will generate about 35,000 pounds of edible flesh per acre, while the grass-fed beef will generate about 75 pounds in the same space.

It is not an unrealistic notion to think at least some portion of our food can be produced in our urban centers. In fact, it is not unusual for city dwellers to grow a meaningful portion of the food they eat. Hong Kong and Singapore already both produce more than 20 percent of their meat and vegetables within the city limits. With aquaponics, production yields are much greater, and done correctly have the potential of allowing a city to basically feed itself.

Climate, Pollution, and Agriculture

A joint statement by 21 national science academies to the G8 summit declared, "It is unequivocal that the climate is changing " (National Science Academy).

The earth is becoming warmer. Studies show that the average temperature of the earth is on the increase. Since thermometer records became available in 1860, the eleven hottest years have all occurred between 1995 and 2011.

However, the climate on earth has always been changing. Sometimes rapidly (e.g., volcanic activity, meteorite hitting earth, etc.). To what extent the past 150 years of human activity (e.g., industrialization, population explosion, rampant natural habitat destruction, etc.) have impacted or are impacting the climate is not an exact science. One would think that the gross amount of habitat destruction and massive pollution humans have been responsible during the past 200 years would have some kind of altering impact on our planet's climate.

A change in the earth's climate would have an impact on our ability to produce food throughout the world. The Food and Agriculture Organization (FAO) warns that a global temperature increase of even two degrees Celsius over preindustrial levels could reduce crop yields as much as 35 percent. An increase of temperatures would result in changes in the weather, including wind patterns, the amount and type of precipitation and the types and frequency of severe weather events. Such climate destabilization could have dramatic unpredictable environmental, social, and economic consequences.

Current conventional agriculture methods are recognized as one of the biggest contributors to air pollution — producing tremendous amounts of carbon dioxide (CO_2), nitrous oxide (N_2O) and methane (CH_4). Carbon dioxide is released by all the fossil fuels. Nitrous oxide comes from chemical-based fertilizers and has 296 times the negative atmospheric impact of CO_2. Methane comes from livestock operations and has up to 25 times the negative atmospheric impact potential of CO_2.

Deforestation

In 2000, nearly 40 percent of the earth's land has already been cleared for agriculture. By 2005, it was closer to 50 percent. The demand for farmland is growing at an unsatiable exponential rate. In our search for more fertile soil, we are turning to the soils of the tropical rain forests.

According to Rainforest Facts, more than an acre and a half of tropical rain forest is being cleared every second of every day. Experts estimate that the last remaining rainforests could be consumed in less than 40 years.

Unfortunately, by clearing tropical rain forests to create more farmland to feed ourselves, and to make way for crops to produce biofuels, we are destroying valuable ecosystems, native plants, and animals at alarming rates, altering natural weather patterns, and destroying a critical air filter our world desperately needs. The rain forests are our greatest source of the air we breathe because of their tremendous efficiency in converting carbon dioxide into oxygen. With less rainforests, our condition only worsens.

Fires to Clear Land = Near-Record Loss of Tree Cover

Tree cover loss, mostly in the tropics, totaled 294,000 square kilometers (113,000 square miles) in 2017, just short of a record 297,000 sq kms in 2016, according to Global Forest Watch. Brazil, Democratic Republic of Congo, Indonesia, Madagascar, and Malaysia suffered the biggest losses based on satellite data.

Tropical forests were lost at a rate equivalent to 40 football fields per minute in 2017, says World Resource Institute (WRI). Burning of forests to make way for farms from the Amazon to the Congo basin caused a loss of global tree cover amounting to an area almost the size of Italy in 2017.

FIGURE 19. Deforestation of native habitat for agriculture. Loss of plants and wildlife habitat. Erosion of topsoil over time.

Vast areas continue to be cleared for soy, beef, palm oil and other globally traded commodities. Much of this clearing is illegal. Unfortunately, until agriculture methods and global consumption habits change the future outlook for forests is not a good one.

Overfishing the Oceans

Before moving on to tilapia farming as part of the solution, it is important to look at one more critical food supply issue: the overfishing of our oceans. Overfishing occurs when more fish are caught than the population can replace through natural reproduction. In 2015, 33% of marine fish stocks were being harvested at unsustainable levels; 60% were maximally sustainably fished, with just 7% harvested at levels lower than what can be sustainably fished Our oceans could arguably be one of the last wild sources of food on our planet, and we are quickly emp- tying them of fish. Today, 85 percent of the world's fisheries are either fully exploited, over exploited or have collapsed. The global fishing fleet is operating at two and a half times the sustainable level—there are simply too many boats chasing a dwindling number of fish. To date, we have lost at least 2,048 fish species that we know of due to overfishing.

Billions of fish worldwide are killed for food every year. Unless current fishing rates are drastically reduced, scientists predict that every species of wild-caught seafood will collapse by the year 2050. Excessive fish depletion can widely be attributed to the dual culprits of advances in fishing technology and techniques on the one hand, coupled with minimal regulations and restrictions to allow fish to repopulate.

Sadly, some reports state we only eat about 10 percent of all the marine life that is killed in order to feed us. And although other reports are more conservative, saying only about 25 percent of marine life is discarded after being caught, that is still nearly 27 million tons of fish.

Large, computerized ships trawl the deep seas with miles of netting that can obliterate 130 tons of fish in a single sweep. Bottom trawlers cause massive destruction, scraping the sea bottom and destroying miles and miles of coral, sponges, and non-target bottom dwelling fish which are simply discarded as collateral damage. The fact is that the depletion we are seeing is happening because we have become incredibly efficient at harvesting the entire depth of the ocean. Even species once left mostly untouched are now in danger of depletion. We now have the technology and fishing fleet capacity to catch four times the current supply of fish.

In fact, fishing is one of the world's most wasteful and destructive industries. Every year, more than seven million tons of so-called "by-catch", (perhaps more accurately described as "by-kill") is inadvertently caught and unabashedly destroyed; including over sea animals such as non-target fish species, sea turtles, dolphins, whales, sharks, albatrosses, and other sea birds. Every year 7.3 million tons of marine life is caught unintentionally by the fishing industry just to be callously thrown back dead, considered an accept- able loss in the industrial pursuit for profit.

Endangered species are also vulnerable to industry nets and other gear. Just as the dolphins still suffocate and die in the tuna industry nets, sea turtles are killed by the millions in the nets of the shrimping industry. In fact, for every pound of shrimp netted in the Gulf of Mexico, four pounds of "by-kill" is wasted and thrown back overboard dead.

Not only are we depleting the oceans of fish at an alarming rate for human consumption, but half the world's fish catch is fed to livestock! In fact, more fish are consumed by U.S. livestock than by the entire human population of all the countries of Western Europe combined.

To solve this crisis, various governmental agencies have attempted to set annual quotas by species to prevent a complete collapse. For example, the International Commission for the Conservation of Atlantic Tuna (ICCAT) sets the limits on bluefin tuna. However, these limits appear to be based more on politics than science. According to many biologists and other scientist these limits are set far above recommended recovery levels. Furthermore, these limits are largely ignored by commercial fishing companies. The WWF estimates that at least 20 percent of the fish caught worldwide, and as much as 50 percent in some areas, are caught illegally.

Therefore, we need to either stop eating so much fish or turn to aquaculture and farm more of our fish on land so the ocean species can recover. Since the health benefits of fish are so compelling, it is unlikely we are going to eat less fish anytime soon. Fish provide an excellent source of omega-3 fatty acids, vitamins and minerals that benefit a person's overall health. The American Heart Association recommends at least two servings of fish per week to help prevent heart disease, lower blood pressure, and reduce the risk of heart attacks and strokes. Compared with other sources of animal-based proteins, all of which are full of saturated fats, fish is the healthy alternative. Fish are also vastly more efficient sources of protein than other forms of animal protein. Currently 37 percent of the world grain harvest is being used to produce animal protein, and in the United States, that number reaches nearly 70 percent. Unfortunately, most of that gain is going to feed cattle, the most inefficient source of animal protein.

The global demand for fish has increased dramatically. In a recent report on "The State of the World's Fisheries and Aquaculture" the FAO revealed that global average consumption of fish has hit a record of over 41 pounds (18 kg) per person per year.

Unfortunately, some types of aquacultures do not relieve any strain on the supply of ocean fish, since the feed used in aquaculture operations uses ocean-harvested fish to create the fish meal which is its protein base. Furthermore, some large-scale ocean aquaculture operations generate more ammonia and feces waste than many human population centers.

Finally, while you would think that the ability to grow fish in ponds and tanks would be great for local fish production, in the United States only 10 percent of the farmed fish we eat is produced domestically. As of 2020, China produces about 70 percent of the farmed fish in the world, harvested at thousands of giant factory-style farms that extend along the entire eastern seaboard of the country. The transport of this product from halfway around the world results in more unnecessary atmospheric pollution and consumption of limited petroleum resources.

Extinction and Loss of Wildlife Habitat is Alarming

Extinction of a particular animal or plant species occurs when there are no more individuals of that species alive anywhere in the world - the species has died out. Endangered animals and plants are at risk of extinction – meaning, there are so few of them that they might soon be wiped out altogether.

More than 99 percent of all species that ever lived on Earth are estimated to be extinct. In the past 500 years, we know of approximately 1,000 species that have gone extinct, but this doesn't account for thousands of species that disappeared before scientists had a chance to describe them. Nobody really knows how many species are in danger of becoming extinct. The International Union for Conservation of Nature (IUCN) has identified 16,928 species of flora, fauna and animals worldwide as currently being threatened with extinction.

Scientists have narrowed down several of the most likely causes of mass extinction. Volcano eruptions, asteroid collisions, and rise in sea level are some of the identified causes of mass extinctions. However, the current dilemma we now find ourselves in is unnatural and is on us – Homo Sapiens. Humans are destroying the natural world; and as a result, wildlife populations have plunged a whopping 60% in just two generations.

The number of wild animals on Earth has halved in the past 40 years, according to a new analysis by the by scientists at World Wildlife Fund (WWF) and the Zoological Society of London found. If half the animals died typical city zoo it would be front page news. Knowing that we have lost one half of the animal population due to human activity should most certainly be wakeup call for us to act now.

The fastest declines among animal populations were found in freshwater ecosystems, where numbers have plummeted by 75% since 1970. Most of the pollution that happens on land ends up in the rivers. The number of animals living on the land has fallen by 40% since 1970. World ocean animal populations have also fallen by 40% overall. The biggest declines in animal numbers have been seen in developing nations. However, the big declines in wildlife in rich nations had already occurred long before the WWF report's baseline year of 1970.

If present trends continue one half of all species of life on earth will be extinct within the next 75 years, as a result of habitat destruction, pollution, and invasive species. Furthermore, a whopping 93 percent of medicinal plants may become extinct due to habitat destruction.

When we talk about extinctions, we need to understand that it's not just about the disappearance of a single specie but also the effects of its disappearance to the environment that it interacts with. When

![Western Black Rhino]

FIGURE 20. Western Black Rhino (Declared extinct in 2011)

FIGURE 21. Pyrenean Ibex (Declared extinct in 2000)

FIGURE 22. *Pyrenean Ibex (Declared extinct in 2000)*

you take a look at the Earth as a whole, people are responsible for the vast majority of its environmental problems – chemical pollutants, destruction through terrorism and wars, radiation, EMF pollution, etc. Human beings do not treat our planet with the respect that it deserves. While it is easy to pass off these issues as not affecting us directly, our collective future will be abysmal if we don't change the direction in which we're headed.

For the first time, a bumblebee has been placed on the endangered species list. But what if they went extinct? Well, if you like to eat, you should be concerned about bumblebees. One out of every three bites of food you eat has been helped along in some way by bees, according to the Natural Resources Defense Council.

The UN's Food and Agriculture Organization recently published a report which shows that 90% of the world's food supply comes from about 100 crop species and 71 of those crops (especially fruits and vegetables) rely on bees for pollination. In the U.S., bee activities generate $15 billion a year. This includes "domesticated" bees such as honeybees.

Bumblebees also pollinate a broad range of native plants that play a vital role in numerous ecosystems. If all bumblebees disappeared it would impact us greatly in terms of the foods we eat, the loss of economic benefits, loss of medicinal plants, and the general integrity of the natural world."

One out of every four species of bumblebee in North America is at risk of extinction, according to the Xerces Society for Invertebrate Conservation. Other bumblebees that are being evaluated for listing as an endangered species include the yellow banded bumblebee, the Western bumblebee and Franklin's bumblebee.

We are living in extremely dangerous times. Between the death of millions of plants and animals, along with massive loss of wildlife habitat at an alarming rate, things seem to be worse than ever.

Causes of Extinction

The biggest cause of tumbling animal numbers is the destruction of wild areas for development, farming and logging: the majority of the Earth's land area has now been impacted by humans, with just 15% protected for nature. Poaching, unsustainable fishing and hunting, and exploitation for food is another major factor, according to recent research. These are extremely bad habits that we have become accustomed to, and they must change for the betterment of the world at large.

Cutting down forests, converting land into fields for farming, overfishing, pollution, and expansion of population centers all put a strain on native plants and wildlife. Below are elaborations of some of the significant causes of extinction.

Agriculture Impact on Extinction

Industrial agriculture disrupts habitats and biodiversity. Habitat loss and unintended chemical runoff are the destructive products of traditional farming practices. Native plants and animals are eradicated on a massive scale.

One example you have likely heard of is the threatened species milkweed, which the vulnerable monarch butterfly relies on for reproduction. Milkweed is killed with agricultural herbicides or mowed away from hedgerows and roadsides. Unfortunately, there are way too many more examples to list.

Beyond the colossal loss of wildlife and native plants, agricultural diversity is also being lost. One estimate suggests that 75 percent of agricultural crops have been lost since 1900. This lack of diversity in food crops is risky for human food security. Agricultural diversity involves not only the production and processing of nutritious food, but also access by individuals to the full range of nutrients needed to maintain an active and healthy life. A greater diversity of genetic agricultural plants also helps to ensure a secure food supply at more stable prices. Greater agricultural diversity also helps prevent massive losses of crops to pests, diseases, and changes in climate conditions.

Habitat Loss

Deforestation and urbanization combine to create two additional reasons why plants and animals become extinct. Deforestation is leveling forests to harvest the wood or create space for building or agriculture, while urbanization is the turning of once-rural areas into cities. As the human population grows, more and more land is being cleared and urbanized for living space. This shrinks habitat for animals and plants. Each year, 36 million acres of natural forest is leveled, according to the World Wildlife Fund. The forest provides habitat for 80 percent of the world's species.

Exotic Species Introduction

When animals and plants that are not native to a region are introduced to the ecosystem, they can cause serious damage to the local plants and animals, which contributes to their extinction. Native species must compete with the exotic species for basic needs such as food and water. If the exotic species is more aggressive than the native species, the native species then runs the risk of extinction.

The introduction of the Nile perch into the Lake Victoria ecosystem in Africa represents a prime example of this, according to "Causes and Consequences of Species Extinctions," a paper published by Princeton University Press. The Nile perch was introduced to the area in the 1950s and by the 1980s, a population boom of these fish contributed to the extinction of between 200 and 400 native fish species.

Overexploitation

Overexploitation, also called overharvesting, is the excessive harvesting of an animal or plant species, making it harder for the species to renew its numbers. The Princeton University Press paper points to the Steller's Sea cow, which was discovered in 1741, over- exploited, and then became extinct in 1768. Save the Frogs, a frog conservation group, notes that several frog species feel the effects of overharvesting for food, pet, and scientific purposes. Fish also fall prey to over- exploitation. According to Greenpeace, more than 70 percent of native habitats worldwide are either "fully exploited, over exploited, or significantly depleted."

Extinction in America

An extinction crisis is rippling through America's wildlife. One-third of species in the US are vulnerable to extinction, a crisis that has ravaged swaths of creatures such as butterflies, amphibians, fish, and bats. According to the National Wildlife Federation, America's wildlife is in a crisis. Fish, birds, mammals, reptiles, and invertebrates are all losing ground at very disturbing rates. More than 1,270 species found in the US are listed as at risk under the federal Endangered Species Act, which includes the grizzly bear, California condor, leatherback sea turtle and rusty patched bumble bee. However, the actual number of threatened species is "far higher than what is formally listed", states the report by the National Wildlife Federation, American Fisheries Society and the Wildlife Society.

Using data from NatureServe that assesses the health of entire groups of species on a sliding scale, rather than the case-by-case work done by the federal government, the analysis shows more than 150 US species have already become extinct while a further 500 species have not been seen in recent decades and have possibly also been snuffed out.

Whole classes of creatures have suffered precipitous drops, with 40% of freshwater fish species in the US now vulnerable or endangered, a third of bat species experiencing major declines in the past two decades and amphibians dwindling from their known ranges at a rate of about 4% a year. Monarch butterfly numbers have dropped by about 90% in recent decades. The true scale of the crisis is probably larger when species with sparse data, or those as yet unknown to science, are considered.

"This loss of wildlife has been sneaking up on us but is now like a big tsunami that is going to hit us," said Thomas Lovejoy, a biologist at George Mason University. Species have been battered by the destruction of forests, prairie and wetlands to make way for mass agriculture, urbanization, roads and mining. The use of pesticides in farming is linked to the decline of key pollinators such as bees.

Meanwhile, improved transportation between states and from other countries has unleashed diseases such as fungal infections that have ravaged certain frogs and bats. Invasive species including feral hogs, nutria and emerald ash borers have torn apart wildlife habitats such as forests and riverbanks, often with little to slow them.

Each year, as they have for thousands of years, millions of waterfowl make their annual fall migration from their breeding grounds in Canada, Alaska, and northern tier of the continental United States (U.S.) to wintering areas farther south. Following traditional flight patterns, by mid-winter more than five million ducks and geese have found their way to their destination in the Central Valley of California, the most important wintering waterfowl area in the Pacific Flyway. This is a remarkable number of birds, but from an historical standpoint, a tremendous decrease, per- haps by a factor of ten, in the total numbers of birds that once "darkened the skies" of the Central Valley. During the twentieth century, this downward trend was seen throughout North America. By 1985, waterfowl populations had plummeted to record lows, not only in the California Valley, but throughout the North American continent. More than half of the original 221 million wetland acres found in the contiguous U.S. had been destroyed, and habitat that waterfowl depend on for survival was disappearing at a rate of 60 acres per hour. The picture was just as bleak across Canada, nesting grounds for a large percentage of the waterfowl that winter in the U.S. And nowhere were the losses greater than in the Central Valley of California, where more than 95% of wetland and riparian habitats had been lost. One can only imagine how awesome it must have been to see so much wildlife—not only the waterfowl, but to see buffalo in herds of 20,000 (according to Lewis and Clark), as well as elk, antelope and so many other amazing animals in such abundance.

Species are being forced into living in smaller patches of habitat. Wildlife is not able to interact with other same species and/or symbiotic species. Extinctions are ramping up. The world is getting increasingly more humanized, and it is happening with colossal negative consequences to wildlife numbers, wildlife biodiversity, and wildlife habitat. Aquaponics greatly helps resolve the problem of extinction and loss of wildlife habit. Aquaponics produces harvest in excess of three times that provided by traditional agriculture methods, per same square area. Aquaponics helps save our planet from overfishing. Aquaponics uses 90% less water than traditional agricultural practices. Aquaponics also coincides well with areas that have already been developed, such as in cities, towns, and community neighborhoods; thus, allowing more land to be preserved for, or converted to, natural habitat for wild animals and our recreational enjoyment (e.g., multiuse trails, sportsman activities, camping, etc.).

Differing Views on the Climate Change and Global Warming Debate

There are six common views regarding 'Global Warming'. Although now the most current politically correct catch phrase, is 'Climate Change'. Regardless of what the most outspoken pundits call it, they are referring to the same thing.

Point of View #1: Many believe that global warming started long before the "Industrial

Revolution" and the invention of the internal combustion engine. They argue that global warming began long ago, as the earth started warming its way out of the 'Ice Age'— a time when much of North America, Europe, and Asia is said to lay buried beneath great sheets of glacial ice- and continues today as part of a natural process.

Point of View #2: Same view as above, adding that the industrial revolution and human activities are now accelerating global warming and climate change.

Point of View #3: The "Industrial Revolution", CO2 producing human activities, and destruction of our natural resources is the cause of global warming, and the world will continue to warm at a devastating exponential rate.

Point of View #4: Global warming is all hype. Planet earth has always experienced variations in climate; and a few decades (or centuries) of warming (or cooling) is just a natural process.

Point of View #5: There is no global warming, it is just bad science and media hype.

Point of View #6: There is no global warming, but the new world order globalist, mainstream media, and government leaders are propagandizing it to push their agenda.

Our Responsibility

Regardless of which view you and I have in regard to the climate change issue, we all share one thing in common. Each one of us has an important moral and ethical responsibility to take good care of this planet during our lifetime. We need to be concerned about the planet, do our part to help out, and reduce our negative impact upon wildlife, oceans, forests, grasslands, and the environment as a whole. We should make every effort to minimize pollution, destruction of natural habitat, consumption of resources, and waste. We should always be striving to do positive things that directly benefit our planet, and the natural environment, regardless of the global warming issue. A good rule of thumb is to always leave a place (and a person) better off than when you arrived. This perspective, when applied, is a win-win for all. Build others up with an encouraging word, a helping hand, good advice, constructive instruction, and/or an empathetic ear and you will make a positive difference in their lives. This positive impact in the life of another in turn spreads into families and communities like the ripples from a rock thrown into a pond.

Being a good steward of this planet — constantly trying to reduce consumption of natural resources, minimizing our pollution, not over consuming or wasting resources, and making a consistent effort to help the environment — likewise benefits earth's inhabitants now and in the future. Such should not be considered as a good deed, but instead viewed as simply honoring our responsibility.

It has been said that a winner is someone who picks up a piece of trash that is not his or hers. As an individual, we cannot dictate government policy, force companies to operate differently, control others, or convince everyone of our climate change viewpoint, but we can make a big difference in regard to our individual impact upon this planet — for better or worse. Our lifestyle will result in either negative consequences or positive benefits for the wildlife, natural habitat, preservation of species, and quality of life for future generations of this planet. The responsibility is ours — an individual choice that truly makes a difference.

Aquaponics vs. Aquaculture

With the projected dramatic decrease of the ocean's fish supply, we must turn to other options to continue enjoying the healthful benefits of eating fish. As with any intensive animal-raising operation though, the central problem is how dispose of the waste without harming the environment. Fortunately, aquaponics solves this problem. Aquaponics takes the potentially toxic waste water from an aquaculture system and creates an organic nutrient for the plants. Plants and the grow bed serve as a biofilter for the aquaponic system (media bed system) and purifies the water that goes back to the fish. By seeking a solution through bio-mimicry techniques and observing nature, scien- tists found the solution in polyculture. Aquaponics is a beautiful intertwining of fish and plant production.

The Aquaponic Solution

Food prices have risen, natural habitats destroyed at outrageous rates; and the supply and demand structures have changed. So, is there hope for the future? While aquaponics cannot address the dual demand pressures of population growth and increasing global standards of living, it does offer solutions to many problems.

Making a Positive Difference

"When the wind changes direction, there are those who build walls and those who build windmills."
—Chinese proverb

In 2010, Mayor Barrett of Milwaukee gave the final approval for a zoning variance to enable Growing Power to build the world's first vertical farm. The five-story structure will be built to grow plants and fish together, with the water flowing from one story to another. It is a building entirely dedicated to the growing of fresh food in an area of Milwaukee surrounded by low-income housing, liquor stores and mini marts.

By learning more about aquaponics, you are choosing to become a part of the solution.

FIGURE 23. *Modern building with plans on balconies and roof. Solar panels on the rgith side of the building also serve as carports.*

CHAPTER 5

Toxic Food vs. Healthy Organic Aquaponic Food

Crop Considerations

Organic food has become a fairly common preference for most people. Despite the growing popularity of organic products there is still a large segment of society, including those who purchase organics, who cannot explain why organic food may be better than non-organic food and do not understand many of the other dangers added to our food: antibiotics, growth hormones, preservatives, arsenic, mercury, and the other 30+ heavy metals commonly found in our foods.

U.S. sales of organic food and beverages grew from $1 billion in 1990 to $47.9 billion in 2019, according to the Organic Trade Association, an industry group. In addition to attracting newcomers, such as Sprouts (a nationwide grocery store chain), the growth in the organic food segment has prompted some traditional grocery stores to rethink their product lineups and are increasingly offering more organic choices. SPINS, a reporting firm which tracks the natural products industry, stated that consumers are becoming more educated regarding the dangers of pesticide use and genetically modified crops. In other words, the demand for organic crops is increasing, and the prices for such continue to rise.

Studies link exposure to many toxins found in our food products to cancer, birth defects, stillbirth, infertility, and damage to the brain and nervous system (including Parkinson's disease). Herbicides, pesticides, and fungicides are designed to kill, and because their mode of action is not specific to one species, they often kill or harm organisms other than pests, fungus, and/or weeds. The application of these toxic chemicals makes its way into our food chain. Even exposure to low doses can cause a range of neurological health effects such as memory loss, loss of coordination, reduced speed of response to stimuli, reduced visual ability, altered or uncontrollable mood and general behavior, and reduced motor skills. These symptoms are often very subtle and may not be recognized by the medical community as a clinical effect. Other possible health effects include asthma, allergies, hypersensitivity, and hormone disruption.

What Are GMOs and Why Are GMOs Bad?

According to the Food and Drug Administration, genetically modified organisms (GMO)—such as plants or animals—have been genetically engineered to create new characteristics. In other words, a specific gene is added to an organism to produce a new trait.

Most of these new unnatural gene alterations allow the plant to be sprayed with pesticides, herbicides, and/or fungicides without being killed. Meanwhile, everything else around the plant dies. Unfortunately, the plant absorbs the toxic chemicals and associated heavy metals, which are then passed on to you and your family. Furthermore, these plants are often used to feed livestock and fish; whereby the toxic substances work their way up the food chain in greater concentrations.

From 2004 through 2017 I lived in the California valley—also known as the Salad Bowl of America since most of the nation's produce is grown here— where it is common to to see a food crop being sprayed with various toxic chemical applications three or four times a season. In addition, with a mild climate farmer are able to grow up to three crops a season, depending on the types of crops being grown. As a result, the same farmland often receives a chemical application many times during the year. These chemicals get more and more concentrated in the soil over time. So, not only are these poisons and associated heavy metals entering the plant through direct application, but they are absorbed by the plant roots from the soil and water.

When we first relocated to California, we were absolutely thrilled to discover such an abundance of fresh fruits and vegetables. Just about every variety of vegetable and fruit can be found at local stores throughout the year. However, it did not take long for our bubble of joy to pop. On just about every drive out of town we saw crops being sprayed or chemicals being added to the water used for irrigation. The amount of chemicals we saw being regularly applied to crops within our area of California alone was truly astonishing. This played a very influential role

as to why I took a much bigger interest in growing a lot of my own food.

The California counties known for growing agricultural crops average over 250 tons of pesticides, herbicides, and fungicides applied to crops annually. That is not a typo—over 250 tons of chemicals are applied annually on farms in each of California's agriculture counties!

Yet Florida applies more than eight times the amount of pesticide and herbicides on tomatoes as does California. In order to get a successful crop of tomatoes, the official Florida handbook for tomato growers lists 110 different fungicides, pesticides and herbicides which can be applied to a tomato field over the course of the growing season, and many of those are what the Pesticide Action Network calls 'bad actors' —the worst of the worst in the agricultural chemical arsenal.

The most recent developments in GMO technology actually programs the plant itself to produce toxic substances that repel or kill insects. Genetically modified organisms are found in a huge variety of food products from baby food to fruit juice, and many believe they are dangerous to your health. Washing produce does minimal good, as the plants actually absorb these chemicals into their cells.

FIGURE 24. Crop duster spraying pesticide on food crop.

GMOs Harmful Health Impacts (Bottom Line)

Studies on GMO are almost infinite. Many studies are performed by companies and industries that profit from GMOs,whereas others are conducted by those that are opposed to GMOs. Therefore, getting a true unbiased and untainted representation of the impacts GMOs have on human health can be a challenge. However, if one will honestly examine the evidence produced from 'true' scientific studies, which are not influenced by agenda driven money backers and tainted with biased data collection or have subjective conclusions, it is obvious that GMOs can result in negative health impacts.

FIGURE 25. *Pesticides being sprayed on an orchard.*

Regardless, basic common sense should be enough to discourage us from the consumption of GMO foods. It does not take a brain scientist, a university study, or a rocket engineer telling us that eating foods sprayed with harmful chemicals is not healthy. Why would any reasonable person want to eat food that contains toxic pesticides, herbicides, and/or fungicides? An excellent resource for accurate scientific evidence on the negative impact GMOs have on human health is the Organic Consumers Association—a non-profit 501(c)3 public interest organization campaigning for health, justice, and sustainability (http://www.organicconsumers.org).

The website "Natural News" (http://www.naturalnews.com) also has many articles based upon unbiased science which provide the real truth about GMO foods. Most people who become educated about the harmful effects of GMOfoods find themselves becoming non-GMO advocates.

GMOs Harmful Environmental Impact

In addition to the potential health risks, there is solid evidence that GMOs are bad for the environment. The Union ofConcerned Scientists (UCSUSA) mentions six ways GMOs might have a negative environmental impact.

1. GMO crops could become weeds.
2. New genes could move to wild plants, causing those plants to become weeds.
3. Crops that produce viruses may lead to new, stronger viruses.
4. GMO plants created to release toxins threaten wildlife.
5. GMO crops could disturb the eco-system in an unpredictable way.
6. GMO crops threaten crop diversity.

The UCSUSA also states there is no consistent monitoring program in the United States, and there may be furthernegative impacts yet to be detected.

Harmful GMOs Everywhere

Currently, 80% of the food supply in North America contains GMOs. Currently, there are no national labeling requirements for GMO identification. While you may associate GMOs with only corn or soy products, they are found in manyothers, especially processed foods, which includes, but is not limited to those listed below.

- Vegetable oils
- Lecithin
- Flavor enhancers
- Cereals
- Sugar
- Dairy products
- Beets
- Papaya
- Squash
- Coffee
- Artificial sweeteners

Some GMO crops have been designed to produce a natural protective pesticide-like by-product which is also detrimental to human health. Aquaponics is about growing organic nutrient dense food in an environmentally friendly way. GMO food and fish feed are contrary to logical reasoning, in regard to good health, concern for the environment, nutrient density, and optimal food production. Educated and responsible citizens try to not do anything that further promotes the GMO industry or proliferates GMO plants.

Being GMO-Free

There are several ways to avoid genetically altered foods:

- Purchase only organic foods.
- Reduce your consumption of processed foods, including store bakery goods wherever possible.
- Avoid artificial sweeteners, especially aspartame.
- Keep in mind that vitamin supplements may also contain GMO soy or corn ingredients. It is prudent to purchase only supplements that are 3rd party lab tested and noted as being non-GMO.
- While genetically modified animals are not currently approved for humans to eat, many GMO crops are used to feed animalsthat are later consumed by humans. The concentration of heavy metals and the toxins increase as they move up thefood chain; with humans being at the end of the food chain. Unfortunately, many of these chemicals and heavy metals are not easily removed from the body after they are consumed—becoming significantly concentrated in us—leadingto a higher propensity to health problems.
- To avoid eating animal products containing GMOs, purchase only organic, wild, or 100 percent grass-fed animals or those that were only fed organic feed.

There is sufficient reason to be concerned about GMO effects on health and the environment. Buying organic andarming yourself with the knowledge necessary to make informed choices, will help you avoid potential health risks to you and those you care about. In addition, every time you buy an organic product, your dollars serve as a voice to further support and strengthen the organic market. Being knowledgeable about GMOs and their negative impacts will also help you better market your produce.

Dirty Produce— Organic Substitute

The following list of produce (in no particular order) has been shown to have the greatest concentration of harmful pesticides and should only be consumed if grown organically. Since the pesticide, herbicide, and/or fungicide is often absorbed by the plant, simply washing the produce will not remove all of the toxic chemicals.

1. Peaches
2. Apples

3. Bell Peppers
4. Celery
5. Nectarines
6. Strawberries
7. Cherries
8. Kale / Lettuce /Spinach
9. Carrots
10. Pears
11. Cucumbers
12. Spinach
13. Blueberries
14. Grapes
15. Potatoes
16. Collard Greens

Most Polluted Fruits and Vegetables

The Environmental Working Group (EWG) studied 100,000 produce pesticide reports from the U.S. Department of Agriculture and the U.S. Food and Drug Administration to create a list of dirtiest produce. The EWG recommends purchasing organic or locally grown varieties of the following products; doing so can lower pesticide intake by as much as 80 percent.

Celery

Research showed that a single celery stalk had 13 pesticides, while a large sample of celery contained as many 67 pesticides. Chemicals cling directly to this vegetable as it has no protective skin, and its stems cup inward, making it difficult to wash the entire surface of the stalk. If you like this crunchy veggie, go organic.

Peaches

Peaches are laced with 67 different chemicals, placing them second on the list of most contaminated fruits and vegetables. They have soft, fuzzy skin; a delicate structure;, and high susceptibility to most pests, causing them to be sprayed much more frequently.

Strawberries

This red, juicy fruit has a soft, seedy skin, allowing easier absorption of pesticides. Research showed that strawberries contained 53 pesticides. Buy organic strawberries or shop for a more naturally grown crop at a local farmer's market.

Apples

Apples are high-maintenance fruit, which means they need many pesticides to stave off mold, pests, and diseases. The EWG found 47 different kinds of pesticides on apples, and while produce washes can help remove some of the residue, they are not 100 percent effective.

Blueberries (domestic)

These antioxidant-rich berries have a thin layer of skin that allows chemicals to easily contaminate the fruit. Domestic blueberries were loaded with 13 pesticides on a single sample, according to the EWG. Imported blueberries had similar contaminants.

Bell Pepper

This vegetable is highly susceptible to pesticides. According to the EWG, sweet bell peppers showed traces of 63 types of pesticides. As with all fruits and vegetables, even though some pesticides can be washed away, many still remain.

Spinach, Kale/Collard Greens

Spinach has been found to be loaded with 45 different kinds of pesticides. Kale/collard greens have been found to be loaded with 57 different kinds of pesticides.

Grapes

These tiny fruit have extremely thin skins, allowing for easy absorption of pesticides. Imported and domestic varieties typically have significant pesticide residue.

Potatoes

The potato is highly laced with an average of 36 different types of pesticides to prevent pests and diseases. Although potatoes will not grow in an aquaponics system, one should avoid consuming potatoes or potato products that are not organic.

Cherries

Cherries, like blueberries, strawberries, and peaches, have a thin coating of skin, often not enough to protect the fruit from harmful pesticides. Research has shown that cherries grown in the U.S. had three times the amount of pesticides as imported cherries. Because cherries contain ellagic acid, an antioxidant that neutralizes carcinogens, they should not be abandoned. However, one would be prudent to buy organic or imported cherries over our domestic varieties.

Coffee's Concealed Secrets

Coffee is one of the most widely traded commodities in the world – with over 12 billion pounds of coffee produced annually. Meeting that demand is no easy task. So over time, farming methods have been developed to maximize production – but often at the expense of human and environmental health.

Conventional coffee is among the most heavily chemically treated foods in the world. It is steeped in synthetic fertilizers, pesticides, herbicides, fungicides, and insecticides. Not only does the environment suffer from this overload, but so do the people who live in it. Farmers are exposed to a high level of chemicals while spraying the crops and while handling them during harvest. The surrounding communities are also impacted through chemical residues in the air and water. These chemical presences are not just unpleasant; many are highly toxic and detrimental to human health. And of course, one would have to conclude that coffee drinkers are also negatively impacted by the ingestion of so much poison.

Most conventionally grown coffee plants are hybrids developed to flourish in open sun. Coffee naturally prefers the shade, but a crop grown in thick forest is more difficult to tend and harvest and cannot be planted as densely.

Forests are cleared to make room for open fields in which to grow mass amounts of this sun-loving coffee variety. Production increases, but the wild ecosystem of flora and fauna is demolished.

If you are going to drink coffee, it is much better to drink organic coffee. Most organic coffee is grown the natural way – within the shade of lush forests, providing a home for wild plants and animals, sustaining soil fertility, and keeping unique regional ecosystems alive.

GMO Labeling

Chemical manufacturers, Big Agriculture and junk food companies spent more than $70 million spreading misinformation in 2012 to narrowly defeat GMO food labeling ballot initiatives in California and Washington. They continue to spend hundreds of millions of dollars in campaigning to defeat state GMO labeling laws in other states.

Currently, 64 countries have policies requiring the labeling of GMO foods, also referred to as Genetically Engineeredfoods, including all our trading partners in Asia, the European Union and even countries where Genetically Engineered (GE) crops are a large part of the economy, such as Brazil. While there may be universal agreement on labeling abroad, here in the U.S. multinational agribusinesses and food corporations spend millions of dollars in campaign contributions, lobbying efforts, and false advertising to block state labeling initiatives.

As a result of this outpouring of cash to defeat GMO labeling, Americans have been inundated with a number of myths intended to defeat state labeling efforts. These myths need to be corrected.

MYTH #1: American consumers will see a huge spike in food prices if companies are required to disclose the GE ingredients

that are already in their products. The fact is companies change their labels all the time without causing a spike in the price of food. In fact, most companies do not print labels more than one year in advance for regulatory or marketing purposes. The establishment of a mandatory labeling standard for GE foods could easily fall within a company's regular label refresh cycle. The cost of modifying food labels is negligible.

MYTH #2: Farmers are opposed to mandatory labeling. While some may oppose labeling, major farm groups like the National Farmers Union, the National Family Farm Coalition and the National Black Farmers Association support mandatory labeling and have opposed legislation intended to block state laws in the absence of a national standard. With mandatory labeling there will be no new financial cost to farmers and given that food companies already produce foods for a variety of markets, there should not be additional segregation costs. Rather the information that is already being captured within the food supply chain will simply be provided to consumers on the end product.

MYTH #3: We can rely on voluntary measures alone. In the 14 years that the FDA has allowed companies to voluntarily label foods produced using genetic engineering, not one single company has done so. Similarly, we cannot merely rely on the use of voluntary absence claims like "GMO-Free." While such marketing claims allow companies to distinguish themselves in the marketplace, they are not a substitution for mandatory disclosure, because consumers are not given the full universe of information. Creating a federal standard for voluntary marketing claims will do nothing to address the overwhelming demand for labeling and likewise will do nothing to address consumer confusion that has festered in the absence of mandatory labeling.

MYTH #4: We cannot label GE foods because there are too many and they are not dangerous. In the U.S. we do not label dangerous food; we take it off the shelf. Rather, foods produced using genetic engineering are fundamentally different at the molecular and genetic level than those produced using conventional breeding methods. Mandatory labeling of GE foods is essential for preventing consumer deception and will allow con- sumers to make informed choices about the products they are buying and feeding their families.

FACT: What is lost in these industry-driven myths (false advertisements) is the fundamental issue of equality. Food issues can all too often turn into issues of class. Each and every person should have the right and the information available to know what they are buying and feeding to their families, regardless of where they shop and where they live.

It is time for Congress and all governments to provide leadership on an issue that impacts each and every person. Any costs would be negligible; and the benefits of labeling are numerous. Establishing a responsible national labeling standard that informs consumers of what is in the food they are buying and feeding their families is only right and fair.

FIGURE 26. Worldwide GMO Labeling, GMOs are not labeled in the USA.

Other Food Label Problems

Food labels are supposed to be there to help you make healthy, informed decisions about what you eat, in terms of notonly the calories, sodium and fat content, but also the ingredients. However, a recent report released by the Government Accountability Office (GAO) gave the FDA a failing grade when it comes to preventing false and misleading labeling. The GAO also reported that the FDA does not track the correction of labeling violations, which means even if a food manufacturer is known to be using inaccurate labels, no one is checking up to make sure the problem is fixed.

Recently, "Good Morning America" hired a lab to test a dozen packaged food products to see if the nutrients matched the labels. All 12 products tested had label inaccuracies of some sort and three were actually off by more than 20 percent on items like sodium and total fat.

The US Government and GMOs

If you are wondering why the United States leads the world in GMO crop acreage, it's because the United States Department of Agriculture (USDA) and the FDA are heavily influenced by *Bayer* (previously known as Monsanto), which spendsmillions of dollars lobbying the U.S. government for favorable legislation that supports the spread of their toxic products every year. *Bayer* spends $1.4 to $2.5 million annually lobbying the federal government. Furthermore, they invest enormous sums of money on campaign contributions to politicians running for office that show favoritism towards their agenda.In addition, the U.S. Food and Drug Administration (FDA), the USDA, and the U.S. Trade Representative all have a special set of revolving doors leading straight to *Bayer*, which has allowed this transnational giant to gain phenomenal authority and influence. Former *Monsanto* and *Bayer* employees currently hold positions in US government agencies such as the Food and Drug Administration (FDA), United States Environmental Protection Agency (EPA) and the Supreme Court. Of few of these include:

- Clarence Thomas, Associate Justice of the Supreme Court.
- Michael R. Taylor, Deputy Commissioner for Foods at the USDA.
- Ann Veneman, former Executive Director of UNICEF, and US Secretary of Agriculture.
- Linda Fisher, Deputy Administrator of EPA.
- Michael Friedman, Deputy Director of the EPA.
- William D. Ruckelshaus, Administrator of EPA.
- Mickey Kantor, US Secretary of Commerce.
- Linda Fisher, Deputy Administrator of EPA. (Ms. Fisher has been back and forth between positions at Bayer and the EPA)
- Former Secretary of Defense Donald Rumsfeld was chairman and chief executive officer of G. D. Searle & Co., which Monsanto purchased in 1985. Rumsfeld personally made at least $12 million from the transaction.

The above list is just a brief summary of the more high-profile positions. Not listed are the hundreds of other GMO former company employees that are now employed in government positions. The cozy relationship our government has to GMO companies is also a two-way streak of opportunities. For instance, the GMO companies make it plain to government employees that wonderful future employment opportunities exist to those employees that are amicable to their agenda. Some of the more high-profile positions include:

- Josh King, former director of production for White house events, is now the director of global communication in Monsanto's Washington, D.C. Office.

- Clayton K. Yeutter, former Secretary of the USDA, former U.S. Trade representative who led U.S. negotiations in the U.S.-Canada Free Trade Agreement and helped launch the Uruguay round of the GATT negotiations, is now a member of the board of directors of Mycogen, whose majority owner is Dow. Mycogen is also the corporation that holds the patent on a technology to genetically alter plants to produce and deliver "edible vaccines."
- Terry Medley, former administrator of the USDA Animal and Plant Health Inspection Serve, former chair and vice-chair of the USDA Biotechnology Council, and former member of the FDA Food Advisory Committee, is now presiding as the director of regulatory and external affairs of Dupont's agriculture enterprise.
- Micky Kantor, former Secretary of the US Dept. of Commerce and former US Trade Representative, is now a member of the board of directors of Bayer.
- Linda J. Fisher, a former Assistant Administrator of the EPA is now Vice-President of Public Affairs for Monsanto.
- William D. Ruckelshaus, the former chief administrator of the US EPA is now (and for the past 12 years) a member of the board of directors of Bayer.
- Lidia Watrud, a former microbial biotechnology researcher at Bayer, is now with the US EPA.
- Margaret Miller, a former laboratory supervisor for Monsanto, is now Deputy Director of Human Food Safety and Consultative Services in the US FDA.

Again, the list above is a very brief summary showing just the more high-profile positions. There are many other employees that could be listed. Such shows a symbiotic culture where favoritism and rewards end up not only influencing but drive public policy. *Bayer* has similar connections with the government, and heavily influences public policy in the pharmaceutical and agricultural industries for their benefit, over that of the public.

Heavy Metals in Our Food Supply

Heavy metal poisoning is becoming a profoundly serious issue in America today, as toxins in groundwater and soils, some of which have persisted there for decades, are increasingly turning up in both drinking water and the general food supply. All across the country, residues of arsenic, lead and other heavy metals have been detected in well water, crop soils and even foods marketed toward the health conscious. Heavy metals are now being found in USDA certified organic foods, superfoods, vitamins, herbs, and dietary supplements at alarming levels. Neither the USDA nor the FDA have limited regulations on heavy metals in foods and organic foods, meaning that products can contain extremely toxic levels of mercury, lead, cadmium, arsenic, copper and even tungsten while still being legally sold across the USA.

The Natural News Forensic Food Lab, a very reputable independent laboratory headed by food researcher Mike Adams (AKA: the Health Ranger) has tested over 1,000 products using inductively coupled plasma mass spectrometry (ICP-MS) instrumentation. Below is a sample of some of the results obtained from the tests performed. A more comprehensive list of results is published at Labs.NaturalNews.com.

- Over 500 ppb Mercury in dried cat treats
- Over 10 ppm Tungsten in rice protein products
- Over 5 ppm Lead in ginkgo herb products
- Over 400 ppb Lead in cacao powders
- Over 500 ppb Lead and over 2000 ppb Cadmium in rice proteins
- Over 6 ppm Arsenic and over 1 ppm Lead in some spirulina products
- Over 100 ppb Mercury in dog treats
- Over 1,200 ppm Copper in children's multivitamins
- Over 200 ppb Lead in brand-name mascara products

- So much mercury contamination found in Maine lobster that the government put a temporary halt on applicable fisheries.

In response to the publishing of these findings some companies have said that they believe heavy metals are actually good for you and that their customers should eat more heavy metals; therefore, they are not going to make any efforts to reduce heavy metals in their products. This response stands at odds with all known environmental science and sound health advise.

The industry desperately needs a standard—even a voluntary standard—to which products can be compared for their heavy metals composition. Neither the USDA nor the FDA have expressed any interest in promoting or enforcing such a standard.

What Levels Are Safe for Consumption?

What is clear to nearly all environmental scientists are that lower exposure to dietary heavy metals is better for your health. All heavy metals interfere with healthy cellular function. At what level they become "dangerous" depends on your genetics, your diet, and your overall health.

Heavy metals bioaccumulate in the human body. When levels become high enough, they substantially interfere with healthy functioning of the brain, liver, kidneys, heart, skin, reproductive organs, and other body systems.

- Learn more about heavy metals toxicity at http://labs.naturalnews.com/Heavy-Metals.html
- For expert clinical assistance regarding heavy metals detoxification, visit American College for Advancement in Medicine (ACAM) website at ACAM.org

Aren't Heavy Metals Safe Because They Naturally Occur in All Foods?

That is a myth promoted by some companies whose products are heavily contaminated with toxic heavy metals. Some of these companies are trying to convince consumers that heavy metals are not concerning by falsely claiming they are "naturally occurring." The claim is scientifically false, and a prime example of scientific fraud perpetrated against innocent ill-informed customers.

As proof of this, consider the fact that rice grown in China is often heavily contaminated with lead, cadmium, and mercury while rice grown in some areas of the USA is incredibly clean, with virtually zero levels of those same heavy metals. If heavy metals were "naturally occurring" in all rice, then levels would be the same no matter where rice is grown. However, this is not the case. This proves that much of the rice being grown in China is grown in areas which are heavily contaminated by industrial pollution containing heavy metals.

The Natural News Forensic Food Lab has also verified huge concentration differences in seaweed products, depending on where they are grown. Wakame grown near New Zealand has almost zero heavy metals, while Wakame grown near China is heavily contaminated.

Arsenic in Our Food Supply

Arsenic exists in both organic and inorganic forms. Both forms of arsenic are naturally occurring and are differentiated simply by the molecules in which the arsenic is attached. In quite simple terms, organic arsenic contains carbon and hydrogen, and inorganic arsenic contains other metals and elements, such as oxygen and sulfur. It has only been in the past few years that arsenic speciation (differentiation between organic and inorganic arsenic) in food has been possible.

Arsenic is the 55th most common element in the Earth's crust. Because arsenic is ubiquitous in the environment, it is unavoidable to have traces in our food supply given the obvious need for soil, air, and water to grow crops needed for direct human consumption and for feeding livestock. Arsenic is designated by the International Agency for Research on Cancer as a Class A human carcinogen.

Many public water supplies are also contaminated with arsenic because public utility filtration systems typically do not remove this toxin before delivering water to customers. This means that untold millions of people who drink unfiltered tap water are consuming arsenic daily.

Consumers Union, the public policy and advocacy arm of Consumer Reports, conducted laboratory tests of arsenic. Their testing, which included 200 samples of more than 60 different products, found inorganic arsenic at concerning levels in virtually every sample.

Contribution of Inorganic Arsenic Intake by Foods

Vegetables — 24%
Fruit, Fruit Juices — 18%
Rice — 17%
Other — 13%
Beer, Wine — 12%
Flour, Corn, Wheat — 11%
Meat, Eggs — 5%

FIGURE 27.

Relative Contribution of Inorganic Arsenic Sources

Food —56%
Water — 42%
Soil — 1%
Air — 1%

FIGURE 28.

Exposure to Low-Level Arsenic is a Major Threat to Human Health

The U.S. Centers for Disease Control and Prevention (CDC) admits that even exposure to low levels of arsenic can cause major health damage over time. "Because it targets widely dispersed enzyme reactions, arsenic affects nearly all organ systems," says the CDC, noting that arsenic is also linked to gastrointestinal effects, renal damage, cardiovascular events, neurological damage, skin problems, anemia, leukemia, reproductive problems and cancer, including several types of skin cancer. "Arsenic can cause serious effects of the neurologic, respiratory, hematologic, cardiovascular, gastrointestinal, and other systems," adds the agency.

The Organic Trade Association research on arsenic revealed that the most commonly cited consequences of chronic exposure to low levels of arsenic include increased incidence of bladder, lung, kidney, and skin cancers, along with elevated levels of heart disease, skin hyperpigmentation, and skin lesions.

Despite it being a carcinogenic and causing so many health problems, there is no standard for arsenic in foods. There are no arsenic testing requirements. Furthermore, there are no regulations placed upon food companies which mandate labeling or warning the public of arsenic dangers in their food products.

Other Toxic Food Considerations

The primary goal is to achieve and maintain a healthy, happy life, devoid of the chronic illnesses and conditions plaguing society today. However, this has become increasingly difficult considering the numerous problems with the current food system in the United States. That is why growing our own food is so important.

The Food Industry

Understanding how the powerful $5+ Trillion-dollar food industry (expected to be $20 Trillion in 2030) works today is critically important for making the necessary decisions to achieve and maintain a healthy life. For example, approximately 90 percent of the money Americans spend on food is spent on 'processed' foods from large food manufacturers such as General Foods and Procter & Gamble. Their food marketers, employing some of the best and brightest minds to study consumer psychology and demographics, do a masterful job at targeting the right population and making it seem like their processed foods are the obvious, even healthy, best choice. But not only are these processed foods "dead" and devoid of any natural nutrition, they are often harmful to one's health and can even be loaded with carcinogenic substances.

The Media

Members of the media are subject to the same disinformation as the populace and therefore are often largely unaware of the problems in our current food system. A major funding source for the media, especially network television advertising revenue, comes from food and drug companies, making the information more unreliable, thus, either promoting unhealthy and dangerous products, or failing to report on the issues with industry. Celebrities and professional athletes often endorse products or participate in advertisements for processed food that they themselves may never or rarely consume, making the products seem more alluring.

Politicians and the FDA

Like the media, our elected officials are consumers who are subject to the same disinformation and are too often unaware of the health issues. Additionally, our politicians have been effectively controlled by the food and drug companies for so long that our government is now a large part of the problem, rather than being poised to be part of a solution. The Food and Drug Administration (FDA), although originally designed to protect consumers from unhealthy products, now often work diligently to protect the very companies it is supposed to regulate by keeping out competition and prolonging the economic life of the drug companies' government-sanctioned patents.

Sadly, government policy is now typically based on data supplied by the food or pharmaceutical industry, lobbyist, and campaign contributions rather than an science from and unbiased source. *USA TODAY* study found that more than half of the experts hired to advise the government on the safety and effectiveness of medicine and food have financial relationships with the companies that will be helped or hurt by their decisions. These experts are hired to advise the FDA on which substances should be approved for sale, and how studies should be designed. To date, the FDA has allowed more than 70,000 chemicals to infiltrate our food supply. Many of these dangerous ingredients are outright toxins, poisoning us, undermining our health, and allowing cancer and diseases to enter our bodies.

Fish

Fish is high in protein, and full of essential nutrients and healthy fats. It is also easily digested, and assimilated, and full of essential nutrients and fats. Unfortunately, the vast majority of fish sold is imported from developing countries, much of which have proven to be contaminated with banned chemicals, poisons, carcinogens, and high levels of antibiotics, often caused by being farmed or caught in contaminated waters.

However, imported fish is not the only fish that is likely to be bad for your health. According to a new U.S. Geological Survey study, scientists detected mercury contamination in every fish sampled in nearly 300 streams across the United States. More than a quarter of these fish were found to contain mercury at levels exceeding the criterion for the protection of people who consume average amounts of fish, established by the U.S. Environmental Protection Agency.

Exposure to mercury can damage your brain, kidney, and lungs. Mercury is especially damaging to your central nervous system (CNS), and studies show that mercury in the CNS causes psychological, neurological, and immunological problems. Furthermore, mercury has an extremely long half-life in the human body that scientist believe is somewhere between 15 and 30 years. Additionally, non-dissipating medications, antibiotics, fungicides, pesticides, herbicides, untreated sewage, and other chemicals are also entering our waterways at alarming rates.

Conventional raised farmed fish often found in grocery stores may not be the answer either. Studies show that farm-raised fish contain more polychlorinated biphenyl and over ten times the amount of dioxin. Raising Tilapia on feed that does not contain toxic chemicals is the way to go, as there are no dangerous substances entering the food supply.

Soy

Unfortunately, numerous so-called experts and the media have extolled soy a healthy food. Supporters claim it as an ideal source of protein. It is also being recommended as a great tool to for lowering cholesterol, protecting against cancer and heart disease, reducing menopause symptoms, and preventing osteoporosis, as well as other things. However, studies based on sound research have found that soy products may increase the risk of breast cancer, cause brain cause damage, contribute to thyroid disorders, promote kidney stones, weaken the immune system and cause fatal food allergies.

One of the most disturbing of soy's ill effects on health has to do with its phytoestrogens that can mimic the effects of the female hormone estrogen. Just moderate consumption of soy has been shown to alter a woman's menstrual cycle. This hormonal disruption is not healthy for men or women. Especially devastating for men, soy is known to lower testosterone levels.

Processed Meat

Processed meats are not a healthful choice for anyone and should be avoided entirely, according to a recent review of more than 7,000 clinical studies examining the connection between diet and cancer. The report was commissioned by The World Cancer Research Fund (WCRF). Virtually all processed meats contain a well-known carcinogen: sodium nitrite. It is a commonly used preservative and antimicrobial agent that also adds color and flavor to processed and cured meats, but this additive can also cause the formation of nitrosamines in your system, which can lead to cancer. Hot dogs, deli meats and bacon are notorious for their nitrite content.

Processed meat is far from being 100 percent beef, besides being loaded with harmful nitrates, it contains some nasty filler and by-product materials, such as other animal parts that most people find repulsive. It is also common for processed meats to contain MSG, high-fructose corn syrup, preservatives, and harmful artificial flavoring or artificial colors.

Processed Food

When discussing processed food, the list of problems is lengthy, but a few specific issues should be discussed. The first is the contaminants in processed food. The FDA, in its long history of managing food safety, has established guidelines for acceptable quantities of a number of contaminants that it will allow in our food supply. Included on the list are various types of mold, flies, maggots, insect eggs or body fragments, rodent hairs and feces pellets, pus pockets, and larvae, to name just a few. No, there is not a typo, the FDA has established acceptable limits of these contaminates.

Another issue with processed foods is the hydrogenated oils used to lengthen the shelf life of products like crackers and cookies, which are also associated with diabetes and heart disease. They are also generally high in sodium, corn syrup and other unhealthy ingredients.

As with charred meats, researchers discovered that a cancer-causing and potentially neurotoxic chemical called acrylamide is created when carbohydrate-rich foods are cooked at high temperatures, whether baked, fried, roasted, grilled, or toasted. The chemical is formed from a reaction between sugars and an amino acid (asparagine) during high-temperature cooking above 212°F. As a general rule, the chemical is formed when food is heated enough to produce a fairly dry and "browned" surface. Hence, it can be found in processed potatoes, grain products and even coffee.

Acrylamide is not the only hazard associated with heat-processed foods, however. The three-year long EU project known as *Heat-Generated Food Toxicants*1 *(HEA*TOX), identified more than 800 heat-induced compounds in food, 52 of which are potential carcinogens. For example, the high heat of grilling reacts with proteins in red meat, poultry, and fish, creating heterocyclic amines, which have also been linked to cancer.

Food Additives

More than 3,000 food additives, such as preservatives, flavorings, colors, and other ingredients, are legally added to foods in the United States, most of which are unhealthy and often dangerous. Many of these additives have been linked to an increased risk of cancer, while recent studies have shown others are estrogen-mimicking xenoestrogens that have been linked to a range of hormonal health effects in males and females. Studies have also shown that a variety of common food dyes and preservatives cause some people to become measurably more hyperactive and distractible and can even do brain damage resulting in a significant reduction in IQ.

International Foods (China)

Generally speaking, quality control and employee health are not issues that the Chinese food industry or the Chinese government are overly concerned about. Without the regulation, China's products often contain plastics, pesticides, herbicides, and other cancer-causing chemicals, in far greater amounts than those produced in America.

The United States imported roughly 4.6 billion pounds of agricultural products from China in 2014. For example, China is responsible for 90 percent of the vitamin (C) consumed by Americans, 78 percent of the tilapia, 70 percent of the apple juice, 50 percent of the cod, 43 percent of the processed mushrooms and 23 percent of the garlic. The top U.S. import commodities from China are fruits and vegetables (fresh/processed), snack food, spices, and tea — the combined which accounts for nearly one-half of the total U.S. agricultural imports from China. According to congressional testimony by Don Kraemer, Deputy

Director of the Office of Food Safety at the FDA, *"The FDA has encountered compliance problems with several Chinese food exports, including lead and cadmium in ceramic-ware used to store and ship food, and staphylococcal contamination of products from China remains a concern for FDA, Congress, and American consumers."* **Less than 1 percent of food imports are examined (laboratory tested) in any given year!**

Artificial Sweeteners

All Artificial Sweeteners are toxic to the human body. They basically trick your body into thinking that it is going to receive sugar (calories), but when the sugar doesn't come your body continues to signal that it needs more, which results in carb cravings. Contrary to industry claims, research over the last 30 years—including several large-scale prospective cohort studies—has shown that artificial sweeteners stimulate appetite, increase cravings for carbs, and produce a variety of metabolic dysfunctions that promote fat storage and weight gain.

The most common artificial sweeteners are Aspartame *(NutraSweet, Equal)*, Acesulfame-K or Ace-K *(Sunett, SweetOne)*, Saccharin *(Sweet'n Low)*, and Sucralose *(Splenda)*. The list of side effects includes, but are not limited to headaches, chronic respiratory disease, dermatologic reactions, tachycardia, cancer, and tumors, enlarged organs, and many neuro-psychiatric disorders, including panic attacks, mood changes, visual hallucinations, manic episodes, isolated dizziness, memory impairment, nausea, temper outbursts, and depression.

Stevia isn't really an artificial sweetener because it is made from one of the extracts of the stevia plant (an herb); and is often marketed as a natural sweetener. However, *Stevia* can negatively interfere with absorption of carbohydrates and can further disrupt the metabolizing and conversion of food into energy.

Food Colorants

Americans are now eating 5 times more food dye than in 1955. There are serious hidden dangers of food colorants. Commonly, they can cause various tumors, allergic reactions, brain gliomas, immune system impairment, and hyperactivity. With their widespread use, they can be found in baked goods, beverages, candies, cereals, treated fruit, ice cream, cosmetics and even dog food. So if you are concerned about your health you should avoid foods with these common label ingredients: Blue #1, Blue #2, Citrus Red #2, Green #3, Red #40, Red #3, Yellow #5 (Tartrazine), Yellow #6 or any other food dyes.

Preservatives

Preservatives are chemicals used to keep food fresh. Although there are a number of different types of food preservatives, antimicrobials, antioxidants, and products that slow the natural ripening process are some of the most common. Despite their function, preservatives can pose a number of serious health risks.

Cancer is a serious side effect associated with the use of preservatives. In fact, the National Toxicology Program reports that propyl gallate—a preservative commonly used to stabilize certain cosmetics and foods containing fat—may cause tumors in the brain, thyroid, and pancreas. Similarly, *InChem*—an organization that provides peer-reviewed information on chemicals and contaminants—notes that nitrosamines, including nitrates and nitrites, can lead to the development of certain cancer-causing compounds as they interact with natural stomach acids. Nitrosamines are found in a variety of foods, including cured meat, beer, and non-fat dried milk.

Hyperactivity in children is another possible side effect associated with the use of preservatives. A study performed by the *Archives of Disease in Childhood* (ADC) noted a significant increase in hyperactive behavior in 3-year-olds who took benzoate preservatives. Children who were enrolled in the study also demonstrated a decrease in hyperactive behavior after they stopped taking benzoate preservatives. While benzoates can be found in a number of foods, they are often used to preserve acidic foods and beverages, like soda, pickles, and fruit juice.

Some people may experience damage to their heart as a result of preservative use. Sodium nitrates can cause blood vessels to narrow and become stiffer. In addition, nitrates may affect the way the body processes sugar and may be to blame for the development of some types of diabetes, the Harvard School of Public Health notes.

Studies have shown and even the FDA has warned that other preservatives, such as Chlorphenesin and Phenoxyethanol, sulfites, BHA (Butylated hydroxyanisole) and BHT (Butylated hydroxytoluene) are toxic and in addition to the above-named effects, can cause depression of the central nervous system, vomiting and diarrhea, severe allergic reactions including anaphylactic shock, stomach irritation, skin sensitivity, and even effects on the body's blood coagulation system.

Flavor Enhancers

Flavor enhancers are used in foods to enhance the existing flavor or modify flavors in the food without contributing to any significant flavor of their own. Food flavor enhancers are commercially produced in the form of instant soups, frozen dinners, and most processed foods. Monosodium glutamate (MSG) is one of the most common flavor enhancers. The FDA has indicated flavor enhancers ingested in low doses are generally regarded as safe (GRAS); however, the list of dangerous side effects is extensive. Most are known to be carcinogenic to humans, but can also cause brain damage, neurological diseases, kidney problems, obesity, eye damage, headaches, depression, fatigue, disorientation, chest pain or difficulty breathing, and severe allergies.

High-Fructose Corn Syrup (HFCS)

Food companies like to use high-fructose syrup, instead of traditional sweeteners because it costs less to make, is sweeter to the taste, and mixes more easily with other ingredients. The average American consumes nearly 63 pounds of high-fructose syrup a year. High-fructose corn syrup is commonly added to many processed foods and beverages. It maybe be listed on food labels as "corn sweetener," "corn syrup," or "corn syrup solids" as well as "high-fructose corn syrup".

Research shows that this liquid sweetener can upset the human metabolism, raising the risk for heart disease and diabetes. Researchers say that high-fructose corn syrup's chemical structure also encourages overeating. It forces the liver to pump more heart-threatening triglycerides into the bloodstream. In addition, it can deplete the body's reserves of chromium, a mineral important for healthy levels of cholesterol, insulin, and blood sugar. Additionally, almost half of tested samples of commercial HFCS contained mercury. Mercury was also found in nearly a third of 55 popular brand-name food and beverage products where HFCS is the first- or second-highest labeled ingredient. Mercury is toxic in all forms, and a poison to the brain and nervous system. At a minimum it causes extreme fatigue and neuro-muscular dysfunction

Food Labels

Food companies know that people are drawn to certain terms like "All Natural" and "Made with Whole Grains." They can make enormous profits if they can market their products as being healthy. "Natural" labeled food generated $219 billion in 2019, and 60 percent of all cereals are now labeled "whole grain," even processed, sugar-laden ones. Misleading food labels regularly dupe consumers with these keywords, questionable advertising practices, misleading packaging statements, and bold statements that appeal to people's dietary preferences and weight loss goals. Sometimes it is impossible to identify the ingredients in a product by reading the label. The FDA allows for ingredients that are present only in small quantities to be labeled as "artificial flavor", "natural flavor", or "spices". Only the manufacturer knows what all the ingredients are in the product. Unfortunately, since the FDA does not regulate all food labels it is unable to keep food manufacturers from using crafty wording.

Antibiotics in Food

Antibiotics are widely used in food-producing animals and is now viewed as a normal operating practice. Animals in factory farms are given hefty doses of antibiotics so that they can remain alive in stressful, unsanitary conditions, and to make them grow faster. Even many grazing animals, not raised in farm lots, are given antibiotics to help them grow faster. The practice of giving animals antibiotics greatly increases profit margins for livestock producers and pharmaceutical companies. As a result, according to the FDA more than 32 million pounds of antibiotics are given to animals annually.

This use contributes to the emergence of antibiotic-resistant bacteria in food-producing animals. These resistant bacteria can contaminate the foods that come from those animals, as these antibiotics work their way up the food chain, and persons who consume these foods can develop antibiotic-resistant infections. Scientists around the world have provided strong evidence that antibiotic use in food-producing animals can have a negative impact on public health. Because of the link between antibiotic use in food-producing animals and the occurrence of antibiotic-resistant infections in humans, CDC encourages and supports efforts to minimize inappropriate use of antibiotics in humans and animals.

In addition to the emergence of antibiotic-resistant bacteria, common side effects from antibiotics include diarrhea, nausea, vomiting, fungal infections, and a variety of allergic reactions.

Fluoride/Chromium-6/Chlorine and Bottled Water (Water Treatments)

Fluoridation is not legal or not used in the overwhelming number of countries including industrialized ones. In fact, 97 percent of Western Europe has chosen fluoride-free water. The United States is one of only eight countries in the entire developed world that fluoridates its water supply. It is added under the guise that it prevents and control tooth decay.

The fluoride added to our drinking water is actually chemical waste product. It is certainly not anything that should be ingested or included in our diet. The chemicals used to fluoridate water in the US are not pharmaceutical grade. Instead, they come from the wet scrubbing systems of the superphosphate fertilizer industry. These chemicals (90 per-cent of which are sodium fluorosilicate and fluorosilicic acid), are classified hazardous wastes and contaminated with various impurities.

Numerous studies have shown that fluoride is dangerous to our health. Five studies from China show a lowering of IQ in children associated with fluoride exposure. The Department of Health in New Jersey found that bone cancer in male children was far greater in areas where water was fluoridated. The U.S. Environmental Protection Agency (EPA) researchers confirmed bone cancer-causing effects of fluoride at low levels in their animal studies. Sadly, 23 human studies and 100 animal studies have linked fluoride to brain damage. Even the US Food and Drug Administration (FDA) has never approved any fluoride product designed for ingestion as safe or effective. Although they still allow it to be put into our drinking water, food, and toothpaste. Read the warning label on your toothpaste about fluoride, then throw it in the trash and start using fluoride free toothpaste and mouthwash.

Fluoride is dangerous, but Chromium-6 (also known as hexavalent chromium) in your water supply may be far worse. Chromium-6 was detected in 31 of the 35 city water supplies tested and confirmed by a number of independent tests by various water utility companies. Hexavalent chromium is classified as "likely to be carcinogenic to humans" by the U.S. Environmental Protection Agency (EPA).

Chlorine is another noxious chemical deliberately put in the water by public health officials. Chlorine is in the same chemical group as fluoride, which has been linked with cancer and osteoporosis. The chemical element chlorine is a corrosive, poisonous, greenish-yellow gas that has a suffocating odor and is 2-1/2 times heavier than air. It can result in arteriosclerosis, heart attack and stroke. Research has shown that individuals who consume chlorinated drinking water have an elevated risk of cancer of the bladder, stomach, pancreas, kidney, and rectum as well as Hodgkin's and non-Hodgkin's lymphoma.

Bottled water has issues, as well. A recent study on more than 250 bottles from 11 leading brands worldwide revealed that a single liter of bottled water can contain dozens or even tens of thousands of microplastic particles, which is much greater than the levels found in tap water samples. Microplastics hold toxic chemicals that can harmfully impact human health, the wildlife, and natural environments.

The best way to ensure that you are drinking healthy water is to install a reputable filtration system. Reverse osmosis filter systems are some of the strongest, most effective filters for drinking water. They are known to remove more than 99% of most dangerous contaminants in the water, including heavy metals, herbicides, pesticides, chlorine, and other chemicals, and even hormones. A good system ranges in cost from $250 to $600 (USD 2020) and can be installed at the kitchen sink. Healthy fish tank water will be addressed later.

Pesticides/Herbicides

As discussed earlier in this chapter pesticides are widely used in producing food to control pests such as insects, rodents, weeds, bacteria, mold, and fungus. Seven of the most toxic chemical compounds known to man are approved for use as pesticides in the production of foods. These toxins are referred to as Persistent Organic Pollutants (POP's). They are called persistent because they are not easily removed from the environment. The greatest risk to our environment and our health comes from the chemical pesticides. In spite of the dangers, the government maintains its approval of the use of toxic chemicals to make pesticides. And science is constantly developing variations of poisons.

Pesticides can be toxic to humans and animals. It can take a small amount of some toxins to kill, and other toxins that are slower acting may take a long time to cause harm to the human body. Even just using pesticides in amounts within regulation, studies have revealed neurotoxins can do serious damage. Several factors determine how your body will react including your level of exposure, the type of chemical you ingest, and your individual resistance to the chemicals. Some possible reactions are fatigue, skin irritations, brain and blood disorders, nausea and vomiting, liver and kidney damage, reproductive damage, breathing problems, cancer and even death.

Herbicides (weed killers) are mixtures of chemicals designed to spray on weeds, where they get inside the plants and inhibit enzymes required for the plant to live. The active ingredient in the most widely used herbicide is glyphosate, and some have the main component of Agent Orange. Until the introduction of GMO crops about 20 years ago, herbicides were sprayed on fields before planting, and then only sparingly used around crops. The food that we ate from the plants was free of these chemicals.

In stark contrast, with herbicide resistant GMO plants, the herbicides, and a mixture of other chemicals (surfactants) required to get the active ingredient into the plant are sprayed directly on the crops and are then taken up into the plant. The surrounding weeds are killed while the GMO plant is engineered to resist the herbicide. Therefore, the food crop itself contains the herbicide as well as a mixture of surfactants.

To accommodate the fact that weeds are becoming glyphosate resistant, thereby requiring more herbicide use, the EPA has steadily increased its allowable concentration limit in food and has essentially ignored our exposure to the other chemicals that are in its commercial formulation.

As a result, the amount of glyphosate-based herbicide introduced into our foods has increased enormously since the introduction of GMO crops. Multiple studies have shown that glyphosate-based herbicides are toxic and likely public health hazards.

New scientific studies link glyphosate to a host of health risks, such as cancer, miscarriages, and disruption of humansex hormones. Other conditions with strong correlations are ADHD, Alzheimer's disease, anencephaly, autism, birth defects, brain, breast and other cancers, celiac disease, chronic kidney disease, colitis, depression, diabetes, heart disease, hypothyroidism, inflammatory bowel disease, liver disease, and many others.

Fungicides are used to kill or prevent the growth of fungi and their spores. They can be used to control fungi that damage plants, including rusts, mildews, and blights.

Fungicide residues have been found on food for human consumption. Modern fungicides that are sprayed on fruit and vegetables have come under fresh scrutiny after scientists found they caused similar genetic changes in mouse neurons. Many experts have provided valid arguments, and shown through reputable studies, that fungicides are dangerous to human health.

Scientists at the University of North Carolina in Chapel Hill performed a comprehensive study on fungicides. To their surprise, they found certain compounds found in fungicides produced some genetic hallmarks of autism and neurodegenerative diseases at the same time.

Irradiation

Irradiation is the process of exposing fresh foods to low amounts of x-rays to sterilize and prolong its life. Commercialized food irradiation is done on a constant basis. Food growers and sellers say that food irradiation is safe. However, studies show the x-ray irradiation destroys vitamins A, E, and K. Some studies show that x-ray irradiation also destroys up to 85 percent of the vitamin C found in vegetables, and fruits. Irradiation also destroy the digestive enzymes in raw foods. Irradiation damages food by breaking up molecules and creating free radicals. Free radicals are unstable atoms that damage cells, causing illness, accelerate the aging process, and contribute to a host of diseases, such as cancer. When high-energy electron beams are used, trace amounts of radioactivity may be created in the food. Some bacteria, like the one that causes botulism, aswell as viruses are not killed by current doses of irradiation.

No one knows the long-term effects of a life-long diet that includes foods which will be frequently irradiated, such as meat, chicken, vegetables, fruits, salads, sprouts, and juices. Studies on animals fed irradiated foods have shown increased tumors, reproductive failures, and kidney damage. Some possible causes are irradiation-induced vitamin deficiencies, the inactivity of enzymes in the food, DNA damage, and toxic radiolytic products in the food.

Bisphenol-A (BPA)

BPA is one of the biggest players in the wrapping industry. ome 9 million tons of BPA-derived chemicals are produced worldwide each year, making it one of the highest produced chemicals worldwide. In addition, BPA has an expected compound annual growth rate of 6% over the period 2019–2024. BPA is deeply imbedded in the products of modern consumer society, not just as the building block for polycarbonate plastic but also in the manufacture of epoxy resins and other plastics. BPA is routinely used to in plastic containers, water bottles, to line cans to prevent corrosion and food contamination. BPA has been used as an inert ingredient in pesticides, as a fungicide, antioxidant, flame retardant, rubber chemical, and polyvinyl chloride stabilizer. BPA contamination has become widespread in the environment in rivers and estuaries throughout the US. Unfortunately, BPA does not readily degrade in the environment. What this all means is that we are constantly being exposed to BPA. A CDC (Centers for Disease Control and Prevention) study found 95 percent of adult human urine samples and 93 percent of samples in children had BPA. However, the FDA has approved the use of BPA and the EPA does not consider it cause for concern.

According to estimates, just a couple of servings of canned food can exceed the daily safety limits for BPA exposure in children. Even low-level exposure to BPA can be hazardous to one's health. There are more than 100 independent studies linking the chemical to serious health problems in humans. Some of the main problems are prostate cancer and breast cancer, diabetes, and obesity, altered immune function, early sexual development in girls and disrupted reproductive function, learning and behavioral problems, including hyperactivity, abnormal heart rhythms and coronary artery disease, asthma, depression, diabetes, heart disease and reproductive disorders.

Growth Hormones

Today's hyper-productive animals are given injections and implants (in the case of cows) or genetic engineering (in the case of salmon), of artificially high levels of sex or growth hormones. This allows them to grow bigger, faster and produce better. Surprisingly, little research has been done on the health effects of these hormones in humans, in part because it's difficult to separate the effects of added hormones from the mixture of natural hormones, proteins, and other components found in milk and meat.

However, many experts have valid concerns that these excess hormones in the food supply are contributing to cancer, early puberty in girls, and other health problems in humans. For years, consumer advocates and public health experts have fought to limit the use of hormones in cows, and some support a ban on the practice. Unfortunately, the FDA continues to approve of growth hormones in animals for human consumption, even though there has been minimal testing to determine whether or not there are any health consequences related to their use.

In 1993, the FDA approved recombinant bovine growth hormone (rBGH), a synthetic cow hormone that increases milk production when injected into dairy cows. Research has found that milk from rBGH-treated cows contains up to 10 times more IGF than other milk. Higher blood levels of IGF have been associated with more than a 50 percent increased risk of breast, prostate, and other cancers in humans.

IGF isn't the only hormone found in the food supply. Ranchers have been fattening up cattle with other sex hormones, most notably estrogen, since the 1950s. Today most beef cows in the U.S, except those, that are raised 'organic', receive an implant in their ear that delivers a hormone, usually a form of estrogen (estradiol) in some combination with five other hormones. Even miniscule amounts of estrogen could affect prepubescent girls and boys. Whether it is related or not, sperm counts in men from America, Europe, Australia, and New Zealand have dropped by more than 50 percent in less than 40 years. The majority of public health experts, health-conscious nutritionist, and most registered dietitians urge consumers to stay away from rBGH-treated milk because of its potentially higher IGF levels.

Biomagnification & Bioaccumulation

Biomagnification, also known as **bioamplification** or **biological magnification**, is the increasing concentration of a substance, such as a toxic chemical, in the tissues of organisms at successively higher levels in a food chain. This increase can occur as a result of:

- **Persistence** – where the substance cannot be broken down by environmental processes.
- **Food chain energetics** – where the substance's concentration increases progressively as it moves up a food chain.
- **Low or non-existent rate of internal degradation or excretion of the substance** – often due to water-insolubility.

Biological magnification often refers to the process whereby certain substances such as pesticides or heavy metals work their way into lakes, rivers, and the ocean, and then move up the food chain in progressively greater concentrations as they are incorporated into the diet of aquatic organisms such as zooplankton, which in turn are eaten perhaps by fish, which then may be eaten by bigger fish, large birds, animals, or humans. The substances become increasingly concentrated in tissues or internal organs as they move up the chain. Bioaccumulates are substances that increase in concentration in living organisms as they take in contaminated air, water, or food because the substances are very slowly metabolized or excreted.

Although sometimes used interchangeably with "bioaccumulation", an important distinction is drawn between the two, and with bioconcentration.

- **Bioaccumulation** – the increase in the concentration of a substance

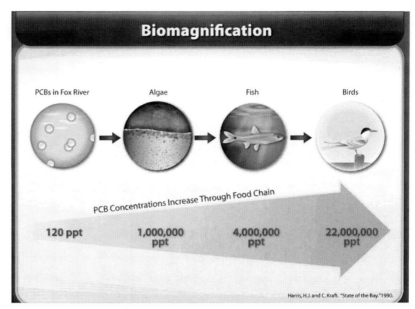

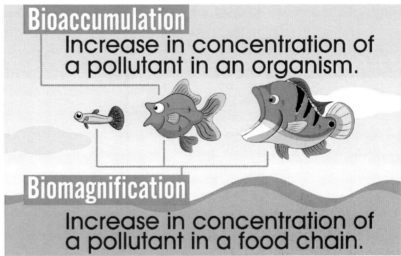

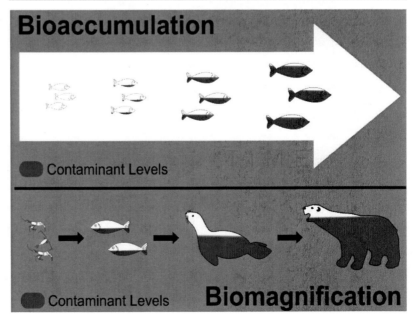

in certain tissues of organisms' bodies due to absorption from food and the environment.

- **Bioconcentration** is defined as occurring when uptake from the water is greater than excretion.

Thus, bioconcentration and bioaccumulation occur within an organism, and biomagnification occurs across trophic (food chain) levels.

Dolphins have been studied by Japanese researchers as a model species for biomagnification because their migratory routes are known, they live in relatively unpolluted waters, and they live a long time (20-50 years). DDT has been found in dolphin blubber in greater concentrations (100 times greater than sardines) than would be expected given the small concentrations present in the water and in sardines, their favorite food. These unexpectedly large concentrations are the result of DDT biomagnification up the food chain.

Biomagnification has serious consequences for all species. It is particularly dangerous for predator species especially if they are at the top of long food chains. Predators are usually at or near the top of their food chain. This puts them at risk because the degree of biomagnification is high by the time it reaches their trophic level. Also, top predators usually consume large quantities of meat which has lots of fatty tissue and contaminants. Polar bears, humans, eagles, and dolphins are examples of top predators, and all of these organisms are vulnerable to the effects of biomagnification. Predators that consume large amounts of wild caught fish have an exceptionally high degree of risk.

Medical Industry vs. Nutrition

Nutrition and diet have long been considered the basis for health. People in the 18th century knew scurvy could only be cured and/or prevented by foods in the diet. So, in today's very advanced age of technology and research, it stands to reason medical professionals would be well-versed in the effects of nutrition on their patients' health. Unfortunately, this is not the case.

Numerous sources report that doctors themselves feel they are inadequately trained to discuss nutrition with their patients. An article titled "A Time for Change: Nutrition Education in Medicine" by nutrition.org states,

"...among a cohort of 930 cardiologists, 90% believe their role includes providing patients with basic nutrition information. In the same group of physicians, though, 90% stated that they had received little-to-no training in nutrition during their fellowship, 59% stated that they had received no nutrition during internal medicine training, and 31% reported no nutrition education in medical school."

Nutrition.org also reported results from a recent survey which indicated 71% of medical schools "failed to meet the minimum nutrition education recommendation of 25 hours, 36% provided 12 or fewer hours, and 9% provided none." Why are medical professionals not being given the training/education they need to advise their patients in this integral part of their health?

One doctor has been quoted as saying, "The problem is that there is not really a consensus on how important nutrition is, and what kind of nutrition should be taught." Dr. Rupy Aujla in his article "Food is medicine – so why aren't our doctors trained in the science of nutrition?" states, "If we don't appropriately educate our health professionals on the breadth and utility of other evidence-based health interventions, the only option they will have heard of is a pharmaceutical one." The pharmaceutical industry is capitalizing on this opportunity through intense marketing strategies that begin when students are in medical school. Rijul Kshirsagar and Priscilla Vu in their article "The Pharmaceutical Industry's Role in U.S. Medical Education" states, "Medical students' exposure to pharmaceutical marketing begins early, growing in frequency throughout their training. Students receive gifts such as free meals, textbooks, pocket texts, small trinketsand even drug samples. Pharmaceutical companies, recognizing the formative nature of the clinical years of medical education, seek to form relationships with medical students years before they are ready to independently practice medicine." Therefore, with little to no nutrition training and constant exposure to pharmaceutical options, many doctors will prescribe a pill to address a symptom rather than discuss nutrition with a patient to address and potentially prevent a problem.

Additionally, physicians receive extraordinarily little education in prevention. As Thomas J. Van Gilder and Patrick Remingtonin their article "Medical education needs to take 'an ounce of prevention' seriously" states "Traditional medical education may include a token course in prevention, but the focus is squarely on how to treat patients."

While many health issues such as obesity, diabetes, congestive heart failure, and other conditions are preventable, the ability to prevent them requires physician knowledge about nutrition and/or a willingness to partner with other professionals knowledgeable about nutrition to form a care team. Unfortunately, it appears there is little funding, training and/or incentives to support preventive care; and the medical community is rewarded greatly though tremendous monetary gains for implementing a pharmaceutical treatment plan.

Overweight & Obesity

Approximately 1/3 of the world's population is either obese or overweight. Obesity is an issue affecting people of all ages and incomes, everywhere. The rise in global obesity rates over the last three decades has been substantial and widespread, presenting a major public health epidemic in both the developed and the developing world.

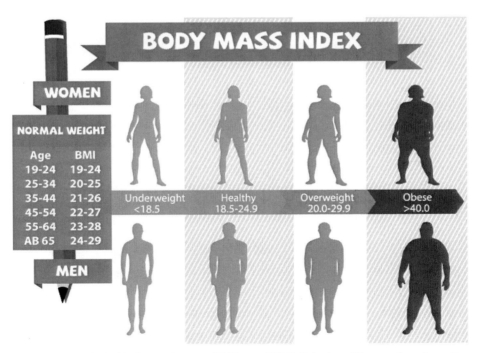

FIGURE 29. NOTE: To determine your BMI enter "BMI Calculator" in your favorite online search engine.

Worldwide obesity has nearly tripled since 1975. More than 50% of the world's 671 million obese live in 10 countries (ranked beginning with the countries with the most obese people): US, China, India, Russia, Brazil, Mexico, Egypt, Germany, Pakistan, and Indonesia. The Middle East showed large increases in obesity. Bahrain, Egypt, Saudi Arabia, Oman, and Kuwait were among the countries with the largest increases in obesity globally. In six countries, all in the Middle East and Oceania – Kuwait, Kiribati, the Federated States of Micronesia, Libya, Qatar, and Samoa – the prevalence of obesity for women exceeds 50%. In Tonga, both men and women have obesity prevalence over 50%. In sub-Saharan

Africa, the highest obesity rates (42%) are seen among South African women. In the United States, more than 71% of all adults over the age of 20 are either overweight or obese.

Overweight and obesity results in substantial health risks -- such as cardiovascular disease, cancer, diabetes, osteoarthritis, dementia, and chronic kidney disease increase substantially when a person is overweight. Children who are overweight or obese are at greater risk for high blood pressure, type 2 diabetes, and heart disease. According to the National Institutes of Health, obesity and overweight together are the second leading cause of preventable death in the United States, close behind tobacco use.

Overweight and obesity is a financial issue. For instance, the obesity crisis costs the United States more than $150 billion in healthcare costs annually and billions of dollars more in lost productivity.

Overweight and obesity is a national security issue. The obesity crisis impacts the United States military readiness. Being overweight or obese is the leading cause of medical disqualifications, with nearly one-quarter of service applicants rejected for exceeding the weight or body fat standards. Obese service members and members of their family who are obese cost the military about $1 billion every year in healthcare costs and lost productivity.

Overweight and obesity is a community safety issue. With millions of obese and overweight Americans serving as first responders, firefighters, police officers and in other essential community service and protection roles, public safety is at risk. Seventy percent of firefighters are overweight or obese, putting them at risk for cardiovascular events — the leading cause of line-of-duty deaths.

Overweight and obesity is a child development and academic achievement issue. Childhood obesity is correlated with poor educational performance and increased risk for bullying and depression.

Overweight and obesity is a top national priority. Americans rated obesity as the top health concern in the country in a recent public opinion survey conducted by the Greenberg, Quinlan, Rosner Research and Bellwether Research groups.

The main driver of obesity is NOT lack of exercise. For years we have been told that a lack of exercise and a sedentary lifestyle are the major factors associated with the obesity crises. However, physical activity levels began to decline before the global obesity rate started to surge — which means changes to the food environment are the prime obesity culprit. Food companies, convenience stores, and fast-food restaurants have made inroads all over the world with cheap, calorie-dense, low-nutrient content food. Soda, candy, processed food, and fast food is loaded with preservatives, additives, sugar, sodium, and other harmful substances. These products are inexpensive, heavily marketed, and are much more accessible than healthier alternatives, like fruits and vegetables. In addition, portion sizes have gone up and people are eating outside of the home more often, which means heavier unhealthy meals.

The government (influenced by millions of dollars in food industry lobbyist efforts and political campaign contributions) and the media (influenced by millions of dollars in food industry advertisements) tell us we need to exercise more as the way to shrink our waistlines. The exercise chant for weight loss is highly misleading. Exercise is excellent for

health; and should be an important part of everyone's day, as should proper stress management, staying hydrated, getting adequate sleep, stretching daily, and avoiding things that are harmful to your body. Although exercise can aid in weight loss and weight control, it is not nearly as important as eating properly on a consistent basis. Eating healthy foods, avoid junk foods and processed foods, implementing portion control, and managing caloric intake are the keys to weight loss and weight management.

What really works for weight loss is not just cutting calories but satisfying your hunger with the right kinds of foods. Eating a diet of healthy fish, fruits, and vegetables, instead of fast food and processed food will do more for weight loss than anything else. In addition, a person on this type of diet feels better and will enjoy a higher quality of life. Coincidently, Tilapia farming provides healthy fish, and exercise.

Thinking Out of the Box - Farming

Santa Monica Encourages Farming

The City of Santa Monica in California is actively encouraging people to pull out their front lawns and replace them with gardens. The city's website for the Office of Sustainability and the Environment offers tips on how to do just that.

Making the Most of Available Land

Curtis Stone is the owner/operator of Green City Acres, a commercial urban farm based in Kelowna, BC. Farming less than half an acre on a collection of urban plots, Green City Acres grows vegetables for farmers' markets, restaurants and retail outlets. After five successful seasons, Curtis has demonstrated that one can grow an extraordinary amount of food in a backyard, and make a good living doing it. During his slower months, Curtis works as a public speaker, teacher, and consultant, sharing his story to inspire a new generation of farmers.

There are 40 million acres of lawns in North America. In their current form, these unproductive expanses of grass represent a significant financial and environmental cost. However, viewed through a different lens, they can also be seen as a tremendous source of opportunity. Access to land is a major barrier for many people who want to enter the agricultural sector, and urban and suburban yards have huge potential for would-be farmers wanting to become part of this growing movement.

The Urban Farmer is a comprehensive, hands-on, practical manual to help you learn the techniques and business strategies you need to make a good living growing high-yield, high-value crops right in your own backyard (or someone else's). Major benefits include:

- Low capital investment and overhead costs
- Reduced need for expensive infrastructure
- Easy access to markets

Growing food in the city means that fresh crops may travel only a few blocks from field to table, making this innovative approach the next logical step in the local food movement. Based on a scalable, easily reproduce business model, The Urban Farmer is your complete guide to minimizing risk and maximizing profit by using intensive production in small leased or borrowed spaces.

Curtis Stone got his start farming other people's yards from a friend's family who owned two houses next door to each other. After one burned down, and the family did not have time to keep up the property, Curtis made a deal with them. He needed a place to farm, and they needed someone to take care of their property.

Various Options Available to New Farmers

In addition to farming yards as discussed above, new farmers have several other avenues available to them to get started farming. Barriers that often prohibit people from entering the farming world typically include the means with which to purchase land and equipment and the lack of available land and mentorship. However, there are various avenues available that allow people to affordably reach their farming goals.

- **Incubators** – These programs allow access to land, infrastructure and mentors. The prospective farmer must have at least three years of farming experience and a solid business plan to be considered. A sample program can be found at https://www.intervale.org/programs#farms-incuabtion.
- **Land Transfer** – These networks match retiring landowners with young farmers. This option includes the retiring famer mentoring the young farmer for a period of time before the young farmer purchases the operation at a low price. A list of land transfer programs can be found on the Center for Rural Affairs website: www.cfra.org/publications.
- **Renting** – Many people initially entering farming are able to secure a lease of land to farm. Another option to consider is lease-to-own.
- **Land Trusts** – These are typically charitable organizations that acquire land for conservation purposes and to ensure land is always available for farming and other activities. Aspiring farmers can access land through these trusts. A list of land trusts in each state can be found at https://www.findalandtrust.org.
- **Farm Management** – Universities, large farm operations, nonprofits, and community groups often hire farmers to oversee their crops. While the aspiring young farmer will not own the land in this position, he/she will have some autonomy, along with a steady income, health care, and a retirement plan.

The Solution

You may be asking yourself why a book about aquaponics has gone into so much detail about tour food industry, toxic food, and the associated problems they cause. There are several reasons why I think it is important that you be armed with this knowledge.

First, it will help you to make better healthy food choices for yourself and your loved ones. Healthier food choices result in a longer, more productive, and better quality of life.

Secondly, understanding the dangers associated with society's food system reinforces the importance of aquaponics and organic gardening. Properly growing our own food lowers the risk that we and our loved ones are exposed to unhealthy toxic foods.

Lastly, being knowledgeable about the dangers of our toxic food system will better enable you to market, barter, and sell your healthy grown product products (fish and vegetables).

Summary

When it comes to evaluating our food purchase options, it is important that we not be duped by mainstream media, fancy packaging, and advertisers. Food companies spend millions of dollars each year to influence consumers.

We also need to skeptics in terms of what the government says on these issues, as well; as so policy, regulations, and government rhetoric is often influenced by special interest groups, lobbying efforts, campaign contributions, political favors, and unscrupulous practices.

Raising public awareness about the presence of arsenic in water and soils is beneficial. We also need to pressure the U.S. Food and Drug Administration (FDA) to set standards for arsenic in food, to prohibit the use of arsenic-containing drugs in livestock and poultry, and to limit the arsenic allowable in manure used on rice fields.

A law requiring mandatory labeling of all GMO food is also needed. Furthermore, the country of origin and tests performed needs to be provided on all food products being sold.

We need to remember that each dollar spent is a persuasive vote. We send a message every time we decide to purchase or not to purchase a product, and by the types of products we purchase. When money goes to organic and environmentally responsible products, then the economy of those sectors improves via of the law of supply and demand.

As individuals it is helpful to maintain a balanced and varied diet of healthy food. Too heavy of a reliance on any particular food can have negative effects on one's health. By varying the types of food we eat, there is a higher probability of obtaining the nutrients the body needs (which is a difficult to do even when being intentional) and reduce the potential of deleterious impact to our personal health.

The diets occf infants, pregnant women and nursing mothers have significant influence at critical developmental stages of human growth. Children are also at a higher risk. Individuals in these sensitive stages need extra protection against toxic food. We all need to share responsibility in helping those that are less able, do what we can to take care of our planet on an individual level, and do what we can to promote healthy food for all.

Obviously, aquaponics removes toxic food concerns. A comprehensive examination of plant species, crop options, associated considerations, and food growing recommendations are addressed in later chapters of this book. Being knowledgeable about our toxic food supply will enable you to take better care of your health, better motivate you to grow your own food, and enable you to better market your aquaponic harvest products.

CHAPTER 6

The Best Locations for Aquaponics

Aqauponics Location Overview

For aquaponics operation to achieve success it needs to be setup and managed utilizing optimal location criteria conditions.

Fortunately, the best location for aquaponics is comprised of many viable options. It can be done in the inner city, suburbs, or country. In can be done in a warehouse, garage, basement, greenhouse, on a rooftop, or outside. A successful aquaponic system can even be set up where part of the system is indoors, and the other part is outdoors.

Plant/Crop Parameters

You should account for sunlight availability during the planning and designing stages. Also, winter and summer season sunlight paths need to be considered when laying out the system. Artificial lighting can be expensive, so it is prudent to plan properly so as to minimize lighting cost.

Sunlight is the perfect balance of wavelengths necessary for plant growth and blooming, but you can also use artificial light to help your plants along. After the summer solace (June 21st), the sunlight hours begin decreasing every day. To extend the growing season for your crops you can use artificial lighting. Artificial lighting does not need to be on all night. It

only needs to be on long enough to trick the plants. Having artificial lighting on just enough helps reduce operational energy cost.

Plants need a minimum of six hours of sunlight a day to grow. However, ideal plant growing conditions for aquaponics is 14 to 16 hours of bright light, followed by 10 to 12 hours of darkness every day. When daylight hours dip below 14 hours, artificial lighting can be used to make up the difference.

The length of day is dependent upon where you are located on the earth in terms of a latitude basis. Obviously, the closer you are to the poles the shorter your days will be, and vice versa.

In general, you should not leave grow lights on 24/7. Plants need a light-dark cycle to develop properly. It's believed that they truly do "rest" during periods of darkness and use this time to move nutrients into their extremities while taking a break from growing.

The following an amazing website has lots of valuable information about the climate and sunlight hours for your specific location: https://www.time-anddate.com

Plants need a minimum of six hours of sunlight a day to grow well. Artificial lighting can be expensive. Therefore, you should account for sunlight availability during the planning and designing stages. Also, winter and summer season sunlight paths need to be considered when laying out the system

Fish Parameters

Fish prefer to be in the shade. The fish tank should never be under direct sunlight, as it can cause increased temperatures and promote algae blooms in the tank. Algae blooms can cause a lack of oxygen which, in turn, kill the fish. Placing the tank under a roof or covering the tank will address this issue.

Furthermore, direct artificial lighting should never be placed directly over the tank. Only use indirect ambient lighting in areas where the fish tank is located. Ambient light is light that is not direct to the fish tank. In other words, the fish should not be able to see the light source.

Growing floating plants on the surface of the fish tank (e.g. incorporating a raft system) will provide, shade, shelter, and hiding places for the fish. Hiding places make fish feel more secure and amounts to less stress on them.

Trees

The aquaponic system should not be set up under trees. Trees drop leaves, sticks, flowers, sap, and insects. Droppings from some tree species can alter pH levels which could be fatal to your fish. And obviously, trees block sunlight which would affect plant growth.

If the aquaponics system is located outdoors, it is a good idea to have a protective cover or shelter to shield the fish tank from debris and airborne contaminants. Clean water is essential for the wellbeing of fish and plants.

Space Allowance and Accessibility

Sufficient space for planting, harvesting and maintenance is a must. Therefore, the aquaponics system should not be adjacent to a fence or wall. Also, the fish tank should not be positioned so close to the grow beds where access would be difficult. Easy convenient access to the entire aquaponics system will save much time and hassle.

Keep in mind that when the grow beds are full of plants, it will be much more difficult to reach the back corners than it is when the grow bed is empty. In addition, plants typically grow over the edge of the grow beds, so take such into consideration when setting up your system. As a general rule of thumb, it is a prudent plan for a minimum distance of 28-inches (70 cm) between grows beds.

It is also very important to have good accessibility to the fish tank for feeding, checking water quality and the health of the fish, as well as harvesting the fish. Since fish tanks are heavy, it is essential that they be properly supported or positioned on solid flooring (e.g., secure ground, concrete, etc.). Elevating fish tanks can be costly and complicated.

Some operators try to maximize space by placing the fish tank directly under the grow beds. This is not a preferred approach as it limits access to the fish tank and puts the grow bed at heights inconvenient to maintain.

Power Considerations

An aquaponics system needs to have access to power for the pump in order to keep the water circulating. Lighting is not always required, but certainly beneficial. Other items for power consideration are temperature management and supplemental grow lights. Power needs for lighting, grow lights, and temperature management is dependent upon the particular aquaponic system set-up, location, and the operator's goals.

Consideration should also be given to for the possibility of long-term power outages due to a storm event, or other infrastructure failure. It is prudent to have a readily available secondary power source, such as a generator or an inverter box connected to an automobile battery, available in the event the power goes out for an extended time. This will ensure the life supporting equipment (e.g., pump, oxygen diffuser, etc.) can continue operating and fish kill risk is minimized.

Some operators prefer to have their aquaponic system off the grid. As a result they obtain their electrical needs system via solar or wind power. Alternative power systems are covered in detail later in this book.

Heating and Insulation

Different fish species have their own optimal temperature ranges. Depending on the location of the aquaponic operation, and the type of fish being raised, it may be necessary to have a submersible heater (which requires electricity) to keep the water temperature within the optimal range. Some operators use heat wire around their water line(s).

Heating is not required if the fish species being raised has an optimal temperature range within the environment being raised. Maintaining the correct temperature range facilitates maximum fish growth and ideal beneficial bacteria conditions.

Furthermore, since plant growth is sped up due to increased availability of nutrients a heater may provide some advantages, so long as the average ambient air temperature remains in the life support range. Plant growth is sped up due to increased availability of nutrients. Hence, even though the cost of electricity is higher, there can be increased yields which results in greater profitability.

If there is a potential for significant temperature fluctuation as a result of location, then insulation and submersible heaters are necessary to keep the water temperature in a constant range; otherwise, the growth and health of fish will be impaired. Also, a consistent proper ambient room temperature range is a required component to ensuring plant and good bacteria thrive at an optimal level. Fish, bacteria, and plant growth can be significantly hindered, more suspectible to disease, and may even die if exposed to tempertures outisde of their ideal conditions.

Ergonomically Correct

It is also helpful to plan a system that is ergonomically correct. In other words, the top of the plant grow beds, top of the fish tank, equipment and devices should be designed to fit the human body and its correct functional abilities. Such will maximize productivity by reducing operator fatigue and discomfort. An ergonomically correct layout will not only be much more convenient and help optimize production, but it will make the entire aquaponics endeavor a much more enjoyable experience.

If the top of the fish tank has to be high, then consider building a platform to stand on. The fish tank can also be partially imbedded in the ground so that the top working surface is at a lower user-friendly height. Grow beds should be positioned so that bending over or reaching high positions are minimized. Keep in mind some vegetables will grow tall, and there will be a need to work within the grow bed media from time to time. Step ladders come in handy occasionally, for instance when harvesting the tops of tall vegetables such as tomatoes growing far above the grow bed. However, the system should be designed so that the use of a step ladder is not a regular requirement.

Also, keep in mind that walking surfaces should be safe, free of tripping hazards, and have a non-slip surface when wet. The design height of all aquaponic components should can be based on a chart, or architectural standard (as will be presented in the system design chapters later in this book), but an even better approach is to construct the system specifically to the operator's body height— that being what is most convenient for the end user.

Storage Spaces

There are a lot of materials, tools, and supplies (piping, tubes, cables, fish food, gardening appurtenances, etc.) needed in order to keep an aquaponics system running smoothly. Easy accessible storage spaces nearby comes in very handy, as there will be frequent trips to this area.

Greenhouses and Net Houses

One of the benefits of having the entire system within the same greenhouse is that the fish tank will serve as a wonderful source of thermal heating in the winter and thermal cooling in the warmer months. Furthermore, many plants do better when they are in an environment with a higher humidity.

However, there is no hard and fast rule as to how the system must be set up. In some parts of the world everything can be located outside. Some operators have the fish tank and grow beds in separate buildings. Other operators may have part of the system outside and the remaining system located indoors. It really depends upon your location, space parameters, the type of plants and fish you desire to grow, and how important energy efficiency is to you. Later chapters in this book discuss greenhouses in more detail (e.g., various types, construction, energy management, etc.).

A greenhouse is a metal, wood or plastic frame structure that is covered by transparent nylon, plastic or glass. The purpose of this structure is to allow sunlight (solar radiation) to enter the greenhouse and then trap it so it begins heating the air inside the greenhouse. As the sun begins to set, the heat is retained in the greenhouse by the roof and walls, allowing for a warmer and more stable air temperature during a 24-hour period. Greenhouses provide general environmental protection from wind, snow and heavy rain. Greenhouses extend the growing season by retaining ambient solar heat, but can also be heated from within. They can keep away animals and other pests, while also serving as a security against theft. Greenhouses are comfortable to work in during colder seasons and provide the grower with protection from the weather. Greenhouse frames can be used to support climbing plants or to hang shade material.

FIGURE 30.

FIGURE 31.

FIGURE 32.

Together, these advantages of a greenhouse result in higher productivity and an extended cropping season.

However, these benefits need to be balanced against the drawbacks of greenhouses. The initial capital costs for a greenhouse can be high depending on the degree of technology and sophistication desired. Greenhouses also require additional operating costs, because fans are needed to create air circulation to prevent overheating and overly humid conditions. Some diseases and insect pests are more common in greenhouses and need to be managed accordingly (use of insect nets on doors and windows), although the confined environment can favor the use of certain pest controls. In some tropical regions, net houses are more appropriate than conventional greenhouses covered with polyethylene plastic or glass. This is because the hot climates in the tropics or subtropics raise the need

for better ventilation to avoid high temperatures and humidity. Net houses consist of a frame over the grow beds that is covered with mesh netting along the four walls and a plastic roof over the top. The plastic roof is particularly important to prevent rain from entering, especially in areas with intense rainy seasons, as units could overflow in a matter of days. Net houses are used to remove the threat of many noxious pests associated with the tropics, as well as birds and larger animals. The ideal mesh size for the four walls depends on the local pests. For large insects, the mesh size should be 0.5 mm. For smaller ones, which are often vectors of viral diseases, the mesh size should be thicker such as mesh 50. Net houses can also provide some shade where the sunlight is too intense. Common shade materials vary from 25 to 60 percent sun block.

Rooftop Aquaponics

Flat rooftops are often suitable sites for aquaponics because they are level, stable, exposed to sunlight and are not being utilized. However, when building a system on a rooftop it is crucial to consider the weight of the system, and whether or not the roof is capable of supporting it. It is essential to consult with an architect or civil engineer before building a rooftop system. In addition, be sure that materials can be transported both safely and effectively to the rooftop site.

Expansion and Transitioning into a Profitable Business

Ideally, when planning your aquaponics system your designed layout will be such that it provides you the flexibility to grow as you gain experience and are ready to scale up. It is easier to manage, operate, troubleshoot problems when things go wrong with a smaller system compared to that of a large aquaponics operation. This is especially important when you are still relatively new to aquaponics. Furthermore, any errors with a smaller system typically do not hurt as much in regards to cost and time. However, mistakes are wonderful opportunities to learn and improve, so they should not be viewed entirely as a bad thing, as they can be excellent teachers. Problems in a smaller system are just easier to recover from. Therefore, starting small and growing as you learn is usually the best approach. Just keep system expansion in mind when you are planning your design layout. Designating and preserving an area for future expansion, during your initial planning phase, will save you a tremendous amount of trouble, expense, and time later, compared to the complexity of relocating or rearranging an existing aquaponic system.

If your desire is to transition into a profitable aquaponic business operation, keep in mind that profit typically progresses with experience. The more you learn, the more you will earn.

FIGURE 33. A media bed unit on a rooftop

FIGURE 34. Variety of vegetables growing on a rooftop in a nutrient film technique system

CHAPTER 7

Nitrogen Cycle

Nitrogen Cycle Explained

Nitrogen is an essential fundamental element necessary for all forms of life on Earth. It is an important constituent in both plant and animal cells. Living organisms need nitrogen to produce proteins, nucleic acids, and amino acids. Although Nitrogen gas (N2) is roughly 78 percent of the earth's atmosphere, it is basically unusable in its natural form. The vast majority of living organisms on earth can only use nitrogen when it is in its 'fixed' state: combined with carbon, hydrogen or oxygen.

One of the most important, yet least understood, aspects of aquaponics is bacteria , and its function in the nitrogen cycle. Basically, fish excrete ammonia. In a lake or ocean the vast volume of water dilutes this ammonia, which is eventually converted by bacteria in those habitats. In a fish tank ammonia must be dealt with properly as it is very toxic to the fish. Decomposing food also creates ammonia. Some effects of excessive ammonia include:

* Extensive damage to tissues, especially the gills and kidneys
* Impaired growth
* Decreased resistance to disease
* Death

Bacteria are the microscopic organisms that are involved in the conversion of fish waste into nutrients for the plants. It is important for aquaponic operators to understand how to create a healthy environment

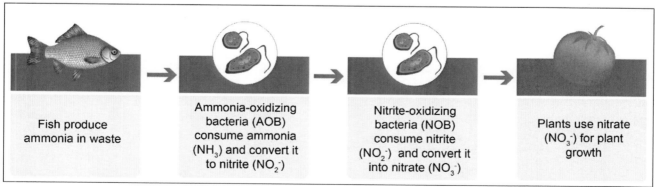

FIGURE 35. *The nitrification process in an aquaponic system*

Fish produce ammonia in waste

Ammonia-oxidizing bacteria (AOB) consume ammonia (NH_3) and convert it to nitrite (NO_2^-)

Nitrite-oxidizing bacteria (NOB) consume nitrite (NO_2^-) and convert it into nitrate (NO_3^-)

Plants use nitrate (NO_3^-) for plant growth

for the bacteria, so they will thrive within the system. A healthy colony of bacteria is essential for an aquaponics system to be successful. A thriving system will contain enough bacteria to break down and convert all the fish waste into nutrients for the plants.

The following factors outline how this process occurs within the aquaponics system. The fish in the tank are fed; they digest and break down the food and produce waste. Fish excrete ammonia through urine, feces (approx 17 percent) and their gills (approx 80 percent). The nitrification cycle is the process by which the ammonia produced by the fish is converted by one type of bacteria to nitrite and then by another type of bacteria to nitrate (the most plant-accessible form of Nitrogen in the cycle—and safest for the fish).

To elaborate further, in regards to more scientific explanation, the Nitrosomonas sp bacterium eats ammonia and converts it to nitrite. Nitrite is much less poisonous to the fish than ammonia, but it is by no means a good thing. It stops the fish from taking up oxygen and will cause damage to their gills. However, another bacterium (Nitrobacter sp.) eats nitrite and converts it to nitrate. Nitrate is a very accessible nutrient source for plants As a matter of fact, plants thrive off nitrate. In addition, the fish will tolerate a much higher level of nitrate than they will ammonia or nitrite. This is referred to as the nitrogen cycle.

When an aquaponics system has sufficient numbers of these bacteria to completely process the ammonia and nitrites, it is said to have "cycled." This process generally takes about a month; however, it can happen much quicker or much slower, depending on environmental conditions associated with the system. The bacteria will increase their numbers (reproduce) as the ammonia load increases, causing an ammonia "spike" when setting up a new tank.

The nitrogen cycle is the most significant process within aquaponics. It is responsible for the conversion of

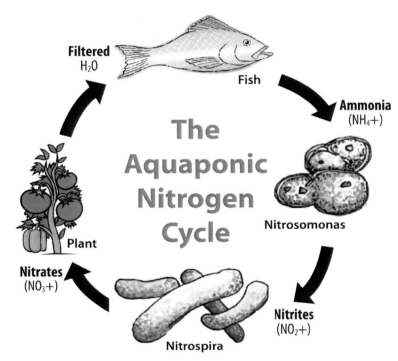

FIGURE 36.

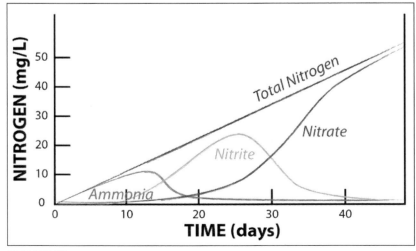

FIGURE 37.

fish waste into nutrients for the plants. Without this process, the water quality would deteriorate rapidly and become toxic to both the fish and the plants in the system. Therefore, the water in aquaponics does not need to be treated chemically to make it "safe," nor does it have to be replaced. In aquaponics, a system is said to have "cycled" when there are sufficient quantities of bacteria to convert all the ammonia into an accessible form of nitrogen for the plants. The bacteria will arrive naturally to a system and colonize the media bed.

A pH of 6.8 to 7 is usually a happy compromise for most fish, plants, and the good bacteria, but again the pH can be slightly more or less depending upon the fish species The nitrogen cycle has a tendency to reduce pH; however, it is fairly easy to keep pH around 7 through the addition of calcium carbonate. Calcium carbonate increases pH but will stop dissolving when the pH level reaches around 7.4, meaning pH will stay fairly stable until all of the available calcium carbonate is depleted. See the section about pH in this book on using calcium carbonate.

With a NFT or DWC system a mechanical or biofilter may be needed to help remove excess waste. *However, no filtration is needed for a properly setup and operating flood-and-drain system.*

Maintaining a Healthy Bacterial Colony

The major parameters affecting bacteria growth that should be considered when maintaining a healthy biofilter in DWC and NFT systems and the grow bed of a flood-and-drain system are adequate surface area and appropriate water conditions.

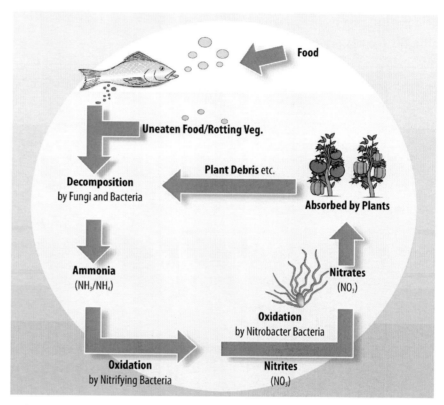

FIGURE 38. Bacteria life-cycle process

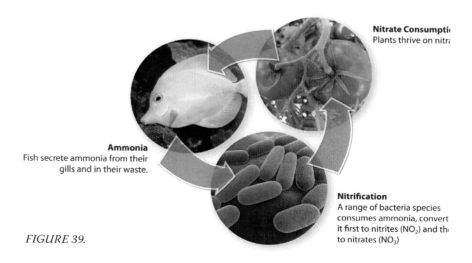

FIGURE 39.

Surface area bacterial colonies will thrive on any material, such as plant roots, along fish tank walls, inside pipes, and media in the grow bed or biofilter. The total area available for these bacteria will determine how much ammonia they are able to metabolize. Depending on the fish biomass and system design, the plant roots and tank walls can provide adequate area. Systems with high fish stocking density require a separate biofiltration component where a material with a high surface area is contained, such as inert grow media including gravel and tough or expanded clay.

Water pH and Bacteria

The pH is a numeric scale used to specify the acidity or basicity (alkalinity) of an aqueous solution. In aquaponics the pH level of the water has an impact on the biological activity of the nitrifying bacteria and their ability to convert ammonia and nitrite.

The noted pH ranges for the two nitrifying groups below have been identified as ideal, yet the literature on bacteria growth also suggests a much larger tolerance range (6–8.5) due to the ability of bacteria to adapt to their surroundings.

NITRIFYING BACTERIA	OPTIMAL pH
Nitrosomonas spp.	7.2–7.8
Nitrobacter spp.	7.2–8.2

However, as mentioned earlier in this chapter, the most **appropriate pH range is 6–7 for aquaponics**, because this range is better for the plants and fish (discussed comprehensively in the Water Quality chapter of this book). Also, a loss of bacterial efficiency can be offset by having more bacteria, thus the biofilter or grow bed needs to be sized accordingly.

Water Temperature and Bacteria

Water temperature is an important parameter for bacteria and aquaponics in general. The ideal temperature range for bacteria growth and productivity is 63-93°F (17–34 °C). If the water temperature drops below 63°F (17 °C), bacteria productivity will decrease. Below 50°F (10 °C), productivity can be reduced by 50 percent or more. Low temperatures have major negative impacts on unit management during winter.

Dissolved Oxygen and Bacteria

Nitrifying bacteria need an adequate level of dissolved oxygen (DO) in the water at all times in order to maintain high levels of productivity. Nitrification is an oxidative reaction, where oxygen is used as a reagent; without oxygen the reaction stops. Optimum levels of DO are 4–8 ppm (4–8 mg/liter). Nitrification will decrease if DO concentrations drop below 2 ppm (2.0 mg/liter). Moreover, without sufficient DO concentrations, another type of bacteria can grow; one that will convert the valuable nitrates back into unusable molecular nitrogen in an anaerobic process known as denitrification.

HMDPHM80 Digital pH/Temp. Meter

- Measures pH and Temperature
- One-touch automatic digital calibration
- Simultaneous temperature display
- Water resistant
- Cost: $45 (USA, year 2020)
- Cost and quality of pH/ Temperature meters vary considerably from approx. $20 to $300+. The meter in Figure 40, or similar from another manufacturer, is sufficient for most aquaponic operations.

FIGURE 40.

TABLE 1. **Water quality tolerance ranges for nitrifying bacteria**

	Temperature	pH	Ammonia	Nitrite	Nitrate	DO
Tolerance Range	17–34 °C	6 — 8.5	< 3 mg/L	< 3 mg/L	< 400 mg/L	4–8 mg/L
	63–93 °F		< 3 ppm	< 3 ppm	< 400 ppm	4–8 ppm

Ultraviolet Light and Bacteria

Nitrifying bacteria are photosensitive organisms, meaning that ultraviolet (UV) light from the sun is a threat. This is particularly the case during the initial formation of the bacteria colonies when a new aquaponic system is set up. Once the bacteria have colonized a surface (3–5 days), UV light poses no major problem. A simple way to remove this threat is to cover the fish tank and filtration components with UV protective material, while making sure no water in the hydroponic component is exposed to the sun, at least until the bacteria colonies are fully formed, and minimizing direct sunlight on the water as much as possible thereafter. Nitrifying bacteria will grow and thrive on material with a high surface area sheltered using UV protective material and under appropriate water conditions.

Balancing the Aquaponic Ecosystem

The term balancing is used to describe all measures an aquaponic operator takes to ensure the ecosystem of fish, plants and bacteria is at a dynamic equilibrium. It cannot be overstated that successful aquaponics is primarily about maintaining a balanced ecosystem. Simply put, this means there is a balance between the amount of fish, the amount of plants and the size of the biofilter, which really means the amount of bacteria. There are experimentally determined ratios between the size of the biofilter or grow bed, planting density, and fish stocking density for aquaponics. It is unwise, and very difficult, to operate beyond these optimal ratios without risking disastrous consequences for the overall aquaponic ecosystem. This section provides a brief, but essential, introduction to balancing a system. Biofilter or grow bed sizes and stocking densities are covered in much greater depth in the Biofilter and Flood-and-Drain chapters of this book.

Nitrate Balance

The equilibrium in an aquaponic system can be compared with a balancing scale where fish and plants are the weights standing at opposite arms. The balance's arms are made of nitrifying bacteria. Therefore, it is fundamental that nitrification is robust enough to support the other two components.

If the fish biomass and biofilter size are in balance, the aquaponic unit will adequately process the ammonia into nitrate. However, if the plant component is undersized, then the system will start to accumulate nutrients. In practical terms, higher concentrations of nutrients are not harmful to plants, but they are an indication that the system is underperforming on the plant side. On the flipside, too few fish will result in insufficient nutrients to adequately meet the plants' needs. This condition eventually leads to stressed plants and lower harvest yields.

The point is that achieving maximum production from aquaponics requires an appropriate balance between fish waste and vegetable nutrient demand, while ensuring adequate surface area to grow a bacterial colony in order to convert all fish waste. This balance between fish and plants is also referred to as the biomass ratio. Successful aquaponic systems have an appropriate biomass of fish in relation to the number of plants, or more accurately, the ratio of fish feed to plant nutrient demand is balanced. Although it is important to follow the suggested ratios for good aquaponic food production, there is a wide range of workable ratios, and experienced aquaponic operators will notice how aquaponics becomes a self-regulating system. Likewise, the aquaponic system provides an attentive operator warning signs in the form of water-quality metrics and the health of the fish and plants, as the system begins to slip out of balance,. All of these are discussed in detail in this book.

Feed Rate Ratio

Many variables are considered when balancing a system (note list below), but extensive research has simplified the method of balancing a unit to a single ratio called the feed rate ratio. The feed rate ratio is a summation of the three most important variables: the daily amount of fish feed in grams per day, the plant type (vegetative vs. fruiting) and the plant growing space in square meters. This ratio suggests the amount of daily fish feed for every square meter of growing space. It is more useful to balance a system on the amount of feed entering it than to calculate the amount of fish directly. Using the amount of feed makes it possible to calculate how many fish based on their average daily consumption.

Main Variables to Consider When Balancing an Aquaponic System

- Method of aquaponic production.
- Capacity (size) of operation.
- Type of fish (carnivorous vs. omnivorous, activity level).
- Type of fish feed (protein level).
- Type of plants (leafy greens, tubers or fruits).
- Proportion of crop (single or multiple species).
- Environmental and water quality conditions.
- Method of filtration (for N.F.T. or D.W.C. systems).

General Feed Rate Ratio:

- Leafy Green Vegetables: 40–50 grams of feed per square meter per day
- Fruiting Vegetables: 50–80 grams of feed per square meter per day

NOTE: The above feed ratio is provided with some reluctance and should only be considered as a very general rule of thumb. There are many other variables that can and will impact the feed rate ratio.

The point being that the proper feed rate ratio will provide a balanced ecosystem for the fish, plants and bacteria, provided the size of the biofilter or grow bed is adequate. Other variables may have larger impacts at different stages of the year, such as seasonal changes in water temperature. One must also be attentive to growth rate needs of the fish. The higher feed rate ratio for fruiting vegetables accounts for the greater amount of nutrients needed for these plants to produce flowers and fruits compared with leafy green vegetables.

Along with the feed rate ratio, there are two other simple and complementary methods to ensure a balanced system: health check, and nitrogen testing. They are described below.

Health Check of Fish and Plants

Unhealthy fish or plants are often a warning that the system is out of balance. Symptoms of deficiencies on the plants usually indicate that not enough nutrients from fish waste are being produced. Nutrient deficiencies often manifest as poor growth, yellow leaves and poor root development. In this case, the fish stocking density, feed (if eaten by fish) and the size of the biofilter (or grow bed) can be increased. Similarly, if fish exhibit signs of stress (gasping at the surface; rubbing on the sides of the tank; showing red areas around the fins, eyes and gills; or, in extreme cases, dying), it is often because of a buildup of toxic ammonia or nitrite levels. This often happens when there is too much dissolved waste for the media in the biofilter or grow bed to process. Obviously, any of these symptoms in the fish or plants indicate that the operator needs to actively investigate and rectify the cause.

Nitrogen Testing

This method involves testing the nitrogen levels in the water using simple and inexpensive water test kits (example shown below). If ammonia or nitrite are high >1 ppm (>1 mg/liter), the media surface area in the biofilter or grow bed is inadequate and should be increased. Most fish are intolerant of these levels for more than a few days. An increasing level of nitrate is desired and implies sufficient levels of the other nutrients required for plant growth. Fish can tolerate elevated levels of nitrate, but if the levels remain high >150 ppm (>150 mg/liter) for several weeks some of the water should be removed and used to irrigate other crops.

- 75 tests can be performed with this kit.
- Cost: $19 (USA, year 2022).
- Cost and abilities of water test kits vary considerably. The below kit, or similar from another manufacturer, is sufficient for aquaponic operations.

FIGURE 41. Seachem Multi-Test Nitrite and Nitrate Test Kit

If nitrate levels are low <10 ppm (<10 mg/liter) over a period of several weeks, the fish feed can be increased slightly to ensure there are enough nutrients for the vegetables. However, increasing fish stocking density may also be necessary. It is worthwhile, and recommended, to test for nitrogen levels every week to make sure the system is properly balanced. Nitrate levels indicate the level of other nutrients in the water.

Fish stocking density, planting capacity, grow bed size and biofilter sizes are explained in much greater depth in their respective chapters of this book. The objective of this chapter was to provide an understanding of the nitrogen cycle, and to emphasize the importance, as well as the strategies, of achieving a balanced system.

CHAPTER 8

The Different Types of Aquaponic Systems

Overview

The three primary methods used in aquaponics are Raft/Deep Water Culture (D.W.C.), Nutrient Film Technique (N.T.F.), and the Flood-and-Drain System. Each of these methods is based on a hydroponic system design with accommodations for fish and filtration.

There are many different aquaponic system configurations. Regardless of the different setups there are two components common to every aquaponic system. These two components are the fish tank and a soil-free plant-growing device. Depending on the type of aquaponics system referenced, the plant growing device is either a conduit, grow bed, or container. The variables include filtration unit, plumbing components, the plant growing device, and the amount and frequency of water circulation and aeration. Generally speaking, systems that utilize a filtration unit to remove the solid fish waste are the N.T.F. system and the D.W.C. system. However, Flood-and-Drain systems, which have an undersized plant grow bed, need supplemental filtration; as the grow bed serves as the filtration unit.

The Flood-and-Drain system is also referred to as an Ebb-and-Flow system or a Media-Filled Bed system. As previously mentioned, there are many different aquaponic arrangements, but they all fall within one of the three primary types of aquaponic system categories listed above.

Below is a brief introduction to these three main aquaponic methods. The latter chapters of this book provide detailed information and design options for each method. The chapters in between, and following the chapters with design details, will provide you with everything you need to know to be successful in aquaponics.

FIGURE 42. N.F.T. System.

Conceptual NFT System

Pump

Oxygenator
(optional – dependent upon system parameters)

FIGURE 43. Cross-Section of a N.F.T. System.

Nutrient Film Technique

The Nutrient Film Technique (N.T.F.) is a commonly used hydroponic method. As a matter of fact the N.F.T. system is one of the most productive hydroponic systems. However, it is not as widespread in aquaponics. In N.F.T. systems, plants are grown in nutrient-rich water pumped down small, enclosed gutters (long narrow channels). The water flowing down the plant channel is only a very thin film, but it provides the plant roots with an abundant supply of essential nutrients, water, and oxygen. Plants are typically grown in small plastic cups, called net cups, allowing their roots to access the water and absorb the nutrients. In some N.F.T. systems, additional water filtration is necessary (discussed in more detail in later chapters).

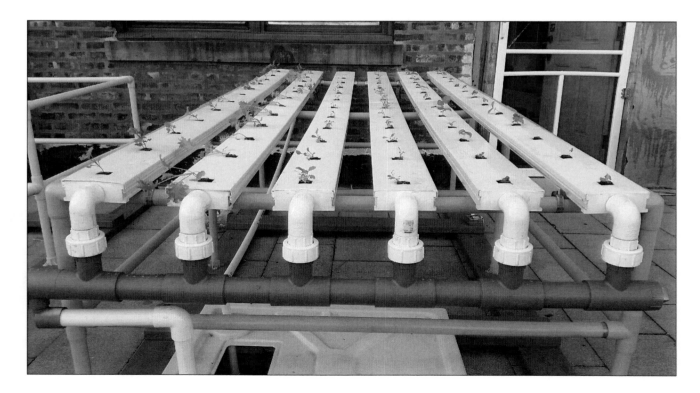

FIGURE 44. *Deep Water Culture Raft System.*

FIGURE 45. *Deep Water Culture Raft System.*

Deep Water Culture (D.W.C.), also referred to as a 'raft system', is done by floating a foam raft (typically a polystyrene board) on top of the fish tank water surface while allowing the roots to hang down into the water. However, another method is to grow the fish in a fish tank and pump the water through a filtration system, then into long channels, or a reservoir, where floating rafts filled with plants float on the water surface and extract the nutrients. Water flows continuously from the fish tank, through filtration components, through the raft tank where the plants are grown and then back to the fish tank. This method is the one most commonly practiced in large-scale commercial operations; but can also be done on a smaller scale.

Flood-and-Drain System

In the Flood-and-Drain System (also referred to as a media-filled bed system or an ebb-and-flow system) the media filled beds use containers filled with rock medium, expanded clay pellets or other similar media. This type of system can be run two different ways: (1) with a continuous flow of water over the rocks; or (2) by repeatedly flooding and draining the grow bed, in a flood and drain or ebb and flow cycle (most common and the recommended option).

This type of aquaponics system is most preferred for those desiring to grow a wide variety of plants, and/or taller plants such as tomatoes and bell peppers. It is also the simplest and most reliable design for a beginner.

With the media filled bed system, all waste, including the solids, is dispersed and eventually broken down within the plant grow bed. (NOTE: media grow bed and plant grow bed are the same, and used interchangeably throughout this book) In some systems, worms are added to the media-filled plant grow bed to enhance the break-down of the waste. The plant media bed serves as a natural water filter that gives the plants everything they need for vibrant growth, while returning filtered water back to the fish tank. This method uses the fewest components and no additional filtration, making it simple to operate. The media-filled bed is used for applications where greater plant diversity is desired, and whereby profit margin is not the primary goal. Not to say that a profit cannot be generated, but that in regards to looking at aquaponics from only a business viewpoint, N.F.T. and D.W.C. offer some revenue advantages to large scale operations. For instance, mass producing lettuce works best in N.F.T. and D.W.C. systems. However, a media-bed (flood-and-drain) system can still be extremely profitable if properly set-up and managed effectively.

Another benefit to a flood-and-drain system is that it can easily be scaled. In other words, it is relatively easy to continue enlarging it over time as you gain experience or develop a desire to produce more product i.e., fish and vegetables. Simply just add more fish tanks and grow beds.

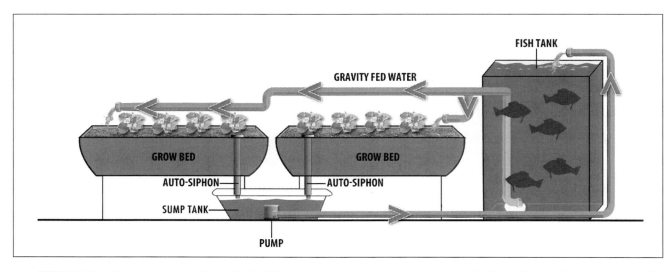

FIGURE 46a Conceptual view of a media-bed flood-and-drain system with a sump tank. **Note: Having the pump located in a sump tank, instead of in the fish task, is the ideal arrangement.**

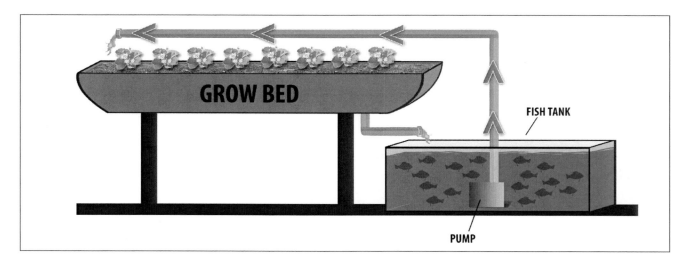

FIGURE 46b Conceptual view of a crude flood-and drain system. **Note: Having the pump located in a sump tank (as shown in FIGURE 30a), instead of the fish tank, is the ideal arrangement.**

PART II

Plants and Fish

CHAPTER 9

Plants and Crops — Keys to Success

Plants for Aquaponics

The most intensive aquaponic systems have been proven to achieve 20–25 percent higher yields than the most intensive soil-based culture. Although there is significant evidence which shows that, with the use of a greenhouse, yields can be anywhere from two to five times higher than traditional agriculture.

It is hard to find anything more rewarding than growing your own fresh, organic produce. With the exception of root vegetables, you can grow just about any type of plant in an aquaponics system. When deciding what plants to cultivate, all you have to ask yourself is what would you like to eat freshly out of your aquaponics farm, and what plants will grow best in your type of system. If you also desire to generate revenue from your aquaponics operation, then you will need to consider which plants are in highest demand and generate the most revenue.

Common plants that are being grown in aquaponics farms include: herbs, parsley, watercress, basil, sage, coriander, green leafy vegetables, (i.e. spinach, lettuce, etc.), and legumes such as peas and beans. Other plants, such as tomatoes, cucumbers, melons lettuce, chili, red salad onions, celery, broccoli, and cauliflower also do well. Some operators even grow

dwarf citrus trees and flowers. For the most part, the sky is the limit.

It is also important to consider your choice of crops and fish together. For example, warm loving plants such as bell peppers would do better with tilapias, which need warmer conditions than say trout, a cold loving fish. If you are thinking of growing tomatoes, you will need to choose fish that do well in a densely populated tank, as tomatoes require a high level of nutrients.

It also makes the most sense to grow crops that are more expensive at the store, rather than those that can be purchased cheaply. In addition, some fruits and vegetables offered at the grocery store are known to usually have high concentrations herbicides, pesticides, heavy metals or other containments. It is always best to grow organic crops instead of purchasing their toxic counterparts at the store. More on this subject will be discussed later.

There are over 300 different aquaponic plants that have been tested which have proven to grow well in an aquaponic system. However, the type of plants that you can grow is dependent on your location and specific system parameters. Keeping this in mind, the following plants have been found to grow well in an aquaponics system.

Plants that do well in Aquaponics

- Amaranth
- Any leafy lettuce
- Arugula
- Basil
- Beans
- Begonias
- Black Seeded Simpson
- Bok choy
- Broccoli
- Cabbage
- Cantaloupe
- Celery
- Chard
- Chinese cabbage
- Chives
- Cilantro
- Collard
- Common Chives
- Coriander
- Corn
- Cucumbers
- Dill
- Eggplant
- Endive
- Flowers
- Ginger
- Impatiens
- Kale
- Lettuce
- Mint
- Most common house-hold plants
- Mustard
- New Tomatoes
- Okra
- Pak Chov
- Parsley
- Peas
- Peppers
- Rapini
- Recao
- Redina Lettuce
- Spinach
- Squash
- Sweet potato
- Swiss Chard
- Taro
- Tatsoi
- Tomatoes
- Watercress
- Watermelon

Following are plants that have higher nutrient demands and typically only do well in a heavily stocked, well established aquaponic system:

- Tomatoes
- Peppers
- Cucumbers
- Beans
- Peas
- Squash
- Broccoli
- Cauliflower
- Cabbage

NOTE: The major groups that do **NOT** grow well in an aquaponic system are root vegetables such as radishes, potatoes, carrots, etc.

Plant Tips & Ideas

There are many resources available to obtain seedlings, starter plants, and cuttings. Sources range from the internet, mail order catalogs, local nurseries, garden centers, etc. It is important to educate yourself upon the source of your product to ensure that you obtain viable product from a reputable source. For instance, make sure you know that the item truly organic. Also, check online reviews to make sure the company does not have a bad reputation for selling old seeds with poor germination rates. Read all seed packages for germinating and pollinating instructions. Beware of potential seed coatings that may not be safe for fish.

Winter plants can be grown during colder weather seasons. Flowers and potted trees can also be grown. Keep in mind that fish and bio-activity will slow down at lower temperatures, which typically correspond with plant activity; which is a good thing.

It is normal for plant sprouts to shoot up quickly and then appear to stall for a few weeks. Don't fret, though. During this time, the plants are actually growing the root system out beyond the initial seed nutrients to support future growth. As the saying goes, patience is a virtue.

Duckweed can be grown directly on top of the water's surface. It multiplies rapidly with proper conditions. Some fish eat it naturally while other fish will take to it eventually. If your fish eat duckweed, be sure to keep some growing in a separate tank so the fish do not ravish your entire supply.

Be sure to grow only organic crops. Heirloom or organic seeds and plants obtained from a trusted reputable source are the best way to go. This will provide you the highest nutrient density and premium value produce.

Plant Design and Layout

A good layout of plant placement and crop design helps maximize production in the available space. Before planting, choose wisely which plants will be grown, bearing in mind the space needed for each plant and the associated growing season. It is prudent to plan the layout of the grow beds on paper in order to have a better understanding of how everything will fit together. Important considerations are: plant diversity, companion plants and physical compatibility, nutrient demands, market demands, and ease of access. For example, taller crops (i.e. tomatoes) should be placed in the most accessible place within the media bed to make harvesting easier.

In general, planting various crops and varieties provides a higher degree of security to the grower. If only one crop is grown, the risk for a serious infestation or epidemic increases. This can unbalance the system as a whole. As such, growers are encouraged to plant a diverse range of vegetables.

Staggered planting, as well as plant diversity, helps to maintain a balanced level of nutrients in the aquaponic system. At the same time, it provides a steady supply of plants to the table or market. Keep in mind that some plants produce fruit or leaves that can be harvested continually throughout a season, such as salad leaf varieties, basil, coriander and tomatoes, whereas some other crops are harvested whole. To achieve a staggered planting process there should always be a ready supply of seedlings. Maintaining a small side plant nursery for this purpose works well for many aquaponic operators.

Not only should the surface area be planned out to maximize space, but also the vertical space and time should be considered. Vegetables, such as cucumbers, are natural climbers that can be trained to grow up or down and away from the beds. Use wooden stakes and/or string to help support the climbing vegetables.

Planting vegetables with short grow-out periods (salad greens) between plants with longer-term crops (eggplant) will generate additional positive results. Lastly, another benefit of aquaponics is that plants can be easily moved by gently freeing the roots from the growing media and placing the plant in a different spot

Planting

Plants may be added to the grow beds as seeds or as seedlings. Most seeds require conditions that are moist (not drowned) and warm to germinate and sprout. Some seeds even require certain amount of light or darkness to germinate. Always be sure you follow seed germination instructions per each plant species. Also, wash off any dirt from plant roots before transplanting them in your system.

When beginning it is prudent to only plant about 1/4th of your grow bed area. Plant another 1/4th of the area after two weeks, and so on. Staggering plant growth will provide you with a continuous harvest (rather than all at once) and helps prevent against all plants dying off at the same time, causing a crash to the system. When the first group dies off, immediately replant the vacant area with something else to keep the rotation going.

Taking Care of the Plants

Caring for plants in the aquaponics farm is much easier compared to a conventional garden. Unlike soil-based farming, you no longer have to battle against weeds which includes constant bending over, resulting in back strain. If grown in a greenhouse, your crop is protected against the pests and wild animals that are often attracted to garden crops. Although bugs can still invade the aquaponics farm, they are far fewer due to its soil-less nature.

For successful pest management, it is helpful to educate yourself on any bugs found on your plants. Some bugs insects are beneficial, whereas others can be harmful to your crops. There are many environmentally friendly and aquaponic safe ways to combat insect problems. For instance, many small bugs, such as aphids, can be easily removed by spraying them with water. Alternatively, if the plant is small, you can even remove the plant from the media and soak it in

the fish tank for a few minutes. This often removes the insects and provides food for the fish. If none of the above techniques work, you might want to consider using some natural, biodegradable foliar spray. You should never use non-organic pest control solutions as they are toxic to the fish, will contaminate the water within your system, and eventually make its way up the food chain to you and others who may consume your produce. There are also a number of natural organic concoctions that can be made and sprayed on your plants that work very well, and in some cases even better, than toxic pesticides. More on this subject later. Never spray your system with pesticides, herbicides, or fungicides, as they will harm or kill your fish. Furthermore, the heavy metals and other toxic pollutants from these toxic chemicals end up in your food supply, negatively impacting you and your family.

Another wonderful thing about aquaponics is that you no longer have to worry about the complexity of fertilizing your crops and whether you are over or under watering them. You are also removed from the problem of having to work with expensive fertilizers or chemicals as in hydroponics farming.

Crops grown in an aquaponics operation are completely organic. The essential nutrients needed by the plants are fully provided by the fish's waste. Bacterial colonies in the media bed convert the fish waste into nitrates and minerals that are readily absorbed by the plants for healthy growth. Supplements are not required in a well-managed aquaponics system. A matter of fact, supplements can be harmful your fish and should be avoided.

It is important, however, to ensure that the water is well-oxygenated and that the pH is maintained within the optimal range of your fish and plants. If the pH range is not optimal, the uptake of nutrients by plant roots as well as bacteria activity will be negatively affected, and waste will build up to toxic levels for the fish. Optimizing oxygen and pH levels will be discussed in more detail later in this book.

Plant Life

Leaves are where photosynthesis occurs. Photosynthesis is the process in which sunlight combines with carbon dioxide (CO2) and water (taken up by the roots) to manufacture food (carbohydrates) for the plant; and oxygen is released as a by-product. Plants regulate small openings, stomata, on leaf undersides to allow CO2, to enter and oxygen (O2) to exit. When open, stomata allows water vapor to escape in the process of transpiration.

Roots anchor a plant in the ground and absorb water, nutrients, and air. Aquaponics allows absorption of water, nutrients, and air at an accelerated rate. Tiny root hairs increase the surface area for absorption. These root hairs are very delicate and must remain moist at all times. Large roots are similar to stems. They transport water and dissolved minerals (fertilizer) in the phloem.

Stems have a vascular system to transport water and nutrients throughout the plant. The xylem carries water and dissolved minerals from roots to leaves. The phloem transports food manufactured by leaves to the stems and roots. The vascular cambium is the growth zone that produces xylem on one side and phloem on the other. The stem also supports the plant and bean leaves, buds, flowers, and fruit

The Three Components of Plant Roots

1. Primary Roots

These are the large diameter roots which first grow from the main body of the plant into the nutrient solution; and which grow so rapidly.

2. Secondary Roots

These are the smaller diameter laterals emerging from the primary roots. The large surface area of these roots enables them to absorb vital nutrients and water from the nutrient solution. By the way, plants don't always take-up nutrients and water from the solution at the same rate. There is a mechanism known as "active" uptake which enables plants to determine what they want to take-up from all that is provided in the solution.

3. Root Hairs

Root hairs are critical to plant health. Root hairs take-up atmospheric oxygen; which is as essential to plants as it is to humans. Root hairs are the lungs of the plant. Most plants cannot absorb sufficient oxygen from the solution for healthy growth so it follows that the roots of your plants should always have roots hairs present and above the solution level in the channel. It is essential to keep the solution from pooling so that roots are not submerged. This is achieved by having an appropriate channel slope, and proper flow of the solution (otherwise known as the fish wastewater). Atmospheric oxygen will always penetrate into the plant root zone of an N.F.T. system, so long as the roots are not completely submerged.

Needs of the Plant

Plants have five basic needs. Each need accounts for 20 percent of the plants ability to grow to its maximum potential. When all of these needs are met at the maximum potential, the result is maximum growth (20% x 5 = 100%). If one of these needs falls short (for instance, only 15 percent), growth is impaired. If two or more of these needs are not met, growth is hampered significantly.

Air 20%
- Temperature
- Humidity
- CO2 and O2 content

Light 20%
- Spectrum (color)
- Intensity
- Photoperiod*

Water 20%   .
- Temperature
- pH
- EC
- Oxygen Content

Nutrients 20%
- Composition
- Purity

Growing Medium 20%
- Air Content
- Moisture Content

*   hours of light per day
**   electrical conductivity—
     a measure of salinity

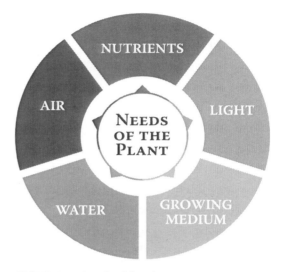

FIGURE 47. Needs of the plant

TABLE 2. **Mineral Elements Required by Plants**

ELEMENT	ABSORBED FORM	MAJOR FUNCTIONS
MACRONUTRIENTS		
Nitrogen (N)	NO_3^- and NH_4^+	In proteins, nucleic acids, etc.
Phosphorus (P)	$H_2PO_4^-$ and HPO_4^{2-}	In nucleic acids, ATP, phospholipids, etc.
Potassium (K)	K^+	Enzyme activation; water balance; ion balance; stomatal opening
Sulfur (S)	SO_4^{2-}	In proteins and coenzymes
Calcium (Ca)	Ca^{2+}	Affects the cytoskeleton, membranes, and many enzymes; second messenger
Magnesium (Mg)	Mg^{2+}	In chlorophyll; required by many enzymes; stabilizes ribosomes
MICRONUTRIENTS		
Iron (Fe)	Fe^{2+} and Fe^{3+}	In active site of many redox enzymes and electron carriers; chlorophyll synthesis
Chlorine (Cl)	Cl^-	Photosynthesis; ion balance
Manganese (Mn)	Mn^{2+}	Activation of many enzymes
Boron (B)	$B(OH)_3$	Possibly carbohydrate transport (poorly understood)
Zinc (Zn)	Zn^{2+}	Enzyme activation; auxin synthesis
Copper (Cu)	Cu^{2+}	In active site of many redox enzymes and electron carriers
Nickel (Ni)	Ni^{2+}	Activation of one enzyme
Molybdenum (Mo)	MoO_4^{2-}	Nitrate reduction

pH and Nutrient Uptake

The water pH has a direct impact upon optimal availability of all essential nutrients for a plant. At extremes in pH, many nutrients occur in forms unavailable for uptake by plant roots. The illustration below shows a relationship between pH and the availability of elements essential to plant growth for most species. Not all plant species will have the same pH/nutrient uptake characteristics. Some plants do better at a higher pH, whereas others absorb more nutrients at a lower pH.

Sowing

For the media-filled bed system (flood-and-drain system) there are a several ways to sow the seeds, dependent upon the type of plants to be grown. One method is to toss or plant the seeds evenly on the surface of the media-filled bed, and then thin them out, as needed, as they grow.

Another way is to germinate the seeds in a wet paper towel before transferring them to the grow media when their roots have grown at least 1 inch long. This also allows you to ensure that the plants are well-positioned in the media bed. This method works best for seeds that germinate very quickly, such as beans, peas, melons and cucumbers.

Seeds can also be sown in seed starting media (such as Rockwool, Peat sponges and Vermicompost) and then transplanted once they are established. This method works better for seeds that are harder to germinate (such as spinach and chard) or delicate plants (such as tomatoes and peppers).

Root cuttings or propagation can also be done on some plants. This works well if you have access to existing plants. It also saves money, as seeds don't have to be purchased.

Some aquaponic operators claim to have success planting crops twice as densely as a traditional soil-based farm. However, other operators find that their crops grow much bigger, wider, and fuller than traditional crops and thus, need more separation

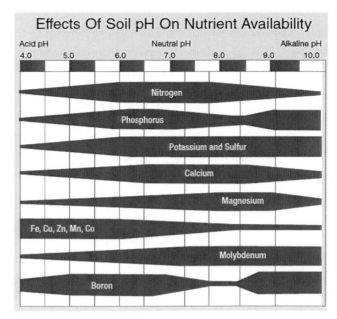

FIGURE 48.

between individual plants. As of now, the best method appears to depend upon the product being grown and system space parameters. My intention is to provide results about both of these methods from current ongoing studies on my forthcoming website **www. FarmYourSpace.com**. Meanwhile, keep in mind that success comes with education and experience. As time goes on, you will know what works best in your system.

Harvesting

Harvest-time brings much excitement, joy, and satisfaction.For many, the harvest is their favorite part of operating an aquaponic system.

Most Profitable Plants for Aquaponics

If growing plants for money, it is prudent to focus on growing those that are in demand are harder to obtain organically, and/or are the more expensive ones at the grocery store. These plants will generate the highest profit margins. Even though not all high value plants are suitable for aquaponics, such as ginseng, there are many viable plant options to choose from that have tremendous revenue potential.

Regardless of whether you are growing plants for revenue or just for personal reasons some of the same principles can be applied. For one, it doesn't make sense to take time and space growing produce that can be inexpensively acquired at your local market. Also, some plants have a lengthy grow period from plant to harvest (months), whereas others can be harvested in a matter of weeks. Furthermore, some plants need lots of space, which will and can limit your available production space.

Most plants do much better in aquaponics than they do through traditional farming methods. For instance, research showed that Basil grew three times better in Aquaponics than it did in a conventional garden. Okra has been found to grow 18 times as well in Aquaponics than in does in soil gardens. To minimize risk, it is best to select plants that have a proven history of successfully growing in aquaponics. However, feel free to experiment with various species and varieties along the way. You may be able to improve upon the latest data available.

Keeping the above in mind, the following is a list of plants that can be grown in an aquaponics system which have the highest earning potential.

- **Bamboo:** Landscapers and homeowners are paying as much as $150 each for specialty potted bamboo plants, and many growers are finding it hard to keep up with the demand. Why is bamboo so popular? It's a versatile plant in the landscape, as it can be used for hedges, screens or as stand-alone "specimen" plants. Bamboo is not just a tropical plant, as many cold-hardy varieties can handle sub-zero winters. If done right, through crop rotation and effective marking, it's possible to grow thousands of dollars' worth of profitable plants in a relatively small area.

- **Flowers:** If you are looking for a high-value specialty crop that can produce immediate income, take a look at growing flowers for profit. A flower growing business has almost unlimited possibilities, from fresh cut flowers to dried flowers — often called "everlastings", for their long life. It doesn't take much to get started growing flowers for profit either, just a few dollars for seeds. Even operators with small systems can produce incredible amounts of flowers and find lots of eager buyers at the local Saturday market held in most towns.

- **Ground Covers:** Due to high labor costs and water shortages, ground covers are becoming the sensible, low-maintenance way to landscape. Growers like ground covers too, as they are easy to propagate, grow and sell. Bringing profits of up to $20 per square foot, ground covers are an ideal cash crop for the aquaponics operator

- **Herbs:** Growing the most popular culinary and medicinal herbs is a great way to start a profitable business. The most popular culinary herbs include basil, parsley, chives, cilantro and oregano. Medicinal herbs have been widely used for thousands of years, and their popularity continues to grow as people seek natural remedies for their health concerns. Lavender, for example, has dozens of medicinal uses, as well as being a source of essential oils. Lavender is quite popular; hundreds of small nurseries grow nothing but lavender plants. The more commonly known herbs are easy to sell, but often don't bring in the higher revenues. Educate your customers on the benefits of other less common herbs and you can enjoy higher profit margins.

- **Ornamental Grasses:** Because ornamental grasses are drought-tolerant and low maintenance, landscapers are using more and more of them, as are homeowners. Because there are hundreds of shapes and sizes, they can be used for everything from ground covers to privacy screens. It's easy to get started growing ornamental grasses, as you simply buy the "mother" plants and divide the root clump into new plants as it grows. It's possible to grow thousands of plants annually with a small system.

Highest Revenue Generating Plants

In regards to produce, table 3 is a list of popular aquaponic plants and their retail average retail cost (USA, year 2016) provided by two reliable sources. For the traditional gardeners and farmers out there, please note that produce producing plants that cannot be grown in an aquaponics system have been omitted from the following list.

TABLE 3. **Highest Revenue Generating Plants**

POPULAR AQUAPONIC PROVEN PRODUCE ONLY	AVERAGE PRICES (Commercial Vendors)			UNITED STATES DEPARTMENT OF AGRICULTURE (USDA) (year 2022 Retail Prices, USA)		
Vegetable	USD Value/ SF (2022) Grocery	USD Value/ SF (2022) Farmers Market	USD Value/ SF (2022) Organic	Avg. Retail Price (per lb. — fresh)	Avg. Retail Price (per 1 cup serving — fresh)	National Retail Price
Artichoke, Globe	$2.91	$3.20	$3.63	$2.67/lb	$2.75	$3.44/each
Arugula-Roquette	$24.22	$26.64	$30.28			
Basil	$6.39	$7.04	$8.00			
Bean, Bush	$2.42	$2.66	$3.04			
Beet	$3.03	$3.33	$3.84			
Broccoli	$0.97	$1.18	$1.47	$3.11/lb	$0.87	$3.41/lb
Brussels Sprouts	$5.82	$6.40	$7.27	$3.35/lb	$1.08	
Cabbage	$0.24	$0.27	$0.41	$0.70/lb	$0.31	$0.75/lb
Cauliflower				$1.49/lb	$0.46	$1.51/lb
Celery				$1.34/lb	$0.48	$1.42/lb
Chard, Swiss	$3.98	$4.37	$6.10			$1.50/lb
Chives	$5.81	$6.40	$7.00			
Choi	$2.72	$3.00	$23.81			$1.85/lb
Cilantro	$12.47	$13.76	$14.91			$1.51/bunch
Corn	$0.80	$0.88	$1.73	$3.26/lb	$2.19	$0.60/ear
Cucumber	$5.48	$7.56	$8.66	$1.58/lb	$0.35	$1.71/lb
Dill	$7.75	$8.53	$9.20			
Eggplant	$2.72	$2.98	$3.82			$2.10/lb
Garlic	$1.94	$2.13	$3.00			
Grass, Lemon	$3.63	$4.00	$4.75			
Green Salad Mix						$3.13/lb
Greens, Mustard	$1.49	$1.64	$2.13	$3.12/lb	$1.21	$3.41/lb
Kale	$6.78	$7.46	$8.23	$2.68/lb	$1.10	$2.85/lb
Kohlrabi	$1.89	$2.10	$3.40			
Lettuce	$4.36	$4.80	$5.50			$2.17/each
Parsley	$4.88	$5.37	$6.04			
Peas, English	$1.81	$1.95	$2.88	$1.23/lb		
Peas, Snow	$2.19	$2.40	$2.25			$0.95/lb
Pepper, Bell	$5.45	$6.00	$6.63	$1.72/lb	$0.46	$1.89/lb
Pepper, Jalapeno	$2.18	$2.40	$3.25			$1.59/lb
Potatoes	$5.45	$6.00	$6.63	$1.65/lb	$0.25	$1.75/lb
Pumpkin	$3.27	$3.60	$4.38			
Rhubarb	$7.53	$8.04	$9.77			
Spinach, Spring/Fall	$1.21	$1.33	$2.25			
Squash, Summer, Yellow	$2.19	$2.40	$3.25	$1.99/lb	$0.85	$1.36/lb
Squash, Zucchini	$2.19	$2.40	$3.25			
Squash, Winter, Acorn	$2.63	$3.30	$3.94	$2.40/lb	$1.16	$2.88/lb
Squash, Winter, Butternut	$1.45	$1.60	$2.50	1.54/lb	$0.89	$2.74/lb
Squash, Winter, Hubbard	$3.88	$4.27	$5.00			
Tomatillo	$1.45	$1.60	$2.50			$0.89/lb
Tomato, Cherry (small & medium)	$9.69	$10.66	$12.00	$3.98/lb	$1.35	$4.14/lb
Tomato, large	$8.41	$9.30	$10.68	$2.10/lb	$0.51	$2.38/lb

NOTE: Two real-world aquaponic business plans that you can edit, plus many other aquaponic business resources (industry trends, operational costs, market data, profitability, aquaponic operation budget information, applicable agricultural economic news, etc.), are available at www.FarmYourSpace.com

Out of Season Crops

Growing out of season produce is another means in which to potentially save money and generate higher revenues. Although some additional artificial lighting may be necessary to trick the plants into thinking, it is their season. The extra cost for lighting is typically negligible and is a very good investment in most cases compared to the cost of out of season produce; and the risk associated with consuming non-organic grocery store food.

The produce considered in or out of season varies considerably from one geographic location to another. For instance, if you live in southern California, Florida, Central America, or Australia, your options in December are far different and greater than someone living in Michigan, Ontario, or Finland.

If you are interested in growing out of season crops it is prudent to obtain seasonal crop statistics from your regional governing agricultural agency, local garden club, and/or your area college/university agriculture department. Keeping in mind that 'seasonal' is geographically dependent. The following fruit and vegetable lists can be used as general guidelines large portions of the United States.

Below Example Represents Most of the United States

(For your specific area, check with your regional agriculture department or local garden groups and nurseries)

TABLE 4. **Seasonal Fruit Planting Guide for most of the United States (not all are conducive to Aquaponics)**

SPRING	SUMMER		FALL		WINTER
Apricots	Apricots	Jackfruit	Black Crowberries	Key Limes	Cactus Pear
Cherimoya	Asian Pear	Key Limes	Catus Pear	Kumquats	Cardoon
Cherries, Barbados	Black Crowberries	Limes	Cherries, Barbados	Passion Fruit	Cherimoya
Honeydew	Black Currants	Loganberries	Apples	Pear, All	Clementines
Jackfruit	Blackberries	Longan	Cranberries	Persimmons	Dates
Limes	Blueberries	Loquat	Feijoa	Pineapple	Grapefruit
Lychee	Boysenberries	Lychee	Gooseberries, Cape	Pomegranate	Kiwifruit
Mango	Breadfruit	Mulberries	Grapes	Quince	Mandarins
Melon, Bitter	Cantaloupe	Nectarines	Grapes, Muscadine	Sapote	Oranges
Oranges	Casaba Melon	Olallieberries	Guava	Sharon Fruit	Passion Fruit
Pineapple	Champagne Grapes	Passion Fruit	Huckleberries	Sugar Apple	Pear
Strawberries	Cherries	Peaches	Jujube		Persimmons
	Cherries, Barbados	Persian Melon			Pummelo
	Cherries, Sour	Plums			Red Banana
	Crenshaw Melon	Raspberries			Red Currants
	Durian	Sapodillas			Sharon Fruit
	Elderberries	Sapote			Tangerines
	Figs	Strawberries			
	Grapefruit	Sugar Apple			
	Grapes	Tomatoes			
	Honeydew Melon	Watermelon			

The seasonal foods listed below in table 5 include all varieties of vegetables (roots, gourds, legumes, etc.), as well as herbs, lettuces and leafy greens. Not all are conducive to aquaponic gardening.

TABLE 5. **Seasonal Vegetable Planting Guide for most of the United States (not all are conducive to Aquaponics)**

SPRING		SUMMER		FALL		WINTER
Artichokes	Greens, Swiss Cha.	Beans, Chinese Lng	Okra	Beans, Chinese Lng	Mushrooms	Brussels Sprouts
Asparagus	Lettuce, Butter	Beans, Green	Peas	Black	Peppers, Jalapeno	Chestnuts
Asparagus, Purple	Lettuce, Manoa	Beans, Lima	Peas, Sugar Snap	Salsify	Pumpkin	Collard Greens
Asparagus, White	Lettuce, Red Leaf	Beans, Winged	Peppers, Bell	Broccoli	Radicchio	Endive, Belgian
Beans, Fava	Lettuce, Spring Baby	Beets	Peppers, Jalapeno	Brussels Sprouts	Squash, Acorn	Kale
Beans, Green	Mushrooms, Morel	Corn	Potatoes, Yukon Gld	Cardoon	Squash, Buttercup	Leeks
Broccoli	Onions, Vidalia	Cucumbers	Radishes	Cauliflower	Squash, Butternut	Squash, Buttercup
Cactus	Pea Pods	Edamame	Shallots	Diakon	Squash, Chayote	Squash, Delicata
Chives	Peas	Eggplant	Squash, Chayote	Radish	Squash, Delicata	Squash, Sweet Dumpling
Corn	Peas, Snow	Endive	Squash, Crooknose	Endive	Squash, Sweet Dumpling	Sweet Potatoes
Endive, Belgian	Radicchio	Garlic	Squash, Summer	Endive, Belgian	Sweet Potatoes	Turnips
Fennel	Ramps	Lettuce, Butter	Squash, Zucchini	Garlic	Swiss Chard	
Fiddlehead Ferns	Rhubarb	Lettuce, Manoa	Tomatillo	Ginger	Turnips	
Greens, Collard	Sorrel			Jerusalem Artichoke		
Greens, Mustard	Squash, Chayote			Kohlrabi		
Greens, Spinach	Watercress			Lettuce, Butter		

Selecting the Right Crops for You

After you have a good idea as to what plants would do well in your geographical location, it's time to decide where to focus your efforts. Chances are you will grow multiple crops, integrating your resources to achieve the annual production goals you have established. Determining the ideal product mix is a task for each individual aquaponics operator based on system parameters and his/her objective, but there are some basic guidelines which will facilitate the process.

Profitability Approach:

1. Known as the 'Profitability Approach', you can grow several crops annually that generate revenue. Estimate the annual income possible from each crop, and total up the amount of sales you think they will generate annually. Subtracting the result from your goal leaves the amount you need to earn in "new sales."

2. Finding the right product mix for your operation means considering not only what you can produce but, more importantly, what you can successfully sell. For example, selling vegetables can involve a lot of direct interaction with the purchaser. Customers at the farmers' market may want to know not only whether your tomatoes have good flavor, but also what culinary uses they might be best adapted. Prepare for this with a printed recipe or two.

3. Customers will engage you in discussions of your growing methods, offer their opinions about crop varieties, and what else you grow. If you find such extensive customer contact daunting, then perhaps you should focus more effort on selling your product to a wholesale buyer or find a few good chefs who will take most of your produce. You could also consider joining or even starting a CSA group. Time constraints will play a crucial role in your decisions, too. If you already have a crowded schedule, you may not be able to spend time running your operation and marshaling a local sales effort. Or maybe your leisure time does not coincide with the optimum sales schedule. Working a farmers' market is similar to having a part-time job. In these situations, selling via the internet may make more sense.

4. The internet has a highly developed community of avid gardeners, foodies, health conscious individuals, herb enthusiasts, and other potential customer groups. The possibilities are limitless. Internet sales also permit scaling your business to match your production capacity. When something is sold out, you can instantly remove it from your website, or even invite customers to put themselves on a "want list" for next year's crop.

5. If your work schedule and leisure time do not coincide with when the farmers' market is open for business then selling via the internet may make more sense. If so, look for products that lend themselves to this approach. You might be best-off developing a product that can be canned or dehydrated and shipped during their winter dormancy rather than having to cope with perishable seasonal vegetables. Again, using the internet is a great way to connect with potential customers.

6. When preparing your start-up plan, examine your own likes and dislikes, the ways you prefer to spend your leisure time, and how much enthusiasm you would truly have for selling your products. Also, consider if you would prefer to sell to others through one-on-one relationships, or prefer a more impersonal experience such as internet sales, or if you would most enjoy talking to a lot of people at a busy farmers market.

7. You must also ask yourself how far you desire to go with your aquaponics operation. If adding value to a product is required to meet your sales goals, are you prepared to take that step? For example, say you realize that you can wring a higher dollar yield with more resources dedicated to canning a particular vegetable. Doing so, however, will require containers, labels, time to grow, harvest, and pack the finished product. Going the distance of actually creating a prepared food product on a large scale requires a commercial kitchen, permits, health inspections, and product liability insurance. Is this something that you really want to do? Do you have the capital for these endeavors? How long will it take to recoup that investment? These are questions that need to be answered before moving forward.

8. Besides the needs of your family and your personal aspirations, consider also the people living around you and your zoning laws. Keeping peace with the neighbors is important. Will your neighbors complain if you have a lot of traffic to and from your house? Will an occasional gift of fresh vegetables be enough to maintain the peace? Will customer parking going to be an issue?

Personal Savings Approach:

9. The 'Personal Savings Approach' is a plan with the objective being more about personal savings than profitability. Given the likelihood that you will probably grow several different crops, estimate the annual savings in grocery store food cost possible from each crop. Subtracting the result from your production cost leaves the amount you amount you will gain through your aquaponics crop selection.

10. Revaluate your crop selection to see if different species or more space may need to be dedicated to a particular species. Next, review the space you have available for expansion and determine how much more product can be produced. Dividing the annual goal of production benefit by the area of this space gives you the productivity you need to reach your production goal, in dollars per square foot. Armed with this number, you can proceed to create a crop plan.

11. Product uses is another determining factor that should be considered. For instance, does your selected tomato variety have only good fresh flavor, or can they also be used for many culinary options? Does plant selection provide you with long term food storage, such as canning, freezing, and dehydration options?

12. One should also consider the time involved for each crop. Some crops are higher maintenance than others. For instance, spinach and lettuce require very little time whereas tomatoes and bell peppers require higher maintenance as they must be supported. It is prudent to ensure that you know what time requirements will be placed upon you and you have the spare time to maintain the crop before making the crop selection.

13. It is also wise to know if the rest of your family is on board. You don't need ongoing resistance on the home front. Farming on any scale is, to some extent, a way of life, and running an aquaponics operation will likely alter some of your accustomed patterns and family activities. Thinking ahead of ways to mitigate potential problems and conflicts now will save a lot of frustration later. With that said, running an aquaponics operation can also bring a family closer together as each member works together towards a common goal that benefits all. Running an aquaponics operation often requires family members to turn off the electronic devices, put away the distractions, and spend time quality together.

These are all issues which should be carefully considered during the planning phase. The more you think through these issues in the beginning, the greater your chance for optimal success and enjoyment.

Identifying the Best Plants to Grow

Every possible product your aquaponics operation might yield has its advantages and disadvantages. Thus, depending upon your particular situation, there are good and bad crop choices. To help sort them out, consider rating different possibilities according to these key criteria:

- **Productivity:** the amount of value or salable crop per square foot cultivated.
- **Market Value:** the price you can obtain and/ or the amount of money you can save by consuming that unit of crop.
- **Estimated Demand:** the volume of a crop you can reasonably expect sell, if earning revenue is one of your objectives.
- **Capital Requirement:** the amount of money and other resources that must be invested in order to bring in a crop to harvest.
- **Personal Zeal:** your familiarity with, or desire to learn about, the cultivation of a particular crop, as well as the enthusiasm you bring to its production and sale. It is much more difficult to be successful if you lack passion.

The ideal crop is one that generates a lot of produce per square foot over the course of a season, has high market value, is in great demand, and is one in which you enjoy growing. Ideally, it is also one with a capital requirement that you can afford or acquire the necessary funding to produce. In addition, growing a top quality product—one that is superior to others on the market— will give you a huge advantage over your competitors.

Time = Money

"Time is money" is an adage that is never more correct than when applied to the business of aquaponics. The operator gets paid for the time required to take a crop from start to salable size. This can range vary significantly, depending upon the type of plant in production.

Each of the crop's "life stages" offers a different level of risk and reward that the entrepreneur must take into account. For example, starting plants from seed is the cheapest way to obtain most species, but also takes longer and will result in the highest percentage of losses.

Production of Annuals

An annual is any plant that completes its life cycle in a single growing season. For the would-be aquaponics operator, product possibilities among the annuals include flower, herb, and vegetable plants. They are usually started from seed. Seedlings are generally grown under cover in order to get a good start, then transplanted to the aquaponics bed to maximize space and ensure that the grow bed is always being utilized by larger plants rather than seeds or sprouts. Larger plants also help filter the water before it returns to the fish tank.

Growing Flowers for Money

"Color," as annual flowers are known in the nursery business, can be a reliable source of income. Locally grown, fresh cut flowers are the fastest growing segment of the U.S. floral market. Approximately 90 percent of the fresh cut flowers sold in the U.S. come from abroad. While foreign growers are great at producing the top three floral crops (roses, carnations and chrysanthemums) at incredibly low prices, the flowers that you buy from your local florist, big box or supermarket are harvested 10 to 14 days before they reach your shopping cart. To achieve this, foreign producers can only grow a limited number of varieties and they have to use an incredible amount of chemical fertilizers, pesticides, and preservatives to make sure that their product looks fresh by the time it reaches the customer.

Most flowers are grown at a huge cost to the environment and the flowers have already lost up to two weeks of vibrant life due to transport and storage. Therefore, with the right kind of marketing, emphasizing locally grown fresh cut flowers, can be a thriving business. Local growers produce a product that is fresher than their foreign competitors. In fact, bouquets can even be sold the same day they are cut. The local grower can also customize his or her offering based on seasonality and local preferences. In addition, the customers of local growers often develop a personal relationship with them. They value knowing who produces their flowers and how that person grew them. When you consider that the local grower does all of this and still keeps prices extremely competitive, you begin to understand why this movement has taken off. Furthermore, as you educate the community as to how your flowers are grown organically through sustainable farming practices, as compared to the way the vast majority of commercial flowers are produced, you will literally have customers begging for your product. Nobody in their right mind would want to give their loved one a flower contaminated with synthetic fertilizers, pesticides, sprayed with chemical preservatives, and produced in ways that cause a great deal of harm to the natural environment.

If you are interested in growing flowers for market, The Association of Specialty Cut Flower Growers (www.ascfg.org) is a great place to start. The ASCFG formed in 1988 to provide information on growing techniques, marketing strategies, and new developments to the field-grown and greenhouse-grown fresh cut flower producer. As of this writing, they have 450 members that specialize in this growing market. While some of these growers are large producers who supply tons of flowers to high-end florists and supermarket chains, the majority is small. These small, independent growers are making a living or supplementing their family income by growing flowers on farms as small as one acre. Many grow, harvest, package, market, and sell directly to their customers. They can provide you with a wealth of valuable information that will save you time, expense, and help you maximize your profit.

Following are some helpful tips on how you can make money growing flowers:

1. Grow good flowers. That sounds obvious, but if you don't have a good product, it'll be harder to make a good profit. So make sure your flowers are grown organically under optimal conditions. Your flowers will be healthier, less susceptible to diseases and look better.

2. Do your research on the best varieties to grow. Spend time on the Association of Specialty Cut Flower Growers website learning what others are doing, talk to florist, search the Internet, and obtain some books on the subject of growing flowers for profit.

3. Educate your potential customers on the disadvantages of buying flowers through the common methods versus your local organic sustainable farming approach.

4. Look into setting up a web-based business or another online mechanism so that customers can easily buy your flowers.

Great Ways to Sell Flowers

- **Farmers' Markets and Flea Markets** — These markets most always draw big crowds. Setup a stand or table with your flowers, and show everyone that stops by why your flowers are the best.
- **Hotels and Restaurants** — Hotels and restaurants often like to make a table, entryway, or

special room look nice by adding some pretty flowers. It is an easy way to spice up any establishment. Talk to local hotels and restaurants and find out what flowers they are looking for. If you are able to grow those varieties, you could open yourself up to a lot of business, as these hotels and restaurants will want to keep their tables and entryways looking nice.

- **Fundraisers** — People will often be more willing to buy your products if they know some of the profits are going to a good cause. That's why fundraisers are an excellent way to sell your flowers. It makes your business look good, while making your wallet happy too.

- **Florists** — Florists have to get their flowers from somewhere, so why not your aquaponic operation? Make the rounds and talk to your local florists, and find out just what they're looking for. Find out what they routinely pay, and see if you can give them a better deal. If you can produce flowers that they can then sell and make good money, they will buy from you repeatedly.

- **Online** — People are more apt to buy from you if it is easy. They can also forward your website's link to to friends, co-workers, and family. Another advantage is that you can capture their contact info (phone number, mailing address, and email address) and reach out to them whenever you have a product to sell. A short, periodic e-newsletter is also a great way to keep your business and products in the thoughts of your customers.

You really can make big money growing flowers. After you get up to speed on all the 'ins' and 'outs', and have your operation running efficiently, your profits will be grown faster than your flowers.

Growing Plants for Money

You'll be facing stiff competition from industrial-scale growers who can turn out plants by the millions, but if you carefully choose a market niche and grow quality plants, you can sell them at a nice profit. However, even common crops can be profitable if grow efficiently. In addition, many customers want variety. A frequent question growers hear is 'what else do you have for sale?'.

Again, the ideal situation would be to find plants that you enjoy growing, can be grown easily in your particular operation, can be grown as efficiently and inexpensively as possible, are ones that you and your family enjoy eating, are in high demand, and produce a high profit margin. However, it is rare for anything to be perfect. Therefore, you may need to pick the plants that will most closely coincide with your main purpose. Keep in mind your primarily objectives and go from there. Another thing to keep in mind, as eluded to previously, is that vast numbers of people are willing to pay more, wait, and go out of their way to purchase a product that is organic, grown locally, and produced without doing harm to the environment; so be sure to emphasize these points to potential customers.

Homemade Organic Pest Control

Pesticides cause undesirable ecological and health impacts. Pest control methods that are relatively non-toxic with few ecological side-effects are sometimes called 'bio-rational' pesticides. The major categories of bio-rational pesticides include botanicals, microbials, minerals, and synthetic materials. However, not all bio-rational pesticides are safe to use in an aquaponic system or integrated into your food supply.

The first thing to keep in mind in regards to introducing any application to your aquaponic system is that of the health of your fish and the good bacteria that are driving your system. Never use non-organic pest control products. Furthermore, all pesticides (whether organic or synthetic) are also harmful to beneficial insects such as ladybugs, honeybees, praying mantas, butterflies and others that are good for your plants. Beneficial insects aid in pollination and/

or eating the harmful insects. For instance, bees pollinate plants and ladybugs feed on aphids. A pesticide should only be used as a last resort.

Although there are organic pesticide products available on the market, the best and least expensive approach is to make your own organic bug spray. A homemade-pesticide-recipe to repel-garden-pests that is suitable to green living can be made from typical kitchen ingredients; even from leftovers. The following sections provide several methods for making your own organic, non-harmful pesticide.

Organic Bug Spray from Onion and/or Garlic Scraps

Simply save your onion skins, peels, and ends in a Ziploc sandwich bag. You can also include garlic leftovers. Keep the leftovers in the refrigerator. Once you have a full bag, place the onion pieces in a pail and fill with warm water. Soak for several days or up to a week. You can keep the pail in a sunlit location to steep, but this is optional. Finally, strain the onion bits out and store the onion water in spray bottles. You can spray this concoction in the plant area as well as directly on the plants.

How to Make Healthy Garlic Spray Pesticide

- 10 cloves minced garlic
- 2 tsp. mineral oil
- 2 1/2 cups water

Soak garlic in mineral oil for 1 day. Strain garlic out and add the water and soap. Mix well. Spray plants.

How to Make Healthy General Organic Pesticide

- 3 hot green peppers (canned or fresh)
- 2 or 3 cloves garlic
- 3 cups water

Puree the peppers and garlic cloves in a blender. Pour into a spray bottle and add the liquid soap and water. Let stand for 24 hours. Strain out pulp and spray onto infested plants, making sure to coat both tops and bottoms of leaves.

How to Make Healthy Pyrethrum Pesticide

Pyrethrum is a natural, botanical insecticide that is environmentally friendly and has several major advantages over chemically synthesized insecticides including its rapid breakdown in the environment and its lack of insect resistance.

Pyrethrum is extracted from a particular type of Chrysanthemum known as the African Daisy (Chrysanthemum cineraria folium). Oil is extracted from the seeds of these flowers.

Ingredients

- 1 tablespoon flower heads of either Chrysanthemum cinerariaefolium or Chrysanthemum roseum.
- 1 liter / 33fl.oz hot water or 1 Quart/32 fl.oz

Steps

- Obtain the flower heads.
- Mix the flower heads with the hot water; allow to stand for one hour.
- Strain off the flower heads.
- Add the soap powder and mix.
- Pour the mixture into a spray bottle.
- Spray lightly on the plants.

Warnings

- Spray with care — this will also impact beneficial insects.
- This is a controversial pesticide. Many web sites say it is harmless to humans and mammals and that it degrades quickly, but some studies indicate that it is very harmful to humans, dogs, cats, and that it lingers in dust. See Cox, Caroline, Insecticide Factsheet Pyrethrins/Pyrethrum, Journal of Pesticide Reform, Vol. 22, No. 1, 14–20.

Human Urine as Fertilizer

For those who are considering a 'hydroponic' system (no fish), or enjoy traditional gardening practices, but the thought of adding synthetic fertilizers to your food supply is a concern, there is a better option. It is also free and effective — human urine.

Yes, that's right, human urine has been proven to be an effective agricultural fertilizer. Researchers say our liquid waste not only promotes plant growth as well as industrial mineral fertilizers, but doing so also helps the environment by eliminating the energy that would otherwise be used to transport (pump) to the sewage treatment facility and treat the urine. In one of several proven experiments, environmental scientists at the University of Kuopio in Finland conducted an extensive study which showed that human urine worked as well as traditional fertilizers.

Fresh urine is high in nitrogen, moderate in phosphorus and low in potassium and can act as an excellent high-nitrogen liquid fertilizer or as a compost accelerator. The nitrogen-phosphorous-potassium ratio (N-P-K ratio) of human urine is typically about $11 - 1 - 2.5$.

Fresh pee can have a pH anywhere from 5 to 9 depending on a person's diet, but it tends to move toward neutral as it ages and breaks down when applied outside. Therefore, the pH of human urine is not really a concern for most garden uses.

Many gardeners have known for years that human urine was an effective, environmental-friendly, and cheap fertilizer. People have been collecting their urine in containers and jugs to spread around their plants for years. Some men even perform the direct application when the urge hits. Ladies may need to be a little more creative if desiring to implement the direct approach.

However, like any fertilizer, too much is too much and can burn up the plants. Fertilizer (and urine) contains salts. Salt draws moisture out of plants. When you apply excess fertilizer to plants, the result is yellow or brown discoloration and root damage. Urine fertilizer burn symptoms may appear within a day or two of over application.

Because urine can contain a lot of salt, especially if you have a diet high in sodium—as well as high nitrogen levels—urine should generally be diluted 10:1 before use on garden crops. Greater dilution – 20:1 or more – is appropriate for more tender plants, seedlings; and potted plants, which are more susceptible to salt build up.

Last word in the sentence --please replace the word "urine" with the word "plants"

Human feces are not sterile. This solid waste can be infected with salmonella and E.coli. Steps should be taken to ensure that your urine isn't contaminated by that solid waste. Also, if you're on any medication that will be present in your urine stream, don't use that urine as it could damage the plants and/or be absorbed into the edible components. Also, don't use your urine if you have a urinary tract infection as the germs from the infection will also contaminate your urine.

If you prefer to have a more natural and cheap alternative to synthetic fertilizers, then human urine is the way to go. Just make sure you have good aim.

CHAPTER 10

Fish — Everything You Need to Know

Importance of Fish

Americans consumed 9.5 billion pounds of seafood in 2017 and to meet that demand, 91 percent of it was imported. In 2019, the US per capita seafood consumption hit 19.2 pounds per person, according to the National Oceanic and Atmospheric Administration (NOAA).

Without increased aquaculture production, the world will face a seafood shortage of 50 to 80 million tons by 2030, according to the United Nations Food and Agriculture Organization. But that production needs to be sustainable by decreasing the use of wild fish according to the USDA.

Fish play a very important role in the aquaponics system. They provide the vital nutrients for vibrant plant development and if you're growing edible fish, then they serve as a valuable source of low-fat, high quality protein, essential omega-3 fatty acids, vitamin D, Riboflavin, and other necessary nutrients. Growing a large population of fish may be a little daunting to some, especially those without any prior experience; however one need not be discouraged. Successfully raising fish in an aquaponic system is just a matter of following some basic fundamental principles. As you follow these simple, proven principles, you will not have any difficulty growing fish from fingerling

size to ready-to-eat fish. Chapter 28 in this book will explain further how you can easily breed and raise your own fish, so as to spare you the cost of having to purchase fingerlings.

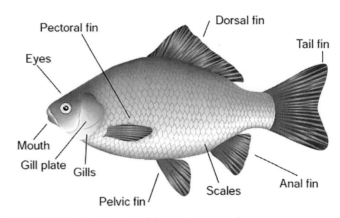

FIGURE 49. *Illustration of the main external anatomical features of fish*

Deciding Upon the Fish Species to Rear

Reiterating an important point, you must clearly define your objectives for getting into aquaponics, and stay true to that vision. Not that you can't change your mind or alter your mission as you learn more along the way and gain experience, but it is important not to be diverted into a different direction due to the random external distractions that pop up in life.

Once you've define your goals, a plan can be established and implemented that will help you achieve optimal success. The following are some ideas that will, hopefully, help you further clearly define your purpose, and the rewards you desire to obtain from aquaponics.

Choosing a Fish Species

There are many different species of fish that can be used in an aquaponic system, depending on your growing environment, available supplies, and in most applications, your local climate.

Do you desire to rear the fish for consumption or for ornamental purposes? If edible fish is the objective, trout or tilapia are excellent choices. Goldfish and koi are good choices for ornamental fish.

If growing edible fish is your objective, and you live in a cooler climate, growing trout year round may make the most sense. In warmer conditions, barramundi or jade perch are often a good option. However, in most warm areas or controlled temperature environments (i.e. inside), tilapia is the fish of choice.

Aquaponic Proven Fish

Ideally, the fish and plants selected for the aquaponic system should have similar needs in regards to temperature and pH. Realistically, a perfect match is rarely achieved, but the closer they match, the higher probability there is for success.

Warm loving fish and leafy crops, such as bush green beans and herbs, typically go well together. Fruiting plants such as tomatoes and peppers—due to their higher nutritional requirements—do the best when supported by a densely stocked fish tank(s).

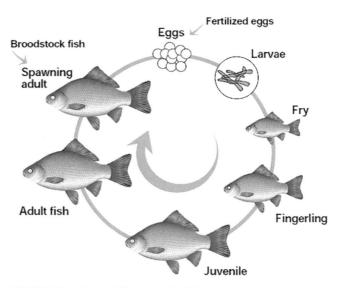

FIGURE 50. *General life cycle of a fish*

Fish known to have excellent results in aquaponic systems are:

- Tilapia
- Blue Gill/Brim
- Sunfish
- Crappie
- Koi
- Fancy Goldfish
- Pacu
- Various ornamental fish such as angelfish, guppies, tetras, swordfish, mollies

Other fish commonly raised in aquaponics:

- Carp
- Barramundi
- Silver Perch
- Golden Perch
- Yellow Perch
- Catfish
- Bass

Best Fish Species for Profitability

When deciding on which species to produce in order to generate the maximum revenue, consider the following issues:

- **Choose a marketable species.** A good example of a species that is easy to produce, but can be difficult to market, is common carp. It is advisable to consider other, more widely accepted species. Of the sixty or so potential fish species used for food, channel catfish, tilapia, crawfish, rainbow trout, and salmon have large, established industries in the United States. Other species such as hybrid striped bass, and various sunfishes also offer considerable potential.

- **Know the complete production cycle.** Without complete production information, trying to raise some species can be a very risky venture. Although species such as walleye, shrimp, and lobsters have wide public appeal and are widely consumed, each has production peculiarities and challenges.

- **Raise a variety of species, if possible.** Many market outlets, for the smaller-scale fish producer, prefer buying a lesser quantity of numerous species. Production of more than one species may offer a competitive edge over single species operations. If production of a variety of species is not feasible, pooling resources with other producers may enhance species' availability.

- **Raise a species that is in high demand.** When choosing what fish to rear, you will need to consider what types of fish are in high demand in the market where you species you like to consume that cost you the most at the store (or which would be most profitable to sell), and ensure that the preferred type of fish is suitable to your climate.

- In addition, you may also consider growing fish, such as goldfish or Koi, which can be sold as pets. Some Koi varieties bring in considerable money per fish.

Fish Details

In working with fish and fish feed it is easier to use metric units, and such is the industry standard; even in the United States. Following is a useful list of proven aquaponic fish with a few details about each species.

Warm Water Fish

BARRAMUNDI

The barramundi or Asian seabass (Lates calcarifer) is a species widely distributed in the Indo-West Pacific region from the Persian Gulf, through Southeast Asia, to Papua New Guinea and Northern Australia. Barramundi grown in the USA are fed a mostly vegetarian diet, and a small amount of fishmeal (which typically comes from herring by-products). They are net protein producers, with a conversion of about 0.9 pounds. This high feed conversion ratio (feed-conversion efficiency), greatly increases return on investment (ROI), which makes it especially attractive to commercial producers.

Growing your own Barramundi excites guests and often generates a lot of stimulating conversation in the community. Barramundi provide a decent harvest at the end of the season and are one of the more majestic species of edible fish.

Barramundi is very popular in Thai cuisine. Barramundi grown in an aquaponic system has an exceptionally clean, crisp taste, with a varying amount of body fat.

TEMPERATURE RANGE: 26–29° C (79–84 ° F)

SIZE: Common between 25 and 100 cm (10 to 40 inches), but can grow to 200 cm (6.5 feet).

BLUEGILL

Bluegill are more sensitive to temperature, pH, and water quality conditions. They prefer a temperature range around 80°F (26.6°C). They can be raised on pellet food and are harvested in 12–16 months.

SCIENTIFIC NAME: Lepomis macrochirus

PRODUCTION POTENTIAL: Easy

MARKETING POTENTIAL: Moderate

MARKET SIZE: Three fish per pound

MARKET: Sport or food

TEMPERATURE REQUIREMENTS: *Growing*: 55–80°F, *Spawning*: 75-80°F, best at 80°F

FEED REQUIREMENTS: *Protein*: 32%, *Fat*: 8–10%

SPAWNING REQUIREMENTS: Spawn in spring, nest builders, 50,000 eggs/lb body weight

CARP

There are many species of carp that could be very well suited to aquaponics. Unfortunately because of their reproductive capabilities, their tough nature, and ability to readily adapt in many areas of the world, carp have become noxious pests to native waterways and disrupt natural ecosystems. As a result, they are listed as an invasive species, not being permitted to be raised or farmed in many regions of the country; doing so could lead to hefty fines, high fees, and/or strict requirements for keeping them.

In most western cultures, carp have a fairly poor reputation as an edible fish. Never the less, carp is still the most widely cultured fish in the world as it's grown throughout most of Asia. They can also be considered as source of revenue in regards to selling them as an animal based food source, if local laws allow. Carp prefer a temperature range of 65–75°F (18–24°C). Carp are omnivorous and consume flake or pellet foods, bugs, plant roots.

SCIENTIFIC NAME: Cyprinus carpio

PRODUCTION POTENTIAL: Easy

MARKETING POTENTIAL: Moderate

MARKET SIZE: 3–5 lbs

MARKET: Food

TEMPERATURE REQUIREMENTS: *Growing*: 55–80°F, *Spawning*: Above 65°F

FEED REQUIREMENTS: *Protein*: 31–38%, *Fat*: 3–8%

SPAWNING REQUIREMENTS: 60,000 eggs/lb. body weight; eggs hatch in 2–7 days

CHANNEL CATFISH

There are many different species of catfish around the world that are well suited to aquaponics. However, channel catfish are the most widely farmed aquaculture species in the United States, so they are readily available in most areas. Catfish don't have scales so they need to be skinned. They are quick growing, and have a good food conversion ratio. Catfish can be harvested in 5-10 months. They are a good fish for warmer climates. Catfish grow best at a temperature of around 80°F (26.6°C). They are very resistant to disease, but are more sensitive to dissolved oxygen (DO) levels. Therefore, it is wise to diligently monitor those levels regularly. Install a good aeration device if DO levels tend to average less than 5 ppm in your system.

SCIENTIFIC NAME: Ictalurus punctatus

PRODUCTION POTENTIAL: Easy

MARKETING POTENTIAL: High

MARKET SIZE: 0.75–2.5 lb.

MARKET: Food or sport

TEMPERATURE REQUIREMENTS: *Growing*: 80–85°F, *Spawning*: 72–82°F

FEED REQUIREMENTS: *Protein*: 28–30%, *Fat*: 6–12%

SPAWNING REQUIREMENTS: Annual spring spawners lay eggs in cavities at a rate of 3,000–4,000 eggs/lb body weight; eggs hatch in 7–8 days at 78°F.

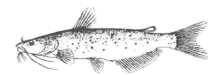

MURRAY COD

Murray cod are a magnificent native Australian fish, known to grow to enormous sizes in their native habitats. Murray cod are widely grown in recirculating aquaculture systems; but can also been grown in aquaponic systems. They are quick growing and deliciously edible fish. They must be well fed, otherwise they cannibalize each other.

SILVER PERCH

Silver perch, a native Australian fish, grow well under a variety of conditions. Perch are omnivorous and eat pellet foods, green scraps, and Duckweed and Azolla. They grow within a wide temperature range. However, they are not as fast growing as many other fish, taking 12–18 months for fingerlings to grow to plate size. They prefer a temperature range around 80°F (26.6°C).

GOLDFISH

Although some people may group these fish with carp, most folks, pet shops, and other fish suppliers refer to them as goldfish. They are generally resilient, withstanding imperfect conditions, and are therefore often used in smaller aquaponic systems by beginners and hobbyist.

If you do not intend to rear aquaponics fish for consumption, rearing goldfish is an option worth consideration. The excess goldfish can be sold to your local pet shop or aquariums for profit.

In many areas they will breed in a tank, although they generally need plant cover within the tank to breed.

Goldfish prefer a temperature range of 65–75°F (18–24°C). Goldfish are omnivorous and consume flake or pellet foods, bugs, plant roots.

COMMON NAME: The comet variety is the most common type of goldfish, but there have been many other varieties developed such as black moors, calico, koi, and shubunkins.

SCIENTIFIC NAME: Carassius auratus

PRODUCTION POTENTIAL: Easy

MARKETING POTENTIAL: Moderate

MARKET SIZE: 1–6 inches for ornamental and 1–2 inches for feeder fish.

MARKET: Ornamental

TEMPERATURE REQUIREMENTS: *Growing*: 70°F, *Spawning*: Above 60°F

FEED REQUIREMENTS: *Protein*: 30–38%, *Fat*: NA

SPAWNING REQUIREMENTS: Instinctively spawns repeatedly from May to June, eggs hatch in 2–8 days, 50,000 eggs/lb. body weight.

An additional note on spawning goldfish. Their spawning period can be modified with artificial lighting. The primary method used is the egg transfer method. In this method, the broodstock spawn on spawning mats which are placed in a separate tank. When mats are covered with eggs, they are then moved to rearing ponds or a tank.

HYBRID STRIPED BASS, SUNSHINE BASS, PALMETTO BASS, WIPER

A hybrid striped bass, also known as a wiper or whiterock bass, is a hybrid between the striped bass (Morone saxatilis) and the white bass (M. chrysops). Hybrid striped bass are known for aggressive feeding habits which makes them highly sought after by anglers. Often schooling by the thousands, these stocked fish will surface feed on baitfish-like shad. Their quality as a hard-fighting gamefish is closely followed by their delicious, firm, white, flaky meat. Many restaurants sell "striped bass" on their menus, but what you are really eating are farm raised hybrid striped bass.

SCIENTIFIC NAME: Morone saxatilis x M. chrysops or M. chrysops x M. saxatilis

PRODUCTION POTENTIAL: Moderate

MARKETING POTENTIAL: Moderate

MARKET SIZE: 1.5–3.5 lbs

MARKET: Food or sport

TEMPERATURE REQUIREMENTS: *Growing*: 77–86°F, *Spawning*: 61–68°F

FEED REQUIREMENTS: *Protein*: 45–50%, *Fat*: 15%

MOST COMMON PRODUCTION SYSTEMS: Ponds, recycle systems, and cages.

SPAWNING REQUIREMENTS: Instinctively spawns in late March through May. Cross made with either female white bass and male striped bass (sunshine bass), or with female striped bass and male white bass (palmetto bass). Female striped bass average 100,000 eggs/lb. body weight (25,000 eggs per ounce of spawn) and white bass females average 50,000 eggs/lb. body weight (100,000 eggs per spawn). Eggs hatch in two to five days. Survival of fry is low, less than 50 percent.

JADE PERCH

This native Australian fish has the highest levels of omega three oils of any fish species in the world. In fact, it's so high that growers are trying to breed a less oily fish because they've found people don't like the high content. They require warm water and an omnivorous diet. They are very well suited to aquaponics and grow quickly. Fingerlings are typically readily available in warmer areas. The ideal temperature for Jade Perch is 23°C (73°F).

Jade perch can tolerate a pH of between 6 and 9, with the desired range between 6.5 and 8.5.

KOI

Another species of carp, but better known as "Koi", are very common within many Asian communities. They are often found in ornamental ponds and public fish tanks throughout the world. For those who love Koi, an aquaponic system is a great proposition for stocking the fish. In terms of revenue, some individuals with distinct color patterns from certain varieties can be quite lucrative. For instance, some KOI with extremely unique color arrangments have been sold for thousands of dollars each. Koi prefer a temperature range of 65–75°F (18–24°C). Koi are omnivores and consume flake or pellet foods, bugs, and plant roots.

LARGEMOUTH BASS

Largemouth Bass can be successfully grown in an aquaponic system, but it requires a vigilant patient grower to do so. They are much less tolerant to unfavorable water conditions than the tilapia. They also take between 16-17 months to produce a table-ready fish. The longer it takes to grow, the higher probability that something will go wrong along the way. They require fairly delicate handling. They are stressed by bright light and cannot tolerate poor nutrition. They are one of the most sensitive fish to raise; and they are more sensitive to water temperature and quality, as well as pH and oxygen levels. The younger fingerlings must be trained to feed on pellets. Largemouth bass prefer temperatures between 77 and 86 degrees. Bass seldom feed at temperatures below 50 degrees and cannot survive for long at temperatures above 98 degrees.

When keeping bass in tanks, it is prudent to use some sort of cover or fencing/netting around the tank as they are prone to jump out.

SCIENTIFIC NAME: Micropterus salmoides

PRODUCTION POTENTIAL: Moderate

MARKETING POTENTIAL: High

MARKET SIZE: 1.0–2.5 lbs.

MARKET: Sport or food

TEMPERATURE REQUIREMENTS: *Growing*: 60–80°F, *Spawning*: 60–65°F

FEED REQUIREMENTS: *Protein*: 40%. These diets are normally fed from fingerlings to adults after fingerlings have been trained to accept commercial diets. *Fat*: NA

SPAWNING REQUIREMENTS: Instinct spawning runs from spring through summer when temperatures are around 75°F (24°C). They are nest egg layers and produce around 13,000 eggs/lb body weight. Eggs hatch in approximately four days.

TILAPIA

Tilapia is a species that is extremely popular in aquaponics systems. They are an ideal species for aquaponics for many reasons. They are easy to breed, fast growing, can withstand poor water conditions, consume an omnivorous diet, and are a delicious edible fish. They are very resilient as well, being less sensitive than other fish species to fluctuations in temperature, pH, dissolved oxygen levels, and a build-up in waste. They can also grow well in crowded tanks. Tilapias have especially high beneficial nutritional ratios of omega-6 to omega-3 fatty acids. Tilapias grow to plate size in about 6-9 months.

A potential downfall is that they may not be the most ideal species for aquaponic systems located in cooler climates as they require warm water. Every breed of tilapia is different, but most tilapia prefer temperatures of 77 to 86°F (25-30°C). They start to lose their resistance to disease and infections below 54°F (12°C). If you live in a cooler area and want to avoid large heating costs, you are much better off growing a fish species that will do well in your temperature range. Tilapias are also a declared an invasive species in many areas, and therefore are prohibited by U.S. Fish and Game laws, and/or other governing agencies in some regions of the country.

There are over 100 different species of tilapia, each with unique characteristics and behavior. Members of the Oreochromis genus are a common choice for aquaponics or aquaculture. In terms of popularity, the Nile tilapia (*O. niloticus*) is the most widely cultured tilapia, followed by Blue tilapia (*O. aureus*),

and Mozambique tilapia (*O. mossambicus*). All can be reproduced fairly easily by a beginner. Refer to the 'Chapter 11: Fish Breeding, Fish Reproduction, and Raising Your Own Crop of Fish' for details on reproducing your own Tilapia.

Tilapias start out as omnivores, but later become more like vegetarians. The Tilapia's digestive system is designed to eat algae, vegetation, other small fish, worms, and insects. The newly hatched, called 'fry', require a lot of protein for fast growth. You can actually stunt their growth by under feeding them, which is what some breeders do to keep their fish in the sellable fingerling size range. As they mature, they require less protein and are not interested in eating their own fry, which is why it's possible to raise fry with adult tilapia in a single tank. Be sure to find a high quality tilapia feed that takes all this under consideration. Be diligent in checking out the protein and fat contents in the fish feed formula when shopping to ensure that it provides the necessary nutrients for each stage of the tilapia's growth.

Tilapias are often fed pellet fish food, duckweed, and green plant products produced from the system. Some operators grow algae and duckweed in separate tanks to feed their tilapia.

Commercial tilapia farms will usually feed their fish pellets made from fishmeal, grain, soybeans or other food products. In the wild, tilapia will eat vegetation, algae, plankton, insects, larvae, decaying organic matter, fish wastes, small fish and just about anything edible that they can get in their mouth. As stated, tilapia can be vegetarians and survive just fine by eating only algae.

Tilapia can be cultured as mixed-sexes (males and females together) or as mono-sex (males only). Most large scale commercial growers prefer to raise only male tilapia because they grow faster than the females. Male tilapia populations can be produced by visual selection, hybridization, sex-reversal, and genetic manipulation. Tilapia with a minimum weight of 25 to 30 g can be separated by visual inspection of the genital papilla.

During the last 10 to 15 years, the most popular way to produce all-male populations is with hormone sex reversal of tilapia fry. Recently hatched tilapia fry obtained by harvest from spawning containers 18 days after brood fish are stocked or hatched from eggs taken from females are fed a powdered diet containing a male steroid for 20 to 28 days. Fry that would have been females if fed a steroid-free diet, will be functional males at the end of the hormone treatment. While all-male populations are hard to produce with sex reversal treatment, 95 to 98 percent males are commonly produced. Tilapia reach sexual maturity at 3 to 5 months of age.

SCIENTIFIC NAME: Oreochromis niloticus, O. aurea, O. mossambicus, O. hornorum

PRODUCTION POTENTIAL: Easy except tilapia grow slowly at temperatures lower than 70°F and die when temperatures drop into the 50°F range.

MARKETING POTENTIAL: High

MARKET SIZE: 1.25–2.0 lbs

MARKET: Food

TEMPERATURE REQUIREMENTS: *Growing*: 80–87°F, *Spawning*: Greater than 72°F, Lethal: 55°F

FEED REQUIREMENTS: *Protein*: 25–30%, *Fat*: 6–8%

SPAWNING REQUIREMENTS: Maternal mouth brooders, spawn twice a month, 2,500 eggs/lb body weight, eggs hatch in 5-7 days. All male hybrids can be produced by crossing female O. niloticus and male O. aurea. or by crossing female O. niloticus and male O. hornorum. Stocking ratios for fingerling production is three females to each male.

Tilapia Feed Conversion Ratio Feeding Rates, Growth Rate, and Harvesting

The feed conversion ratio (FCR) or feed conversion efficiency (FCE), to define it simply, is a measure of an animal's efficiency in converting feed mass into increased body mass. Tilapia have an average feed conversion rate of 1.7. This 1.7 to 1 ration is incredibly efficient, especially compared to cattle which have a FCR of 8:1 (8-lbs of feed for every 1-lb of mass).

It takes between 7 and 9 months for a tilapia to reach harvest size of 1.25-lbs (0.57-kg or 567-grams) which produces two, 4-ounce (113-grams) fillets, or enough for a meal for two people. Commercial growers, using supplemental feedings and intensive management techniques, are able to achieve harvest of a 500-gram fish within five months. Keep in mind, though, that premium prices for your fish will only be achieved via being able to honestly market your fish as being grown through sustainable farming practices, fully organic (no artificial supplements & organic based feed products), in an animal friendly environment.

Tilapia can be harvested anytime they reach a marketable size of 1 to 2 pounds. Tilapia grow fast and usually reach market size in 6 to 12 months, depending on the feed and conditions. Large commercial operators generally harvest all of their fish at one time; whereas smaller operators typically harvest their fish over a period of time. Both options have their advantages. Harvesting all at once is more efficient, and the fish usually are sold to one buyer (i.e. a food company). For the small to mid-size operator, harvesting over time relieves system overcrowding, minimizes water quality challenges, and proves a steady supply of fresh fish for meals and/or an ongoing revenue stream.

Tilapia are most commonly processed into skinless, boneless fillets. The fillet yield is typically 30 to 37 percent of their total body weight, depending on fillet size and final trim. [1-ounce = 28.3 grams]

Tilapia is an Excellent Source of Protein and Nutrients

Tilapia is a pretty impressive source of protein . In 3 .5 ounces (100 grams), it packs 26 grams of protein and only 128 calories. Even more impressive is the amount of vitamins and minerals in this fish. Tilapia is rich in niacin, vitamin B12, phosphorus, selenium, and potassium. A 3 .5-ounce serving contains the following:

- Calories: 128
- Carbs: 0 grams
- Protein: 26 grams
- Fats: 3 grams
- Niacin: 24% of the RDI
- Vitamin B12: 31% of the RDI
- Phosphorus: 20% of the RDI
- Selenium: 78% of the RDI
- Potassium: 20% of the RDI

Tilapia is also a lean source of protein, with only 3 grams of fat per serving.

Another thing to keep in mind, especially if you are looking for farm-raised fish fed with non-GMO feed: The USDA does not currently have guidelines for classifying seafood as organic.

TABLE 6. **Tilapia Growth and Feeding Rates**

MONTH	START WEIGHT (g)	END WEIGHT (g)	GROWTH RATE (g/day)	FEEDING RATE (% weight)
1	1	5	0.2	15–10
2	5	20	0.5	10–7
3	20	50	1.0	7–4
4	50	100	1.5	4–3.5
5	100	165	2.0	3.5–2.5
6	165	250	2.5	2.5–1.5
7	250	350	3.0	1.5–1.25
8	350	475	4.0	1.25–1
9	475	625	5.0	1

TABLE 7. **The Most Common Edible Fish Raised in Aquaponics**

LIFE SUPPORT	BASS	TROUT	TILAPIA
Thriving Temp.	74°–80°F 24°–26°C	55°–65°F 13°–18°C	74°–80°F 24°–26°C
Surviving Temp.	40°–90°F 5°–32°C	38°–68°F 4°–20°C	60°–95°F 16°–35°C
Carnivore or Omnivore	Carnivore	Carnivore	Omnivore
Oxygen Needs	Low	High	Low

TABLE 8. **Potential growth rates of tilapia in one tank over a year using a progressive harvest technique**

MONTH	DEC	JAN	FEB	MAR	APR	MAY	JUN	JUL	AUG	SEP	OCT	NOV	DEC
STOCKING ROUND	WEIGHT (KG)												
1	1.5	3.75	6.0	8.25	10.5	12.75	15.0*						
2				1.5	3.75	6.0	8.25	10.5	12.75	15.0*			
3							1.5	3.75	6.0	8.25	10.5	12.75	15.0*
4										1.5	3.75	6	8.25
5													1.5
Total fish mass (kg)	1.5	3.75	6.0	9.75	14.25	18.75	24.75–9.75	14.25	18.75	24.75–9.75	14.25	18.75	24.75–9.75
Action							Restock harvest			Restock harvest			Restock harvest

NOTES: Fingerling tilapia (1.5 kg = 50 g/fish x 30 fish) are stocked every three months. Each fish survives and grows to harvest size (15g = 500 g/fish x 30 fish) in six months. The asterisk indicates harvest. The range during harvest/stocking months accounts for the range if not all 30 fish are taken at once, i.e. the 30 mature fish are harvested throughout the month. This table serves only as a theoretical guide to illustrate staggered harvest and stocking in ideal conditions.

TABLE 9. **Potential growth rates of tilapia in one tank over a year using a progressive harvest technique**

MONTH	DEC	JAN	FEB	MAR	APR	MAY	JUN	JUL	AUG	SEP	OCT	NOV	DEC
STOCKING ROUND 1													
Number of fish in tank	80	80	70	60	50	40	30	10					
Fish weight (g)	50	125	200	275	350	425	500	575					
Cohort biomass (kg)	4	10	14	17	18	17	15	5.8					
STOCKING ROUND 2													
Number of fish in tank							80	80	70	60	50	40	30
Fish weight (g)							50	125	200	275	350	425	500
Cohort biomass (kg)							4	10	14	17	18	17	15
Total tank biomass (kg)	**4**	**10**	**14**	**17**	**18**	**17**	**19**	**15.8**	**14**	**17**	**18**	**17**	**15**

NOTES: Tilapia fingerling are stocked every six months. Staggered harvest starts from the third month to keep the total fish below the maximum stocking biomass of 20 kg/m³. The table shows the theoretical weight of each batch of harvested fish along the year if fish are reared in ideal conditions.

Table 8, using tilapia as an example, outlines the potential growth in one tank over a year using the staggered stocking method. The important aspect of this table is that the total weight of the fish varies between 10–25 kg, with an average biomass of 17 kg. This table is a basic guideline depicting optimum conditions for fish growth. In reality factors such as water temperature and stressful environments for fish can distort the figures presented here.

If it is not possible to obtain fingerlings regularly, an aquaponic system can be still managed by stocking a higher number of juvenile fish and by progressively harvesting them during the season to maintain a stable biomass to fertilize the plants. Table 9 shows the case of a system stocked every six months with tilapia fingerlings of 50g. In this case, the first harvest starts from the third month onward. Various combinations in stocking frequency, fish number, and weight can apply providing that fish biomass stands below the maximum limit of 20 kg/m3. If the fish are mixed-sex, the harvest must firstly target the females to avoid breeding when they reach sexual maturity from the age of five months. Breeding depresses the whole cohort. In the case of mixed-sex tilapia, fish can be initially stocked in a cage and males can then be set free in the tank after sex determination.

It is important to note that adult tilapia, catfish, and trout will predate their smaller siblings if they are stocked together. Although, tilapia are not as likely to eat their young compared to other species, they will do so under certain conditions. A technique to keep all of these fish safely in the same fish tank is to isolate the smaller ones in a floating frame. This frame is essentially a floating cage, which can be constructed as a cube with PVC pipe used as frame and covered with plastic mesh. It is important to ensure that larger fish cannot enter the floating cage over the top, so make sure that the sides extend at least 6-inches (15 cm) above the water level. Each of the vulnerable size classes should be kept in separate floating frames in the main fish tank. As the fish grow large enough not to be in danger, they can be moved into the main tank. With this method, it is possible to have up to three different stocking weights in one tank, so it is important that the fish feed pellet size can be eaten by all sizes of fish. Caged fish also have the advantage of being closely monitored to determine the feed rate ratio by measuring the weight increment and weight of the feed over a period.

Fish Overview — Common Aquaponic Edible Fish

Nearly all freshwater fish are edible, but their taste, production potential, and growing parameters must be taken into consideration. It is vital to take good care of your fish since they are the lifeline of your

---

Cold Water Fish

TROUT

Trout are a good choice of fish for aquaponic systems located in cooler climates, where water temperatures can efficiently be kept cooler. Trout are best suited for water temperatures between 50°F (10°C) and 60°F (20°C). They have extremely fast growth rates and excellent food conversion ratios. They can be trained to be carnivorous, but will typically always eat smaller fish given an opportunity. They require high dissolved oxygen levels. They are sensitive to pH changes and water quality. Most aquaponic operators who raise trout feed them pellet fish food. They reach plate size in 12-16 months.

SCIENTIFIC NAME: Oncorhynchus mykiss

PRODUCTION POTENTIAL: Easy

MARKETING POTENTIAL: High

MARKET SIZE: 0/5—1.5 lbs.

MARKET: Food or sport

TEMPERATURE REQUIREMENTS: *Growing*: 50—60°F, *Spawning*: 50—55°F, *Lethal*: Greater than 70°F

FEED REQUIREMENTS: *Protein*: 45—50%, *Fat*: 12—15%

SPAWNING REQUIREMENTS: Spring and fall spawning strains, 500—10,000 eggs depending on size of female, eggs hatch in 24—31 days at 50—55°F.

For more information on how to successfully raise and breed tilapia the following book covers every aspect of tilapia farming in an easy-to-follow format.

FIGURE 51. *Acclimatizing fish. Juvenile fish are transported in a plastic bag (a) which is floated in the receiving tank (b) and the fish are released (c).*

aquaponics system. Managing water quality and using only top-rated fish food helps ensure that your fish stay.

Another thing to consider is whether to buy fry or fingerlings. Fish fry is cheaper, but takes longer to mature; which means that they take longer to produce adequate nitrate levels for plants to absorb. On the other hand, fingerlings are more expensive but they produce more waste in the early stage optimization stages, which means an earlier start in growing vegetables.

Acclimatizing Fish

Acclimatizing fish into new tanks can be a highly stressful process for fish, particularly the actual transport from one location to another in bags or small tanks. It is important to try to remove as many stressful factors as possible that can cause fatality in new fish. There are two main factors that cause stress when acclimatizing fish: changes in temperature and pH between the original water and new water; therefore, differences in pH and temperature from the previous fish environment to the new tank must be kept to a minimum for the fish to have the best chance at survival during the transfer.

The pH of the culture water and transport water should ideally be tested. If the pH values are more than 0.5 different, then the fish will need at least 24 hours to adjust. Keep the fish in a small aerated tank in their original water and slowly add water from the new tank over the course of a day. Even if the pH values of the two environments are fairly close, the fish still need to acclimatize. The best method to do this is to slowly allow the temperature to equilibrate by floating the sealed transportation bags containing the fish in the culture water. This should be done for at least 15 minutes. At this time small amounts of water should be added from the culture water to the transport water with the fish. Again, this should take at least 15 minutes, so as to slowly acclimatize the fish. Larger volumes of transfer water require longer water temperature adjustment times. Finally, the fish can be added to the new tank.

Stocking Density

The recommended stocking density is 1 pound of fish per 5–7 gallons of tank water (0.5 kg per 20-26 liters). However, a lighter fish stock density has been found to be more forgiving if things go wrong (pump malfunction, water leak not immediately discovered, etc.).

Fish selection should take into account the following:

- Edible (e.g., tilapia, trout, etc.) vs. ornamental (e.g., koi, goldfish, etc.).
- Water temperature based upon your climate (recommended).
- Diet of fish: Carnivore vs. omnivore vs. herbivore
- In order to maintain the perfect balance between fish and plant population density, it is best to

progressively harvest the fish as soon as they are big enough.

Keep in mind that there are other factors affecting the number of fish that can be grown in an aquaponic system, such as the species of fish and feed rates. The more the fish are fed, the more waste they produce. It is important to monitor system parameters such as water flow-rates, oxygen levels, pump rates, and water temperature as they all play a critical role as well. However, don't let these things intimidate or discourage you from getting into aquaponics. This book will provide you the information needed so that you may be successful. All these issues are addressed in detail in their respective chapters of this book.

Harvesting and Staggered Fish Stock

A constant biomass of fish in the tanks ensures a constant supply of nutrients to the plants. This ensures that the fish eat the amount of feed calculated using the feed rate ratio. The next chapter, which covers feed conversion rates, will show how the feeding ration depends on the size of the fish, and small fish are not be able to eat enough feed to supply the full growing area with adequate nutrients. To achieve a constant biomass in the fish tanks, a staggered stocking method should be adopted. This technique involves maintaining three age classes, or cohorts, within the same tank. Approximately every three months, the mature fish (500 g each) are harvested and immediately restocked with new fingerlings (50 g each). This method avoids harvesting all the fish at once, and instead retains a more consistent biomass. Important Notes Regarding Fish

- Add fish only after the fish-less cycling process is complete (media-bed systems only).
- Feed the fish as much as they can eat in 5-10 minutes, two times per day. Always remove uneaten feed after 30 minutes. Record total feed added. Balance the feeding rate with the number of plants using the feed rate ratio, but avoid over or under feeding the fish.
- Fish appetite is directly related to water temperature, particularly for topical fish such as tilapia, so remember to adjust feeding during colder winter months.
- A fingerling tilapia (50 g) will reach harvest size (500 g) in 6–8 weeks under ideal conditions. Staggered stocking is a technique which involves stocking a system with new fingerlings each time some of the mature fish are harvested. It provides a way of maintaining relatively constant biomass, feeding rate and nutrient concentration for the plants.

Other Aquatic Species for Aquaponics

There are other fish species which are quite suitable for aquaponics, which might be available in your local area. In Europe, many different species of carp are grown; within the United States species such as Bluegill are often available, while in Australia there are a number of other native species like Sleepy cod which would be suitable.

Other aquatic animals that are sometimes used in an aquaponic system are fresh water mussels, fresh water prawns, and fresh water crayfish. Mussels are a filter-feeder, and do a great job of helping to clean the water. They will grow in flooded grow beds, or can be incorporated into fish tanks. Crustaceans make a nice addition to an aquaponic system. There are a few different species available depending on your location and water temperatures.

Consideration for those that live in tropical areas is Redclaw, a fast growing native Australian species. For those in cooler areas there's Yabbies or Marron as a viable option.

Aquatic Animals to Avoid

Animals such as turtles and snails may work for general pond watching activity, but they are not good for an aquaponics system. Turtles eat fish while snails eat algae; they usually reproduce beyond control, can plug pumps filters, pipes, and will eat certain plants and plants roots. Growing snail shells will also deplete your system of carbonates causing a drop in pH level. It is also important to keep domestic pets out of your system.

Keeping Fish Healthy

An aquaponic system fish tank has inputs of food, water, and oxygen. The fish tank has outputs of urine, ammonia, carbon dioxide, feces, and uneaten food.

Although each fish species is unique in regards to the ideal growing conditions, there are some generalities that are common for all fish. For instance, most fish need the pH to be somewhere between 6 and 8 (although the pH range of 6.8-7.0 is optimal for plants and fish) . Ammonia and nitrites are very toxic to fish. Nitrates are fairly safe for fish (and great for plants). Fish need oxygen (they will die within 30 minutes without it). Drastic temperature changes can cause health issues and even result in death. Fish are sensitive to light, and do best when not exposed to direct light. Fish need to be temperature matched to the water before releasing them into the tank.

Fish Maintenance

The following are general rules to keep in mind:

- Feed fish 2-3 times a day, but don't overfeed.
- Fish eat 1.5-2.0 percent of their body weight per day.
- Only feed fish what they can eat in 5-10 minutes.
- Fish won't eat if they are too cold, too hot, or stressed.
- Check water quality regularly.
- Add water or do partial water changes when necessary.
- In addition to checking water conditions of the fish tank, observe fish behavior and appearance. After becoming familiar with your fish, you will often be able to tell if there is something wrong or different.
- Some fish desire to be your friend and will regularly "greet you" at the tank.

Types of Fish Disease

Fish ailments can be separated into four general types:

- Bacterial Diseases
- Fungal Diseases
- Parasitic Diseases
- Physical Ailments

TABLE 10. **Cause and symptoms of stress in fish**

CAUSES OF STRESS	SYMPTOMS OF STRESS
Temperature outside of range, or fast temperature changes	Poor appetite
pH outside of range, or fast pH changes (more than 0.3/day)	Unusual swimming behavior, resting at surface or bottom
Ammonia, nitrite or toxins present in high levels	Rubbing or scraping the sides of the tank, piping at surface, red blotches and streaks
Dissolved oxygen is too low	Piping at surface
Malnourishment and/or overcrowding	Fins are clamped close to their body, physical injuries
Poor water quality	Fast breathing
Poor fish handling, noise or light disturbance	Erratic behavior
Bullying companions	Physical injuries

How to Prevent Fish Diseases

Precautions can and should be taken to reduce the possibility of your fish getting a disease. Following these precautions can also help keep fish diseases from spreading if they do occur:

- Buy only good quality, compatible fish, and then breed/raise your own fish thereafter.
- Quarantine new fish in a separate tank before adding them to your aquaponic system.
- Avoid stressing the fish with rough handling, sudden changes in conditions, or "bully" tank mates.
- Do not overfeed your fish.
- Remove sick fish to a separate tank for treatment.
- Disinfect nets used to move sick fish.
- Do not transfer water from the quarantine tank to the main tank.
- Do not let any metal that has the propensity to rust come in contact with your system's water.

Recognizing Disease

Diseases may occur even with all of the prevention techniques listed above. It is important to stay vigilant and monitor and observe fish behaviour daily to recognize the diseases early. The following lists outline common physical and behavioural symptoms of diseases.

External signs of disease:

- Ulcers on body surface, discoloured patches, white or black spots,
- Ragged fins, exposed fin rays,
- Gill and fin necrosis and decay,
- Abnormal body configuration, twisted spine, deformed jaws,
- Extended abdomen, swollen appearance,
- Cotton-like lesions on the body,
- Swollen, popped-out eyes (exophthalmia).

Behavioural signs of disease:

- Poor appetite, changes in feeding habits,
- Lethargy, different swimming patterns, listlessness,
- Odd position in water, head or tail down, difficulty maintaining buoyancy,
- Fish gasping at the surface,
- Fish rubbing or scraping against objects.

Abiotic Diseases: Most of the mortalities in aquaponics are not caused by pathogens, but rather by abiotic causes mainly related to water quality or toxicity. Poor water quality conditions can induce opportunistic infections that can easily occur in unhealthy or stressed fish.

Biotic Diseases: In general, aquaponics and recirculating systems are less affected than pond or cage aquaculture farming by pathogens. In most cases, pathogens are actually already present in the system, but disease does not occur because the fishes' immune system is resisting infection and the environment is unfavourable for the pathogen to thrive.

Healthy management, stress avoidance, and quality control of water are thus necessary to minimize any disease incidence. Whenever disease occurs, it is important to isolate or eliminate the infected fish from the rest of the stock and implement strategies to prevent any transmission risk to the rest of the stock. If any cure is put into action, it is fundamental that the fish be treated in a quarantine tank, and that any products used are not introduced into the aquaponic system. This is in order to avoid any unpredictable consequences to the beneficial bacteria. More details on this subject are available from regulatory agencies, such as the U.S. Fish and Wildlife Service, online research, and most local fishery organizations.

Beware of Fish Disease Treatments

Many recommended ailment treatments, although effective, are not conducive to an aquaponic system. For instance, antibiotics will kill beneficial bacteria and copper treatments can be harmful to your plants.

These treatments should only be used in a quarantine situation, and the water from the quarantine tank should never be added to the aquaponics system. All recommended treatments need to be carefully scrutinized to ensure that they will not negatively impact the aquaponics system, as the vast majority of fish experts address disease and treatments based upon isolated conditions (i.e. aquaculture, aquarium, quarantine tank), and not within the scope of an aquaponics system.

Steps to Treating Sick Fish

If a significant percentage of fish are showing signs of disease, it is likely that the environmental conditions are causing stress. In these cases, check levels of ammonia, nitrite, nitrate, pH, and temperature in order to respond accordingly. If only a few fish are affected, it is important to remove the infected fish immediately in order to prevent the spread of the any disease to the other fish. Once removed, inspect the fish carefully and attempt to determine the specific disease and cause.

However, it may be necessary to have a professional diagnosis carried out by a veterinarian, extension agent, or other aquaculture expert. Knowing the specific disease helps to determine the treatment options. Place the affected fish in a separate tank, sometimes called a "quarantine" or "hospital tank", for further observation. Kill and dispose of the fish if appropriate.

Disease treatment options in small-scale aquaponics are limited. Commercial drugs can be expensive and/or difficult to procure. Moreover, antibacterial and antiparasite treatments have detrimental effects on the rest of the system, including the plants, media bed and/or biofilter. If treatment is absolutely necessary, it should be done in a hospital tank only; antibacterial chemicals should never be added to an aquaponic system. One effective treatment options against some of the most common bacterial and parasite infections is a salt bath.

Salt Bath Treatment: Fish affected with some ecto-parasites, moulds, and bacterial gill contamination can benefit from salt bath treatment. Infected fish can be removed from the main fish tank and placed into a salt bath. This salt bath is toxic to the pathogens, but non-fatal to the fish. The salt concentration for the bath should be 1 kg of salt per 100 liters of water. Affected fish should be placed in this salty solution for 20–30 minutes, and then moved to a second isolation tank containing 1–2 g of salt per liter of water for another 5–7 days.

With bad white-spot infections, all fish may need to be removed from the main aquaponic system and treated this way for at least a week. During this time, any emerging parasites in the aquaponic unit will fail to find a host and eventually die. The heating of the water in the aquaponic system can also shorten the parasite life cycle and make the salt treatment more effective. Do not implement a salt bath treatment within the aquaponic system, or use any salt bath water when moving the fish back into the aquaponic system as the salt concentrations would negatively affect the beneficial bacteria and plants.

CHAPTER 11

Fish Feed

Fish Feed and Nutrition

Fish require the correct balance of proteins, carbohydrates, fats, vitamins, and minerals to grow and be healthy. This type of feed is considered a whole feed. Commercial fish feed pellets are readily available from numerous sources from online suppliers to local feed stores.

Protein is the most important component for building fish mass. In their grow-out stage, omnivorous fish, such as tilapia and common carp, need 25–35 percent protein in their diet, while carnivorous fish need up to 45 percent in order to grow at optimal levels. In general, younger fish (fry and fingerlings) require a diet richer in protein than during their grow-out stage. Proteins are the basis of structure and enzymes in all living organisms. Proteins consist of amino acids, some of which are synthesized by the fishes' bodies, but others have to be obtained from the food. These are called essential amino acids. Of the ten essential amino acids, methionine and lysine are often limiting factors, and these need to be supplemented in some vegetable-based feeds.

Lipids are fats, which are high-energy molecules necessary to a fish's diet. Fish oil is a common component of fish feeds. Fish oil is high in two special types of fats, omega-3 and omega-6, that have health benefits for humans. The amount of these healthy lipids in farmed fish depends on the feed used.

Carbohydrates consist of starches and sugars. This component of the feed is an inexpensive ingredient that increases the energy value of the feed. The starch and sugars also help bind the feed together to make a pellet. However, fish do not digest and metabolize carbohydrates very well, and much of this energy can be lost.

Vitamins and minerals are necessary for fish health and growth. Vitamins are organic molecules, synthesized by plants or through manufacturing, that are important for development and immune system function. Minerals are inorganic elements. These minerals are necessary for the fish to synthesis their own body components (bone), vitamins, and cellular structures. Some minerals are also involved in osmotic regulation.

Pelletized Fish Feed

There are a number of different sizes of fish feed pellets. Obviously, the recommended size of pellet depends on the size of the fish. Fry and fingerlings have small mouths and cannot ingest large pellets, while large fish waste energy if the pellets are too small. If possible, the feed should be purchased for each stage of the lifecycle of the fish. Alternatively, large pellets can be crushed with a mortar and pestle to create powder for fry and crumbles for fingerlings. Some operators use the same medium-sized pellets (2–4 mm) so that their fish continue to eat the same-sized pellet from the fingerling stage right up to maturity.

Fish feed pellets are also designed to either float on the surface or sink to the bottom of the tank, depending on the feeding habits of the fish. It is important to know the eating behaviour of your specific fish and supply the correct type of pellet. Floating pellets are advantageous because it is easier to identify how much the fish are eating. It is often possible to train fish to feed according to the food pellets available; however, some fish will not change their feeding culture.

Feed should be stored in dark, dry, cool, and secure conditions. Fish feed will attract rodents and other vermin, if not securely contained. Warm wet fish feed can rot, being decomposed by bacteria and fungi. These micro-organisms can release toxins that are dangerous to fish; spoiled feed should never be fed to fish. Fish feed should not be stored for too long, should be purchased fresh, and used immediately to conserve the nutritional qualities, wherever possible.

Avoid overfeeding your fish. Uneaten food waste should never be left in the aquaponic system. Feed waste from overfeeding is consumed by heterotrophic bacteria, which devours substantial amounts of oxygen. In addition to wasting money, decomposing fish feed can increase the amount of ammonia and nitrite to toxic levels in a relatively short period. Finally, the uneaten pellets can clog the mechanical filters, leading to decreased water flow and anoxic areas. In general, fish eat all they need to eat in a 10 minute period. If uneaten food is found, lower the amount of feed given at the next feeding.

Fish Feed

The following provides some general information about fish feed:

- Live foods are a good source of supplements and provide variety for carnivorous fish.
- Fish typically eat all their food within 3 minutes. If feed remains after 10 minutes it is a good indication that they are being overfed. Overfeeding will lead to food decomposition toxicity problems. Feeding a variety of different feed brands helps ensure proper nutrition.
- Most commercial fish feeds contain exact protein, carbohydrate, and other vitamin requirements for specific fish.
- Plant based proteins can include soy meal, corn meal, wheat meal, etc.
- Most commercial feeds are between 10 to 35 percent protein.
- Alternative feeds should be considered like duckweed, insects, worms, or black soldier fly larvae.
- Avoid fish meal based feeds as this source is not sustainable or derived from environmental friendly practices. Fish meal feed can also come from animals raised on growth hormones, antibiotics, pesticides, herbicides, and fungicide laced feed, which then enters your food supply.
- Most fish feed is GMO based, which can entail the presence of heavy metals. In turn, this is passed on up the food chain to you and your family in higher concentrations. Heavy metals wreak havoc on our health and well-being. Therefore, try to use only fish feed that is made entirely from non-GMO, USDA certified organic ingredients, is free of terrestrial animal parts, and contains no fish meal or soy. There are many suppliers of organic fish feed. An Internet search for organic fish feed will provide numerous options.
- Many online vendors will provide you with the nearest retail outlet that sell their feed, saving you the shipping cost. Depending upon your location, though, having it shipped to you may be the only option. Teaming up with other aquaponic or aquaculture operators in your area could enable you to get better bargains via buying in bulk and sharing the shipping cost.

Feeding Fish — Parameters and Other Considerations

In some operations, feed costs can add up to half or more of the total annual operating costs. For this reason, it is important to use the proper feed and to take measures to be sure that the conversion of feed to fish flesh is efficient. The Feed Conversion Ratio (FCR) describes how efficiently an animal turns its food into growth. It answers the question of how many units of feed are required to grow one unit of animal. FCRs exist for every animal and offer a convenient way to measure the efficiency and costs of raising any given animal.

Fish, in general, have one of the best FCRs of all livestock. The FCR is expressed as the number of pounds of feed required to produce one pound of flesh. Depending on the species being grown, it may take 1.75 to produce 1 pound of fish. In good conditions, tilapias have an FCR of 1.4–1.8, meaning that to grow a 2.2 pound (1.0 kg) tilapia, 3-4 pounds (1.4–1.8 kg) of food is required.

Tracking FCR is not essential in small-scale aquaponics, but it can be useful to do in some circumstances. When changing feeds, it is worth considering how well the fish grow in regard to any cost differences between the feeds. Moreover, when considering starting a small commercial system, it is necessary to calculate the FCR as part of the business plan and/or financial analysis. Even if not concerned about the FCR, it is good practice to periodically weigh a sample

FIGURE 52. Weighing a sample of fish using a weighing scale

of the fish to make sure they are growing well and to understand the balance of the system.

This also provides a more accurate growth rate expectation for harvest timing and production. As with all fish handling, weighing is easier in darkness to avoid stressing the fish. Following is a list of simple steps for weighing fish. Weighing fish of the same age, growing in the same tank, is more preferable than heterogeneous cohorts of fish as the measurement should provide more reliable averages.

Simple Steps for Weighing Fish

1. Fill a small bucket with 2.5 gallons (10 liters) of water from the aquaponic system.

2. Place the bucket on a weighing scale and record the weight (tare).

3. Scoop 5 average size fish with a landing-net, drain the landing-net of excess of water for a few second-ds then place the fish into the bucket.

4. Weigh again and record the gross weight.

5. Calculate the total weight of the fish by subtracting the tare from the gross weight.

6. Divide this figure by 5 to retrieve an average weight for each fish.

Repeat steps 1–6 as appropriate. Try to measure 10–20 percent of the fish (preferably no duplicates) for an accurate average.

Periodic weight measurements will give the average growth rate of the fish, which will be obtained by subtracting the average fish weight, calculated above, over two periods. The FCR is obtained by dividing the total feed consumed by the fish by the total growth during a given period, with both values expressed in the same weight unit (i.e. ounces and pounds, or gram or kilogram).

Total Feed / Total Growth = FCR

The total feed can be obtained by summing all the recorded amount of feed consumed each day. The total growth can be calculated by multiplying the average growth rate by the number of the fish stocked in the tank.

At the grow-out stage, the feeding rate for most cultured fish is 1.5–2 percent of their body weight per day. On average, a 3.5 ounce (100 gram) fish eats 0.04 to 0.07 ounces (1–2 grams) of pelletized fish feed per day.

For example, if you have 75 lbs (34kg) of fish in your tank, multiply 75 lbs x 1.5% (0.015) = 1.125lbs of fish feed daily (34kg x 1.5% (0.015) = 0.5kg).

If the fish still appear to be consuming all of the feed, then increase the amount to 1.75 percent and then to 2 percent (a multiplier of 0.0175 and 0.02, respectively). As mentioned in the previous chapter, in working with fish and fish feed, it is easier to use metric units; such is the industry standard, even in the United States.

Monitor the feeding rate and FCR to determine growth rates and fish appetite helps maintain overall system balance. However, don't just rely the calculations. Observe your fish eating to help determine the proper amount of feed needed above or below the recommended amount. If they rapidly devour all of the feed, they most likely need more. If the fish are showing little interest and much of the feed is being wasted on the bottom of the tank, then they are probably being overfed.

As a friendly reminder to an important and often overlooked issue mentioned earlier in this chapter, **in selecting a proper feed, it is important to match the feed size to the size of the fish being fed. Smaller particle or pellet size is required for smaller fish, while larger pellets will be more efficiently used by larger fish.**

The feed must also be suitable to meet the nutritional needs of the species being cultured. A commercially manufactured feed is available for most species.

Feeding rates will vary by species and production system, but a few common factors contribute to determining these rates:

- Water temperature.
- Water quality.
- Size of the feed particles.
- Palatability of the feed to the fish.
- Frequency of feeding.
- Technique for feed delivery.
- Type of feed used (i.e., floating, sinking, etc.).

Feed can be delivered in a variety of ways, including feeding by hand, using automated stationary feeders, or by allowing the fish to feed themselves using "demand" feeders. The choice of feed delivery system used will be dictated by logistical needs, resources available, amount of feed to be delivered, number of fish to be fed daily, and the size, scope, and type of operation.

Keep carnivorous fry (newborns) separated from bigger fish so they are not eaten. Feed fry a diet of micro worms (nematode), brine shrimp, or soaked oatmeal (soft things). Feed fingerlings (between newborn and mid-grown) small fish flakes.

Extruded trout feed is a proven favorite of the North American trout industry. Formulated to allow controlled growth and deliver excellent feed conversions, extruded trout feed can lead to more efficient production. It can be fed to numerous species including trout, perch, bass, sturgeon, catfish, and tilapia. The typical composition is shown in table 11:

TABLE 11. *Typical Composition*

GUARANTEED ANALYSIS

Crude Protein, min.............................40%
Crude at, min 12%
Crude Fiber, max 3%
Ash, max..................................12%

INGREDIENTS

Fish Meal, Soybean Meal, Wheat Flour, Stabilized Fish Oil, Wheat Midds, Poultry By-Product Meal, Blood Meal, Hydrolized Feather Meal, Corn Gluten Meal, Poultry Oil, Vitamin A Acetate, D-Activated Animal Sterol (D_3), Vitamin B12 Supplement, Riboflavin Supplement, Niacin, Folic Acid, Menadione Sodium Bisulphite Complex, Calcium Pantothenate, Pyridoxine Hydrochloride, Thiamine, Biotin, DL Alphatocopherol (E), L-ascorbyl-2-polyphosphate (C), Betaine, Zinc Sulfate, Copper Sulfate, Ferrous Sulfate, Manganese Sulfate, Ethylenediamine Dihydriodide, Ethoxyquin (Anti-Oxidant).

Practical Aspects of Feeding Fish

Hand-feeding Techniques

Hand and mechanized feedings are the two widely practiced techniques. Of these, hand feeding is the recommended one. Calibrated spoons and hand shovels should be used in order to ensure exact and uniform portions of feed.

Loss of appetite among fish is one of the most obvious symptoms of many different problems. It indicates, among others concerns, insufficient oxygen content of water or a developing disease in fish. Therefore, regular daily feeding is an excellent opportunity to observe fish, detect problems, and diagnose diseases.

Demand and Automatic Feeders

Demand feeders are those that release feed according to the appetite of fish. Because some fish species are very greedy, these feeders may allow unnecessary overfeeding of fish unless the portions are controlled.

The advantage of mechanized and automatic feeders is that they save on labor. The most typical

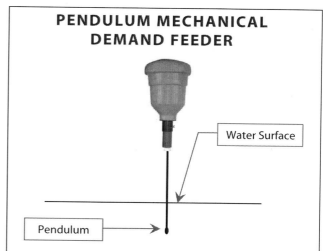

PENDULUM MECHANICAL DEMAND FEEDER

Water Surface

Pendulum

Batteries or an external power sources, are not needed. As fish bump the pendulum, feed drops into the water. Most of these feeders come with a unique twist-lock lid, which is wind- and varmint-proof. Furthermore, the better feeders are made with UV-resistant polyethylene. There are four common sizes, which accommodate #4 crumble to ¼-inch pellets.

Typical Cost (year 2022, USD)

Demand Feeder 22 lbs (10 Kg)	**$395.00**
Demand Feeder 44 lbs (20 Kg)	**$478.00**
Demand Feeder 88 lbs (40 Kg)	**$521.00**
Demand Feeder 132 lbs (60 Kg)	**$746.00**

FIGURE 53. *Pendulum Mechanical Demand Feeder*

mechanized and automatic feeders are the demand bar feeder, used for fish size 50 g, and the clock-driven feeding belt.

Signs of Feeding Problems

Obvious signs of feeding problems are the increasing differences in individual sizes, growing aggressiveness, and cannibalism. Lack of sufficient feed manifests itself in bitten/damaged fish and dead fish.

TABLE 12. **Estimating Feed Cost/lb Gain**

Cost/ Ton	Cost/ 50 lb bag	Cost/ lb 0.9	Feed Conversion (lb feed required for lb gain)										
			1	1.1	1.2	1.3	1.4	1.5	1.6	1.7	1.8	1.9	2
$400	$10	$0.20	$0.20	$0.22	$0.24	$0.26	$0.28	$0.30	$0.32	$0.34	$0.36	$0.38	$0.40
$440	$11	$0.22	$0.22	$0.24	$0.26	$0.29	$0.31	$0.33	$0.35	$0.37	$0.40	$0.42	$0.44
$480	$12	$0.24	$0.24	$0.26	$0.29	$0.31	$0.34	$0.36	$0.38	$0.41	$0.43	$0.46	$0.48
$520	$13	$0.26	$0.26	$0.29	$0.31	$0.34	$0.36	$0.39	$0.42	$0.44	$0.47	$0.49	$0.52
$560	$14	$0.28	$0.28	$0.31	$0.34	$0.36	$0.39	$0.42	$0.45	$0.48	$0.50	$0.53	$0.56
$600	$15	$0.30	$0.30	$0.33	$0.36	$0.39	$0.42	$0.45	$0.48	$0.51	$0.54	$0.57	$0.60
$640	$16	$0.32	$0.32	$0.35	$0.38	$0.42	$0.45	$0.48	$0.51	$0.54	$0.58	$0.61	$0.64
$680	$17	$0.34	$0.34	$0.37	$0.41	$0.44	$0.48	$0.51	$0.54	$0.58	$0.61	$0.65	$0.68
$720	$18	$0.36	$0.36	$0.40	$0.43	$0.47	$0.50	$0.54	$0.58	$0.61	$0.65	$0.68	$0.72
$760	$19	$0.38	$0.38	$0.42	$0.46	$0.49	$0.53	$0.57	$0.61	$0.65	$0.68	$0.72	$0.76
$800	$20	$0.40	$0.40	$0.44	$0.48	$0.52	$0.56	$0.60	$0.64	$0.68	$0.72	$0.76	$0.80
$840	$21	$0.42	$0.42	$0.46	$0.50	$0.55	$0.56	$0.63	$0.67	$0.71	$0.76	$0.80	$0.84
$880	$22	$0.44	$0.44	$0.48	$0.53	$0.57	$0.62	$0.66	$0.70	$0.75	$0.79	$0.84	$0.88
$920	$23	$0.46	$0.46	$0.51	$0.55	$0.60	$0.64	$0.69	$0.74	$0.78	$0.83	$0.87	$0.92

Economics of Feeding Fish

Economics of production is related primarily to efficiency of the system and market price. Two of the most predictable and significant variable costs are fish and feed. Feed cost to produce a one-pound fish is related to conversion rate and cost of the feed.

Table 12 shows cost of feed per pound of fish flesh produced, using Rainbow Trout as an example. Trout will require from 1.2 to 1.7 lb of feed for one pound of gain for food size animals. Please note that the costs below are based upon buying in bulk, and are geographic specific. Prices will vary when buying in smaller quantities and your location.

Reducing Feed Cost

To offset cost, many operators report having success growing earth and blood worms in the media bed. Some operators maintain a nearby compost bin for worms or raise solder grubs. Others grow crickets, roaches, or other insects as feed. Some operators even grow maggots and feeder fish for food for their aquaponics fish.

If the fish tank is located outdoors, a low voltage submersible LED light can be integrated into the fish tank to attract bugs at night. If trying this method, be sure to shield the light so that the fish are not exposed to any direct lighting.

Duckweed is a popular aquaponics feed. Duckweed can be raised by those of the do-it-yourself crowd or purchased from a multitude of sources. Duckweed is addressed comprehensively later in this chapter.

It is perfectly acceptable to feed your fish store bought food or table scraps so long as it is corresponds to their diet. Research the eating habits of your fish, realizing that some fish only eat a plant based diet, while some species only eat smaller animals (fish, worms, insects, cut-up meat scraps, etc), and some fish eat both. This approach will greatly lower your feed cost.

Real World Commercial Aquaculture Data Farming Striped Bass

Table 13 is based on a real world hybrid striped bass commercial aquaculture businesses operating in the United States using a recirculating tank system. Labor, oxygen, and biocaronate line items used in commercial aquaculture operations have been omitted to better reflect a commercial aquaponic operation. Hybrid striped bass are generally harvested at a weight of 1.5 to 2.5 pounds when they are 18 to 24 months old. In controlled growing environments water temperature and quality can be controlled, not ponds where conditions are subject to change, growth is faster (harvest at18 months).

Reducing the above mentioned commercial aquaculture operation down to the typical size of a small backyard aquaponic operation (raising bass) in a 250 gallon fish tank, the economics would more closely resemble the following for one harvest cycle:

$200	Total Operational Cost.
$8	Cost per lb. (Cost is higher per lb. in smaller systems).
26.5	Pounds of ending biomass.
$13.54	Average retail market value for striped bass.
$5.54	Net profit per lb.
$146.81	Total Net Profit (250 gallon fish tank).

NOTE: Aquaponic economics, and cost-benefit analysis and earning revenue from aquaponics are addressed compressively my 650+ page 'Aquaponics for Profit' book. That book also has real world aquaponic business plans and critical financial data.

In deciding what is the best species for you to grow, you should take a few factors into account; most importantly is what you want from your system. Another important factor

Fish Enterprise Budget 'Go-By' Example

TABLE 13. **Annual Bass Fish Production Cost/Profit (Year 2022, USA)**

INVENTORY & INPUT USE	
Beginning number of fish	250
Ending number of fish	212
Beginning biomass (grams of fish, 250 grams at 1 gram each)	250
Beginning biomass (lbs. of fish)	0.6
Ending biomass (lbs. of fish)	265
Max. standing biomass (lbs./gal.)	0.12
Feed used, lbs.	718
Kwh used	1,102

COSTS	
Fingerlings (each)	$0.85
Fingerlings (total quantity)	250
Fingerlings (total cost)	$212.50
Feed	$480
Electricity	$230
Total of above costs for this unit	$922.50
Cumulative cost per lb.	$3.48

NOVEMBER 2022 MARKET VALUE	
Market value for bass at current retail prices (price/lb)	$23.50

EST. NET PROFIT/2,500 GALLON FISH TANK	
Ending biomass (lbs. of fish)	265
Cumulative cost per lb.	$3.48
Market value for bass at current retail prices (price/lb)	$23.50
Net profit per lb.	$20.02
Total net profit/tank	**$5,305.30**

depends on the type of fish that is available your area. You need to be able to buy fish to stock your system. Even if you plan to breed your own fish with a species such as tilapia that reproduces readily, you need to be able to get your broodstock in the first place.

In some areas of the United States, such as parts of northern California for instance, it is illegal to have tilapia, if they are located in indoor tanks; thus, shipping of Tilapia to the areas is prohibited. Therefore, it is important to check with your regional US Fish and Game office, or the governing regulatory agency in your region, to ensure that you are in compliance with all applicable laws in your area. Desiring to raise a species that is not common in your area or country will likely be very expensive to obtain.

Tilapia and trout are among the most popular aquaponics fish. Other commonly raised aquaponic species include cod, perch, and striped bass. Goldfish are frequently raised in smaller systems that have a fish tank of 50 gallons or less.

Always keep in mind that in order to achieve maximum benefits with plants and fish, the aquaponics system must be sized correctly and fish population maintained at the optimal stocking density. Following is a tilapia commercial aquaculture fish tank efficiency table based upon a recirculating aquaculture operation. Check your local feed cost for a more accurate cost of feed.

TABLE 14. **Tilapia Fish Tank Efficiency**

Water volumne, galloons	2,500
Size stocked (grams)	1
Size harvested (grams)	567
Size harvested (lbs)	1.25
Survival rate	85%
Feed cost, per pound	$0.52

NOTE: Most backyard aquaponic systems have fish tanks ranging in size from about 250 to 1,000 gallons.

Feeding Summary

- A good rule of thumb is to feed your fish as much as they will eat in 5 to 10 minutes, 1 — 3 times per day. An adult fish will eat approximately 1 percent of its bodyweight per day. Fish fry (babies) will eat as much as 7 percent. Be sure that your fish are being fed enough. However, be cognizant of the fact that over feeding fish will negatively affect water quality, is wasteful, and is an unnecessary increase in cost.

- If your fish are not eating as they should, it is a good indication that they are stressed or unhealthy. **Some factors that may result in fish not eating as they should:**
  - » Living in conditions that are outside of their optimal temperature range.
  - » Water quality issues: Improper pH range, too much ammonia in the system, inadequate dissolved oxygen.
  - » Loud or irritating noises and vibrations.
  - » Direct lighting upon the fish tank.

Commercial Fish Feed Problem and a Possible Solution

About half of the world's seafood now comes from fish farms. From the environmental perspective, that is creating a major problem: millions of tons of wild fish like anchovies, sardines and mackerel are being caught in the ocean to feed farm-raised fish like salmon. Most anchovies and sardines don't end up on pizzas. Instead, they go to processing plants where they are turned into pellets to feed farmed fish. We are depleting the world's oceans to make a cheap protein.

Up to 90 percent of tiny harvested forage fish from the oceans go into pet food, poultry feed and fishmeal, never destined for human consumption. Small, filter feeding fish were traditionally used because they were inexpensive. But as wild fish stocks diminish, the cost of these forage fish increases. Meanwhile, the price for plants like corn and soy has decreased.

Now scientists and entrepreneurs are finding ways to create vegetarian diets for species like trout, which may lessen the strain on over-fished oceans. To avoid using wild fish in farmed fish diets, the United States Department of Agriculture has spent the past ten years researching alternative diets that include plants, animal processing products, insects and single-cell organisms like yeast, bacteria, and algae. "We have been hit over the head with the notion that farming carnivorous fish means that you have to catch fish in the ocean for its diet, but that's wrong," says Michael Rust, science coordinator of the NOAA Fisheries' Office of Aquaculture.

Recent advances in aquaculture research have shown that farmed carnivorous fish do not require any fishmeal or fish oil in their feeds. The USDA has proven that many species of fish can get enough nutrients from these alternative sources without eating other fish. If widely adopted by the aquaculture industry, this plant-based diet could significantly reduce the amount of wild fish that are harvested and turned into fish meal pellets.

Fish, like people, don't need specific foods but rather specific nutrients in order to stay healthy. In fact, all animals essentially need the same forty nutrients—a combination of amino acids, fatty acids, vitamins and minerals. With this in mind a pair of entrepreneurs started a company called 'TwoxSea'. They have found that aquaculture facilities were concerned about the environmental impact of traditional fish feed, future availability and cost of such; and as result were very open to replacing fishmeal with alternative feeds like corn, soy and algae. They now have several large commercial customers feeding their fish nothing but TwoxSea's nutritionally complete vegetarian feed. By all accounts, there is now hope that we can have a growing aquaculture industry that is sustainable and we won't have to rely on the ocean to get our fish.

Alternative Fish Feed

Fish feed is one of the most important and expensive inputs for any aquaponic system. It can be purchased or self-made. Purchasing a quality manufactured whole food fish feed is certainly the easiest way to go and ensures the nutritional needs of the fish are being met. Even so, below is an example of supplemental fish feed that can be easily produced domestically, which can help save money or used temporarily if manufactured feeds are not available.

Duckweed

Duckweed is the second smallest flowering plant in the world (watermeal being the smallest). It floats and grows directly on top of water. Not all fish take to duckweed immediately, but most herbivorous fish adjust quickly. Duckweed grows in calm waters. It produces oxygen for the water when in sunlight, and consumes oxygen from the water when shaded and at night.

FIGURE 54. *Growing duckweed for fish feed for mostly herbivorous fish, such as Tilapia, Goldfish, and Koi.*

Duckweed is a fast-growing floating water plant that is rich in protein and can serve as a food source for carp and tilapia. Duckweed can double its mass every 1–2 days in optimum conditions, which means that one-half of the duckweed can be harvested every day. Duckweed should be grown in a separate tank from the fish because otherwise the fish would consume the whole stock. Aeration is not necessary and water should flow at a slow rate through the container in which the duckweed is grown. Duckweed can be grown in sun-exposed or half-shaded places. Surplus duckweed can be stored and frozen in bags for later use. Duckweed is also a useful feed for poultry.

Duckweed consumes more nutrients than most plants. Duckweed can consist of up to a 45 percent protein, which even surpasses the protein concentration of soybeans. It also has all the essential amino acids. Duckweed can be obtained from a variety of sources online simply by performing an Internet search.

It is a useful addition to an aquaponic system, especially if the duckweed growing container is located along the return line between the plant grow devices (i.e. flood-and-drain grow beds, N.F.T. grow channels), and the fish tank. Any nutrients that escapes the plant's grow beds fertilize the duckweed, thereby ensuring the cleanest water possible returning to the fish.

Azolla (Water Fern)

Azolla is a genus of fern that grows while floating on the surface of the water, much in the manner as duckweed. The major difference is that Azolla is able to fix atmospheric nitrogen; essentially creating protein

FIGURE 55. *Azolla spp. growing in a container as fish feed supplement*

from the air. This occurs because Azolla has a symbiotic relationship with a species of bacteria, Anabaena azollae, which is contained within the leaves.

As well as providing a free source of protein, Azolla is an attractive feed source because of its exceptionally high growth rate. Like duckweed, Azolla should be grown in a separate tank with slow water flow. Its growth is often limited by phosphorus, so if Azolla is to be grown intensively an additional source of phosphorous is needed such as compost tea.

Insects

Insects are considered undesirable pests in many cultures. However, they have an enormous potential in supporting traditional food chains with more sustainable solutions. In many countries insects are already part of people's diets and sold at the markets. In addition they have been used as animal feed for centuries.

Insects are a healthy nutrient source because they are rich in protein and polyunsaturated fatty acids and full of essential minerals. Their crude protein content ranges between 13 and 77 percent (on average 40 percent) and varies according to the species, the growth stage, and the rearing diet. Insects are also rich in essential amino acids, which are a limiting factor in many feed ingredients. Edible insects are also a good source of lipids, as their quantity of fat can range between 9 and 67 percent. In many species, the content of essential polyunsaturated fatty acids is also high. These characteristics together make insects a healthy and ideal option for both human food, and feed for animals or fish.

Given their enormous number and varieties, the choice of the insect to be reared can be tailored to their local availability, climatic conditions/seasonality and type of feed available. The source of food for insects can include staple husks, vegetable leaves, vegetable wastes, manure, and even wood or cellulose-rich organic materials, which are suitable for termites. Insects also make a great contribution to waste biodegradation, as they break down organic matter until it is consumed by fungi and bacteria and mineralized into plant nutrients.

The culturing of insects is not as challenging as other animals since the only limiting factor is feed and not rearing space. Sometimes insects are referred to as "micro-livestock". The small space requirement means that insect farms can be created with very limited areas and investment costs. In addition, insects are cold-blooded creatures, this means that their feed conversion efficiency into meat is much higher than terrestrial animals and similar to fish. Lots of possible options and additional knowledge on insect farming as feed is available on the internet. Among the many species available, an interesting one to be used as fish feed is the black soldier fly.

Black Soldier Fly

The larvae of black soldier flies, Hermetia illucens, are extremely high in protein and thus, a valuable source for various livestock types, including fish. The lifecycle of this insect makes it a convenient and attractive addition to an integrated homestead farming system in favorable climate conditions. The larvae feed on manure, dead animals, and food waste. When culturing black soldier flies, these types of waste are placed in a compost unit that has adequate drainage and airflow. As the larvae reach maturity, they crawl away from their feed source through a ramp installed in the compost unit that leads to a collection bucket.

Essentially, the larvae devour wastes, accumulate protein and then harvest themselves. Two-thirds of the larvae can be processed into feed while the remaining one-third should be allowed to develop into adult flies in a separate area. The adult flies are not a vector of disease; adult flies do not have mouthparts, do not eat, and are not attracted to any human activities. Adult flies simply mate and then return to the compost unit to lay eggs, dying after a week. Black soldier flies have been shown to prevent houseflies and blowflies in livestock facilities and can actually decrease the pathogen load in the compost. Even so, before feeding the larvae to the fish, the larvae should be processed for safety. Baking in an oven (170 °C for 1 hour) destroys any pathogens, and the resulting dried larvae can be ground and processed into a feed.

Moringa or Kalamungay

Moringa oleifera is a species of tropical tree that is very high in nutrients, including proteins and vitamins. Classified by some as a super food and currently being used to combat malnutrition, it is a valuable addition to homemade fish feeds because of these

FIGURE 56. Black soldier fly (Hermetia illucens) adult (a) and larvae (b)

essential nutrients. All parts of the tree are choice edibles suitable for human consumption, but for aquaculture it is typically the leaves that are used. In fact, there has been success in several small-scale aquaponic projects in Africa using leaves of this tree as the only source of feed for tilapia.

These trees are fast-growing, drought-resistant, and easily propagated through cuttings or seeds. However, they are intolerant of frost or freezing and not appropriate for cold areas. For leaf production, all of the branches are harvested down to the main trunk four times per year in a process called pollarding.

Making Homemade Fish Feed

As mentioned previously, fish feed is one of the most expensive inputs in aquaponics. Feed is also one of the most important components of the whole aquaponic ecosystem because it sustains both the fish and vegetable growth. Therefore, it is necessary that operators understand its composition. Also, if commercial pelleted feed is not available, it is important to understand how to make it.

Composition of Fish Feed

Fish feed consists of all the nutrients that are required for growth, energy, and reproduction. Dietary requirements are identified for proteins, amino acids, carbohydrates, lipids, energy, minerals, and vitamins. A brief summary of major feed components are listedas follows.

Protein

Dietary protein plays a fundamental role for the growth and metabolism of animals. A combination of more than 100 amino acids joined by peptides forms a protein; they are the building blocks of protein. Only some amino acids can be synthesized by animals while others cannot, so these must be supplied in the diet. Non-essential amino acids can be synthesized internally. However, this does not mean they are unimportant. It is just that the body is capable of producing a sufficient amount to meet the demands for growth and tissue repair. Essential amino acids cannot be synthesized by the body and must be acquired through outside sources.

For aquatic animals, there are ten essential amino acids (EAAs): arginine, histidine, isoleucine, leucine, lysine, methionine, phenylalanine, threonine, tryptophan, and valine. Therefore, feed formulation must find an optimal balance of EAAs to meet the specific requirements of each fish species. Non-compliance with this requirement would prevent fish from synthesizing their own proteins, and also waste the amino acids that are present. The ideal feed formulation should thus take into account the EAA levels of each ingredient and match the quantities required by fish.

Recommended protein intake of fish depends on the species and age. For tilapia and herbivorous fish the optimal ranges are 28–35 percent; carnivorous species require 38–45 percent. Juvenile fish require higher-protein diets than adults due to their intense body growth.

Besides any optimal amino acid content in the feed, it is worth stating the importance of an optimal dietary balance between proteins and energy (supplied by carbohydrates and lipids) to obtain the best growth performance and reduce costs and wastes from using proteins for energy. Although proteins can be used as a source of energy, they are much more expensive than carbohydrates and lipids, which are preferred.

In aquaponics, any increase in dietary proteins directly affects the amount of nitrogen in the water. This should be balanced either by an increase in plants grown in the system or the selection of vegetables with higher nitrogen demands.

Carbohydrates

Carbohydrates are the most important and cheapest energy source for animals. They are mainly composed of simple sugars and starch, while other complex structures such as cellulose and hemicellulose are not digestible by fish. In general, the maximum tolerated amount of carbohydrates should be included in the diet in order to lower the feed costs. Omnivorous and warm-water fish can easily digest quantities up to 40 percent, but the percentage falls to about 25 percent in carnivorous and cold-water fish. Carbohydrates are also used as a binding agent to ensure the feed pellet keeps its structure in water. In general, one of the most used products in extruded or pelleted feed is starch (from potato, corn, cassava, or gluten wheat), which undergoes a gelatinization process at 140-185°F (60–85 °C) that prevents pellets from easily dissolving in water.

Lipids

Lipids provide energy and essential fatty acids (EFAs), indispensable for the growth and other biological functions of fish. Fats also play the important role in absorbing fat-soluble vitamins and securing the production of hormones. Fish, as with other animals, cannot synthesize EFAs, which have to be supplied with the diet according to the species' needs. Deficiency in the supplement of fatty acids results in reduced growth and limited reproductive efficiency.

In general, freshwater fish require a combination of both omega-3 and omega-6 fatty acids, whereas marine fish need mainly omega-3. Tilapias mostly require omega-6 in order to secure optimal growth and high feed conversion efficiency. Most diets are comprised of 5–10 percent lipids, although this percentage can be higher for some marine species. Lipid inclusion in the feed needs to follow optimal protein/energy ratios to secure good growth, to avoid misuse of protein for energy purposes (lack of fat/carbohydrates for energy purposes), and to avoid fat accumulation in the body (diet too rich in lipids).

Energy

Energy is mainly obtained by the oxidation of carbohydrates, lipids and, to a certain extent, proteins. The energy requirements of fish are much lower than warm-blooded animals owing to the reduced needs to heat the body and to perform metabolic activities. However, each species requires an optimum amount of protein and energy to secure best growth conditions and to prevent animals from using expensive protein for energy. It is thus important that feed ingredients be carefully selected to meet the desired level of digestible energy (DE) required by each aquatic species.

Vitamins and Minerals

Vitamins are organic compounds necessary to sustain growth and to perform all the physiological processes needed to support life. Vitamins must be supplied with the diet because animals do not produce them. Vitamin deficiencies are most likely to occur in intensively cultured cages and tank systems where animals cannot rely on natural food. Degenerative syndromes are often ascribed to an insufficient supply of these vitamins and minerals.

Minerals are important elements in animal life. They support skeletal growth and are also involved in osmotic balance, energy transport, neural, and endocrinal system functioning. They are the core part of many enzymes as well as blood cells.

Fish require seven main minerals (calcium, phosphorus, potassium, sodium, chlorine, magnesium, and sulphur) and 15 other trace minerals. These can be supplied by diet, but can also be directly absorbed from the water through their skin and gills. Supplementing of vitamins and minerals can be done according to the requirements of each species.

The production of feed requires a fine balance of all of the nutrient components mentioned above (protein, lipids, carbohydrates, vitamins, minerals, and total energy). An unbalanced feed will cause

TABLE 15. *Common feed ingredient sources of the most important nutrient components*

NUTRIENT COMPONENTS	FEED INGREDIENT SOURCES
Protein	*Plant-based sources*: algae, yeast, soybean meal, cottonseed meal, peanuts, sunflower, rapeseed/canola, other oil-seed cakes *Animal-based sources*: fishery by-products (fishmeal or offal), poultry by-products (poultry meal or offal), meat meal, meat and bone meal, blood meal
Carbohydrates	Wheat flour, wheat bran, corn flour, corn bran, rice bran, potato starch, cassava root meal
Lipids	Fish oil, vegetable oil (soybean, canola, sunflower), processed animal fat
Vitamins	Vitamin premix, yeast, legumes, liver, milk, bran, wheat germ, fish and vegetable oil
Minerals	Mineral premix, crushed bone

reduced growth, nutritional disorders, illness and, eventually, higher production costs.

Fishmeal is regarded as the best protein source for aquatic animals because of its very high protein content and it has balanced EAAs. However, it is an increasingly expensive ingredient, with concerns regarding sustainability. Moreover, fishmeal is not always available. Proteins of plant origin can adequately replace fishmeal; however, they should undergo physical (de-hulling, grinding) and thermal processes to improve their digestibility. Plant ingredients are, in fact, high in anti-nutritional factors that interfere with the digestion and the assimilation of nutrients by the animals, which eventually results in poor fish growth and performance.

The size of the pellets should be about 20–30 percent of the fish's mouth in order to facilitate ingestion and avoid any loss. If the pellets are too small, fish exert more energy to consume them; if too large, the fish will be unable to eat. A recommended pellet size for fish below 50 g is 2 mm, while 4 mm is ideal for pre-adults of more than 50 g.

The use of any raw ingredient of animal origin (fish offal, blood meal, insects, etc.) should be preventively heat treated to prevent any microbial contamination of the aquaponic system.

Homemade Fish Feed for Omnivorous and Herbivorous Fish

Two simple recipes for a balanced fish feed containing 30 percent of crude protein (CP) are provided in tables 16 and 17. The lists of the ingredients for each diet are expressed in weight (kilograms), enough to make 10 kg of feed. The first formula is made with proteins of vegetable origin, mainly soybean meal (see table 16) . The second formula is mainly made with fishmeal (see table 17).

Step-by-Step Preparation of Homemade Fish Feed

1. Gather the utensils noted in table 18.
2. Gather the ingredients shown in tables 16 and 17. Purchase previously dried and defatted soybean meal, corn meal, and wheat flour. If these meals are unavailable, obtain whole soybeans, corn kernels, and wheat berries. These would need to be dried, de-hulled, and ground. Whole soybeans need to be toasted at 240°F (120 °C) for 1–2 minutes.
3. Weigh each ingredient following the quantities shown in the recipes above.
4. Add the dry ingredients (flours and meals) and mix thoroughly for 5–10 minutes until the mix becomes homogeneous.
5. Add the vitamin and mineral premix to the dry ingredients and mix thoroughly for another

5 minutes. Make sure that the vitamins and minerals are evenly distributed throughout the whole mixture.

6. Add the soybean oil and continue to mix for 3–5 minutes.

7. Add water to the mixture to obtain a soft, but not sticky, dough.

8. Steam-cook the dough to cause gelatinization.

9. Remove the dough, divide into manageable pieces, and pass them through the meat mincer/pasta maker to obtain spaghetti-like strips. The mincer disc should be chosen according to the desired pellet size.

10. Dry the dough by spreading the strips out on aluminium trays. If available, dry the feed strips in an electric oven at a temperature of 140–185 °F 60–85 °C for 10–30 minutes to gelatinize starch. Check the strips regularly to avoid any burn.

11. Crumble the dry strips. Break or cut the feed on the tray with the fingers into smaller pieces. Try

TABLE 16. **Recipe for 10 kg of fish feed using vegetable-based protein, including proximate analysis**

FEED INGREDIENTS	WEIGHT (kg)	% OF TOTAL FEED	PROXIMATE ANALYSIS	%
Corn meal	1.0	10	Dry matter	91.2
Wheat flour	1.0	10	Crude protein	30.0
Soybean meal	6.7	67.2	Crude fat	14.2
Soybean oil	0.2	2	Crude fiber	4.8
Wheat bran	0.7	7.8	Ash	4.6
Vitamin and mineral premix	0.3	3	Nitrogen-free extract (NFE)	28.3
Total amount	10.0	100	-	-

TABLE 17. **Recipe for 10 kg of fish feed using animal-based protein, including proximate analysis**

FEED INGREDIENTS	WEIGHT (kg)	% OF TOTAL FEED	PROXIMATE ANALYSIS	%
Corn meal	1.0	10	Dry matter	90.9
Wheat flour	4.0	40	Crude protein	30.0
Soybean meal	1.5	15	Crude fat	10.5
Soybean oil	0.2	2	Crude fiber	2.1
Fishmeal	3.0	30	Ash	8.3
Vitamin and mineral premix	0.3	3	Nitrogen-free extract (NFE)	34.5
Total amount	10.0	100	-	-

TABLE 18. **Utensils**

COMPONENT	QUANTITY	SPECIFICATION
Weighing scale	1	Capacity 2–6 lbs. (1–3 kg), Divisions in ounces or grams
Grinder	1	Electric coffee-type grinder
Metal sieve	1	5–10 U.S. Sieve Size, 0.2–0.4 cm (2–4 mm) mesh
Mixing bucket	1	Capacity 3-gallon (10 liters)
Plastic bowl	1	Capacity 2-quart (2 liters)
Meat mincer / pasta maker	1	Manual or electric
Mixing spoon	1	Large size
Aluminum baking tray	10	Large baking tray

to make the pellets the same size. Avoid excessive pellet manipulation to prevent crumbling. Pellets can be sieved and separated in batches of homogeneous size with proper mesh sizes.

12. Store the feed.

Storing Homemade Fish Feed

Once prepared, the best way to store fish feed is to put pellets into an airtight container soon after being dried and broken apart. Containers must be kept in a cool, dry, dark and ventilated place, away from pests. Keeping pellets at low levels of moisture (less than 10 percent) prevents them becoming mouldy and developing toxic mycotoxins. Depending on the temperature, the pellets can be stored for as long as two months.

Another way to keep pellets for long periods is to close them in a plastic container and store them in the refrigerator. Feed kept in this way can last for more than one year.

Feed must be used on a "first in, first out" basis. Avoid using any feed showing signs of decay or mould, as this could be fatal for fish.

Specific Nutritional Requirements for Tilapia

The low trophic level and the omnivorous food habits of tilapia make them a relatively inexpensive fish to feed, unlike other finfish, such as salmon, which rely on high-protein and lipid diets based on more expensive protein sources like fish meal. In addition, tilapias are similar to channel catfish (Ictalurus punctatus), in that they can tolerate higher dietary fiber and carbohydrate concentrations than most other cultured fish. To ensure high yield and fast growth at least cost, a well-balanced prepared feed is essential to successful tilapia culture. Slight variations exist among tilapia species, but nutrient requirements are primarily affected by the size of the fish.

Composition of Fish Feed

Fish feed consists of all the nutrients that are required for growth, energy, and reproduction. Dietary requirements are identified for proteins, amino acids, carbohydrates, lipids, energy, minerals, and vitamins. A brief summary of major feed components is listed as follows.

Protein

Dietary protein plays a fundamental role for the growth and metabolism of animals. A combination of more than 100 amino acids joined by peptides forms a protein; they are the building blocks of protein. Only some amino acids can be synthesized by animals while others cannot, so these must be supplied in the diet. Non-essential amino acids can be synthesized internally. However, this does not mean they are unimportant. It is just that the body is capable of producing a sufficient amount to meet the demands for growth and tissue repair. Essential amino acids cannot be synthesized by the body and must be acquired through outside sources.

For aquatic animals, there are ten essential amino acids (EAAs): arginine, histidine, isoleucine, leucine, lysine, methionine, phenylalanine, threonine, tryptophan, and valine. Therefore, feed formulation must find an optimal balance of EAAs to meet the specific requirements of each fish species. Non-compliance with this requirement would prevent fish from synthesizing their own proteins, and also waste the amino acids that are present. The ideal feed formulation should thus take into account the EAA levels of each ingredient and match the quantities required by fish.

The profile of dietary protein is important when formulating diets for tilapia. Recommended protein intake of fish depends on the species and age. For tilapia and herbivorous fish, the optimal ranges are 28–35 percent; carnivorous species require 38–45 percent. Juvenile fish require higher-protein diets than adults due to their intense body growth.

TABLE 19. **Protein requirements (dry basis) of tlapia of various species and sizes.**

Species	Size (g)	Requirement (% of diet)	Reference
0. niloticus	0.5-68.3 45.0-76.3	40 40	Al Hafid (1999)
	0.84-22.8 40.4-108.0	40 30	Siddiqui et al. (1988)
0. niloticus x 0. aurevs	21.3-81.5	28	Twibelll and Brown (1998)
0. aurevs	2.5-16.6	56	Winfree and Stickney (1981 }
S. mossambicus	1.83-8.5	40	Jauncey (1981)

TABLE 20. **Amino acid requirements (dry basis) of tilapia.**

Amino acid	% of dietary protein	
	0. niloticus"	0. mossambicus>
Arginine	4.20	2.82
Histidine	1.72	1.05
Isoleucine	3.11	2.01
Leucine	3.39	3.40
Lysine	5.12	3.78
Methionine	2.68	0.99
Phenylalanined	3.75	2.50
Threonine	3.75	2.93
Tryptophan	1.00	0.43
Valine	2.80	2.20

Dietary proteins are used continuously by fish for maintenance, growth, and reproduction functions. When fed in excess, protein may be used as energy; however, the latter function is not desirable because of the expensive cost of proteins. The protein requirement of tilapia decreases with age and size, with higher dietary CP concentrations required for **tilapia fry (30–56%)** and **juvenile (30–40%)** tilapia but lower protein levels **(28–30%)** for larger tilapia.

Besides any optimal amino acid content in the feed, it is worth stating the importance of an optimal dietary balance between proteins and energy (supplied by carbohydrates and lipids) to obtain the best growth performance and reduce costs and wastes from using proteins for energy. Although proteins can be used as a source of energy, they are much more expensive than carbohydrates and lipids, which are preferred.

Carbohydrates

Carbohydrates provide a relatively inexpensive source of energy compared to protein, and their inclusion can improve the quality of pelleted feeds. A matter of fact, tilapia can effectively utilize carbohydrate levels up to 30 to 40% in the diet, which is considerably more than most cultured fish.

Carbohydrates are mainly composed of simple sugars and starch, while other complex structures such as cellulose and hemicellulose are not digestible by fish. In general, the maximum tolerated amount of carbohydrates should be included in the diet in order to lower the feed costs. Omnivorous fish (tilapia) can easily digest quantities up to 40 percent, but the percentage falls to about 25 percent in carnivorous and cold-water fish. Carbohydrates are also used as a binding agent to ensure the feed pellet keeps its structure in water. In general, one of the most used products in extruded or pelleted feed is starch (from potato, corn, cassava, or gluten wheat), which undergoes a gelatinization process at 140-185°F (60–85 °C) that prevents pellets from easily dissolving in water.

Lipids

Lipids provide energy and essential fatty acids (EFAs), indispensable for the growth and other biological functions of fish. Fats also play the important role in absorbing fat-soluble vitamins and securing the production of hormones. Fish, as with other animals, cannot synthesize EFAs, which have to be supplied with the diet according to the species' needs. Deficiency in the supplement of fatty acids results in reduced growth and limited reproductive efficiency.

In general, freshwater fish require a combination of both omega-3 and omega-6 fatty acids, whereas marine fish need mainly omega-3. Tilapias mostly require omega-6 in order to secure optimal growth and high feed conversion efficiency.

Dietary lipids provide a major source of energy, facilitate the absorption of fat-soluble vitamins, play an important role in membrane structure and function, serve as precursors for steroid hormones and prostaglandins, and serve as metabolizable sources of essential fatty acids. For tilapia up to 2.5 g, the optimum dietary lipid concentration is 5.2%, decreasing to 4.4% for fish up to 7.5 grams. **To maximize protein utilization, dietary fat concentration should be between 8 and 12% for tilapia up to 25 grams, and 6 to 8% for larger fish.** As with most fish, tilapia appear to have a requirement for n-6 (linoleic) fatty acids, and to a lesser extent, a requirement for n-3 (linolenic) fatty acids. Studies have shown that dietary lipids should supply at least 1% of n-6 fatty acids. When dietary lipids contain considerable amount of polyunsaturated fatty acids, attention should be given to prevent oxidation of the dietary lipids. The resulting products of lipid oxidation are toxic, reduce the availability of other nutrients, and impact the quality of fish-flesh products.

Energy

Energy is mainly obtained by the oxidation of carbohydrates, lipids and, to a certain extent, proteins. The energy requirements of fish are much lower than

TABLE 21. **Common feed ingredient sources of the most important nutrient components**

NUTRIENT COMPONENTS	FEED INGREDIENT SOURCES
Protein	*Plant-based sources*: algae, yeast, soybean meal, cottonseed meal, peanuts, sunflower, rapeseed/canola, other oil-seed cakes *Animal-based sources*: fishery by-products (fishmeal or offal), poultry by-products (poultry meal or offal), meat meal, meat and bone meal, blood meal
Carbohydrates	Wheat flour, wheat bran, corn flour, corn bran, rice bran, potato starch, cassava root meal
Lipids	Fish oil, vegetable oil (soybean, canola, sunflower), processed animal fat
Vitamins	Vitamin premix, yeast, legumes, liver, milk, bran, wheat germ, fish and vegetable oil
Minerals	Mineral premix, crushed bone

warm-blooded animals owing to the reduced needs to heat the body and to perform metabolic activities. However, each species requires an optimum amount of protein and energy to secure best growth conditions and to prevent animals from using expensive protein for energy. It is thus important that feed ingredients be carefully selected to meet the desired level of digestible energy (DE) required by each aquatic species.

Vitamins and Minerals

Vitamins are organic compounds necessary to sustain growth and to perform all the physiological processes needed to support life. Vitamins must be supplied with the diet because animals do not produce them. Vitamin deficiencies are most likely to occur in intensively cultured cages and tank systems where animals cannot rely on natural food. Degenerative syndromes are often ascribed to an insufficient supply of these vitamins and minerals.

Minerals are important elements in animal life. They support skeletal growth and are also involved in osmotic balance, energy transport, neural, and endocrinal system functioning. They are the core part of many enzymes as well as blood cells.

Fish require seven main minerals (calcium, phosphorus, potassium, sodium, chlorine, magnesium, and sulfur) and 15 other trace minerals. These can be supplied by diet but can also be directly absorbed from the water through their skin and gills. Supplementing of vitamins and minerals can be done according to the requirements of each species. The production of feed requires a fine balance of all of the nutrient components mentioned above (protein, lipids, carbohydrates, vitamins, minerals, and total energy). An unbalanced feed will cause reduced growth, nutritional disorders, illness and, eventually, higher production costs.

Fishmeal is regarded as the best protein source for aquatic animals because of its very high protein content and it has balanced EAAs. However, it is an increasingly expensive ingredient, with concerns regarding sustainability. Moreover, fishmeal is not

TABLE 22. **Mineral requirements of tilapia.**

MINERAL	SPECIES	REQUIREMENTS (MG/KG)
Calcium	0. aureus	7000
Phosphorus	0. niloticus	< 9000
	0. niloticus	4600
	0. niloticus x 0. aureus	7000
	0. aureus	5000
Potassium	0. niloticus x 0. aureus	2100-3300
Magnesium	0. aureus	500
	0. niloticus	600-800
Zinc	0. niloticus	30
	0. niloticus	79
	0. aureus	20
Manganese	0. nilolicus	12
Iron	0. niloticus	60
Chromium	0. niloticus x 0. aureus	139.6

always available. Proteins of plant origin can adequately replace fishmeal; however, they should undergo physical (de-hulling, grinding) and thermal processes to improve their digestibility. Plant ingredients are, in fact, high in anti-nutritional factors that interfere with the digestion and the assimilation of nutrients by the animals, which eventually results in poor fish growth and performance.

The size of the pellets should be about 20–30 percent of the fish's mouth in order to facilitate ingestion and avoid any loss. If the pellets are too small, fish exert more energy to consume them; if too large, the fish will be unable to eat. A recommended pellet size for fish below 50 g is 2 mm, while 4 mm is ideal for pre-adults of more than 50 g.

The use of any raw ingredient of animal origin (fish offal, blood meal, insects, etc.) should be preventively heat treated to prevent any microbial contamination of the aquaculture system.

Fiber – Tilapia (Do not exceed 5%)

Fiber is usually considered indigestible, as tilapia do not possess the required enzymes for fiber digestion. For this reason, and to attain maximum growth, crude fiber levels in tilapia diets should not exceed 5%.

TABLE 23. **Vitamin requirements and deficiency symptoms of tilapia.**

VITAMIN	FISH SPECIES	REQUIREMENT (MG/KG)	DEFICIENCY SYMPTOMS
Niacin	0. n x 0. a	26 121	Haemorrhage. deformed snout Gill and skin oedema. fin and mouth lesions
Biotin	0. n x 0. a	0.06	
Choline	0. n x 0. a	1000	
Pantolhenic Acid	0. aureus	10	Low growth, haemormage. anaemia, sluggishness, hilt! mor1ality, hyperplasia of epithelial cells of gill lamellae
Thiamin	0. m x 0. n	2.5	I ow growth and low food efficiency, low hacmatocrit
Riboflavin	0. aureus	6	Anorexia, low growth, hilt! rnort.ality, fin erosion, loss of body cdour, cataract, dwarfism
Aiboflavin	0. m x 0. n	5	
Pyridoxine	0. n x 0. a	1.7-9.5 15-16.5	Low growth, high mortality, abnormal neurological signs, anorexia, convulsions, caudal fin erosion, mouth lesion
VitaminC	0. aureus 0. n x 0. a 0. nil0ticus 0. n x 0. a 0. n x 0. a 0. n x 0. a 0. spilurus	50 79 420 41-48 37-42 63.4 11- 200	
D	0. n x 0. a	374.S IU	
E	0. aureus	10 25	Low growth and FCR, skin haemorrhage, muscle dystrophy, impaired erythropoiesis, oeroid in liver and spleen, abnoonal skin coloration
E	0. nil0ticus	50-100 500	
E	0. n x 0. a	42-44 60-66	
A	0. nil0ticus	5000 IU	Low growth, resdess, abnormal movement, blindness, exophthalmia, haemorrhage, pot-belly syndrome, reduced mucus secretion, high mortality
Inositol	0. n x 0. a	400	

PART I I I

Components Used in Aquaponics

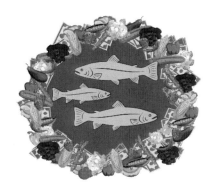

CHAPTER 12

Equipment & Component Overview

Overview of Aquaponic Equipment and Components

Following is a list of equipment that is available for an aquaponics system. Some components are necessary, whereas other items are optional, or may not even be applicable to your particular set-up. The list is provided for consideration. All of these items are available via the internet, and many can be obtained through your local home improvement store. Prices vary greatly, depending on the quality of parts and materials used and how sophisticated you want to go, i.e., automation vs. manual.

Only use food-grade plastics and materials typically used for potable water such as PVC. Some plastics will degrade from weather and break down or leak chemicals into your system. Avoid using copper or other metals in any part of the system exposed to water, as they can negatively affect the fish.

Some aquaponic operators use recycled items for system parts. This is a great way to lower costs; however, it is important to refrain from using materials previously used with chemicals or when their prior use is unknown. Even used parts with marine grade paint or galvanized coatings can leak chemicals and oxidized metal into your system. Inspect and thoroughly rinse all parts thoroughly before

integrating them into your system. For additional protection certain parts can be encased with a safe marine grade epoxy coating.

Below is a list of items used in aquaponics. These items will be addressed in much greater detail in the following chapters, with the most prominent components (pumps, grow media, plumbing, fish tanks, liners, etc.) having an entire chapter dedicated to providing more comprehensive information.

Plumbing

Plumbing supplies which may include piping, elbows, bends, sleeves, pipe joint compound, gaskets, flares, reducers, tees, Y-joint, etc. will be needed. In 'Chapter 16: Plumbing', all aspects of plumbing will be addressed in detail.

Grow Bed

Grow beds can be made from any number of materials including wood, fiberglass, steel, concrete, bricks, etc. A liner can be installed to retain the water if necessary. The grow bed can also be made from totes, purchased directly from a vendor, or custom made. Grow beds are addressed in much greater detail in the Part V: Flood-and-Drain System Design and Layout chapters.

Grow Bed Stand

Keep in mind that a stand will most likely be needed for the grow bed. The stand should be firmly supported and strong enough to support the weight of the grow bed filled with media, water plants, and most likely the weight of the operator leaning against it.

Float Switches

Float switches are inexpensive devices used to control the pump depending on the water level (see figure 57 below). If the water level in the fish or sump tank falls below a certain height, the switch will turn off the pump. This prevents the pump from pumping all of the water out of the tank. Similarly, float switches can be used to fill the aquaponic system with water from a hose or water main. A float switch similar to a toilet ballcock and valve can ensure the water level never falls below a certain point. It is very important to know that in certain types of loss-of-water events, such as a broken pipe, a float switch can actually make the flooding much worse, and this needs to be carefully considered in indoor applications and other situations where flooding could cause significant property damage or electrical shock dangers.

Hi-Low Water Level Sump Pump Controller (Dual Float Switch)

A Hi-Lo Pump Controller is a dual float device with a universal switch that works with all types of sump pumps and utility pumps. Its two sensors give you complete control of where your pump turns on and off. Using this type of controller with the right utility pump allows you to set the turn on level as low as 1/2" of water and turn off as low as 1/8" of water. When used with a sump pump the controller enables you to adjust the turn on and turn off levels to get the longest run time for the pump, which saves energy and lengthens the service life of the pump.

One example of a Hi-Lo pump controller switch is the HC6000 by HydroCheck. It is currently available on Amazon.com for $89 (USD, year 2022), and has excellent reviews. This particular make/model Hi-Lo pump controller switch is presented as an example and hopefully a helpful starting point (resource) for the reader (see figure 58). There are also other Hi-Lo switches on the market with various features and degrees of quality, and cost.

Water Detector and Hi-Low Water Alarms (Optional)

There is a wide variety of water alarms available with a range of features, quality, and cost. They are available with battery, solar, and/or AC/DC power supply. Most units under $100 have sound alarms, but some also have a light 'on' alarm. More expensive units can be obtained that make a phone call, send an email, and/or a text message alert.

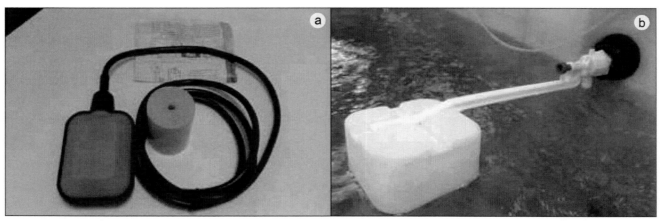

FIGURE 57. *Float switch controlling a water pump (a) and a ballcock and float valve controlling the water main (b)*

Water detection and hi-low water alarm devices are not mandatory in aquaponics but can provide the operator with a higher level of protection and peace of mind. They can also help prevent a disaster, saving the aquaponics operator from potential system-related loss (fish, pump burn out, plant) and/or property damage (flooding).

For instance, a water detector sensor alarm could be used where water could damage the surrounding environment (i.e. indoor applications). A hi-low water alarm can alert the operator 'immediately' of any water balance problems. Discovering the problem later during a routine operational check may be too late.

Again, these devices are entirely optional. They range in cost from under $10 to over a $1,000 (USD, year 2022. This expense needs to be weighed against risk factors, budget, and peace of mind.

Other Monitoring Alarms

Automatic monitoring devices for water temperature, water level, pumps, pH, blower, lights, air temperature, dissolved oxygen, or the entire system and system environment are available. Alarms can even call, text message or email you the status of conditions and alert you if there is a problem.

Water Quality Testing

Monitoring water quality in aquaponics is an important procedure. There are diverse water quality test kits and meters available, manual and automatic, in a wide price range. Water quality testing devices can be acquired which will monitor just one, several or all of the following components. Although all of these water parameters should be tested, budgetary constraints may determine how many tools are used to gather this data.

- pH
- Ammonia
- Water Temperature
- Dissolved Oxygen

- Works with all types of sump pumps and utility pumps
- Precise control of turn on and turn off levels
- Wide control range from 1/2" to 20' (Not timed based like other dual-float switches)
- Small profile fits in small or crowded spaces
- Sensors not affected by minerals and debris in water — Never has to be cleaned

- Part Number HC6000
- Product Dimensions 2.8 x 3.8 x 2.5 inches
- Voltage 120 volts; Wattage 2.4 watts; Amperage Capacity 14 A
- Cord Length 12 Feet
- UL Certified
- HC6000 is for indoor applications.

NOTE: For outdoor applications refer to HC6100 by HydroCheck.

FIGURE 58.

NOTE: Please refer to Chapter 31: Water Quality for a comprehensive examination on these components and associated monitoring equipment.

Inline Water Heater

Allows the operator to establish the desired water temperature. Most devices are fully equipped with a digital control mechanism that will provide precise all-season temperature regulation. They also come with a flow switch and safety thermostat and are easy to install with the option of water flow from either direction.

Ammonia Nitrogen Test Kit

Used for determining ammonia and nitrogen concentrations in water.

Water Hardness Test Kit

A portable testing kit to measure total hardness, calcium, and magnesium hardness in water.

Fish Tanks

Avoid tanks that have hollow pockets as they will collect fish waste that will go anaerobic and cause water quality problems. Also ensure that there is adequate circulation delivering dissolved oxygen throughout the tank. Please also refer to 'Chapter 14: Fish Tanks'.

Sump Tanks

A "sump" is an area where liquid run-off accumulates. In an aquaponics system the sump (when necessary) is positioned at a point lower than the grow beds and is where the grow beds drain. A sump is not necessary if the grow bed drains via gravity directly into the fish tank.

Grow Lights

Grow lights are necessary when growing plants where adequate sunlight is not readily available. They are also beneficial during winter months and/or when there is a desire for longer growing periods for plants.

Using grow lights to supplement the natural sunlight in a greenhouse can increase plant production by up to 40 percent. If you are growing indoors, you will need a high quality, full spectrum grow light. Metal halide lights and LED lights are available. Both offer an excellent light spectrum. The LEDs use less electricity but cost more to purchase. The metal halides use more electricity but cost substantially less to purchase.

Grow Media

There are many different types of growing media that can be used for a flood-and-drain aquaponic system. The ideal grow bed media will anchor the plants, will not decompose, will have enough space to provide a good circulation of air and water, will be beneficial for bacteria growth, and will have close to a neutral pH level so as not to impact the overall pH level of the system. Furthermore, oxygen should be able to move freely to lower levels of the grow bed and the plants. The most commonly used growing media includes gravel, clay aggregate, lava rock, packing foam, sponges, perilite, and vermiculite. See 'Chapter 16: Growing Media' for Plants for a comprehensive examination of grow media.

Liner

A liner is an impermeable geotextile used for water retention commonly referred to as pond liner, water garden liner, greenhouse cover material, hydroponics pond liner, aquaponics bed liner, and polyethylene tarp material.

Materials include LDPE (Low Density Polyethylene), PVC (Poly Vinyl Chloride), PVC with internal reinforcement, and HDPE (High Density Polyethylene). HDPE is frequently noted as the best, but it is the most expensive and hardest to work with because of its rigid nature. LDPE is most preferred by small to mid-size aquaponic operators. Avoid EPDM as it emits toxins harmful to the beneficial bacteria in your system, and the toxins will eventually make their way into your food supply. Also avoid vinyl liners (they are too stretchy) and any product that does not specifically identify what it is made of.

The liner thickness should range anywhere from 20 to 40 mils. Obviously the thicker the better in terms of protection against tears. However, the thicker the liner the more difficult it is to handle and work with during installation; thicker will also be more expensive.

The ideal liner will be UV resistant, fiber reinforced, have one side white for easier installation, food grade quality, and thick enough to not tear easily during installation or regular use. See 'Chapter 15: Liner Material' for a comprehensive examination of liners.

Vertical Gardening

Vertical gardening is a revolutionary new garden system that provides proven methods and techniques for growing up, not out, thus maximizing space. There are a variety of containers and systems available, with more being introduced at increasing rates. Vertical gardening aquaponics will be addressed in full detail at the **www.FarmYourSpace.com** website.

FIGURE 59. Vertical gardening

Pumps

The correct pump for your aquaponics systems is just as important as choosing the right fish, selecting bed material, and determining tank and grow bed size. Some ill-informed people simply purchase a pump at the local home improvement store or order one online before gaining an understanding of their system's parameters. This is a big mistake. Please do not buy your aquaponics pump this way. It is rare to find a sales representative or a retailer that knows aquaponics (growing fish and plants together). A pump needs to be selected based upon compatibility of pump specifications to the system parameters, such as how much water is in your system, how high the pump needs to raise the water (head), desired flow rate, and whether or not a siphon or timer system is being used. If you desire to have your system off the grid, then efficiency becomes a very critical factor as well. Even if you have your system on the grid, efficiency should be considered to minimize operating costs. Refer to 'Chapter 18: Pumps & Choosing the Right Pump' for more specific and detailed helpful information on pumps.

Aeration

Aeration devices are sometime needed, or just included for additional benefit, in order to raise dissolved oxygen levels. Oxygen is introduced into the aquaponics system naturally through the plant life, waves, cascades, and other water turbulence methods, such as fountains and waterfalls. If water turbulence and natural aeration methods, such as plant life, are insufficient then an aeration device is necessary. Aeration devices are also used if dead spaces in a tank are a problem such as bottom corners of square tanks, end of a long run, etc. Mechanical devices include air pumps, tubing, oxygen injectors and oxygen diffusers.

Net Pots

Net Pots are used in floating raft culture, N.F.T. and sometimes flood and drain systems. They are used  to help hold and support plants. They can be purchased online or at hydroponic stores.

Heating and Cooling

Maintaining ambient room temperature for plants, as well as your comfort is important. There are multitudes of heaters, air conditioners, fans, misting devices, and evaporation systems that can be used to achieve this goal; however, it is important to ensure that whatever is used is not counterproductive to plant health.

Timing Controllers

Timing Controllers enable you to run your aquaponic system according to your preferences and needs. They can be set up to work a pump, multiple pumps, water heaters, lighting, fish feeding, humidity, and anything else you desire to automate. A time controller is really only necessary for pump operation, but having other components on an automatic timer controller is a nice convenience. It allows the operator to maintain the system on a consistent schedule and better enables one to make clearly defined adjustments to various system elements (flow rate, water temperature, feeding schedule, lighting preferences, etc.). Timing controllers come with a wide range of features and in many price ranges.

Dehumidifier

Depending upon the environment and the type of plants to be grown, a dehumidifier may be necessary. This is a rare item, but it is one that should be considered if trying to grow arid loving plants in a room where there is high humidity, or if there are extensive mold problems.

Ambient Lighting

Room and work lighting is also an important consideration. Just remember not to have any direct lighting impacting the fish tank.

Backup Energy

In case of an extended power outage it is essential to have a back-up energy source. Keep in mind that if your power is out for several days, others in your community will also most likely be without power, resulting in a run on generators from area rental companies and home improvement stores. Fish will perish quickly as oxygen becomes insufficient and waste begins to accumulate.

An electric generator is a device that converts mechanical energy to electrical energy, typically via burning some type of fossil fuel (gas, diesel, propane, etc.). Typically, the only items that must be provided power through an emergency event are pumps, aerators, and heaters. The remaining aquaponic components being without power through an extended outage will typically not result in catastrophic problems.

For small to mid-size systems, a pump can simply be plugged in to a power inventor box, which is in turn connected to any DC power source (typically just a 12-volt automobile battery). The AC output voltage of a power inverter device is often the same as the standard power line voltage, such as household 120AC. This allows the inverter to power numerous types of equipment designed to operate off the standard line power. Most often, if it is just a matter of a few hours, survival can be maintained by just keeping the pump in operation.

Alternative Energy

Alternative energy for aquaponics is referred to as any energy source that provides off-the-grid power supply. This back-up power can be used in case there is a disruption of service of the main public utility supply, or as a primary means in which to power the electrical components associated with an aquaponic system (i.e. pumps, lighting, heat, fans, etc.). Following is an example of one back-up alternative power supply which is relatively affordable.

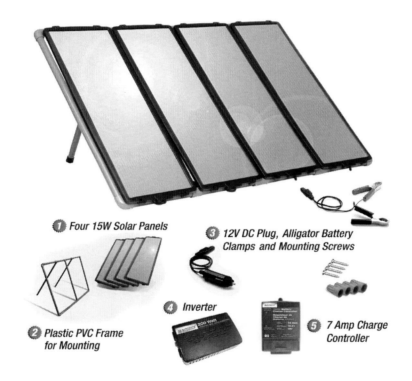

Alternative Energy Supply Source (one example)
Sunforce 50048 60W Solar Charging Kit
Available on online for approximately $350 (USA, year 2022)

① Four 15W Solar Panels

③ 12V DC Plug, Alligator Battery Clamps and Mounting Screws

④ Inverter

② Plastic PVC Frame for Mounting

⑤ 7 Amp Charge Controller

Features:
- Amorphous solar charging kit provides up to 60 watts of clean, free, renewable power
- Designed for back-up and remote power use
- Weatherproof, durable solar panels.
- Built-in blocking diode helps protect against battery discharge at night
- Complete kit includes four 15W amorphous solar panels, a PVC mounting frame, a 7-amp charge controller, 200-watt inverter, and wiring/connection cables

FIGURE 60.

CHAPTER 13

Fish Tanks and Ponds

Fish Tank Shape

Although any shape of fish tank will work, round tanks with flat bottoms are recommended. Square tanks with flat bottoms are perfectly acceptable but require more active solid-waste removal. Tank shape greatly affects water circulation. There is a risk to having tank with poor circulation. Artistically shaped tanks with non-geometric shapes (featuring many curves and bends, such as a Jacuzzi) can create dead spots in the water with no circulation. These areas can gather wastes and create anoxic, dangerous conditions for the fish. If an odd-shaped tank is to be used, it may be necessary to add water pumps or air pumps to ensure proper circulation and remove the solids. It is also important to choose a tank to fit the characteristics of the aquatic species reared because many species of bottom dwelling fish show better growth and less stress with adequate horizontal space.

As mentioned above, the fish tank can be of almost any shape, but the most commonly used are circular. The round shape allows water to circulate uniformly and transports solid wastes towards the center of the tank by centripetal force. A round tank is structurally stronger than any other shape, so given that the tank may be holding 250 plus gallons of water, the round shape allows for better structural integrity and less reinforcement. Therefore, round tanks don't have to be as heavy and bulky as square or rectangular

FIGURE 61. Round fiberglass tanks

163

FIGURE 62.

shaped tanks. As a result, round tanks, such as the fiberglass tanks shown in the two images (figure 63), are usually the least expensive tanks.

Round tanks have several distinct benefits for water quality and fish health, such as:

- Allows for better water circulation.
- Water circulation prevents thermal layering and thus helps to improve water quality.
- A good flow of water provides the fish with a current to swim against, which promotes health and muscle growth. This in turns makes raising fish for food better for consumption.
- Fish appear to naturally enjoy some moving water.
- Water movement aids in the exchange of gases between the air and the water (CO_2 exiting the fish tank, and oxygen entering the fish tank). Surface water constantly changing dramatically increases the rate of oxygen exchange.

- Increased oxygen through water movement benefits not only the fish, but also the de-nitrifying bacteria in the system, as well as inhibiting harmful bacteria that thrive in an anaerobic environment.
- In a rounded tank, solid waste has a tendency to gravitate toward the bottom-center of the tank. Strategic placement of the pump at this point will enable the collection and transport of this solid waste to the grow bed.

NOTE: I highly recommend that you avoid bolt-up fiberglass tanks, similar to the one in figure 62. I have had lots of experience with these types of tanks, as well as many other types of fish tanks. Bolt-up fiberglass tanks are highly problematic. There is a strong probability for leakage with bolt up tanks (eventually, if not initially). I have seen bolt up tanks leak way too many times in my career. I will never use or recommend a bolt up tank. Even if obtained for free, they will cost you time, and most likely product, when you have to eventually address a leak. Lastly, I believe bolt up tanks can be a safety hazard as well, should leaked water make its way to an electrical source (e.g., extension cord on the ground, etc.).

Square or rectangular fish tanks are also common and are especially useful if there is limited space. Care should be taken to ensure there is adequate water circulation so dead air pockets (low dissolved oxygen levels) do not form in the corners. Square tanks with rounded corners will assist in the water movement.

FIGURE 63. *Rectangular and square tanks.*

FIGURE 64. IBC (Intermediate Bulk Carrier) Tote

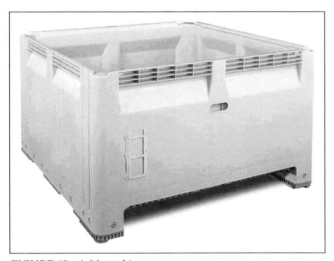

FIGURE 65. A Macrobin

IBC and Macrobin Tanks

IBC (Intermediate Bulk Carrier) totes (or high quality, food grade bulk shipping containers such as Macrobins) are commonly used for fish tanks. A used or reconditioned 275 or 330-gallon food grade IBC tote works great and can be acquired at a relatively low cost. Most standard size micro-bins can hold about 400 gallons of water.

Liner Tanks

Another practical and relatively inexpensive type of tank that works well is a DIY frame (wood, brick, concrete block, earthen, etc.) lined with a LDPE (Low Density Polyethylene) or HDPE (High Density Polyethylene) liner. The liner should range anywhere from 20 to 40 mils in thickness. Obviously, the thicker the liner, the better in terms of protection against tears. However, the thicker the liner the more difficult it is to handle and work with during installation, and the more expensive it will be.

The ideal liner would be UV resistant, fiber reinforced, have one side white for easier installation, be of food-grade quality, and be thick enough so as to not tear easily during installation or regular use. However, a liner that is made of LDPE or HDPE material, is 20 to 40 mils in thickness, and UV resistant is certainly satisfactory.

FIGURE 66. Liner tanks

Fish In and Predators Out

Regardless of what type of tank is used, it is important to ensure that small children and predators cannot enter the tank, and that fish cannot exit the tank. To keep fish in the tank, the water level can be lowered to approximately eight inches below the rim (this works for most species). However, doing so greatly decreases valuable volume capacity. A better method is to install netting or a fence around or over the fish tank. Keep in mind that it is also important to have quick access to the fish tank to check on the water quality, and for maintenance purposes.

I worked with a large aquaculture farm in California that raised several different types of fish in both ponds and 50-foot diameter tanks. One species raised in the tanks was largemouth bass. Although the surface water level was about a foot below the rim of the tanks, they had to keep a net stretched tightly over the bass tanks, because during feeding (when they dispersed feed on the surface of the water) the fish would get so excited--the water became extremely turbulent--the fish would literally jump out of the tank if it were not for the net.

Multipurpose Fish Tank (Pond)

Planned correctly, a fish tank can serve several valuable purposes. The benefits of each should not be overlooked or taken lightly. Using a fish tank for more than just containing fish can significantly increase production, profits, and lower cost. And although I am using the 'tank' term, the same principles apply to a pond or any vessel used to raise fish. Furthermore, a fish tank's value increases when each of the following items are implemented.

- **Fish tank used for radiating heat and/or the cooling of the greenhouse.** Radiation is the process of heat transfer resulting from the temperature difference between elements. Standing next to a hot fire (or standing outside on a hot sunny day), you can feel radiation heating the

FIGURE 67. Net over fish tank

FIGURE 68. fence around fish tank

surface of your skin. Similarly, in a greenhouse, a fish tank radiates energy to the surrounding environment. In the summer, the tank helps cool the greenhouse, and in the winter the tank helps generate heat. This process helps to lower heating and cooling utility costs and helps maintain a more consistent temperature balance within the greenhouse.

- **Fish tank used with an aquaponic DWC raft.** A D.W.C. plant raft on the water surface of the fish tank provides shade and security for the fish, while at the same time allows for the growing of certain beneficial plants. Besides providing you plant product without sacrificing space, the raft helps the fish feel more secure, and as a result, lowers fish stress thereby improving their health. Just be sure to allow some spacing between the edge of the plant raft and the side of the tank for fish care and tank maintenance.

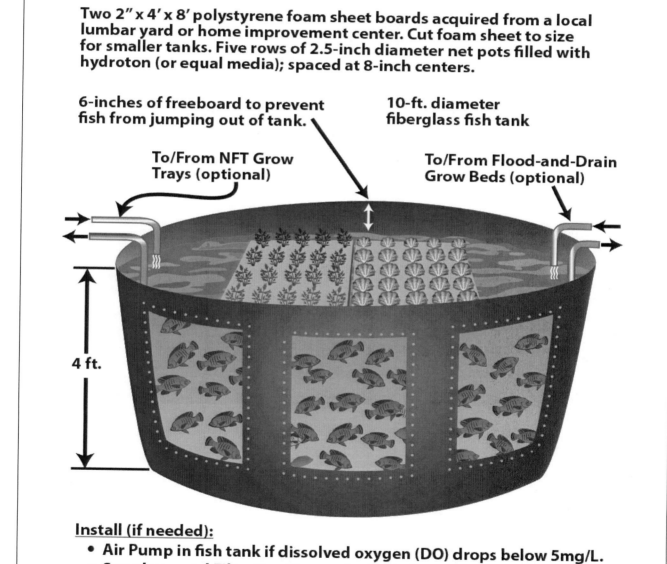

Two 2" x 4' x 8' polystyrene foam sheet boards acquired from a local lumbar yard or home improvement center. Cut foam sheet to size for smaller tanks. Five rows of 2.5-inch diameter net pots filled with hydroton (or equal media); spaced at 8-inch centers.

6-inches of freeboard to prevent fish from jumping out of tank.

10-ft. diameter fiberglass fish tank

To/From NFT Grow Trays (optional)

To/From Flood-and-Drain Grow Beds (optional)

4 ft.

Install (if needed):
- **Air Pump** in fish tank if dissolved oxygen (DO) drops below 5mg/L.
- **Supplemental Filtration** if grow beds and/or NFT grow trays are not able to maintain clear water. Refer to Chapter 19 on Filtration for additional guidance on filtration.

FIGURE 69. Fish tank integrated into an aquaponic system, providing multiple uses. The plant raft serves as a Deep Water Culture (DWC) for plants and fish shading. Grow beds elsewhere can be utilized for plants and help filter the water.

- **Fish tank used for multiple types of aquaponic systems.** Most aquaponic resources in the marketplace refer to the three different types of systems (D.W.C., N.F.T., and Flood-and-Drain). However, if planned properly, a system can be set up to be more than just one system, thus providing much greater flexibility and product yield.

Figures 69 and 70 show how a fish tank/pond can be utilized to provide "multiple-use" options, and thereby maximizing production without sacrificing space.

NOTE: Introducing increased oxygen into the water, via aeration tubes, not only helps keep the plants healthy, but it also accelerates plant growth.

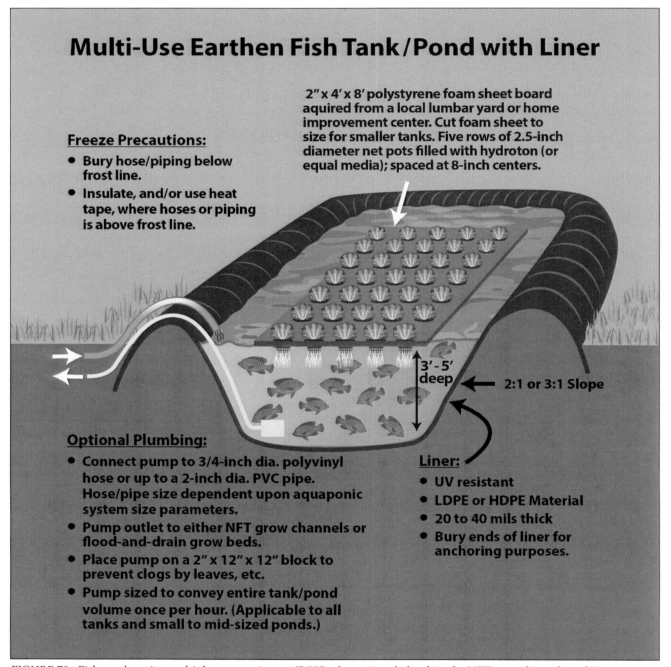

Multi-Use Earthen Fish Tank / Pond with Liner

2" x 4' x 8' polystyrene foam sheet board aquired from a local lumbar yard or home improvement center. Cut foam sheet to size for smaller tanks. Five rows of 2.5-inch diameter net pots filled with hydroton (or equal media); spaced at 8-inch centers.

Freeze Precautions:
- Bury hose/piping below frost line.
- Insulate, and/or use heat tape, where hoses or piping is above frost line.

3' - 5' deep

2:1 or 3:1 Slope

Optional Plumbing:
- Connect pump to 3/4-inch dia. polyvinyl hose or up to a 2-inch dia. PVC pipe. Hose/pipe size dependent upon aquaponic system size parameters.
- Pump outlet to either NFT grow channels or flood-and-drain grow beds.
- Place pump on a 2" x 12" x 12" block to prevent clogs by leaves, etc.
- Pump sized to convey entire tank/pond volume once per hour. (Applicable to all tanks and small to mid-sized ponds.)

Liner:
- UV resistant
- LDPE or HDPE Material
- 20 to 40 mils thick
- Bury ends of liner for anchoring purposes.

FIGURE 70. *Fish pond serving multiple aquaponic uses (DWC, plus optional plumbing for NFT grow channels and/or Flood-and-Drain media-beds).* **NOTE: *In some circumstances an air pump may be necessary in order to deliver additional oxygen to the DWC plant roots.***

Birds of Prey

As mentioned in the introduction of this book, I served as the Engineering Manager over four large aquaculture farms, which produced 80 percent of the Nation's caviar and seven-plus tons of meat annually, which we also shipped meat and caviar all over the world. True caviar is harvested from sturgeon when they are ten-plus years old. In my case, we raised white sturgeon fish from egg to harvest. By the time they were old enough to produce caviar, they typically weighed anywhere from 125 to 300 lbs. (four to seven-plus feet in length). One of our farms was inside a steel building, and the other three farms were outdoors. All four farms had a water recirculation system, and the fish were raised in round tanks; most tanks ranged in size from 20 to 50 feet in diameter, with a depth of four to six feet. However, the larger tanks were ten feet deep. These tanks held a lot of fish. We had to keep all outdoor tanks with fish under about two years of age (less than 18-inches in length) covered with a net or shade cloth to prevent hawks and eagles from stealing them. The tanks were checked a least three times a day (feedings, maintenance, etc.), so employees had to regularly partially uncover the tanks to gain access. There were hundreds of tanks.

On rare occasions, an employee would fail to tightly seal the tank cover, after which we would sometimes find the remains of a partially eaten fish where a bird of prey took advantage of the opportunity for an easy meal. If you live in a location where hawks and eagles are common, you may need to install a cover over your tank, if you find these awesome birds of prey are stealing your fish. It is doubtful that a scarecrow would work, as these birds will try to steal a fish off of a fishing line should they encounter a fisherman reeling in his catch.

FIGURE 71. A hawk with his catch.

FIGURE 72. A shade covers over a fish tank helps regulate water temperature, shields fish from direct sunlight, and provides protection against birds of prey taking fish.

FIGURE 73. An eagle stealing a fish off of a fishing line.

Fish Tank Materials

Fish tanks are made via many different methods, and with a variety of materials. Some of the most common are food-grade plastic, fiberglass, and HDPE liner. However, concrete tanks and earthen structures are also used. All have their advantages and disadvantages. For practicality, in consideration of cost and ease of installation, plastic, fiberglass and HDPE liner materials make the most sense if the tank is going to be located on grade. The materials for these types of tanks are light weight, easy to handle, and readily available throughout most of the world. Concrete and earthen tanks are most practical if the tank is below grade. Some creative aquacponic enthusiasts have even successfully converted swimming pools into viable aquaponic systems.

Wooden frames (or any other type of material for that matter) can also be built and turned waterproof via a HDPE liner, fiberglass, or an epoxy-based substance. These methods are certainly acceptable, but care needs to be taken to ensure that the frame has the structural integrity to withstand the lateral pressures, downward force, and stresses of the water weight against the structure; and the potential of several adults leaning against the tank. Water alone is extremely heavy by volume. Add to that a grown person leaning against the tank, and it is easy to understand that the tank must be fabricated using strong materials and heavy-duty construction methods.

Ponds are also used in aquaponics. With ponds extra precautions should be taken as an outside pond may contain and spread undesirable bacteria and/or sediment throughout the aquaponics system via the recirculating pumped water. This would compromise the water quality of the system and, at the least, require more frequent cleanings.

Concrete needs to be carefully considered and managed, as it can negatively impact water composition by causing imbalances in the pH. As water interacts with concrete, the water can dissolve various minerals present in the hardened cement paste or within the concrete aggregates. If the solution is unsaturated, dissolved ions such as calcium ($Ca2+$) are leached out and can be detrimental to the aquaculture system as a whole. If concrete is used, it should be sealed with a food-safe, commercially available sealant

If constructing an aquaculture system with a previously used tank or materials, care needs to be taken to ensure that the tank is food grade, materials don't have any toxic residues, and there are no elements associated with what is being used that may be harmful to fish, plants, and human consumption. If the tank will be outdoors, it should also be of material that will not breakdown easily via UV light (UV resistant). If you are unsure about the material or tank, then it would be prudent to pass on it as potential problems are not worth the risk, could end up being a costly mistake, would be a major drain on your valuable time, and negatively impact on your peace of mind.

Ideally, the fish tank will be of an opaque material (not transparent), as direct sunlight will encourage algae growth. Algae is detrimental to an aquaculture system (primarily because algae are a prolific grower that also needs oxygen to multiply, thus depleting your system of the available oxygen needed by your fish, bacteria, and plants).

A window on the side of a tank can bring much pleasure, and also serves to make monitoring water quality and fish health much easier. It also makes aquaponics that much more fun for both adults and children. However, it is best if such a window is not located on a side of the tank that is exposed to direct sunlight, but if so, install a curtain so the sunlight can be blocked when the window is not in use.

Small aquariums that one finds in homes or businesses are able to use standard glass because they are micromanaged and have specific aquarium filters which address algae. Even so, a small aquarium can develop algae if in direct sunlight or if the filter is inadequate.

Fish Tank Size

There are several different issues that must be considered pertaining to fish tank size selection. Below is a summarized list:

Objectives, goals, and long-term plan.

What is your purpose for getting into aquaculture? What are your immediate and long-term production goals (e.g., amount of fish you want to harvest each year)? Do you want to install your system and be done with it, or do you want to have the ability to enlarge it over time? Is your objective to just partially supplement your grocery store food with healthy, home-grown food, grow enough for yourself and/or others in your circle, or also grow enough to barter and/or sell for a profit?

Location, facilities, and available space.

Will your tank be indoors or outdoors? A fish tank in a greenhouse works great because it helps maintain the temperature in the greenhouse. Will you need a greenhouse or green room to grow vegetables in the winter? How much space do you have available for both the fish tank and plants? Will your fish tank require temperature control during all or part of the year?

Start-up and operational budget (feed cost, utilities, etc.)

The larger the system, the greater the start-up and operational cost. How much are you willing to invest in creating your system? What is your budget for feeding the fish, and potentially pay for increased utility cost (for temperature control and lighting)?

Maintenance and operational resources (e.g., your time, available assistance, etc.)

The larger the system, the more time and attention will be required. It is great to have big ambitions, but if you don't have the time or resources to keep up with it, success will be hindered. Sometimes it is better to start off small and then grow in phases.

Regardless of the type of system or size of the fish tank, a certain level of water quality must exist. Adequate filtration must occur, whether it is through aquaponic grow beds, a bio-filter, mechanical filtration, or a combination of these filtration methods. If growing fish in a pond, will the fish be negatively impacted by runoff surface water contaminants entering the pond, extreme fluctuations in water levels, or predators (including poachers)? Water quality and specific details of system design are addressed later in this book

Redundancy

The optimal planned aquaculture system will have redundancy integrated within, where possible. Using a minimum of two fish tanks, two pumps, and two filtration systems. Redundancy offers many advantages when it comes to addressing emergencies, harvesting operations, and maintenance issues.

Fish Tank Placement

A common perspective of aquaculture is that of having the fish tank downstream of the filtration system. Although there is nothing wrong with this layout, it is by no means the only option. As a matter of fact, sometimes it is a big advantage to have the fish tank outdoors.

The fish tank is the heaviest component in the aquaculture system. Each gallon of water weighs 8.34 lbs., which means a 300-gallon fish tank would weigh about 2,502 pounds (slightly less because of the fish). Since the fish tank will be too difficult to be move once it is filled, it is important to carefully consider its location. Furthermore, the fish tank should be located within or on the ground, or on solid flooring, since a structure to support all the weight would have to be enormous and very costly. In short, due diligence in determining fish tank location is paramount.

Fish Tank Safety Considerations

Regardless of the tank system being implemented or its size, remember that safety is a priority. If you have small children on your property then fencing, nets, and/or locked doors should be intact to prevent children from potentially drowning in the fish tank.

Water in contact with electrical components, electrical outlets, breaker boxes, and extension cords combine for an extremely dangerous situation. All electrical items should be securely protected from water and potential fish tank leaks. Thus, all electrical components, including extension cords, should be kept a safe distance off the floor.

In summary, take all necessary safety precautions to protect yourself and others. Be aware of all electricity and water combinations. Follow all National Electric Codes.

Fish Tank Selection

In summary, your fish tank choice will be influenced by space, budget, available time for maintenance, and aquaponic goals (desired yield). There is a wide variety of choices; deciding upon a fish tank can seem bewildering at first, but if you keep focused on what you desire to achieve out of aquaponics, then the size issue is easily resolved.

1. A 250-gallon (1000 liters) or larger fish tank has been proven to create a more stable system. Larger volumes are especially better for beginners because they allow more room for error. With larger volumes, changes to water quality happen more slowly than they do in smaller systems.

2. To raise a fish to "plate size" a fish tank volume of at least 50 gallons is required.

3. The recommended stocking density is one pound of fish per five to seven gallons of tank water (0.5 kg per 20-26 liters).

4. Determine fish tank volume from the stocking density rule above (one pound fish per five to seven gallons of fish tank volume or 1 kg per 40-80 liters).

Constructing an Inexpensive Fish Tank

A fish tank is nothing more than an above ground container filled with water. Examples for backyard aquaponic fish tanks are swimming pools, IBC totes, fiberglass hot tubs, and lined plywood troughs. Of course, there are more industrial tank options (e.g., commercial fish tanks, concrete walls, etc.).

Tilapia (the most common fish raised in aqaponics) need 0.5 cubic foot of water, or 3.74 gallons, for every pound of their body weight at harvest. So, if you want to keep 144 pounds of fish in the same pond, you will need to have one that holds 72 cubic feet of water, or 538.56 gallons. At harvest, average weight of a tilapia is approximately 0.5 pounds (220 grams).

A lined plywood trough that is 4 feet wide and 8 feet long, with 2.25 feet of water depth, would fit the size needed in this example. Of course, you can expand this pond to any size that you want. And there is nothing wrong with having more water volume per pound of fish than what is needed. Yes, your pump and filter will have to do more work, but unless the tank is extremely larger than what is necessary, the extra pumping and filtering that needs to be done is negligible. To figure out how many cubic feet, or gallons, you will need, decide on how many pounds of fish that you want to harvest every six to nine months, depending on species of tilapia fingerlings that you select, and then divide that weight in half to get the cubic feet. Then multiply the cubic feet by 7.48 to get gallons. For example: if you want to have 144 pounds of tilapia in your tank at harvest time, you take 144 and divide it by two to get 72 cubic feet (144 / 2 = 72). Then, to get the gallons, you just have to take the cubic feet, and multiply by 7.48 to get 538.56 gallons (72 x 7.48 = 538.56).

Once you know how many cubic feet or gallons you need, it is simply a matter of finding the right container to hold that much water; with a little lip at the top, so that your tilapia don't swim over the edge. To get the cubic feet of a rectangular pond, you multiply the length, times the width, times the water depth. To get the cubic feet of a circular pond, multiply the radius times the radius (R^2), times 3.14 (pi), then multiply the result times the water depth.

Determine Your Fish Tank Construction

The simplest solution to making a fish tank, is to use an above ground swimming pool. A twelve-foot diameter pool filled with 24 inches of water holds 1,696.46 gallons and is very inexpensive. However, there are a few of drawbacks to using one of these small pools as a tank. First, as the vinyl ages it tends to get very brittle, and it will eventually split down the side. You can support the sides after the pool is filled by surrounding it with thin plywood, or similar flexible material, but this will only buy you a second season of use. The best thing to do is replace the pool (or liner) every 24 months, or sooner. The second potential drawback to using a swimming pool as a fish pond has to do with whether or not the fish are affected by the vinyl leaching chemicals into their water.

A lined plywood trough has many advantages. It is durable and will last a long time. It can be built to any size. It makes harvesting fish extremely easy. It is relatively inexpensive to build. And, if you want to expand into a commercial aquaponic operation, it can be easily made with readily available FDA approved materials.

Wood Framed Tank Construction

Duct tape is used on plywood joints.

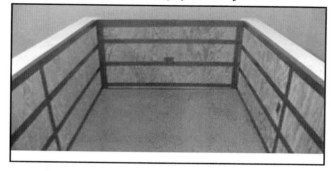

Finished wood tank with pond liner material for a watertight fish tank.

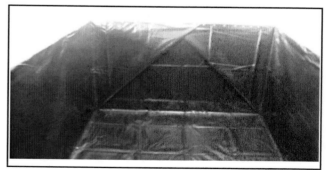

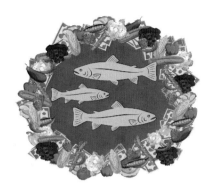

CHAPTER 14

Liner Material

Liner Overview

A liner is an impermeable geotextile material used for water retention. They are commonly referred to as pond liner, water garden liner, greenhouse cover material, hydroponics pond liner, aquaponics bed liner, and polyethylene tarp material. However, liners are also used in many other types of industries in a wide variety of applications.

Liners are often used in aquaponics for flood-and-drain grow beds, D.W.C. tanks, fish tanks, and fish ponds. With the aid of structural support a liner has the ability to contain large volumes water, even against significant pressure. The advantage of using a liner over other materials is lower cost, ready availability, and ease of use.

There are many different types of liners available on the market. As matter of fact, there are well over 24 different types of common liner materials. However, only some materials are suitable for aquaponics.

Materials include LDPE (Low Density Polyethylene), PVC (Poly Vinyl Chloride), PVC with internal reinforcement, and HDPE (High Density Polyethylene). HDPE is frequently noted as the best, but it is the most expensive and hardest to work with because of its ridged nature. LDPE is most preferred by small to mid-size aquaponic operators.

Avoid EPDM as it emits toxins that are harmful to the beneficial bacteria in your system and the toxins will eventually make their way into your food supply. Also avoid vinyl liners as they are too stretchy as well as any product that doesn't specifically identify what is made of.

The liner thickness should range anywhere from 20 to 40 mils. Obviously, the thicker the better in terms of protection against tears. However, the thicker the liner, the more difficult it is to handle and work with during installation, and more expensive it will be.

The ideal liner will be UV resistant, fiber reinforced, have one side white for easier installation, be of food grade quality, and be of thick enough to avoid tears during installation or regular use.

Liner Installation Precautions

Whether installing a liner in a pond, tank, or grow bed care, needs to be taken to ensure that the piece is large enough to do the job. Allow excess to overlap grow bed rims and tanks or to be buried in the ground for anchoring purposes. In other words, measure twice, cut once.

Refrain from walking on or laying tools or supplies on the liner. Avoid installing liner material outdoors on windy days or make sure you have enough people to assist you. Also, don't let pets walk on the liner material either. Any of the above can cause a puncture and result in a major hassle when discovered after the system is filled with water.

Liner Modifications

Occasionally, two separate pieces of liner material need to be joined in order to have a piece large enough to do the job. The following are directions from the Colorado International Lining Company (www.coloradolining.com) for field seaming liner material.

RECOMMENDED GUIDELINES FOR FIELD SEAMING

Temperatures for seaming should be as follows:

- Minimum ambient temperature: 50° F.
- Liner surface temperature: 90-100° F.
- Solvent adhesive should be 70-80° F.

1. Before adhesive is applied, surfaces to be seamed must be dry and free of dirt and foreign materials. The contact surfaces of the panels should be wiped clean to remove all dirt, dust, or other foreign materials. A clean cloth or grout brush may be used to help clean.

2. Adhesion of one liner panel to another is accomplished by lapping the edges of panels a minimum of 3 -6" inches (6" up to 1' is more desirable).

3. If using a seaming board, it should be placed below the liner panels to be joined. Only the pull rope should be exposed through the seam.

4. To commence seaming, fold the upper sheet back and apply adhesive to both sheets at the overlap area using a 3" wide paintbrush. Only apply about a body width (shoulder to shoulder width) of adhesive at a time. The adhesive should be applied to reach the outer edge of the seam and be 2-3" wide (within the overlapped area). Use enough solvent to make the liner surface appear wet and shiny (not flooded or inundated). Once the solvent is brushed-on, the brush should be replaced in a can (not on the liner) and the seam be rolled flat with a seam-roller once both surfaces become tacky. Roller strokes perpendicular to the liner seam should be made to push out excess adhesive and air pockets. Some adhesive should barely start to ooze from under the top overlapped edge. Once 100 percent is burnished down, the next shoulder to shoulder width area can be adhered with the same repeated process. The seaming board shall be advanced as needed.

5. Always keep the solvent adhesive can sealed. Only remove the lid long enough to wet the seaming brush. Failure to do so will result in the adhesive losing its "solvent grab" through evaporation of volatiles and seam quality will deteriorate to unacceptable quality. One option is to have a separate paint style can with a slit carefully cut into the lid allowing the brush to fit snugly within. Once brushes begin to stiffen-up, they should be replaced.

6. Using too much PVC bonding solvent in a wide area could result in a poor quality seam and make repairs difficult.

7. About one hour after seaming is performed it is advisable to manually probe the seam. Any loose edges should be peeled back and re-glued or patched if necessary. All repaired areas should be identified with a crayon or marker for re-inspection after glue dries.

8. Seams typically require 24 hours to completely cure. They can reach 90 percent of their final cure strength in just a few hours.

TOOLS SUPPLIES LIST FOR FIELD SEAMING

- PVC bonding solvent specially formulated for liners (i.e. LO-VOC X-15™ PVC Solvent, or equal). Purchase enough for your job. Read product label for coverage specifications.
- Typical solvent adhesive yield is: One gallon of adhesive should bond 75' — 100 lf of seam.
- Safety glasses or safety goggles.

- Rubber gloves.
- Well ventilated area.
- Knee pads.
- Cotton rags.
- Several 3" wide paint brushes
- One (1) whisk broom (or fox tail brush).
- One (1) 10" x 6' -8' long Douglas Fir clear board, rounded off on both ends as

well as all edges, with a rope tied to one end.
- One (1) Stanley Knife.
- One (1) yellow crayon for marking liner surface.
- One (1) pair of scissors with rounded-off points.
- One (1) 2' plastic or wood wallpaper seam-roller per each field seaming crew.

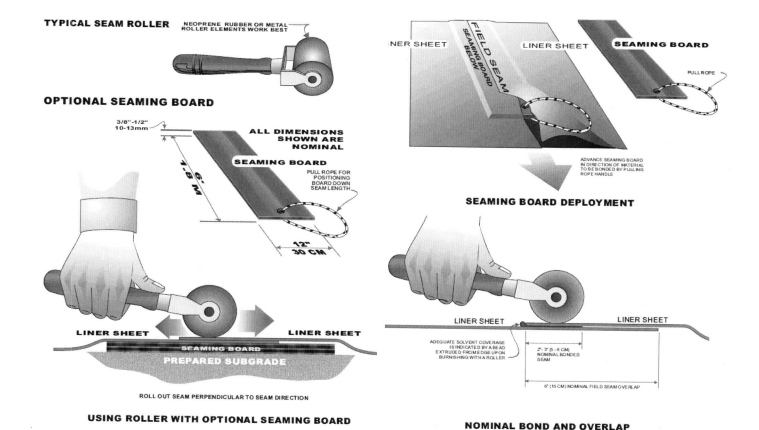

FIGURE 74. *Joining two liners with a watertight seam.*

Liner Repairs

To repair small rips or puncture holes, follow the instructions for sealing a seam above, but using the method described in the illustration (see figure 76).

Liner Plumbing Penetrations

Although this topic is addressed in greater detail within 'Chapter 16: Plumbing', along with the methods described in this chapter, for a watertight pipe penetration through a liner.

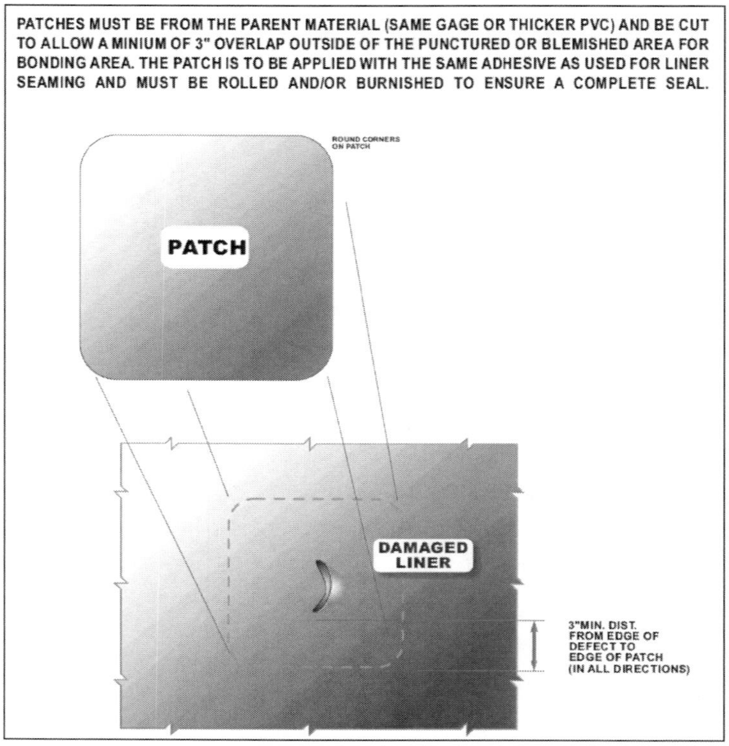

PATCHES MUST BE FROM THE PARENT MATERIAL (SAME GAGE OR THICKER PVC) AND BE CUT TO ALLOW A MINIUM OF 3" OVERLAP OUTSIDE OF THE PUNCTURED OR BLEMISHED AREA FOR BONDING AREA. THE PATCH IS TO BE APPLIED WITH THE SAME ADHESIVE AS USED FOR LINER SEAMING AND MUST BE ROLLED AND/OR BURNISHED TO ENSURE A COMPLETE SEAL.

FIGURE 75. Patching a damaged liner.

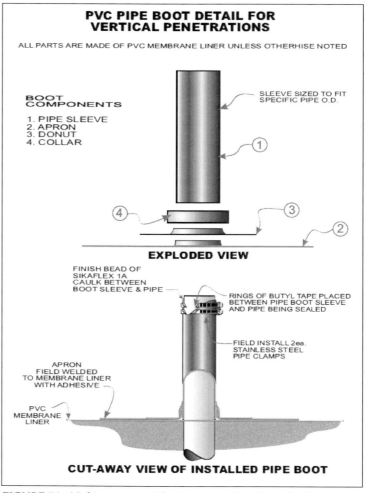

FIGURE 76. Making a watertight pipe protrusion through a liner.

CHAPTER 15

Plumbing

Overview of Plumbing

Plumbing your aquaponics system requires careful consideration of many different factors and will depend on your own design and the type of aquaponics method being implemented (i.e. N.F.T., D.W.C., and Flood-and-Drain system). Nevertheless, there are some basic principles that are applicable on almost every system which need to be applied. Therefore, issues pertaining to plumbing infrastructure are addressed in this chapter with the hope of providing you the best possible, user-friendly assistance.

Plumbing is an integral part of an aquaponics system and needs to be considered from the very beginning. In other words, one should consider plumbing to be just as important and as much as a priority as the fish tank and the grow beds. A common mistake is to develop the fish tank and grow beds (or grow channels), and then attempt to plumb in afterwards only to find a major problem. This chapter, as well as sections in the following design chapters of this book, will help you avoid those time consuming, and sometimes costly, mistakes.

Water Conveyance

It should be understood that water pressure and water volume rate are two separate and distinct issues. Water pressure is the force that water flows from a plumbing fixture. Water volume rate is the amount of water present to fill a tank or grow bed. Water pressure is typically noted in pounds per square inch (psi) or Kilopascal (kPa). Water volume rate is typically presented in gallons per minute (gpm), gallons per hour (gph), liters per second (L/s), or cubic meters per hour (m3h). Volume of water is normally described simply in terms of gallons, cubic feet, litters, or cubic meters.

Piping can be classified into two categories: (1) those delivering water to the grow beds, and (2) those removing it from the grow beds. As a general rule, drain pipes conveying water from the grow bed(s) to the fish tank are typically larger and function via gravity, whereas pipes or tubes conveying water from the fish tank to the grow bed are typically pressurized by the pump and can be smaller in diameter.

Pipe diameter size will depend on system parameters, but it is always better to go with a slightly larger sized diameter pipe than the minimum size needed. There are a number of engineering related calculators online that can help you work out the ideal pipe diameter to use and it is prudent to review these during the planning phase. The following are internet links to two such online calculators that can used to determine pipe size:

- http://irrigation.wsu.edu/Content/Calculators/ General/Pipe-Velocity.php
- http://www.calctool.org/CALC/eng/civil/ hazen-williams_g

Flow rate decreases as the length of pipe increases, so keep this in mind if conveying water or wastewater a considerable distance (i.e. an outdoor pond to a greenhouse is usually a considerable distance away, etc.). The line itself provides resistance to the water flow. Therefore, the length of the run is a major factor. The longer the run, the less gallons per minute that can flow through the line.

Length of run actually has a dramatic affect on the conveyance of fluid. As an example, a typical water line will lose approximately 33 percent of its water delivery capability when the length of the run is increased from 30 linear feet to 60 linear feet. As a specific example, 1-¼ inch diameter pipe can deliver approximately 21 gallons per minute over a run of 30 linear feet, yet only 14 gallons, approximately, per minute over a run of 60 linear feet. While the length of run is a major factor for water line size calculations, it becomes more of factor when the run is unusually long.

Table 24 is another helpful guide to determine the pipe size needed based upon the required amount of water that will be conveyed to empty the fish tank once per hour.

TABLE 24. **Water Flow Rate**

PIPE LENGTH (ft)	WATER FLOW RATE IN GLM Pipe Diameter in Inches									
	0.5	0.75	1	1.5	2	2.5	3	4	5	6
5	23	66	140	407	868	1560	2520	5371	9659	15601
10	16	45	96	280	597	1073	1733	3694	6643	10730
15	13	36	77	225	479	862	1393	2968	5337	8620
20	11	31	66	193	410	738	1192	2541	4569	7380
40	7	21	46	132	282	508	820	1747	3142	5076
100	4	13	28	81	172	309	500	1065	1916	3095

PIPE LENGTH (m)	WATER FLOW RATE, m³/hr Pipe Diameter in mm									
	12	20	25	40	50	65	75	100	130	150
1	5.6	21.5	38.6	133.0	239.2	477.0	694.9	1481	2953	4302
2	3.9	14.8	26.6	91.5	164.5	328.1	478.0	1019	2031	2959
4	2.7	10.2	18.3	62.9	113.2	225.6	328.7	700.5	1396.7	2034.9
6	2.1	8.2	14.7	50.6	90.9	181.3	264.1	562.8	1122	1635
12	1.5	5.6	10.1	34.8	62.5	124.7	181.6	387.1	771.7	1124
30	0.9	3.4	6.2	21.2	38.1	76.0	110.7	236.0	470.5	685.5

Additional Pipe Sizing Considerations

Increasing the pipe to just one size larger makes a dramatic difference. Those not in the plumbing trade or engineering field do not realize that there is strong correlation between length and pipe diameter.

As an example, a 1-¼ inch diameter pipe is only 25 percent larger in diameter than 1-inch diameter pipe, but there is an area difference of 56 percent between these two slightly different pipe diameter sizes. Another example of this size/area relationship can be seen when examining the difference of the areas inside a 1-¼ inch diameter pipe compared to a 2-inch diameter pipe, which is about 77 percent.

When examining the flow-rate (gallons per minute), the differences are even more dramatic. Basing calculations of an average run of pipe of 50-feet in length, a 1-¼ inch diameter pipe will convey up to about 16 gallons per minute. On the other hand 1-inch diameter pipe only provides about 9 gallons per minute. Therefore, a 1-¼ inch diameter pipe provides almost 77 percent more gallons per minute than a 1-inch diameter pipe.

What does all this mean to the aquaponic operator? It means that for a nominal amount of money, increasing pipe diameter by just one size provides dramatic benefits. The table below clearly illustrates this point.

Pipe Size (Sch. 40)	I.D. (range)	O.D.	GPM (w/ min. PSI loss & noise)	GPH (w/ min. PSI loss & noise)
1/2"	0.5 - 0.6"	0.85"	7	420
3/4"	0.75 - 0.85"	1.06"	11	660
1"	1 - 1.03"	1.33"	16	960
1-1/4"	1.25 - 1.36"	1.67"	25	1,500
1-1/2"	1.5 - 1.6"	1.9"	35	2,100
2"	1.95 - 2.05"	2.38"	55	3,300
2-1/2"	2.35 - 2.45"	2.89"	80	4,800
3"	2.9 - 3.05"	3.5"	140	8,400
4"	3.85 - 3.95"	4.5"	240	14,400
5"	4.95 - 5.05"	5.563"	380	22,800
6"	5.85 - 5.95"	6.61"	550	33,000
8"	7.96"	8.625"	950	57,000

Assume Gravity to Low Pressure. About 6 f/s flow velocity, also suction side of pump

FIGURE 77. *Typical flow rates for common pipe sizes used in aquaponics.*

This is probably a good place to mention that the above noted plumbing principles apply to both tubing and pipes. There are minor head loss difference for each type of material being considered (i.e. PVC, steel, copper, polyvinyl, etc.). Furthermore, fitting and bends also impact conveyance of the fluid being delivered. However, for the vast majority of aquaponic systems, the head loss differences between material type and the number of fittings used are of such minor consequence that these differences can be ignored. Head loss needs to be considered, but not to the extent of examining each minor difference when planning and designing an aquaponic system. Pipe diameter, elevation difference, and length of pipe run are going to be the critical factors that need to be considered in the planning and design phases.

Over time, debris can build up on the inside of the pipes and this will negatively impact the flow rate. Pipes may need to be cleaned periodically in order to ensure an unimpeded flow rate. The necessity to clean some sections of plumbing should influence your decision as to how you connect pipe and fittings (i.e. glue, installing a cleanout fitting(s) at certain plumbing points, etc.). Feeding a domestic garden hose through the pipe (with the water turned on) will sufficiently clean the pipe in most cases. A power washer does wonders, as well.

PVC Piping

The most commonly used plumbing materials used in aquaponics are PVC or UPVC pipes and irrigation tubing. Garden hoses are also used fairly often, especially when the fish tank is located a significant distance from the plant grow beds or channels.

Occasionally, there is an article questioning the safety of PVC, but after years of study by scientists all over the world, there is still very little evidence to prove that it is harmful; as such, it has been certified as safe for use in drinking water plumbing by government agencies throughout the world. In reality, all evidence suggests that the risk of harm from using

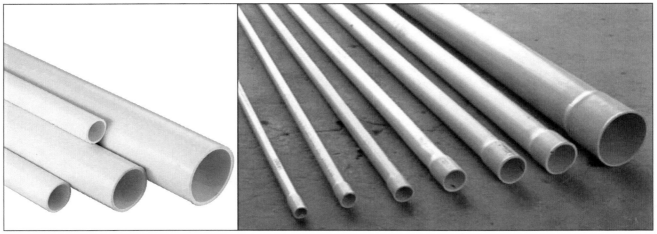

FIGURE 78. Straight (left) and bell end (right) PVC piping.

PVC pipes in food and water supply is so slight as to be negligible. Because of this, it is almost universally used for agriculture, aquaculture, hydroponics, and aquaponics.

Below are several beneficial features:

• PVC Pipe is almost universally available.
• PVC Pipe is usually extremely cost effective (low cost).
• PVC Pipe comes in standard sizes throughout the world.
• PVC Pipe has a wide range of adapters and connectors available.
• PVC Pipe is easy to use, cut and adapt.
• PVC Pipe is durable and long lasting.PVC Pipe is light weight.

Although other piping can be used in aquaponics (such as agricultural pipe, flexi-pipe, bamboo, hosepipe, etc.,) it important to make sure that it is safe for use in a system that grows food for human consumption, and make sure that it will not be harmful to fish or plants. As an example, it is prudent to avoid using metal piping, especially copper piping, as it can be highly toxic to fish. Also, if installing used plumbing materials, make sure that it was not used to covey any toxic or harmful substances in the past. If in doubt, it is best to pass on it, especially since PVC pipe piping and fittings are relatively inexpensive.

Schedule 40 vs Schedule 80 PVC

If you've been shopping around for PVC you may have heard the term "schedule". Despite its deceiving title, schedule doesn't have anything to do with time. A PVC pipe's schedule has to do with the thickness of its walls. Maybe you've seen that schedule 80 pipe is slightly more costly than schedule 40.

Though the outside diameter of a schedule 80 pipe and a schedule 40 pipe are the same, an 80 pipe has thicker walls. This standard of measuring pipe came from a need to have a universal system for referring to PVC. Since different wall thicknesses is beneficial in different situations, the ASTM (American Society for Testing and Materials) came up with the schedule 40 and 80 system for classifying the two common types.

The main differences between Schedule 40 (Sch 40) and Schedule 80 (Sch 80) are:

• Water Pressure Rating
• Sizing & Diameter (Wall Thickness)
• Color
• Application & Use

Water Pressure for Sch 40 vs. Sch 80

Both schedule 40 and 80 PVC are used widely around the world. Each one has its benefits in different applications. Schedule 40 pipe has thinner walls, so it is best for applications involving relatively low water pressure. In the vast majority of situations, schedule 40 is sufficient for aquaponics.

Schedule 80 pipe has thicker walls and is able to withstand higher PSI (pounds per square inch). This makes it ideal for industrial and chemical applications. To give you an idea of the size difference, 1" schedule 40 PVC pipe has a .133" minimum wall and 450 PSI, while schedule 80 has a .179" minimum wall and 630 PSI.

Sizing & Diameter

As mentioned earlier, both schedule 80 and schedule 40 PVC pipe have the exact same outside diameter. This is possible because schedule 80's extra wall thickness is on the inside of the pipe. This means schedule 80 pipe will have a slightly more restricted flow, even though it may be the same pipe diameter as an equivalent schedule 40 pipe. This means schedule 40 and 80 pipe do fit together and can be used together if necessary.

The only thing to be careful of is that the lower pressure handling schedule 40 pipe meets the pressure requirements of your application. A pipeline is only as strong as its weakest part or joint, so even one segment of schedule 40 pipe used where a higher pressure schedule pipe is needed can cause problems. However, it is rare to have such high pressures in aquaponics. An exception may be a back-up or supplemental pipe directly from another water supply source.

Schedule 40 and Schedule 80 Color

Generally, schedule 40 pipe is white in color, while schedule 80 is often gray in order to distinguish it from 40. PVC is available in many colors though, so be sure to check labels when purchasing.

Which Schedule PVC do I Need?

So what schedule PVC do you need? For aquaponics, home repairs, or irrigation projects, schedule 40 PVC is the way to go. Even schedule 40 PVC is capable of handling impressive pressure, and it is likely more than adequate for light to moderately heavy applications.

Using schedule 40 will save you money, especially if you plan on using large diameter parts. For large commercial, industrial, or chemical applications, it would be wise to use schedule 80 pipe and fittings. These are applications that will likely cause higher pressure and stress on the material, so thicker walls are imperative.

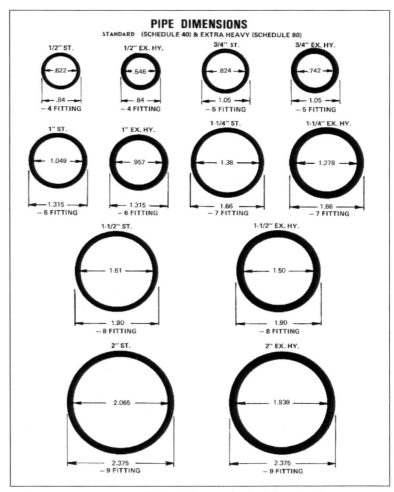

FIGURE 79. Dimensions of Schedule 40 and Schedule 80 PVC pipe.

Pipe Connections and Fittings

There are two commonly used PVC fittings in aquaponics—threaded connectors and slip connectors. Threaded connectors are ones that screw into one another and are designated as male and female. Slip connectors, as the name suggests, just slip into one another. In order to preserve pipe diameter, avoid restricting flow, and minimize clog points, it is prudent to use only female fittings. Female fitting fit over the outside of the pipe, whereas male fittings fit inside the pipe. Examples of common connectors are:

- 90° elbows
- 45° elbows
- 90° Tee fittings
- Ball Valves
- Bulkheads
- Reducers
- Couplings
- Wyes

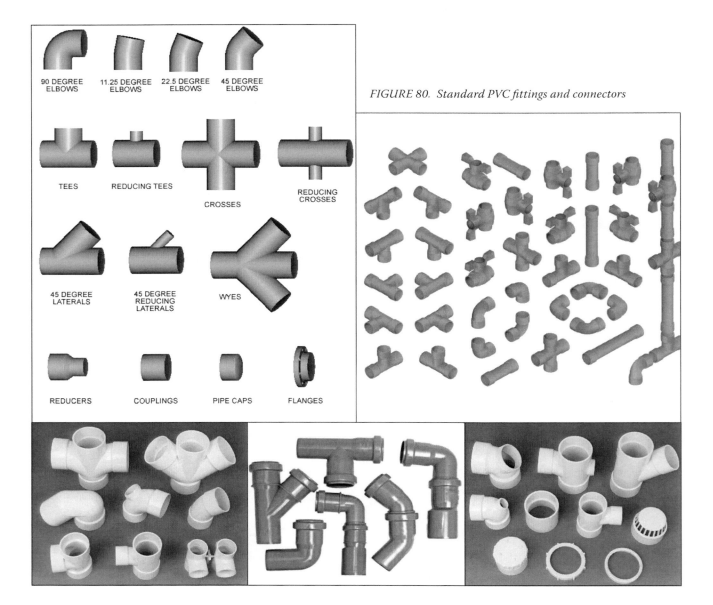

FIGURE 80. Standard PVC fittings and connectors

Irrigation Supplies

Irrigation materials are also commonly used in aquaponics. There are several good reasons as to why irrigation materials are integrated into aquaponics. They are inexpensive, require minimal effort in learning how to install them, they are safe for plants, fish and people, they are easy to install, and are effective conduits of aquaponic fluids.

However, not all irrigation materials are created equally. Some have thin walls, and are so light they are basically a cheap low grade inferior solution. As inexpensive as irrigation materials are, it is better to invest in the higher grade premium materials sold commercially to professionals from an irrigation supply store, rather than the typical residential stuff commonly sold at home improvement stores. Also, no more than what is typically used in a standard size aquaponics system, the extra cost for premium materials is nominal. The result for paying slightly more for premium irrigation supplies is that your aquaponic system will be much more reliable (less prone to leaks and not easily disrupted because of accidental damage). Premium irrigation materials are also much easier and faster to install than light weight residential materials.

It is also helpful to stick with the same name brand of irrigation materials, as they will be more interchangeable. Furthermore, it is helpful to shop at the same store so as to develop a solid working relationship with qualified staff. *Ewing Irrigation and Landscape Supply*, for instance, has expert staff on board eager to provide a wealth of information and assistance. And, no, I am not getting compensated for endorsing them. Nor do not have any friends or family working for Ewing, or benefiting from my praise of Ewing Irrigation and Landscape Supply Co. I say this as one consumer to another with the sole purpose of helping you. I have shopped for irrigation supplies for my nursery, aquaculture, hydroponics, and aquaponic operations for many years. I've been to many different supply stores (Ewing's competitors, several different large chain home improvement stores, Wal-Mart, etc.), and have tried many different products.

Bottom line: I am of the opinion that Ewing has the best quality products, and all the stores I have visited (as well as my phone calls), they have provided me with the most knowledgeable professional advice. Ewing is located throughout the southern half of the United States, as well as the west coast. They also have a very user-friendly website, and provide accredited education opportunities for those aspiring to learn more of development further professionally.

In summary, irrigation supplies offer a good alternative or supplement to PVC for plumbing of an aquaponics system. It is prudent to purchase premium quality irrigation products over cheaper residential type irrigation materials. It is also beneficial to shop at a store in which sound expert advice can be obtained, and build a positive relationship with the staff. Following are some of the more common irrigation materials used in aquaponics:

FIGURE 81. *90-degree elbow, tee fitting, coupling*

FIGURE 82. *¼-inch tube tee, ¼-inch tube elbow, ¼-inch tube coupling*

FIGURE 83. **Tubing**, *also called Poly Tubing, Poly Pipe, Supply Line, Trunk Line; all of which are common terms for this flexible polyethylene pipe (shown above). Common sizes are ½" (aka ⅝") or ¾" tubing. Emitters can be inserted into tubing or connected via ¼-inch diameter size micro tubing.*

FIGURE 84. *Two different types of ¼-inch tube to ⅝-inch tube connections*

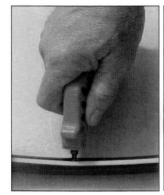

FIGURE 85. *Two different kinds of hole punches used to install ¼-inch tubing in larger dia. Irrigation poly tubing.*

Hoses

In addition to piping and irrigation tubing, hosing can also be used for water conveyance in aquaponics. The disadvantages of hoses are that they can kink, and some can be relatively expensive. Nevertheless, there is a wide variety of hose material types that can be used in aquaponics (see figures 83–90). Having clear (see through hose) will provide you the benefit of being able to watch your aquaponics system plumbing at work, which is both helpful and fun.

Use a hose clamp (figure 91) to obtain a secure watertight connection of the hose to pipes and fittings.

Fluid Dynamics

There are a few things to consider that influence how fluid actually flows through a pipe. The pipe and fittings causes friction to what would otherwise be smooth movement of the water, so the water in the very middle of the pipe is conveyed somewhat faster than the water flowing near the sides of the pipe. The difference is small, but it exists nonetheless.

In addition, comparing the flow rate through a straight length of PVC pipe, versus that of a pipe with a series of bends, the water flows more quickly through the straight pipe. There is no need to use complicated engineering equations; just recognize that there are some factors that will determine the flow rate through the aquaponics plumbing system, which in turn impacts what size diameter piping or tubing should be used. Simply put, in a given amount of time you can move a greater volume of water through a big pipe than you can through a small pipe. Also, if moving water over a significant distance (i.e. from an outdoor fish tank to a greenhouse grow bed), then it is especially important to caution on the side of using larger diameter piping or tubing instead of a smaller size, even if a reducer must be used at both ends (i.e. reducer at the pump and a reducer at the grow bed).

FIGURE 86. Flex hose

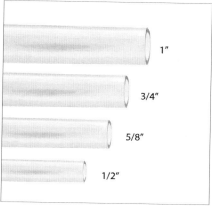

FIGURE 87. Clear vinyl tubing

1"
3/4"
5/8"
1/2"

FIGURE 88. Reinforced PVC hose

FIGURE 89. Braided PVC hose

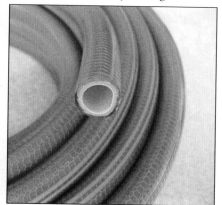

FIGURE 90. 5/8 to 1-inch diameter garden hose

FIGURE 91. Hose clamp

Many pumps suitable for an aquaponics system come with a ½-inch outlet. Rather than convey the pump outflow through a ½-inch irrigation line, it is better to install a reducer at the pump. For example, at the pump, install a short ½-inch irrigation tube about an inch in length, then add a ½-inch to ¾-inch reducer, and connect it to a ¾-inch poly irrigation tube to convey the fish tank waste water to the flood-and-drain plant grow bed (or grow channels if referring to a N.F.T. system).

Another thing to consider is gravity. Gravity will exert a constant downward pressure on the water in the aquaponics system. A pump used to lift water will be a fight against gravity. This means that the amount of water a pump can push will be reduced the more it has to lift the water. This will be discussed in more detail in the chapter covering pumps.

Gravity can also be used to provide a great advantage. It can be used to move water with no mechanical intervention. For instance, if a grow bed or grow channel is higher than the fish tank, then the overflow water can return to the fish tank directly through the use of gravity in a well designed system.

When considering plumbing, think about all the water that will be in your system. Such includes the water in the fish tank, grow beds or channels, sump if applicable, and in the pipes. The sum of that volume is the amount of water in the aquaponics system. As a general rule, for a flood-and drain system, the entire volume of water in the fish tank(s) should be moved every hour in order to maintain good water quality for the fish. This issue will be addressed in more detail in the water quality, pump, and flood-and-drain chapters.

As discussed in this chapter, and addressed in more detail later in the book, the 'head' of the system is how high in elevation the pump must move the water. Another item to consider is whether the system is to have a pump running continuously, or if it will have a timed flood and drain system. All of these factors together determine how much water

187

needs to be moved, and the time it takes to move it. Therefore, due diligence is important in plumbing design and pump size selection. The pumps, pipes and/or tubing need to be large enough to sufficiently convey the required volume of water, but not over-sized to the point where other problems are created.

Also, a well-designed system needs to have various controls and safety measures in place just in case there is any problem. Not to worry, as these issues can easily be determined, and they will be addressed in a user-friendly way later in this book. This chapter is meant to serve only as an introduction into these issues, and to emphasize that when selecting piping and/or tubing, it is better to pick slightly larger diameter plumbing component when possible.

Watertight Pipe Protrusion through Grow Beds and Fish Tanks

To achieve a watertight connection when passing a pipe or polyvinyl tubing through a fish tank wall, grow bed wall, or a N.F.T. grow channel a bulkhead fitting or a Uniseal can be used. Bulkheads are sturdier and work better for thick-walled applications, but also cost more than Uniseals.

The average price for a PVC bulkhead is approximately 25 percent more than a Uniseal.

Also, additional fittings are needed to connect the pipe to the bulkhead, whereas with a Uniseal, the pipe will slide through the opening (no additional fittings are needed).

For additional protection or if a drip leak is discovered after installation, with a Uniseal or a bulkhead fitting, heavily applied silicon caulking will often resolve the problem.

Bulkheads

Bulkheads come in a very wide variety of sizes and shapes, but can be easily assembled from parts readily available in most plumbing supply stores and home improvement centers, as well as online. Bulkhead fittings are identified by the size of the pipe it connects to, not the hole size. The bulkhead is a good, sturdy option for plumbing through a fish tank or grow bed. Bulkhead fittings are typically made of polyethylene, CPVC, PVC, polypropylene, Polytetrafluoroethylene (PTFE), and of various metallic materials. All types will work for aquaponics, so it makes sense to select the more common and inexpensive types, such as polyethylene, CPVC, or PVC.

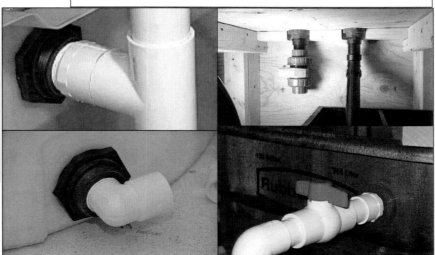

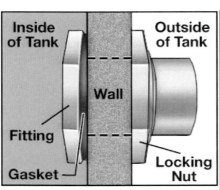

FIGURE 92. Bulkheads

Grommets (Uniseal®)

Grommets (Uniseal⁾ are rubber rings that fit into the holes that have been drilled into the tank. Uniseal is a company trade name. A uniseal is a grommet, but they are so common that most people refer to all grommets as 'unseals'. It is similar to people referring to drywall as sheetrock. Sheetrock is a company name. Drywall (also known as plasterboard, wallboard, sheetrock, gypsum board) is a panel made of gypsum plaster pressed between two thick sheets of paper. It is used to make interior walls and ceilings. Since most people in aquaponics and plumbing refer to a grommet as a 'unseal', the same will often be done throughout this book so as to hopefully help the reader better relate to the message being provided.

A uniseal clamps around the hole making a watertight connection; the PVC pipe can then be slotted into the seal. The seals usually allow the pipe to be installed in only one direction, thus providing a watertight seal between the pipe and the connector. Unseals are inexpensive, costing anywhere from about $2 to $15 (USA, year 2020), depending upon quality, size, and where it was purchased. They make it easy to put a pipe through a tank, and they can also be used with rounded surfaces thus making them particularly useful for plumbing into barrels and other like rounded containers.

Uniseals will even allow you to plumb directly into five gallon buckets, brute trash cans, or any type of round surface. They accept standard Sch. 40 or Sch. 80 PVC and allow DIY projects that once may have been very costly to complete much more affordable.

Uniseals are used to attach pipe to just about any container in situation where bulkheads will not work, or not preferred. The most common use for uniseals is on curved surfaces such as storage drums, buckets, or even other pipes.

The advantage to using a uniseal is that it is inexpensive, and provides for a quick and easy installation. A hole is cut in the side of the tank or grow bed, and then the rubbery black uniseal is inserted. Next, a

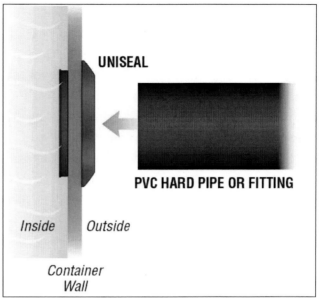

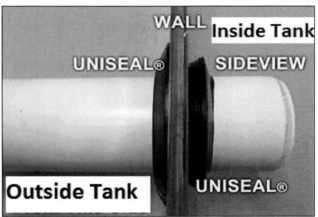

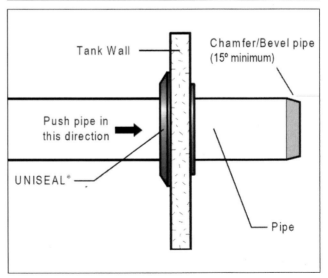

FIGURE 93. Grommets (Uniseal⁾)

slippery detergent film (i.e. dish soap) is applied to the exterior of the pipe. The pipe is then pushed through the seal completing the installation. When the pipe is pushed through the rubber-like uniseal from the outside, the uniseal becomes thin enough to allow the pipe to slip through. With this simple design, the uniseal solves many complex problems.

The disadvantage to using a uniseal is that it is prudent to replace them anytime you need to take out or reinstall the pipe, as they lose their watertight structural integrity. Also, they cannot be used in thick-walled applications. Lastly, in high pressure situations (for instance, in extremely tall tanks, but rare in aquaponics) a bulkhead would be a better choice.

Grommets (uniseals) have more than one dimension to consider. They are measured with both an inside and outside diameter; basically the thickness of the "wall" changes. Plus there is the thickness of the material the grommet is being used it as well.

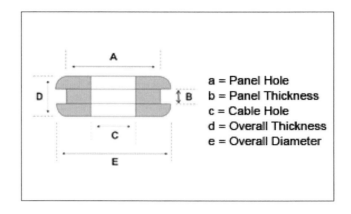

FIGURE 94. Grommet (Uniseal)

Uniseal Specifications

½" Uniseal
Fits Schedule 40 or 80, ½" pipe
Pipe ID — ½"
Hole saw size: 1 ¼" or 31.7mm (32mm)

¾" Uniseal
Fits schedule 40 or 80, ¾" pipe
Pipe ID — ¾"
Hole saw size: 1 ¼" or 31.7mm (32mm)

1" Uniseal
Fits schedule 40 or 80, 1" pipe
Pipe ID — 1"
Hole saw size: 1 ¾" or 44mm

1¼" Uniseal
Fits schedule 40 or 80, 1¼" pipe
Pipe ID — 1¼"
Hole saw size: 2" or 50.8mm

1½" Uniseal
Fits schedule 40 or 80, 1½" pipe
Pipe ID — 1 ½"
Hole saw size: 2½" or 64mm

2" Uniseal
Fits schedule 40 or 80, 2" pipe
Pipe ID — 2"
Hole saw size: 3" or 76mm

3" Uniseal
Pipe ID — 3"
Hole saw size: 4" or 102mm

4" Uniseal
Pipe ID — 4"
Hole saw size: 5" or 127mm

6" Uniseal
Pipe ID — 6"
Hole saw size: 7" or 177.8mm

Uniseal Installation Instructions

- Cut hole to the hole saw size indicated for the uniseal below.
- Ensure that the hole is clean with no sharp edges. Irregularities can cause a poor seal and leaks.
- Insert the uniseal into the hole with the wide flange on the outside of the container.
- Ensure the pipe end that will be inserted is clean of burs or sharp points. File the edges if needed.
- Insert the pipe into the uniseal. You can lubricate the pipe end with Windex. Most of it will be squeezed off during installation, but be sure to wash it out thoroughly after the pipe is inserted.

FIGURE 95.

Watertight Pipe Protrusion through a Liner

There are a number of devices that can be used to ensure a watertight seal where a pipe protrudes a liner. One item is a PVC liner boot. The PVC liner boot can either be built into the liner or made separate for field installation. A pipe coupler can also be used. A conduit flashing pipe boot (cone image below) also works well. The items can easily be obtained from your local plumbing supply store, hardware store, or home improvement center at a relatively low cost.

Pipe Maintenance

Periodic cleaning of pipes is a maintenance chore that should not be neglected. It will ensure that your aquaponics system continues to run efficiently, and that no unnecessary stress being placed upon pumps, plants, and fish. Pipe cleaning will remove blockage due to accumulation of algae, mosses, or other debris. Since each system is different, there is no hard and fast rule as to how often this should be done, but it is prudent to do it sooner and regularly rather than waiting until a problem occurs.

FIGURE 96.   *Several methods for making a watertight pipe protrusion through a liner.*

A drain snake is the most standard pipe cleaning method used. Drain snakes are available as either a manual or power operated tool. Running water through the pipe during and after the process is recommended. However, it is best to detour the cleaned waste debris out of your system, or catch it in a bucket, rather than allowing it to enter back into your system. Never use chemicals.

A power pressure spraying machine is ideal for cleaning pipes. They can typically be rented from home improvement centers, as well as tool rental stores. However, most backyard aquaponic setups are too small to warrant the rental cost.

A built in debris trap located underneath the grow bed on the fish tank return line will greatly help reduce accumulation of pipe clogging debris. The following figure provides several examples of debris traps and cleanouts:

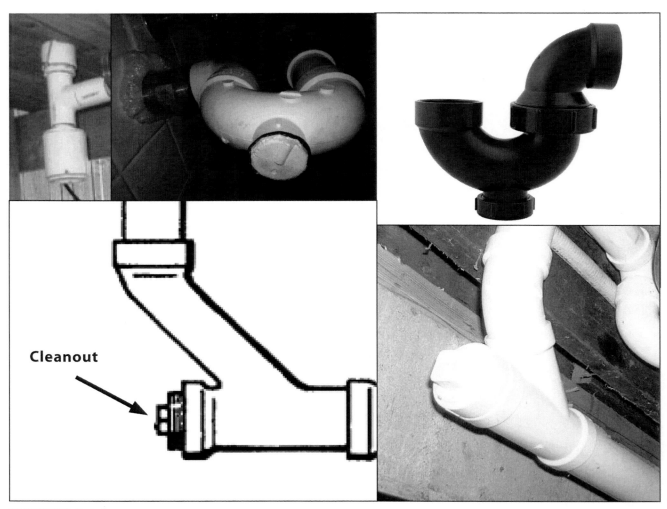

FIGURE 97. Debris traps

CHAPTER 16

Making a Water Tight Container

Making a Water Tight Wood Frame Container (DIY)

In addition to using a liner, as discussed previously, there are a variety of other waterproofing options available. The waterproofing materials discussed in this section are in the epoxy or resin categories, and adheres to the wood structure.

There are a variety of options available to seal a wood framed tank. Structural support is primarily achieved via a wood frame. Plywood and/or other boards are typically used for the walls and floor. The next step is to waterproof the container so that it will hold water.

The point of this section is not to endorse a particular product or method, but rather to provide comprehensive, unbiased, and reliable information about the primary methods that can be successfully implemented so that you can ultimately make your own educated decision. The following are other main methods in which to make a water-tight, sealed container (i.e. fish tank, grow bed, D.W.C. grow tank).

1. Two Part Epoxy Paint

A commonly used and reliable epoxy paint for plywood container builds is 'Sweetwater' epoxy available from Aquatic Ecosystems. It is non-toxic when cured and has good adhesion to lumber materials. This epoxy paint has solvents mixed in and is only 65-72 percent solids. It has strong, toxic fumes while curing, so a well-ventilated workspace is essential when using this product. It has a nice consistency and is very easy to work with and apply. Sweetwater can be used as a stand-alone product for waterproofing a wood container. It is important to have a well built structure when using this product as excessive flex could potentially contribute to leaks. Silicone will adhere well to Sweetwater so when sealing a tank with this method you should first apply the Sweetwater and then silicone (i.e. fish viewing windows, grommets, bulkheads, pipes, etc.).

Epoxy Paint Summary

PROS: Easy to apply, available in a range of colors, silicone will stick to it making window installation easy.
CONS: Toxic solvent requires well ventilated workspace, does not add structural strength to a container. Potential risk of failure in an inadequately supported tank with excessive flex.

2. Fiberglass Resin with Epoxy Paint Top Coat

Reinforcing a wood container with fiberglass is an excellent way to add structural strength to the build and impact resistance to a non-structural epoxy coating. An inexpensive way to apply fiberglass to a wood container is to apply a fiberglass resin to wet out the cloth. Lightweight fiberglass cloth and fiberglass resin are available from online vendors and are also generally easily found in home improvement centers such as *Home Depot* and *Lowes*, as well as in hardware stores such as *Ace Hardware*.

Fiberglass resin is generally a polyester resin and requires a small amount of hardener to be added as a catalyst. Effective application of fiberglass takes a little skill, but is fairly easy to learn with some practice. It is important to avoid bubbles in the fiberglass layer, which may ultimately pop and compromise the watertight seal. Polyester fiberglass resin is fairly inexpensive. It has a very strong toxic smell and requires a well ventilated workspace. In addition, it is not sufficient as a standalone waterproof barrier coating and will leach out chemicals into your system. Therefore, it is important to finish a fiberglass resin coated container with a non toxic, waterproof topcoat. Sweetwater epoxy (noted above) is an excellent product for this purpose. Using Sweetwater over a layer of fiberglass overcomes most of the potential cons of Sweewater alone.

Fiberglass Resin + Epoxy Paint Summary

PROS: A relatively inexpensive way to add structural strength and impact resistance to a wood container. The epoxy topcoat is available in a range of colors. Silicone will adhere to the epoxy topcoat.

CONS: Fiberglass application requires some practice and skill. Toxic fumes in the resin and paint require well ventilated workspace. Fiberglass resin is not sufficient as a stand-alone barrier coating.

3. Two-Part Marine Epoxy Resin

There are many different brands of epoxy resin available, but only true two-part marine epoxies should be used for wood frame aquaponic containers. These epoxies have a long established and successful history in waterproofing wooden boats. They differ from epoxy paints in that they are 100 percent solid. Several brands are available, but some tried and true options include:

- *West Systems 105* (one of the more expensive products).
- *US Composites* (an inexpensive option).
- *Max ACR* (relatively affordable epoxy being marketed specifically for aquatic applications)

There are many other marine epoxy brands available that can be used in aquaponics. The three noted above cover the spectrum of price and have all been successfully used in waterproofing wood containers.

Marine epoxies come as two-parts, a resin and a separate hardener, which have to be mixed in a precise ratio. It is best to use slow hardeners when sealing a wood container with these products so as to be provided a longer working time and better penetration into the wood. It is strongly recommend that instructions be thoroughly read, and a 'how to' video on the internet be watched before beginning to work with these products. An instructional video will be posted on the **www. FarmYourSpace.com** website.

Marine epoxies can be used as a standalone product to provide a completely waterproof and non-toxic coating for wood containers. However, they are fairly brittle when cured, can be susceptible to stress fractures at seams, and damage from impact which will compromise the barrier coating. The best way to avoid these issues is to incorporate a layer of fiberglass cloth into the epoxy resin. Epoxy resins can be used to wet out fiberglass cloth in much the same way as polyester fiberglass resin, but offer several advantages.

There is not a strong smell. The cured resin layer is completely waterproof, non-toxic, and is slightly less brittle than polyester resin. With the exception of cost, epoxy resin is an all around better option than polyester fiberglass resin. As discussed above, wetting out fiberglass cloth does take a little practice, but with a little skill is an excellent way to add significant structural strength to a wood container.

When used with thickening agents such as colloidal silica, marine epoxy can also function as an excellent adhesive, particularly for slightly loose joints or joints where high clamping pressure cannot be applied. It can therefore also be useful as a waterproof adhesive during the construction and assembly of a wood container.

Silicone will adhere well to epoxy resin, so waterproof the wood container first and then silicone in your any viewing windows, bulkheads, grommets, etc. Epoxy resins can be tinted with a coloring coating agent but will usually still show wood surface grain and joints. Sweetwater epoxy, mentioned above, can be used as a topcoat if solid color is desired.

Two-Part Marine Epoxy Summary

PROS: Can add significant structural strength to a wood container, particularly when used with fiberglass. Minimal smell. Effective standalone waterproof barrier layer. Silicone will stick to it making window installation easy.

CONS: Expensive and it can suffer from stress fractures if used without fiberglass on an inadequately supported structure.

4. Pond Shield

Pond Shield is a 100 percent solid, two-part epoxy resin available from Pond Armor. It is different enough from the marine epoxies described above that it is discussed here as a standalone waterproofing option. Pond shield is non-toxic, is almost odorless, and is safe to apply indoors. Pond shield is an extremely

thick epoxy which can make it somewhat challenging to work with. The black pond shield is the thickest and has a consistency slightly thinner than honey. It can be thinned marginally with denatured alcohol to make it more workable, but thinning also increases the risk of not getting the required thickness in a single coat. One 1.5qt kit of Pond Shield claims to cover 60sq ft at 10mil thickness. For many applications, a single coat is sufficient to get a 10mil coat that is completely waterproof.

Pond Shield is best suited for waterproofing well-supported structures with no flex. If there are concerns about the structural integrity of seams, it is best to fiberglass them in order to prevent the formation of potential stress fractures.

Pond Shield is ideal for sealing concrete and masonry tanks. While it adheres to wood, it holds even better to concrete and masonry. Therefore, one option when using it on a wood tank is to first line the inside with Hardiboard. If you instead choose to apply it directly to a wood tank, it is best to first do a light wash with 30-40 percent alcohol-thinned Pond Shield to get better penetration into the wood. Follow this with a single coat of un-thinned, or very slightly thinned, Pond Shield.

The thick consistency of Pond Shield can make it challenging to work with and may require touching up in some areas after the initial coat. Careful inspection and touch up is critical to the success of using this product.

Pond Shield Summary

PROS: Completely non-toxic and odor free. Available in a range of colors. Requires only a single coat and touch up. Silicone will stick to it making window installation easy.

CONS: Thick consistency can make it difficult to work with. While it remains somewhat flexible after curing, it is susceptible to stress fractures in poorly supported structures.

5. Liquid Rubber

These waterproofing products are elastomeric emulsions that remain highly flexible after curing. While there are a number of these products available, some examples of those that have been successfully used with wood containers are:

- *Zavlar* (named to Permadri Pond Coat in the US).
- *Ames Blue Max*.

These products have minimal odor and are easy to apply. *Zavlar* (Permadri Pond Coat) requires several coats to achieve a waterproof barrier of 40mil thickness. One gallon will cover 30 square feet at 40mil thickness.

The primary advantage of these products is that they're incredibly flexible, which allows them to stretch and resist fractures in inadequately supported structures. However, it is still a good idea to use drywall tape on seams while applying these products in order to reduce potential stress on the coating at these spots.

Zavlar (Permadri Pond Coat) will initially appear brown, but will dry to a black coating. However, this black coating will gradually turn back to brown after being submerged for a period of time. *Ames Blue Max* dries to a translucent blue color.

Zavlar (Permadri Pond Coat) will not cure when applied over silicone. Similarly, silicone will not adhere to cured *Zavlar* (Permadri Pond Coat). This incompatibility with silicone is a disadvantage of these products, but can be easily overcome. One strategy is to use butyl rubber, polyurethane caulk, or *3M 5200* instead of silicone when double waterproofing a viewing windows, grommets, and bulkheads.

As an additional measure of security, it is advisable to use a small amount of epoxy to first waterproof the area where a viewing window or bulkhead will be installed, such that epoxy layer bridges the seam between the *Zavlar* (Permadri Pond Coat) and silicone caulk. This way, in the event the *Zavlar* (Permadri Pond Coat) separates from the silicone caulk, the epoxy provides an additional waterproof layer that will prevent leakage.

Liquid Rubber Summary

PROS: Highly flexible coating resists fractures even in poorly supported tanks. Easy to apply. Minimal smell.
CONS: Limited choice of colors (brown in the case of *Zavlar*/Pond Coat, bright blue in the case of *Ames*). Incompatibility with silicone slightly complicates fish tank viewing window installation and backup waterproofing of grommets and bulkheads.

CHAPTER 17

Pumps & Choosing the Right Pump

Pumps: Overview

Choosing the right pump is often a challenging decision for the new comers to Aquaponics who desire to build their own system. The pumps main purpose is to lift water to a certain height and move a specified amount of water over a unit of time (i.e. gallons per minute, etc.). The perfect mechanical device for this purpose is energy efficient, inexpensive, reliable, and will last a long time with minimal maintenance.

As a general rule, the pump should circulate all of the water from the fish tank in the aquaponic system at least every two hours, but preferably closer to every hour, 24 hours a day, seven days a week. Make sure the pump you choose will meet this standard of cycling half your system's water every hour. For example, if you have 300 gallons of water in your fish tank, you will need a pump that can move at least 150 gallons per hour (2.5 gallons per minute).

An efficient and reliable pump for your aquaponics system is essential. Without a good quality pump that is specifically right for your system, you simply will not succeed.

The flow rate of your aquaponics pump will either be measured in gallons per hour (gph), gallons per minute (gpm), liters per hour (lph) or liters per minute

(lpm). **The flow rate will change depending on the head or the height the water must be pumped.** As the head increases the flow rate of your pump will decrease. Be sure to keep this in mind when deciding on your pump. The more head in your system, the more electricity will be required to move a specific amount of water. It takes one pound of pressure per square inch (PSI) to move water up 2.2 feet. The more head, the more pressure required to lift the water.

All pumps are different. One pump may take 100 watts to move five gallons per minute up 10 feet while another might only use 30 watts. The difference is how much energy is consumed and how much heat is produced. Daily power usage equals wattage of pump multiplied by 24 hours. Watt hours = wattage of pump x hours of operation.

Just as you need a powerful enough pump to do the job, make sure you do not get a grossly oversized pump. An oversized pump may move too much water out of your system or overly draw down the fish tank. It will also cause you unnecessary operating expense. Do not hastily jump in and find the first second-hand submersible pump that you see on the internet. You need the right pump for the specific operational characteristics of your system. Taking the time and doing your due diligence in selecting the right pump in the beginning will save you a lot of headache later. Your system must operate the way it is supposed to so you will not lose plants and/or fish.

When designing your system, strive to make it as efficient as possible in regards to pumping requirements. Keep the following in consideration:

- The higher the flow rate (amount of water being pumped), the more electricity will be required.
- The higher the water must be pumped (the higher the head), the higher the electricity consumption.
- A timer system will use less electricity than a siphon system as the pump will operate less.
- Keep in mind that the longer the pipe or hose run, the more turns, elbows, bends and fittings that are is the pump outflow line, the greater the friction head (pumping resistance), and thus, the harder the pump will need to work to overcome this resistance.

Steps for Selecting the Right Pump

1. Know the volume of your fish tank.
2. Determine how high (elevation difference) you need to pump the water. This is referred to a 'head', technically speaking. A pump simply capable of moving 40 gallons an hour could be suitable if the tank and the growing beds were adjacent on the same level, but an increase in height and distance between the tank and the growing beds will indicate you need a stronger pump. To calculate what size you need in regards to 'head', measure from the level of the pump intake up to the highest the water needs to be lifted which will be either over the rim of the growing beds, or over the rim of the filter-tank, depending on the system you will be using.

Evaluate the pump's efficiency, and don't be intimidated by this process. It is easy to learn about pump curves.

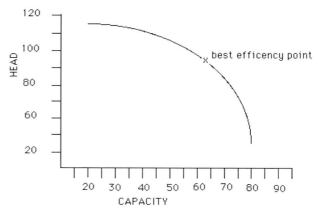

FIGURE 98. Pump efficiency curve.

How to Read a Pump Curve:

Figure 98 above shows the head of the pump with its capacity and optimal operating efficiency point. The head of a pump is read in feet or meters. The capacity units will be either gallons per minute, liters per minute, or cubic meters per hour. You can think of the above illustration in metric or imperial units, however you see fit.

The maximum head of this pump is 115 units. This is called the maximum shutoff head of the pump. Also note that the best efficiency point (BEP) of this impeller is between 80 percent and 85 percent of the shutoff head. This 80 percent to 85 percent is typical of centrifugal pumps. The pump manufacturer will typically provide you with the pump curve that will show the exact best efficiency point for the pump in consideration.

Ideally a pump would run at its best efficiency point all of the time, but we seldom hit ideal conditions. As you move away from the BEP, the shaft will deflect and the pump will experience some vibration. You'll have to check with your pump manufacturer to see how far you can safely deviate from the BEP and still get satisfactory operation (a maximum of 10 percent either side is typical)

The pump manufacturer typically states the maximum height the pump can efficiently move the water. Be wary of buying a model that does not supply that information. You may also want to consider using a pump that has a larger head than is strictly necessary for your aquaponics set-up. This will provide you with the option of diverting the water, should you ever have the need to do so, for maintenance or repair reasons.

Aeration of the water is extremely important and will affect the growth of both plants and fish. Water circulation through pumping action is typically the only way aeration is done in aquaponics, although some operators do use aerators. A good efficient pump may cost a little more to purchase, but plant and fish production can be maximized, and operating cost reduced; which can amount to a significant economic advantage over time.

Don't be fooled by advertisers boasting about horsepower, wattage, or voltage. Pump selection should never be made based upon these characteristics. Instead, selection of the pump needs to based entirely on flow rate, head, and pump efficiency. When these parameters closely match your system's parameters, then horsepower, voltage, and wattage will follow.

Customer reviews are helpful. Pumps that are extremely loud or produce a great deal of vibration can impede fish health via stress. User reviews are one of the best ways to determine if this may or may not be a problem with the pump you are considering. **Always have a spare pump on-hand.**

Check your pump regularly to ensure that the inlet is not clogged or partially clogged. As the pump pulls in water, debris can sometime cling to the inlet hole(s), inlet grate, or pump impeller. Some operators build a screen box for their pump to be housed in to help prevent clogging. Even so, it is wise to inspect and clean the screen box and pump regularly.

Maintain some type of back-up power system just in case your electricity is disrupted for an extended time. Imagine having to keep your pump working if the power went off for three weeks. Have an alternative plan in place and the necessary equipment readily available, just in case this happens. Refer to 'Chapter 22' for detailed information on back-up power, associated equipment and alternative energy options.

Shop around for the best pump at the best price. There are many places online where pumps can be purchased. Also remember that sometimes we get what we pay for, so be wary of exceptionally low priced pumps, as well as those on sale at a big discount store or have had the price reduced remarkably. Do your research.

Word of Caution

When buying a pump, or any other product, it is helpful to read product reviews by previous customers. Beware, though, as there are companies with large staffs, mostly located overseas, in which their business is influencing public opinion. For a fee, they will bombard various online retail outlets with positive comments, provide "Likes" or "Dislikes", give a thumbs up or down, and perform other such measures to sway opinion.

Some of the retail, media, and social websites they assail with this service is Facebook, Yelp, mainstream news articles, Yahoo, Google, Amazon, and various other online sites. Many manufacturers, suppliers, and even the federal government, use these companies to push their product or agenda. Coincidently, just before publication of this book I read a solicitation posting on Craigslist offering payment to individuals for posting positive reviews on certain Amazon product listing pages.

Therefore, read product and news article reviews with a skeptical eye. Sometimes it can be more helpful to read the negative product reviews. Obviously, those reviews noted as being from a 'verified purchase' are the most reliable.

CHAPTER 18

Filtration
(Mechanical, Biofiltration, Natural)

Filtration

All cultured organisms, vertebrates or invertebrates, finfish or shellfish, produce waste as a result of the nutrition they receive. Fish excrete ammonia (NH^3), mostly from their gills, and it dissolves in the water in which the fish must live. This waste product is toxic to the fish and is an environmental stressor that causes reduced appetite, reduced growth rate, and death at high concentrations.

Maintaining water quality is imperative for fish health. Even with the perfectly designed aquaponic system, it is not a bad idea to have a spare or supplemental filtering mechanism available. If water quality is becomes a concern (regularly or approaches threshold limits on occasion), supplemental filtration can be used (regularly, intermittently to maintain water quality, or just switched on as needed in those rare occasions until water quality reaches optimal conditions). Some aquaponic operators make their own biofilter while others purchase a filtration system. Supplemental filtration is usually needed with D.W.C. and N.F.T. systems; and sometimes necessary systems.

Natural Filtration

Of course the best filtration one can have in an aquaponic system is the grow beds themselves. Sized correctly, kept in a favorable temperature range year-round, and plants maintained properly, the flood-and-drain grow beds serve as the best natural filtration system one could hope to have for the fish tank. Even if the system is primarily set up to be a D.W.C. or N.F.T. system, adding grow beds as a supplemental filtration mechanism can help clean the fish tank while also producing healthy organic vegetables.

Grow beds are addressed in much more detail in the chapters of 'Part IV: Flood-and Drain System Design and Layout'. However, pertaining to our discussion here regarding the sole purpose of using grow beds for natural filtration it is prudent to consider the following guidelines:

- **Size the grow bed using a 1:1 ratio of grow bed volume to fish tank volume.**

The grow bed media should be at least 12-inches deep to allow for growing the widest variety of plants and to provide complete filtration. A grow bed with a freeboard of 1 to 2-inches above the top of the media is helpful in terms of practical application. This allows the operator to work within the media bed without spilling media or water on the floor. Therefore, a media bed 14-inches deep with 12-inches of media is recommended for optimal success.

Design the grow bed to be a working height that best suits the operator. An ergonomically correct height not only reduces strain on the back, arms and shoulders, but makes the aquaponics experience that much more enjoyable.

Turning over or stirring the bulk of the media within the grow bed every 4 to 12 months is beneficial. If using a liner, be sure not to get too close with your shovel or do anything else that may risk puncturing or tearing the liner.

Use a media guard around all plumbing fixtures. A media guard can be made from a wide variety of common hardware supplies, such as: window screen material, larger pipes, wood, aluminum, plastic, paint strainer, etc. A media guard will greatly facilitate cleaning and repair of plumbing fittings.

Mechanical Filtration

The easiest, but most costly, approach is to purchase a filtration unit. The size of filtration unit(s) is dependent upon the volume and operational characteristics of your system (i.e. numbers/size of fish, plant grow area/plant density, size of fish tank, etc.).

With so many variables, there is no easy formula for determining the size and number of filtration units needed, or how often they should be used. It is a trial and error process. One method however, is to purchase a filtration unit that is specified to address the volume of water contained within the fish tank.

For instance, assume you have one 400 gallon tank of fish within the normal recommended stocking density range (stocking density is addressed in Chapter 11), then the following type of filtration unit would be a wise choice. It is designed to for aquariums up to 400 gallons.

The Fluval FX6 High Performance Canister Filter has very good reviews (figure 99 on the following page). At the time of this writing , it is being sold by Amazon, Petco, Big Als Pets, Pet Mountain, Marine Depot, and other retailers for around $300 USA dollars (2022 prices). The author is not providing a recommendation to any of these merchants, just listing them as options. Furthermore, there are other similar product options which will also work equally as well. The referenced Fluval FX6 is provided here only as one viable option. Tank volumes in excess of 400 gallons would need multiple Fulval FX6 units or a larger filtrer.

Biofiltration

Biological filtration is the use of beneficial bacteria to eliminate organic waste compounds from a body of water. It is differs from mechanical filtration in that it is a process whereby water is strained and suspended material is physically removed from the water.

Adequate filtration (used to trap and remove solid waste) is especially important for N.F.T. and D.W.C. systems. **The minimum volume of this biofilter container should be one-sixth that of the fish tank.** Without proper filtration, solid and suspended waste will build up in the grow channels and canals and will clog the root surfaces. Solid waste accumulation causes blockages in pumps and plumbing components. Finally, unfiltered wastes will also create hazardous anaerobic spots in the system. These anaerobic spots can harbor bacteria that produce hydrogen sulphide, a very toxic and lethal gas for fish, produced from fermentation of solid wastes, which can often be detected as a rotten egg smell.

Biofiltration is the conversion of ammonia and nitrite into nitrate by living bacteria. A lot of fish waste is not filterable using a mechanical filter because the waste is dissolved directly in the water, and the size of these particles is too small to be mechanically removed. Therefore, in order to process this

Fluval FX6 High Performance Canister Filter

Product Overview:

- Super-capacity canister filter for aquariums up to 400 gallons
- Enhanced filter performance for superior aquarium water quality
- Includes all essential filtering media to streamline aquarium filtration

High performance canister filter boasts enhanced performance and setup ease. Fluval FX6 High Performance Canister Filter makes aquarium fish keeping easier and more convenient. A 1.5-gallon media capacity filter is powered by an energy-efficient pump with a 925-gph pump output that draws just 43 watts. The result is cleaner and healthier aquarium water while reducing operating costs. Fluval FX6 Canister Filter comes with all the essential filtering media to provide complete 3-stage filtration.

Multistage filter features removable media baskets precision engineered to eliminate water by-pass for efficient filtration. Each media basket is lined with a mechanical foam insert for effective mechanical pre-filtering. Instant-release T-handles let you lift and separate the baskets quickly and easily, making routine maintenance simpler. For freshwater or marine aquariums up to 400 gallons.

DIMENSIONS	PUMP GPH	MECHANICAL AREA	FILTER GPH	HEAD HEIGHT	WATTS
17" dia x 21" high	925 gph	325.5 in²	563 gph	10.8 ft	43W

FIGURE 99.

microscopic waste an aquaponic system uses microscopic bacteria.

In an aquaponic system, the biofilter is a deliberately installed component to house a majority of the living bacteria. The dynamic movement of water within a biofilter will break down very fine solids, which prevents. Biofiltration is unnecessary in the media bed systems (flood-and drain, ebb-and-flow) because the grow beds themselves serve as perfect biofilters.

The bacteria that do the work in a biological filter are part of the 'nitrogen cycle', which is compressively covered in 'Chapter 7: Nitrogen Cycle'. To summarize, fish constantly and continually excrete highly-toxic nitrogenous liquid waste from their bodies in the form of ammonia. If ammonia becomes too prevalent in the water, the fish will die. The ``nitrogen cycle'' (more precisely, the *nitrification* cycle) is the biological process that converts ammonia into other, relatively harmless nitrogen compounds. Several species of bacteria are involved in this process. Some species convert ammonia (NH_3) to nitrite ($NO2-$), while others convert nitrite to nitrate ($NO3-$). Thus, cycling the tank refers to the process of establishing bacterial colonies in the filter that convert ammonia -> nitrite -> nitrate.

Nitrates are one of the three forms of nitrogen found that plants use to grow and produce chlorophyll and proteins. It is a component of DNA, which transfers genetic information cell reproduction and plant reproduction.

By eliminating the organic waste compounds in the water, biological filtration detoxifies the water and makes it safe for fish. Additionally, by removing the organic waste compounds, algae is controlled because those compounds are the nutriment that algae require in order to grow.

A biological filter or "biofilter" is simply a home for the beneficial bacteria that perform the nitrogen cycle. The filter provides surface area that the bacteria can live on and a recirculating water pump ensures that water flows over the bacteria so they can obtain the nutrients and oxygen needed for survival.

The bacteria occur naturally in a fish tank or pond. They live on fish and other underwater surfaces. So if the bacteria occur naturally, then why is a bio filter necessary? It is because fish tanks have a much higher concentration of fish than would occur in nature, and the fish are usually fed a high-protein food. Hence, there is a higher concentration of organic waste (e.g. ammonia) than then naturally occurring bacteria can deal with. A biofilter houses a higher concentration of beneficial bacteria, so that ammonia and the other nitrogen compounds can be reduced to levels which are safe for the fish.

Why do tanks/ponds turn green?

Ammonia is at the root of most green water (algae) problems. As discussed above, ammonia forms naturally in fish tanks and ponds, and is toxic to fish. Ammonia can be reduced or eliminated by the beneficial bacteria in a properly operating bio-filter, but if it is not, the water could become toxic were it not for algae. Algae help protect fish—up to a certain point. As ammonia levels rise, algae will colonize the pond or tank by taking up the ammonia as nutrient. However, too much algae makes for an unsafe environment for fish. Some algae produce toxic chemicals that pose a threat to fish. The toxins are released into the water when the algae die and decay. However, algae's biggest threat to fish is its ability to deplete dissolved oxygen in the water; thus, causing the fish to suffocate.

Types of Biological filters

There are two basic types of bio-filters: in-tank/pond and out-of-tank/pond. Out-of-tank/pond filters are divided into two types — pressurized and non-pressurized. The main function of any type of bio-filter (i.e. providing a home to bacteria), is the same regardless of design. The differences are in cleaning, space requirements, and add-on enhancements. Out-of-tank/pond filters work best for aquaponics.

A bio-filter can be a manufactured purchased unit or constructed as a Do-It-Yourself (DIY) project. Both types will be discussed later in this chapter.

The primary purpose of a bio-filter is to provide surface area for beneficial bacteria to live on, the size of the filter depends upon the amount of organic waste the bacteria have to deal with. In aquaponics, the amount of waste is a function of the fish population and uneaten feed.

If the bacteria colony is not thriving, ammonia will accumulate and algae will colonize the tank or pond. The most common problems with bio-filters are allowing it to be depleted in wastewater, improper cleaning, chlorine or chloramine in the water supply and copper leaching into the water from copper pipes. Winter weather (cold temperatures) can also reduce or kill off bio-filter bacteria.

How to Make a Make a Low-Budget Media Ball Biofilter

The filter is made up of a specially designed inert material such as ceramic or plastic. Plastic is less expensive. Commonly used biofilter mediums are Bioballs®, Kaldnes® Bio Media®, and BioMax Balls®, which are proprietary products available from aquaculture supply stores, aquarium stores, and online. There are many other equally reliable brands on the market, as well. These products are designed to serve as ideal biofilter material, because they are small, specially shaped plastic items that have a very large surface area for their volume. Other media can be used, including volcanic gravel, plastic bottle caps, nylon shower poufs, netting, polyvinyl chloride (PVC) shavings and nylon scrub pads; however the plastic bio media balls work best. Any biofilter needs to have a high ratio of surface area to volume, be inert and be easy to rinse. Biofilter balls have almost double the surface area to volume ratio of volcanic gravel, and both have a higher ratio than plastic bottle caps. When using suboptimal biofilter material, it is important to fill the biofilter as much as possible, but even so the surface provided by the media may not sufficient to ensure adequate biofiltration. It is always better to oversize the biofilter, but secondary biofilters can be added later if necessary.

Biofilters occasionally need stirring or agitating to prevent clogging, and occasionally need rinsed if the solid waste has clogged them, creating anoxic zones. For cleaning, not all the media has to be removed. Removing and power washing approximately 75 percent of the media is usually sufficient. Leaving some media will help jump start good bacteria growth

standard type cleaning solvents. Cleaning solvent residue remaining on the balls can kill the good bacteria and introduce undesired contaminants into the aquaponic system.

Another required component for the biofilter is aeration. Nitrifying bacteria need adequate access to oxygen in order to oxidize the ammonia. One easy solution is to use an air pump, placing the air stones at the bottom of the container. This ensures that the bacteria have constantly high and stable DO concentrations. Air pumps also help break down any solid or suspended waste not captured by the mechanical separator by agitating and constantly moving the floating bio filter media balls. To further trap solids within the biofilter, it is also possible to insert a small cylindrical plastic bucket full of nylon netting (such as Perlon®), sponges or a net bag full of volcanic gravel at the inlet of the biofilter. The waste is trapped by this secondary filter. The trapped waste is also subject to mineralization and bacterial degradation.

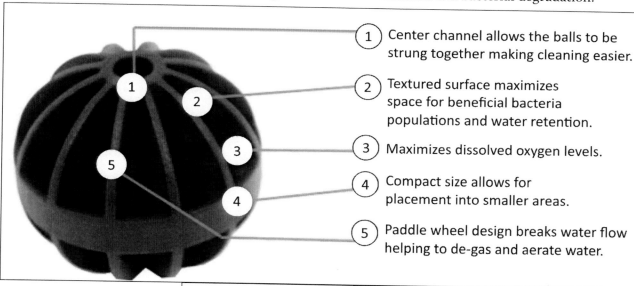

1. Center channel allows the balls to be strung together making cleaning easier.

2. Textured surface maximizes space for beneficial bacteria populations and water retention.

3. Maximizes dissolved oxygen levels.

4. Compact size allows for placement into smaller areas.

5. Paddle wheel design breaks water flow helping to de-gas and aerate water.

FIGURE 100.
Plastic biofilter media material.

How to Make a Low-Budget Polyester Woven Biofilter

A biological filter needs to be constructed out of non-corroding material such as plastic, fiberglass, ceramic or rock that has large amounts of surface area nitrifying bacteria cells can colonize. To make bio-filters more compact, material that has a large surface area per unit volume is usually chosen. This unit of measure is usually referred to as the specific surface area (SSA) of the biofilter media. Simply stated, the more surface area available, the more bacteria cells can be grown and the greater the nitrification capacity, which means that higher feed rates can be achieved. A biofilter with a higher SSA will be more compact than one with a lower SSA. Keep in mind, however, that some biofilter media with a higher SSA can become clogged with bacteria. Thus, there must be a balance between a high SSA and an operationally reliable biofilter media.

Below is an illustration of a homemade biofilter, followed by step-by-step instructions.

Steps to making a biofilter:

1. Determine if a biofilter is necessary. The necessity of a biofilter will vary greatly between D.W.C., N.F.T., and Flood-and-Drain systems. In some systems a biofilter may be an essential life support component that is in operation the all or the majority of the time (D.W.C. and N.F.T.), and in other systems, such a flood-and-drain system, the biofilter may just be a supplemental or backup component to ensure the integrity of water quality for the fish should the grow beds fail to keep up with filtration demands (e.g. during winter months, maintenance purposes, etc.). In some systems additional filtration may not be necessary at all.

There are two methods to determine if a biofilter (or any additional filtration) is needed. The first method is just a common sense approach. Take a look at the system (preferably during the design and planning phases) in regards to the volume of the fish tank, planned stocking density, plant grow areas, and consider whether or not the

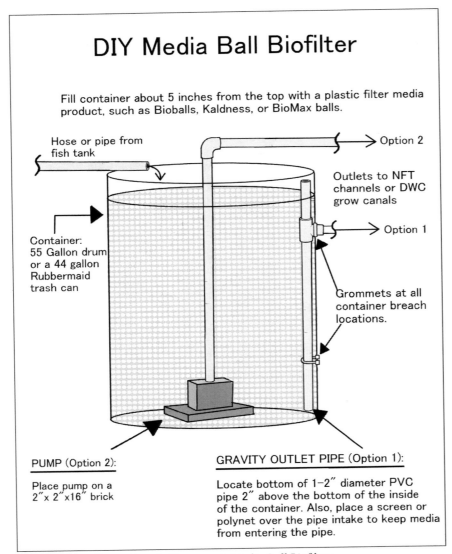

DIY Media Ball Biofilter

Fill container about 5 inches from the top with a plastic filter media product, such as Bioballs, Kaldness, or BioMax balls.

Hose or pipe from fish tank

Option 2

Outlets to NFT channels or DWC grow canals

Option 1

Container: 55 Gallon drum or a 44 gallon Rubbermaid trash can

Grommets at all container breach locations.

PUMP (Option 2):

Place pump on a 2"x 2"x16" brick

GRAVITY OUTLET PIPE (Option 1):

Locate bottom of 1–2" diameter PVC pipe 2" above the bottom of the inside of the container. Also, place a screen or polynet over the pipe intake to keep media from entering the pipe.

FIGURE 101. Illustration of a Homemade Media Ball Biofilter

system has enough plant grow area to provide adequate filtration. In most cases, it is easy to determine whether or not additional filtration is necessary just by taking a close look at the system.

The second approach is based upon water quality observations. Problems with water quality and/or algae are typically good indicators that additional filtration is needed. This can typically be addressed by either adding filtration or increasing plant filtration area (e.g. more N.F.T. grow trays, larger flood-and-drain grow bed volume).

It is possible to determine the size biofilter needed. This is no easy task, though, as size will vary greatly dependent upon the type of system and the need for additional filtration. For a densely stocked tank it is ideal to size the pump so that the tank is pumped out every hour. For a flood-and-drain system, this volume should pass through the grow bed(s) every hour. If the beds are sized properly, and working properly (not partially dormant because of cold temperatures, etc.), then additional filtration will not be necessary. However, for systems where additional filtration is needed, then the biofilter can be sized accordingly:

FIGURE 102. Above View of a Homemade Media Ball Biofilter (located between the fish tank and D.W.C. canals.

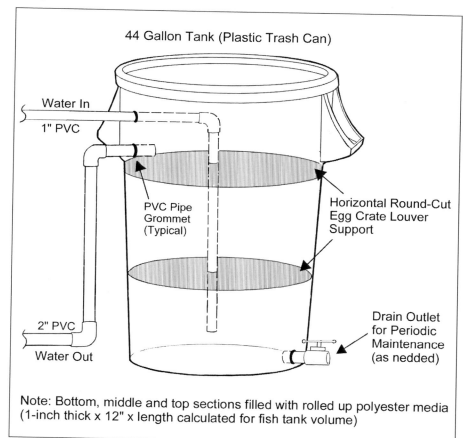

FIGURE 103. Homemade biofilter

- The ideal rate of filtration is 1/2 gallon of water per minute per square foot of biofilter bed. If your filtration is too fast it will result in insufficient exposure time to the bacteria.

- To calculate the size of your filter, figure the tank volume in gallons and divide by 60 (minutes). This equals the square footage of your biofilter material. This 'area' is the TOTAL area of filter material put it in biofilter unit. It will be cut to size and rolled up.

- Acquire the supplies needed:
  - » One 44-gallon Rubbermaid (or equal) round trash can. See figure 104 below.

FIGURE 104.   Standard 44-gallon plastic drum.

  - » A roll of 1-inch thick HVAC cleanable reusable filter (typically polyester). See figure 105 below.

FIGURE 105.   HVAC cleanable reusable filter material.

NOTE: Any of the media materials described in Chapter 20 'Growing Media for Plants' would work. However, the advantage of using rolled up HVAC cleanable reusable filter material is that in addition to the micro-surface area it provides for bacteria adhesion and growth, it is easy to clean — just unroll it and blast it with water. Use a pressure sprayer to blast it clean if it becomes too clogged for a garden hose to do the job.

Another option is 1-inch thick dual sided poly fiber filter made of 100 percent polyester specifically for Koi ponds (see figure 106). It is washable or inexpensive enough that it can simply be replaced. It cost approximately $12 for a 12-inch by 120-inch roll (year 2022 USA dollars). It is available on line through eBay, Amazon, and various aquarium supply websites. Many local aquarium shops also carry it, or can order it for you.

FIGURE 106.
Dual sided poly fiber filter filter material.

- PVC plumbing pipe and fittings:
  - » 3/4" PVC Pipe (2)
  - » 2" PVC Pipe (1)
  - » 1" PVC Pipe (1)
  - » 2" 90 Degree Elbows (2)
  - » 2" Male Adapter, for 1/2 of bulkhead adapter
  - » 2" Female Adapter, for 1/2 of bulkhead adapter

» 1" Male Adapter, (2), for 1/2 of bulk-head adapters

» 1" Female Adapter, (2), for 1/2 of bulk-head adapters

» 1" 90 Degree Elbows (1)

» 1" PVC Pipe to Garden Hose Fitting (2)

» 3/4" 90 Degree Elbows (8), for supports

» 3/4" Kris Cross Fitting (2), for supports

» 3/4" PVC fittings to get from the pump to a garden hose on the outside of the box.

• Egg Crate Louver from overhead fluorescent light fixture, for supports. Cut to fit horizontally in the 44-gallon trash can. See photos below for various examples.

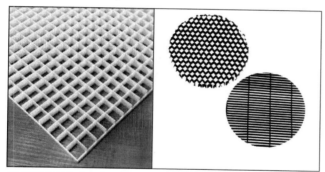

FIGURE 107. *Dual sided poly fiber filter made of 100 percent polyester.*

• Install the plumbing as shown in the DIY illustration below.

• Cut the HVAC cleanable reusable filter area previous calculated.

• Install ¼ of the previously determined HVAC cleanable reusable filter area in the bottom third of the 44-gallon can (this filter material should be rolled up like a newspaper).

• Place a round-cut egg crate louver support horizontally on top of the rolled-up reusable filter material.

• Install ½ of the previously determined reusable filter area in the middle third of the 44-gallon can (this filter material should also be rolled up) on top of the round-cut egg crate louver horizontal support.

• Place the second round-cut egg crate louver horizontally on top of the rolled-up reusable filter material that was placed in the middle section of the can.

• On top of the second horizontally placed round-cut egg crate louver support, install the remaining ¼ of the reusable filter area in the top third of the 44-gallon can (this filter material is also to be rolled up).

Purchasing a Biofilter

Or those aquaponic operators would rather purchase a biofilter than make one, there are many options available. Below is one option that works well for aquaponic systems. The cost for the below biofilter is approximately $90 (USA, year 2022).

TetraPond Clear Choice Biofilter PF1
by Tetra Pond (figure 108)

• Works with fish tanks up to 500 gallons.

• Mechanical pre-filter sponges remove suspended debris to improve water clarity.

• Interchangeable .75" and 1" diameter intake fittings.

• Bio Ring media provide large surface areas for beneficial aerobic bacteria.

• Easy out-of-tank accessibility and simple maintenance.

• *ClearChoice* biofiltration removes these contaminants and ammonia using its advanced Trickle Flow and and Bio Ring technologies.

The *TetraPond ClearChoice BioFilter* works to keep your pond clean through biological and mechanical filtration. This easy-to-use system filters coarse debris and provides biological filtration media with massive surface area for beneficial bacteria to colonize and remove harmful pollutants. The *ClearChoice BioFilter* utilizes a unique Venturi system, which draws air into the in-flowing water, creating ideal

FIGURE 108. TetraPond Clear Choice Biofilter PF-1.

conditions for the beneficial bacteria to decompose waste. Take a look at the information below to see how the *ClearChoice BioFilter* could benefit your aquaponic system.

How the TetraPond Clear Choice Biofilter PF1 Works

STAGE 1: Fish water is pumped into the filter. It passes through the foam, which sieves coarse suspended debris from the water (Mechanical Filtration).

STAGE 2: The water from stage 1 then passes through the finer foam, which provides further filtration.

STAGE 3: The final purification process of the water occurs on the surface of the biological filtration media. Beneficial bacteria will naturally colonize on this massive surface area and convert the harmful pollutants in the water into relatively harmless nitrates, which are absorbed by the aquatic plants or removed in partial water changes.

The Tetra Venturi and Trickle-Flow System

The water inlet into your filter is fitted with an advanced Venturi system, which draws air into the in-flowing water, creating ideal conditions for the beneficial bacteria to decompose waste. This, when combined with the use of "Trickle Filtration" encourages the prolific growth of beneficial bacteria, which helps to keep the pond free of pollutants.

Recommended Pump

TetraPond recommends the *TetraPond Water Garden Pump* 325 GPH or 550 GPH. Do not use pumps with flows that exceed 550 gallons per hour unless a flow control valve is used.

CHAPTER 19

Growing Media for Plants (Flood-and-Drain System)

Grow Media

Grow media is used in most aquaponic systems. It is even used in N.F.T. and D.W.C. aquaponic operations. In N.F.T. and D.W.C. operations net containers are typically filled with media to help anchor the plants.

However, it is used in abundance in flood-and-drain systems, as the grow beds are filled with media. The media is needed for anchoring of the roots to support the plants and to increase the surface area on which the beneficial bacteria cling to and live. With the help of bacteria and plants, the media also acts as a bio-filter. With the right media, and a balanced system, the grow bed becomes a very suitable habitat for the beneficial bacteria.

The most commonly used media to fill the grow beds in a flow-and-drain system are expanded clay pellets and gravel. The grow media anchors plants, is home to beneficial bacteria, and in some cases can even be used to raise worms. Some operators add worms to further aid in the break down accumulated solids and sediment. A surplus of worms to feed to the fish is a bonus for those raising carnivorous fish.

Factors to Consider when Choosing the Media

Particle size should be 8-16 mm (3/8–5/8 inches). If the particles are too small, the air space in between the particles is limited and the flow of water can be obstructed. Plant roots require oxygen and good water circulation. If the particles are too big, the surface area is greatly reduced and the plant roots would not be as well-anchored.

The pH of the media should be neutral. Expanded clay and most river stones are pH neutral. However, not all gravel is pH neutral. Some local crushed rocks or gravel contain limestone or other pH minerals, which are undesirable. Therefore, always know what you are getting before purchasing media.

For a flood-and-drain system, since gravel, plus the weight of water, is so heavy it is important to design and build strong supporting stands to withstand the weight. Expanded clay is lighter, but it is considerably more expensive than gravel. To reduce cost, it is perfectly acceptable to fill the bottom portion of the grow beds with gravel and the top with clay.

Growing Media Options

Table 26 below is a summary of several different growing media types, and their various pro's and con's.

TABLE 15. **Media Comparison Chart (Pros and Cons)**

	COST	WEIGHT	pH IMPACT	WATER RETENTION	DUST/ DEBRIS	AVAILABILITY
Gravel	Low	High	Possibly	Lowest	Needs Initial Rinse Only	Common
Sand	Low	Highest	Possibly	Low	Possibly	Common
Lava Rock	High	Medium	No	Medium	Needs Initial Rinse Only	Uncommon
Coir	Medium	Lowest	Yes	Medium	Yes	Common
Rockwool	Medium	Low	No	High	No	Uncommon
Hydroton	High	Medium	No	High	Needs Initial Rinse Only	Uncommon
Perlite/ Vermiculite	Low	Low	No	Medium	Needs Initial Rinse	Common

NOTE: Only the most common media options are listed in this table. Other viable media options are discussed in this chapter. In addition, various media options can also be combined into one media mix.

Expanded Clay Pellets

Expanded clay is lightweight and porous, allowing an abundance of air, water, and nutrients to reach the plants. It holds roots well and supports the beneficial bacteria necessary to convert the ammonia waste from the fish tank into nitrogen for the plants. Expanded clay mixes well with gravel. Expanded clay pebbles are often referred to as Hydroton, which is a really just a company's brand name for the product. It

FIGURE 109. Image shows a close-up view of Expanded Clay Pellets

is also relatively easy to work with, although usually the most expensive of all mediums.

Expanded Slate

Expanded slate is mostly used as a traditional gardening soil additive, but it works well as a medium in aquaponics since it has a large surface area for the roots to grip; however, it is still lightweight. It is also less expensive than expanded clay. Expanded slate mixes well with pea gravel.

Gravel

Pea gravel contains small particles of gravel, most commonly produced by running gravel through a screen. Pea gravel and crushed gravel, another common aquaponics medium, provide additional substrate to mix with larger aquaponics media and serve as biofilter for the fish waste and home for the bacteria that nitrify it. Gravel is an excellent choice of aquaponics medium when mixed with other mediums that retain water, but it doesn't work well on its own because it doesn't hold water well. It also isn't large or heavy enough to provide the plant roots the support they need and can easily damage them. Crushed basalt is frequently used in place of gravel, although it provides both the same benefits and drawbacks. River stones are a slightly larger alternative (about the size of marbles) which provide many of the same benefits without the drawbacks.

Avoid gravel that has points or sharp edges as it can wreak havoc on hands, liners, and plant roots. Plant roots move about when exposed to running water through a flood-and-drain system. Gravel with sharp edges will damage or even cut the roots if gravel with sharp edges or points are used. Again, remember that it is heavy and stronger supports than usual will be needed to hold the weight of the gravel and water. As mentioned above, be sure to rinse the gravel well before adding it to your system.

Sand

Media beds filled with coarse larger type sand (not silt or fine sand) can make a good aquaponic sub-strate because sand retains and circulates water well. However, be sure to have a screen, which can be easily accessed for regular cleaning, so as to prevent sand from entering the fish tank and/or doing damage to the pump. Also, sand can sometimes be contaminated with with clay particles. Clay particles are very fine and will mix with the water causing silt problems through the system.

Perlite

Perlite is a naturally occurring volcanic glass produced by hydrating obsidian. Perlite is a popular growing medium used by itself or as a mixture with other mediums. Perlite is commonly used with vermiculite (as a 50 — 50 mix), and is also one of the major ingredients of within a soilless mix. Perlite is also relatively inexpensive. Perlite does not retain water well, which means that it will dry out quickly between watering.

Unfortunately, perlite dust is bad for your health, so you should always wear a dust mask when handling it. Another drawback is that without proper screening at the drain outlet and/or via of a filter cage around the pump, the pump and emitters can become clogged and rendered useless.

Coconut Fiber

Coconut fiber (also called 'Coir') is rapidly becoming a popular growing medium. Coconut fiber is essentially a waste product of the coconut industry. It is the powdered husks of the coconut itself.

There are many advantages. It maintains a large oxygen capacity, yet also has excellent water holding ability, which is a real advantage for most systems that have intermittent watering cycles.

Coconut fiber is also high in root stimulating hormones and offers some protection against root diseases including fungus infestation. A large contingent of growers in the Netherlanders have found that a mixture of 50 percent coconut fiber and 50 percent expanded clay pellets is the perfect growing medium.

One word of caution, you must be careful not to purchase the commonly available, lower grade coconut fiber that has a high concentration of sea-salt and is very finely grained. This lower grade coconut fiber will lead to disappointing results for plants, and can negativity impact water quality, thus being detrimental to the fish. Also, coconut fiber tends to only last 3 to 4 years before it biodegrades.

Pumice

Siliceous material of volcanic origin, inert, has high water-holding water capacity, and high air-filled porosity.

Scoria

Porous, volcanic rock, fine grades used in germination mixes, lighter, and tends to hold more water than sand.

Polyurethane

Polyurethane is a relatively new material for aquaponics which typically holds 75 to 80 percent air space and has about a 35 percent water-holding capacity.

Composted Pine Bark

Composted pine bark combines an optimum water-retentive capacity together with good drainage. A medium size product does not need to be mixed The problem is that sawdust from certain treeswith any other media types. It is cost effective and it works.

Sawdust

The right kind of sawdust, with medium to course texture, is good for short-term uses, has reasonable water-holding capacity, and good aeration qualities. The problem is that sawdust from certain trees (i.e. western red cedar, etc.) can be harmful to plants and fish. Furthermore, the lumber industry sometimes uses chemical sprays on their materials. So unless you know for certain that your sawdust will not impact your pH and be harmful to fish or plants, it is best to stay away for it.

Vermiculite

Vermiculite is most frequently used in conjunction with perlite as the two complement each other well. Vermiculite retains moisture (about 200 percent–300 percent by weight), which is the opposite of perlite, so it is easier to balance your growing medium so that it retains water and nutrients well, but still supplies the roots with plenty of oxygen. A 50/50 mix of vermiculite and perlite is a very popular medium for drip type hydroponic and aquaponic systems. Vermiculite is inexpensive. It should never be used alone, as is it retains too much water and can suffocate the roots of plants if used straight.

Soilless Mix

There are many kinds of soilless mix's containing a vast assortment of ingredients. These mixes can be purchased or created by the do-it-yourself enthusiast. Many operators create their own mix using a wide variety of ingredients such as expanded clay pellets, sphagnum moss, perlite, and vermiculite.

Beware to take the proper precautions when using a soil mix as they can have some very fine particles that will clog pumps and drip emitters. If using any ingredient with fine particles, be sure to install a good filtration system. Panty hose and paint strainers serve as good filters when used on the return line and/or on a small cage around the pump. This will prevent fine particles from damaging the pump and interfering with emitters.

Most soilless mixes retain water well and have great wicking action while still holding a good amount of air, making them a good growing medium for aquaponic grow beds.

Sphagnum Moss / Peat Moss

Peat moss (also referred to as 'Sphagnum Moss') is the partially decomposed remains of formerly living sphagnum moss from bogs. Peat moss has long strands of highly absorbent, sponge-like material that hold and retain large amounts of water while simultaneously having good aeration. Sphagnum is usually purchased in dry, compressed blocks, and works best if soaked for approximately one hour before use.

A problem with this growing medium is that it can decompose over time and will shed small particles that can plug up your pump or drip emitters. Although, the biggest problem with peat moss is that it's environmentally bankrupt. Peat moss is mined, which involves scraping off the top layer of living bog. A sphagnum peat bog is a habitat for plants and animals; common as well as rare and endangered animals. Despite manufacturers' claims that the bogs are easy to restore, the delicate community that inhabits the bog cannot be quickly re-established. Yes, peat moss is a renewable resource, but it can take hundreds of years for the natural habitat and ecosystem to be restored. Like all precious wetlands, peat bogs purify fresh air and even mitigate flood damage. Many conservationists, gardeners, and wetland scientists from all over the world have recommended a boycott of peat. Coir (a natural fiber extracted from the husk of coconut) has been touted as a sustainable alternative to peat moss as a growing media. Another viable peat moss alternative is manufactured in the USA (California) from sustainably harvested redwood fiber.

Rice Hulls

Rice hulls are a lesser known and underutilized substrate in most parts of the world, but they have proven to be as effective as perlite for the production of a wide range of crops. Rice hulls are a by-product of rice production and are typically inexpensive in rice production areas.

This free-draining substrate has low to moderate water-holding capacity, a slow rate of decomposition and low level of nutrients. However, rice hulls have a tendency to build up salt and decompose after one or two crops, so they should be replaced often.

Rockwool/Stone Wool

Made from rock that has been melted and spun into fibrous cubes and growing slabs, rockwool (also referred to as 'Stone Wool') has the texture of insulation and provides roots with a good balance of water and oxygen. Rockwool is suitable for plants of all sizes, from seeds and cuttings to large plants.

Rockwool is considered by many commercial growers to be the ideal substrate because of its unique structure. Rockwool can hold water and retain sufficient air space (at least 18 percent) to promote optimum root growth. Since Rockwool exhibits a slow, steady drainage profile, the crop can be manipulated more precisely between vegetative and generative growth without fear of drastic changes in pH.

Note that some Rockwool products require an overnight water soak before usage, as the bonding agents used to form slabs can result in high pH. Additionally, there has been a growing concern about disposing Rockwool after use because it never truly decomposes.

Oasis cubes

These lightweight pre-formed cubes are designed for propagation. A very popular medium for use when growing plants from seed or from cuttings. This product has a neutral pH and retains water very well. The cubes are meant to be a starter medium only. They typically come in three sizes, up to 2" x 2". They can be easily transplanted into practically any kind of hydroponic system or growing medium (or into soil).

CHAPTER 20

Greenhouses

Do you need a controlled plant-growing environment (a greenhouse)?

No matter how well your aquaponic system constructed it will not function to maximum capacity if the environmental conditions are outside the comfort zone for the fish and plants. A controlled environment greenhouse can provide natural sunlight, proper temperature, humidity and ventilation. Greenhouses can be designed for every climate, from the tropics to northern climates with extreme winters. Artificial lighting can also be utilized for up to a few hours each day during winter months allowing for production of any crop. Greenhouses can also include bio-security features.

Bio-Security

Bio-security is a combination of equipment and procedures that you implement to keep your food safe. Essentially, bio-security is an implemented process that keeps pathogens and pests out of the greenhouse so that plants stay healthy and your food is never contaminated via air-borne pollutants. It is astonishing to learn about all of the air-borne contaminates that can settle on our fruit and vegetables when planted outdoors. Needless to say, the more we can do in

regards to taking precautionary measures to prevent pollutants and toxins from coming into contact with our food, the better. Greenhouses provide an extra measure of security against toxic food.

Greenhouse Basics

A greenhouse is used to increase crop production and ensure that produce can be enjoyed throughout the year. It can also be a means of giving plants a head start on spring outdoor planting.

The costs of building a greenhouse can vary from several hundred dollars to tens of thousands of dollars. Likewise, operating costs can be relative low or very high depending upon location, regional climate, type of greenhouse constructed, materials used, energy supply system(s), and how much additional heating, cooling, or lighting is required.

A greenhouse can be built using traditional methods, purchasing a kit, or installed by a contractor. Before you decide whether to build or buy, determine your needs in regards to preferred size, available space, and desired level of production. A greenhouse is a long-term investment that should provide the growing area and service desired while blending well with the home and landscape. Also, keep in mind the option to expand the greenhouse size at a later date, should such be a possibility. With an open mind, examine as many greenhouse styles and equipment options as possible in person, books, and through the Internet before making a decision.

Greenhouse Kits

Kits are the most common method of establishing a greenhouse. Greenhouse kits are available in a wide range of costs and with a wide range of features. Prices range from a few hundred dollars to well over $25,000 depending on the size, style, accessories, and type of construction materials.

Greenhouse manufacturers and vendors are numerous. Some reputable, and others not. Some offer affordable, reliable, and practical greenhouses, and others offer products that are in the poor investment category. Thorough research is a must. My book on 'Greenhouses' addresses these issues, will save you enormous amounts of time, and will help you avoid a costly mistake.

Compare costs and features for the style and size you are interested in. Generally, plastic-covered greenhouses are easier to assemble than glass houses. If any aspect of the assembly is beyond your skills and/or available time, many manufacturers and contractors will erect their products on-site for an additional fee.

Building Your Own Greenhouse

A kit, although common, is certainly not the only way to go. A greenhouse can be constructed easily and inexpensively by anyone able to use simple hand tools. Most of the construction materials can be purchased at building supply stores. Materials may also be available inexpensively at construction sites, through Craigslist, Facebook Market Place, and building supply salvage yards. If any aspect of the construction is beyond your skills, you can hire a local carpenter or handyman to help. Plans for different styles of hobby greenhouses can be acquired online and through most libraries.

When you do decide to build a greenhouse, choosing the type of structure, covering, and environmental control equipment can be confusing. This book will empower you with a user-friendly approach that will address your needs your needs can help you organize the planning and implementation of your hobby greenhouse.

Greenhouse Needs

When deciding upon a greenhouse you need to consider what type of plants you prefer to grow, what seasons of year you will use the greenhouse, and how a greenhouse fits into your lifestyle. For example, you might want to use the greenhouse in one of the following ways:

- To start vegetable or flower seeds or propagate cuttings in the spring to plant in the garden. On a small scale, this can be accomplished with a structure as simple as an outdoor cold frame or hotbed. A freestanding greenhouse can also be used for this purpose. This would be a simple and inexpensive model.

- To grow year-round tropical foliage in a conservatory setting. A greenhouse for this purpose will probably be more permanent and formal.

- To grow specialty flowers or ornamentals. Many greenhouses are constructed because owners develop an interest in specialty flowers or ornamentals that have unique requirements, such as orchids, African violets, or bromeliads. These greenhouses should be designed with the needs of the particular plant in mind.

- A greenhouse can be a part of your home in the form of a sun-room or porch. Sunrooms or porches usually have clear covering on one or more sides but not on the roof. A greenhouse can also be attached to the house, with an entrance to the living area. Plants, walks, furniture, a water pond, or a fountain may also be included and arranged formally or informally as an extended living room. Plants may "spill over" from the greenhouse through a sliding glass door into the living area of the home. This type of greenhouse can be used for relaxing, reading, or family gatherings.

- A greenhouse can be used as a production facility providing year-round produce. In this case, it is also good to consider allocating a portion of the greenhouse as a work area.

Greenhouse Location Importance

Often, there may be a limited choice of locations that will have adequate sunlight, adequate soil drainage, easy access for people and materials, access to utilities, and a pleasing blend with the landscape. For many homeowners, the appearance of the structure is most important, so compromises must be made to meet other location requirements. The exact size and shape of the property will have a direct impact upon the size of greenhouse that can be erected.

An extremely important location considerations is sun exposure. Many plants require full sun to perform well. A freestanding greenhouse for these plants should be constructed with the long sides of the building facing southeast to southwest (Figure 110). Vegetable and flower seedlings for transplanting outdoors in the spring need maximum sunlight, so choose a location that receives full sun. For plants requiring less light, the greenhouse can face northeast to southeast or northwest to southwest.

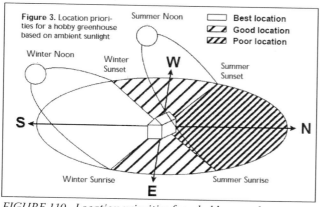

FIGURE 110. *Location priorities for a hobby greenhouse based on ambient sunlight*

Exposure is particularly important for attached greenhouses. Consider these locations in order: first—south or southeast, second—east, third—southwest, fourth—west, and last—north.

Keep in mind that a western exposure can be too hot in summer, and a northern exposure usually does not receive enough light for most plants. Also, be aware that tall structures and trees near the greenhouse may block light for parts of the day.

Falling limbs can also be a major problem if the greenhouse is located too close to trees.

Other location considerations include ensuring that the site is level and that the soil drains well. Many locations may have to be graded to ensure that the foundation is level. Slope the soil away from the greenhouse to drain rainwater away. If drainage is a problem, consider installing drainage tile before constructing the greenhouse.

Avoid low areas with poor air circulation, especially those surrounded by woods or buildings. Cold, humid air can stagnate in these locations and increase heating costs. Conversely, avoid high elevations with direct exposure to strong winter winds. Convective heat loss through the covering material can increase heating demand. Wind can also wreak havoc on polyethylene film coverings.

The greenhouse should be convenient to a driveway to receive supplies and to haul away plants or garbage when needed. Walkways to and from the garden, house, and storage areas and access to water, fuel for heating, and electricity should all be considered.

The greenhouse should contribute to the appearance of the home and landscape and not be an eyesore either to the owner or neighbors. Consider room for expansion if you think you may be so inclined in the future.

Commercial Greenhouse Considerations

If you plan to have a commercial retail operation then it is important to be visible and easily accessible to customers. It is also prudent to plan for expansion. Therefore, make sure there is enough room to grow until you can afford to purchase more property for the business. Make sure the property is zoned for business. Check to see if zoning is likely to change in the near future or if it has been disputed in the recent past. Also, check to see if there are any special restrictive clauses that may inhibit future expansion, as well as regulations on the size or height of signs would be needed to promote your business.

The business should be close enough to major roads for delivery and transport trucks to have easy access. Check to see if there are any weight limits or restrictions on large trucks that would need to access your business. For a retail greenhouse, locate the business so customers can see it from at least 200 feet and can get to the business easily and safely. A lot of shopping is done on impulse. The more customers have to cross major barriers or make a special effort to get to your business, the less likely they will do business with you.

Water quality and availability for a Commercial Greenhouse Operation

Is city water available or will you have to dig a well? If you dig a well, how much water is available and how long will it last? Most commercial greenhouses require about 6 acre feet of water per year for every acre of greenhouse production area. Regardless of the source, have a water quality test performed. This is an inexpensive, easy procedure that may save a lot of money in the future.

Private labs or your County Extension Agent will usually provide assistance in taking a water sample and have it analyzed. Check the level of soluble salts and bicarbonates. Low soluble salts, a level below 0.75 mmhos/cm, is best because fertilizer is often added to the water during irrigation. When present in excess amounts, some salts are toxic to plants. Water bicarbonate level is important in plant production.

A bicarbonate level of less than 100 ppm (parts per million) is recommended for growing most plants. It is also prudent to to create a plan for water collection and a plan for water runoff from your greenhouse.

Proper Size Greenhouse for Your Needs

Available space and cost usually have a large impact on the choice of size for a greenhouse. Keep in mind, however, that a greenhouse that is too small may cost more to operate than the initial cost of building a larger one. The obvious problem with a small greenhouse is that it is too small to meet the needs of the owner. In addition, temperatures can fluctuate rapidly in a small greenhouse, and heat losses can be as high as they are in a larger greenhouse. Small greenhouses may also have limited headroom and be hard to work in. A taller, larger greenhouse obviously has more space, and it heats and cools more uniformly than a shorter, smaller one.

As a starting point for a small greenhouse, 100 square feet would be a minimum size, but 200 square feet is better. A house 9 to 14 feet wide by 20 feet long can be managed in a few hours per week. A larger greenhouse can also cost less to cover per square foot than a small greenhouse, so choose a size slightly larger than you think you need. On the other hand, ask if you have the time and dedication to maintain a large greenhouse, now and in the future.

Utilities and Permits for Your Greenhouse

It is best to check with your local governing agency planner and/or local building codes before building a greenhouse on your property. Some county or city codes prohibit greenhouses or place restrictions on size, type, covering, or construction materials. Some agencies have restrictions on property location placement. Most utility companies require that a permit for a structure be shown to them before they will connect utilities to it.

It is also a good idea to check with the local electric company. In some areas, the utility company may request a utility pole and separate meter for the greenhouse. Be sure all electrical work is performed by a licensed electrician according to code.

Water can usually be plumbed from the home supply line as long as the volume and pressure are adequate. Install a backflow prevention valve in the water supply line to prevent the possibility of contaminating the water in your home.

Greenhouse "Do's" and "Don'ts."

Finally, consider the following points. They are intended to prevent problems and to make life with a greenhouse more enjoyable.

Do's

- Keep the greenhouse and surrounding areas clean and organized.
- Allot enough time to the greenhouse weekly to be successful.
- Learn more about greenhouses and growing plants by reading, conducting research online, and talking to others.
- Keep the greenhouse in a good state of repair.
- Discard weak, diseased, or badly insect-infected plants.
- Enjoy the greenhouse; arrange work intelligently so it doesn't become a chore.
- Experiment—try new methods.
- Plants in a greenhouse are a responsibility. Properly care for them for good results.

Don'ts

- Don't accept sick plants from friends or family. You're asking for trouble if you do!
- Don't start with the most difficult plants. Gain experience with plants that are easier to grow before trying the difficult ones.

NOTE: This chapter provides a general overview about greenhouses. To obtain a comprehensive understanding about greenhouses, to save yourself a lot of time and money, it is highly recommended that you read the book I created exclusively about greenhouses.

Greenhouse Types, Designs, and Energy Management

by David H. Dudley, PMP, PE

Paperback ISBN: 978-1-7350055-4-6
eBook ISBN: 978-1-7350055-5-3
Published: April 2021

Book Summary:

Everything you need to know about greenhouses. All different kinds of greenhouse covered. What you need to know before building or buying a greenhouse. How to make money with your greenhouse. Tips for owning a hobby greenhouse. Easy plants for greenhouse beginners. Making a greenhouse a profitable commercial operation. Options for watering plants. How to minimize energy costs. Things to include inside your greenhouse. Greenhouse shading. Lighting, fans, heaters, and ventilation systems. Automation systems. Greenhouse material options. Pollinating plants. Natural and safe pest management methods. Energy management and lowering operational costs. Greenhouse types, construction processes, heating, and cooling options; shading, seeds & seedlings, environmental control systems, permitting, greenhouse uses, reducing operational costs, managing and maintaining a greenhouse, pros and cons of greenhouse options, and much more. Everything you need to know about greenhouses and achieving optimal success with your greenhouse.

Chapter 1 ¦ **Overview of Greenhouses**

Chapter 2 ¦ **Greenhouse Types**

Chapter 3 ¦ **Walipini Greenhouse**

Chapter 4 ¦ **Before You Build Your Greenhouse**

Chapter 5 ¦ **Greenhouse Covering Materials**

Chapter 6 ¦ **Greenhouse Construction Options**

Chapter 7 ¦ **Temperature Control**

Chapter 8 ¦ **Lighting**

Chapter 9 ¦ **Greenhouse Energy Management**

Chapter 10 ¦ **Questions & Answers**

Chapter 11 ¦ **Greenhouse Hobbyist Tips**

Chapter 12 ¦ **Greenhouse Business Considerations**

Chapter 13 ¦ **Plants**

Chapter 14 ¦ **Pollination**

Chapter 15 ¦ **Organic and Natural Pest Control**

APPENDIX

Different Types of Greenhouses

Greenhouse design styles vary widely and include Quonset, tri-penta, dome, gothic arch, slant-side, A-frame, gable roof, straight-side lean-to, curved-side lean-to, and slant-side lean-to structure. Some styles are more suited to flexible coverings like polyethylene, such as the dome, gothic arch, Quonset, curved-side lean-to, and tri-penta. Others work better with rigid coverings like glass or plastic, including the A-frame, gable roof, slant-side, and straight- or slant-side lean-to.

Likewise, some design styles are more efficient to heat and cool, such as the gable roof and Quonset. Others may look unusual and attractive but are difficult to construct or heat and cool, such as the dome and tri-penta. The A-frame style is easy to construct and is inexpensive, but the usable growing area is small and awkward, and the shape may not blend well with normal surroundings. The most commonly used styles are the gable roof, gothic arch, Quonset, and slantside lean-to. In addition to deciding what style your greenhouse should be, you need to decide whether it will be freestanding or whether it will be attached to your home. Freestanding greenhouses stand alone in the landscape. They can be constructed in a wider range of styles, can be larger, and can offer greater flexibility in location than attached greenhouses can. These greenhouses can be placed almost anywhere in the landscape where the ground is level and adequate light is available. The most widely used styles are the gable roof, gothic arch, Quonset, and slant-side. Attached greenhouses are attached to the home and may or may not have an entrance to the home. They can be designed to blend with the architecture and landscape of the home and are useful where space is limited.

An attached greenhouse typically cost less per square foot to build than a freestanding greenhouse. With an inside entrance, you can maintain the greenhouse without going outside during bad weather. Utilities such as electricity, water, and heat can be

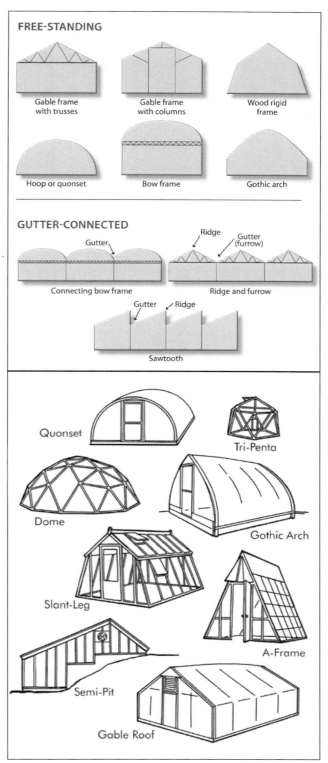

FIGURE 111. *Freestanding greenhouse options.*

shared with the home. If the greenhouse is not on the home HVAC system you may need an additional heater because greenhouses lose heat five to ten times faster than an equivalent area of an average sized residential dwelling. However, the cost of heating an attached greenhouse may be less than that of heating a freestanding greenhouse of the same floor area because one wall is not exposed; although, attached greenhouses usually receive less light for the same reason. Straight-side lean-to, slantside lean-to, and curved-side lean-to styles are ideally suited for small, easy-to-construct attached greenhouses, although the Quonset, gothic arch, slant-side, and gable roof freestanding styles can also be attached. A solid foundation similar to the house foundation is often required or highly desirable for attached greenhouses. Joining and sealing the greenhouse to the house needs special attention. In some cases, it is best to consult an architect or building contractor to determine the method of attachment.

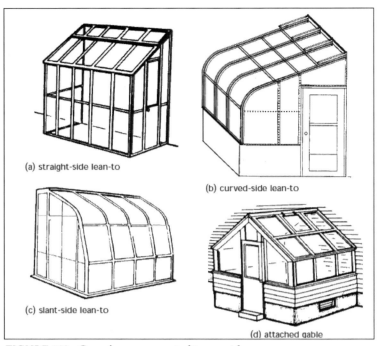

(a) straight-side lean-to

(b) curved-side lean-to

(c) slant-side lean-to

(d) attached gable

FIGURE 112. Greenhouse connected to a residence.

Net House

In some tropical regions, net houses are more appropriate than conventional polyethylene plastic or glass covered greenhouses. This is because the hot climate in the tropics or subtropics increases the need for better ventilation to avoid high temperatures and humidity. Net houses consist of a frame over the grow beds that is covered with mesh netting along the four walls and a plastic roof over the top. The plastic roof is particularly important to prevent rain from entering, especially in areas with intense rainy seasons, as units could overflow in a matter of days. Net houses are used to remove the threat of many noxious pests associated with the tropics, as well as birds and some animals. The ideal mesh size for the four walls depends on the local pests. For large insects, the mesh size should be 0.5 mm. For smaller ones, which are often vectors of viral diseases, the mesh size should be thicker (e.g. mesh 50). Net houses can provide some shade if the sunlight is too intense. Common shade materials vary from 25 to 60 percent sun block.

FIGURE 113. Net house structure to house a
small aquaponic unit

What is a Nature Greenhouse?

The Nature Hobby Greenhouse features a green or silver powder-coated aluminum frame with clear twin-wall polycarbonate panels that are virtually unbreakable, and 100% UV protected. These panels provide excellent heat retention and even diffused light to keep your plants safe and healthy. An adjustable roof vent and hinged door provide excellent ventilation.

Greenhouse Examples

Walipini Greenhouse

The Walipini (also referred to as a geothermal greenhouse or a pit greenouse), in simplest terms, is a rectangular hole in the ground 6 to 8 feet deep with a translucent covering. Walipini greenhouses are common in South America, but are becoming more ordinary elsewhere.

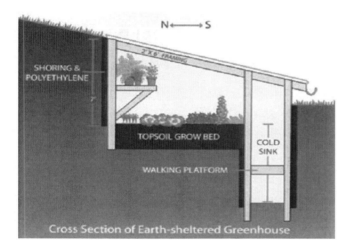

Cross Section of Earth-sheltered Greenhouse

The longest area of the rectangle faces the winter sun – to the north in the Southern Hemisphere and to the south in the Northern Hemisphere. A thick wall of rammed earth at the back of the building and a much lower wall at the front provide the needed angle for the translucent roof. The roof seals the hole and allows the sun's rays to penetrate creating a warm, stable environment for plant growth.

The Earth maintains a fairly constant temperature 3+ feet below the surface in most areas. In the US, that temperature is typically around 45-50 degrees Fahrenheit in the northern states and 50-70 in the south. Harnessing the existing geothermal heat by digging 6-8 feet underground and capturing and solar radiation creates a near-ideal growing climate that's resistant to surface-level temperature changes.

Benefits of a Walipini Greenhouse

Besides the energy savings and ideal growing conditions, there are others benefits to using a Walipini greenhouse. The most obvious benefit is an extended season, providing a year-round growing opportunity.

This type of greenhouse is also a great option for those with a prepper mindset. It's lower profile is not so conspicuous can be better hidden from view. In addition, it can be built in a way so that it is not obvious what's in it; providing another element of protection for one's food supply.

Walipinis can also be built in such a way that they can be used for multiple food sustaining purposes. They can be a self-sustaining unit containing animals, aquaculture, aquaponics, and/or hydroponics, as well as for edible plants, herbs, and money generating non-edible plants, such as flowers.

If you live in a dry climate, another advantage is that the Walipini will typically to hold moisture in. This can be facilitated by using water along the wall. Most plants typically do better in an environment with warm moist air.

Having an underground greenhouse will keep the temperatures hot in the winter and help prevent overheating in the summer. This energy saving arrangement makes it possible to grow plants all year at a low-cost.

The final advantage that a Walipini or pit greenhouse has is that you can usually build it at a low cost. Even less, if you have the right kind of geotechnical conditions, when a retaining wall is not necessary.

PART IV

Flood and Drain System Design and Layout

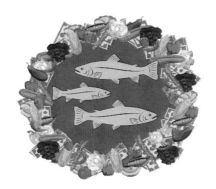

CHAPTER 21

Flood-and-Drain System Instructions & Procedures

Flood-and-Drain System (Media-Filled Bed System)

In the Flood-and-Drain System (also referred to as a media-filled bed system and an ebb-and-flow system), plant grow beds are containers filled with various types of media through which the fish tank wastewater passes through. This style of system can be setup two different ways: 1) with a continuous flow of water through the grow bed(s), or 2) by flooding and draining the grow bed(s.

This chapter addresses the Flood-and-Drain System aquaponics from a Do-It-Yourself (DIY) perspective. The objective is to provide you with the information needed to be successful in developing a system that operates at optimal capacity. Although this chapter primarily refers to a Flood-and-Drain system many of the principles covered also apply to NFT and DWC/Raft systems as well. Additionally, even though the term flood-and-drain is used extensively throughout this chapter, most everything discussed applies to a continuous flow system as well. If there is a difference between the flood-and-drain system and a continuous flow system, the difference will be noted.

As discussed in the first several chapters of this book, aquaponics is a great way to grow your own organic produce, free of pesticide and chemicals. You can have fresh clean fish free of mercury, lead, and many other contaminates common to fish purchased at grocery stores and restaurants; while at the same time helping the environment. Aquaponics can be done easily in your backyard, greenroom of your home, or in a small greenhouse.

Once established, the symbiotic relationship between the fish, plants and nitrifying bacteria does most of the work, practically self-regulating and requiring minimal maintenance. Aquaponics gardening saves tons of time and effort compared to the traditional soil-based gardening.

There are also many other benefits in addition to the health and economic advantages. With aquaponics the joys of gardening and rearing fish are combined. Moreover, you will find aquaponics also enriches your social and family life and is also a positive way to stay active. It is an edifying endeavor to share with children and can help you bond closer with your significant other.

After your system has been set up and running efficiently, all you need is just a few minutes a day to tend to the plants and fish. You can even integrate many automatic controls to reduce your time further. Automated temperature and water quality control devices, as well as grow lights and dispersion of fish feed set via a timer, can further eliminate the time needed to manage the system. Although, like most everything else, the more you put into it, the more you will get out of it.

Beginner Basics

The flood and drain configuration is the simplest and most reliable aquaponics design making it the best suited for beginners. It requires minimal care and can be constructed using a wide range of containers, tanks, materials and sizes. Media also provides better plant support than the other types of aquaponic systems and is more closely related to traditional soil gardening. The cost of building the system can be relatively inexpensive, because there are fewer components and so many material options.

Flood-and-Drain System for the Beginner

The media-filled bed provides the ideal environment for beneficial bacteria to thrive and serve as a reliable natural bio-filter where all of the ammonia-rich fish waste is converted to soluble nitrates on which plants thrive. Any remaining solid waste decomposes into mineral nutrients that also benefit the plants. This design eliminates the need for expensive filtration to keep the water clean and free of toxins for the fish. It is also worth mentioning that some aquaponic operators have success growing worms in their media grow beds.

A properly set up system has good and even distribution of the incoming nutrient-rich water throughout the grow bed, thus delivering nutrients to all the plant roots. The periodic flood-and-drain method produces better results than the continuous flow method for these purposes. The draining of the aquaponics system increases aeration to the media, hence increasing oxygen supply to the plant roots and bacteria living in the media-filled bed. The circulating water picks up oxygen molecules as it makes its way through all of the cavities within the media bed. The returning water further aerates the fish tank water via turbulence as it strikes the tank water surface.

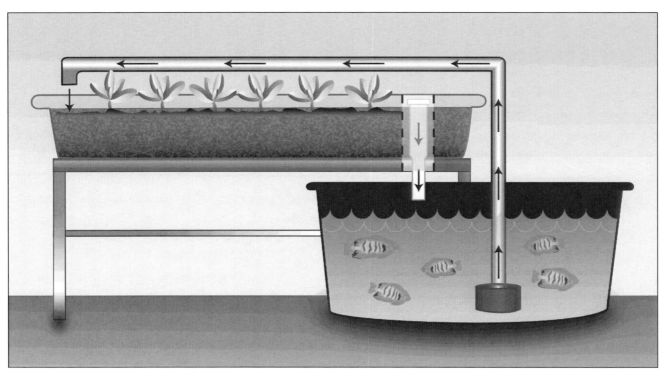

FIGURE 114. Basic media-bed flood-and-drain system without a sump tank. NOTE: Using a sump, rather than having the pump in the fish tank, is the ideal arrangement.

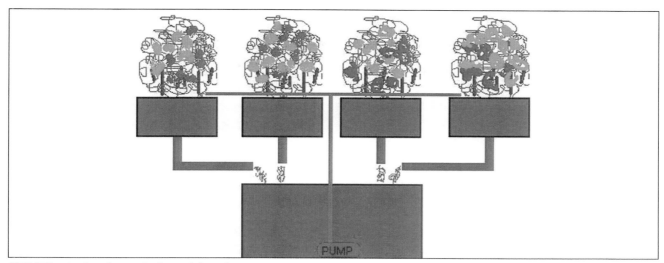

FIGURE 115. *Simple growbed over fish tank setup*

Flood-and-Drain System Fundamentals

A basic flood-and-drain aquaponics system consists of a media-filled plant grow bed placed above the fish tank so water is able to return to the fish tank via gravity flow. A submersible pump is typically installed in the fish tank to pump water up to the grow bed. This design layout is the most energy efficient configuration as it requires the use of only one (1) pump. Another benefit is that the media grow bed and the fish tank can easily be set up so that they are at an ergonomically correct height for the operator (easy to maintain without a lot of bending over). It is a relatively simple design.

The flood-and-drain system can be set-up many different ways. The grow bed can be set up where it partially overhangs the fish tank, set-up a distance from the fish tank, or even in a completely separate building from the fish tank. For instance, the grow beds can be in a greenhouse or even outdoors if you live in a year-round warm weather climate. The fish tank can be located near the grow beds, outside, or in a separate building such as a shed, barn, or garage. The variety of possible configurations are only limited by the owner's local climate conditons and available space.

There are also no rules regarding the size of a flood-and-drain system. Some systems are so small they are located in an apartment, whereas other systems can be larger than an acre, or operate out of a large warehouse-type building. It all just depends upon your goals and available resources. If the space is available, a system can be set up and built upon over time, with the addition or phasing in of more tanks and media beds as experience and resources allows.

With the media-filled bed system all waste, including solids, is dispersed and eventually broken down within the plant bed. As mentioned previously, in some systems, worms are added to the gravel-filled plant bed(s) to enhance the break-down of the waste.

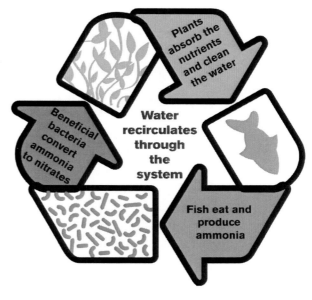

FIGURE 116. *Aquaponics nutrient cycle.*

The grow bed serves as a natural water filter that gives the plants everything they need for vibrant growth. It is important to note, however, that production of measurable, edible produce from a media-filled bed operation is typically lower than the other two methods described below. However, a much wider variety of plants can be grown in this type of system; therefore, the media-filled bed is typically used for applications where a greater amount of plant diversity is desired. Large commercial operators typically use deep water culture (or Raft System) and the Nutrient Film Technique (NFT) to grow lettuce quickly and repeatedly.

Pros:

- It is very basic to build and maintain
- It has an easily customizable design with much flexibility in materials and configurations.
- Self-Cleaning — The grow media filters out the fish waste by performing three (3) filtering functions:
  » Removal of solids from fish tank
  » Mineralization (the release of plant-available compounds such as ammonium during decomposition)
  » Bio-filtration

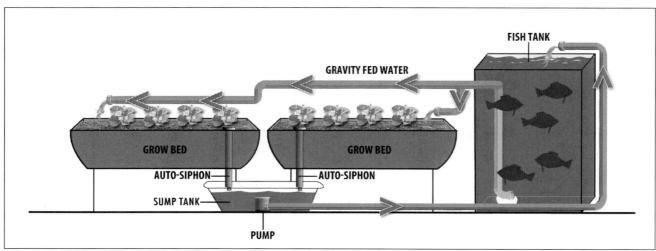

FIGURE 117. Media-bed flood-and-drain system with a sump tank. **Having the pump located in a sump tank, instead of in the fish task, is the ideal arrangement.**

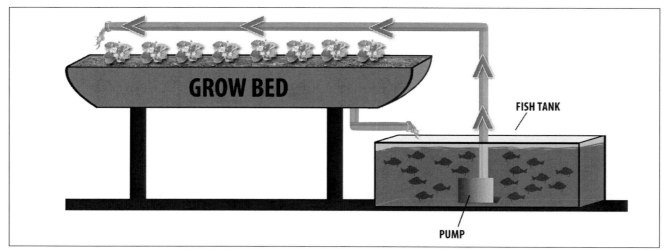

FIGURE 118. Basic Flood & Drain System. Note: Having the pump located in a sump tank, instead of in the fish task, is the ideal arrangement.

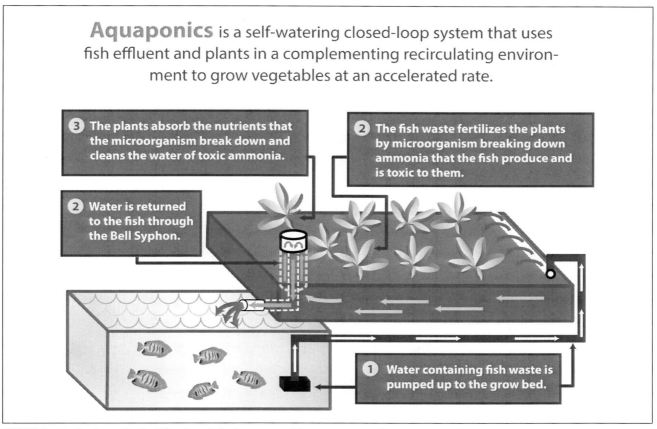

Aquaponics is a self-watering closed-loop system that uses fish effluent and plants in a complementing recirculating environment to grow vegetables at an accelerated rate.

3 The plants absorb the nutrients that the microorganism break down and cleans the water of toxic ammonia.

2 The fish waste fertilizes the plants by microorganism breaking down ammonia that the fish produce and is toxic to them.

2 Water is returned to the fish through the Bell Syphon.

1 Water containing fish waste is pumped up to the grow bed.

FIGURE 119. Basic media-bed flood-and-drain system without a sump tank.

- Media provides better plant support and is more closely related to traditional soil gardening, because there is a media in which to grow plants.
- It does not require a sump tank (low space used for collecting undesirable liquids and/or increasing water volume), although, some operators do integrate a sump set-up in their system.

Cons:

- Adding more grow beds or fish tanks can disrupt system balance. Expansion requires maintaining the grow bed to fish tank ratio. For instance, if you decide to just increase your grow beds there will be too much water drained in every flood cycle from your fish tank, unless you use an indexing valve. Low water levels could mean more stress for your fish.
- The upfront media cost can be expensive.

Do-It-Yourself Aquaponics

Even with the help of the internet, quality aquaponics plans and Do-It-Yourself (DIY) guides are hard to find; thorough books, plans, and other helpful resources are in short supply. Specific information can be obtained, but at a substantial cost. Training, workshops, and educational programs provided by professional consultants, successful aquaponic companies, and educational institutions can cost thousands of dollars, and it can take months or even years to acquire the desired knowledge. While it is possible to purchase ready-made aquaponics kits, they are expensive, and technical support can be non-existent.

In consideration of the issues noted in the above paragraph, one of the best options is to design and build your own aquaponics system using the basic fundamentals. If you educate yourself, create a plan, and adequately prepare, it is not as dauntingly difficult

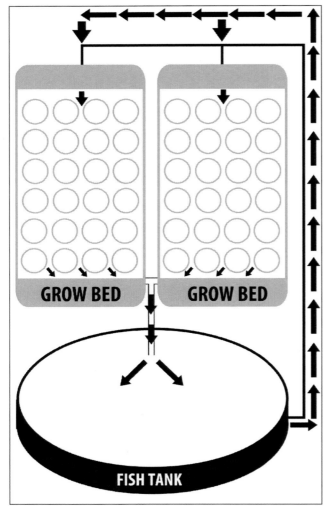

FIGURE 120. *Media-bed flood-and-drain system showing one simple flow pattern option.*

Whether you are planning to purchase a ready-made aquaponics system or build it yourself, it is important to understand the types of aquaponic designs available and which suits you best. If you are purchasing a system understand what you will be getting for your money. Like any endeavor, it is always prudent to determine your cost and time involvement up front. The design of an aquaponics system can be as simple or as complicated as you make it. As mentioned previously, the Flood-and-Drain System is the most common and simplest aquaponics design. This type of system has been adopted by most backyard aquaponics operators, those just desiring to feed their family, and smaller commercial applications (small businesses). The media-filled bed aquaponics design can also be subdivided into two configurations — continuous flow system and the flood and drain system (also known as ebb-and-flow cycle), based on the way the water is being re-circulated.

Flood-and-Drain Configuration vs. Continuously Flooded Configuration

There are two different configurations of recirculating water between the fish tanks and media-filled grow beds that must be considered, namely the flood and drain (also known as ebb and flow) and the continuously flooded systems.

The flood-and-drain configuration is the method of choice among most aquaponic operators. This configuration has been proven to provide good and even distribution of the incoming nutrient-rich water throughout the grow bed. The periodic flooding and draining of the aquaponics system also increases aeration to the media as well as the water returning to the fish tanks. Hence, it helps increase the oxygen supply to the fish, plant roots and bacteria living in the media-filled bed. Furthermore, since the pump does not have to work around the clock, there is a small energy savings compared to a continuous flow system.

as it may at first seem. Building an aquaponic system yourself also allows you to gain much valuable hands on experience with all details of your system, before fish and plants are added. Furthermore, you can save yourself costly mistakes if you start small and grow with knowledge, versus starting big as with some kits.

Aquaponics Types and Design Alternatives

If you desire to get into aquaponics, you need to first consider your long-term goal and what type of system will best enable you to successfully achieve that goal.

System Setup

System design is critical. Although aquaponics is a fairly straight-forward process, it is possible to set it up wrong. An example of an incorrect set up is when a great deal of the system water is in the grow beds with little in the fish tank. It is important that proper planning be done in advance of beginning any work to avoid such problems.

The grow beds need to be set up so the maximum water flood level is at least 1-inch (25mm) below the top of the grow bed media. This helps prevent algae, as most algae needs light to grow. It also helps guard against accidental splashing of water out of the system. A separate sump container is sometimes used which allows for a constant water height in the fish tank. A back-up overflow pipe can also be installed to ensure water never exceeds the designed maximum water level height of the grow bed should the main drain outlet become clogged. This ensures good circulation and returns a full dose of oxygen to the fish.

Another approach implemented by some aquaponic operators is to install a ball valve on each grow bed inlet to control the speed of fill time. However, since this approach will produce backpressure on the water pump, it is important to provide a water return back into the fish tank from the water pump in order to eliminate undue stress on the pump.

Take precautions to ensure the water pump will not completely drain the fish tank should another part of the system fail to return water due to an unforeseen problem or leak. A low water alarm in the fish tank or a backup overflow pipe installed from the grow bed to the fish tank will provide an additional measure of safety against such problems.

If you have the pump in the fish tank, be sure to raise it off the bottom an inch or two; this will help prevent clogging. Furthermore, always make sure the pump is secure and will not move around. The author's preferred design is to keep the pump out of the fish tank to provide a more natural environment for the fish without the hum and vibration of the pump; however, I am not aware of any studies that indicate the pump is actually stressful to the fish or impedes normal, healthy growth. I just feel that keeping the pump out of the fish tank is a more humane way to rear fish.

Be sure to provide sufficient support for the grow bed and fish tank. For the grow bed, account for the weight of the media, water, the operator's leaning body weight, full grown plants, and plant supports. Keep in mind that 100 gallons of water is about 800 pounds. In short, due diligence is needed in planning and constructing the supports of all raised structures (grow beds, stands, stairs, piping, grow light supports, etc.).

Shade fish tanks to prevent algae growth and to reduce stress to the fish. Remember, fish prefer dark hiding places. Including at least one object in the water, in addition to shading the top, will help them feel more secure. Avoid direct lighting on the fish tank.

For initial system material cleansing, route the water through a clean towel/sock free of fabric softeners or other laundry residuals to catch any silt, chemical residue, or other contaminants that may be associated with the materials used to build the system. Better yet, when cleaning the unit after construction, discharge all water out of the system.

Design Layout Overview

An internet search for aquaponics will quickly show the diversity of aquaponic systems out there in regards to types, sizes, and setup configurations. As a matter of fact, it would be a challenge to find two identical systems. Even aquaponic operators who purchased package units typically have different combinations of fish and/or plants growing in them and may integrate various components into their system, such as a greenhouse, artificial lighting, temperature control devices, automation controls, etc. Much of this depends on local climate conditions, the owner's growing and the operator's preferences.

There is no one type of aquaponic setup arrangement that is perfect for everyone. Your climate, goals, local regulatory parameters, and available resources (space, time, family, etc.) are driving forces to consider when planning an aquaponic system.

Although there are many different types of systems, various setup configurations, and a multitude of package units for sale, some operators have much more success than others, even when using similar setups in generally similar climate conditions. Yes, one can construct an aquaponic system that produces fish and plants using a multitude of ways. However, there is a big difference in just producing product and consistently producing product at an optimal level. The difference can be measured in hundreds of pounds of fish, bushels of vegetables, and/or thousands of dollars in profit a year. Therefore, it is very important to not just set up a system that works and produces, but to setup a system properly that will provide maximum results.

Among other critical factors, this chapter will address design specifications essential for achieving the most productive aquaponic systems proven to generate the highest yields of product on a consistent basis. Keep in mind that the system instructions provided in this chapter will only attain optimal effectiveness if the principles (fish tank to grow bed ratio, water quality conditions, fish care, etc.) discussed elsewhere in this book are not followed. The various layouts presented in this book and on the www.FarmYourSpace.com website can be uniformly sized according to your space parameters and goals.

Flood-and-Drain System Design Layout

The following layouts have proven to be the most effective systems in regards to generating the highest yields of product on a consistent basis. System details are provided elsewhere in the book; and those basic principles need to be followed as well in order to maximize success.

Basically, there are two types of schematics for a Flood-and-Drain system, with many variations of each. The two types of Flood-and-Drain schematics are

- Pump located in the fish tank;
- Use of a sump with the pump located in the sump.

Both have advantages and disadvantages. Having the pump located within the fish tank simplifies the process, as you only have two major components—the fish tank and the grow bed. However, a pump located within the fish tank has a higher probability of becoming clogged due to fish waste and uneaten food. Clogging can be minimized by placing the pump on a brick, putting a screen around the pump, and/or through periodic tank maintenance cleanings with a standard swimming pool cleaning net or pool leaf rake. **The best approach is to have the pump located in a sump, and not in the fish tank.**

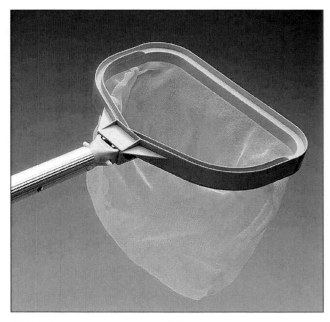

FIGURE 121. A swimming pool cleaning net serves as an excellent fish tank cleaning tool.

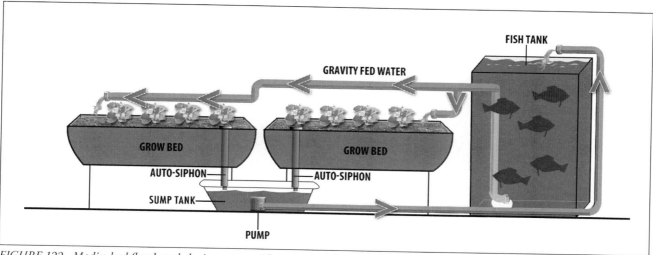

FIGURE 122. Media-bed flood-and-drain system with a sump tank. **Having the pump located in a sump tank, instead of in the fish task, is the ideal arrangement.**

Basic Set-Up Fundamentals:

- Fish Tank at the lowest point.

- Pump in the Fish Tank — Pump up to the grow bed(s).

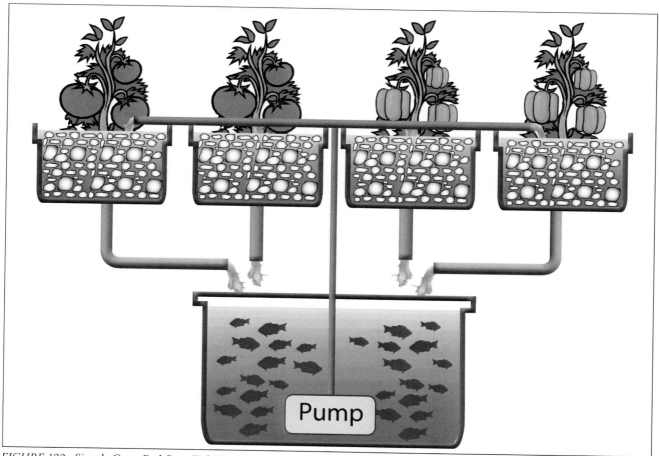

FIGURE 123. Simple Grow Bed Over Fish Tank Setup

Some aquaponic operators prefer to use a sump because they do not want the pump in the fish tank, as they believe the buzz and vibration of the pump causes needless stress to the fish; they feel it is not being friendly to our animals. The author is still studying the issue, but as of now I am not aware of any studies or data that suggest that a pump in the fish tank stresses the fish, harms them in any way, or interferes with optimal growth. However, **placing a mechanical pump in the fish tank is unnatural and could place the fish under an element of unnecessary stress.** Chronic stress does negatively impact the health of any creature. For animaltarian reasons, the pumps should be located in a sump, and not in the fish tank.

Water is a much better conductor of sound than air. If you have ever gone swimming in a lake when motor boats or jet skis are in the general proximity, you can appreciate this fact. The engine of these crafts may sound nearby underwater, even though they may be hundreds of yards away. Although we plan to harvest our fish for consumption and market, we do not want them to suffer in any way during their life or be exposed to unnecessary stress. As soon as I am able to obtain factual data on this issue, I will post it on the website: www.FarmYourSpace.com

> **The author's preferred and recommended approach is to use a sump tank so as to keep the pump out of the fish tank.**

Sump Set-Up Fundamentals:

- Sump located at the lowest point
- Simple gravity flow to a Sump Tank
- Water Pump in the Sump — Pumps to the Fish Tank
- Pump in sump controlled by timer or a float

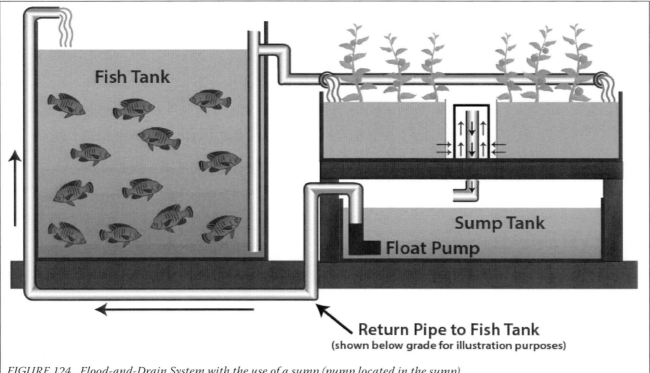

FIGURE 124. *Flood-and-Drain System with the use of a sump (pump located in the sump).* *Pipe shown under floor for illustration purposes only.*

Gravity flow from the Fish Tank to the Grow Bed(s) using a Solids Lift Overflow (SLO)

Several previous illustrations throughout this book have eluded to the method of conveying water from the fish tank to the grow bed via gravity flow, but it has not yet been discussed. This option works well and has the advantage of reducing the probability of the pump becoming clogged with fish waste and uneaten food which accumulates at the bottom of the fish tank where a pump might otherwise be located. The disadvantage of this setup is the fact that elevated fish tanks full of water need heavy duty structural support, or the fish tank needs to be taller to maintain the recommended tank to grow bed volume ratio. Nevertheless, the solid lift overflow method works great, and it certainly needs to be considered as an option.

When the fish tank is positioned above the grow bed(s), gravity can be utilized to efficiently convey the outflow water and fish waste to the grow bed(s). If an outflow is simply located out the side of the fish tank, the water will indeed flow out of the tank and directly into the grow beds. However, the problem is that since the nutrient-rich, solid waste is heavier and at higher concentrations closer to the bottom of the fish tank, using just an outlet in the top half of the fish tank does not move these rich nutrients, and it never makes it to the grow bed(s). So in essence, just having an outlet in the upper half of the fish tank deprives the grow bed(s) and plants of nutrients and exacerbates undesired water quality problems for the fish, since the waste continues to build up in the fish tank.

To resolve this problem, a Solids Lift Overflow (SLO) can be implemented. The SLO draws the water

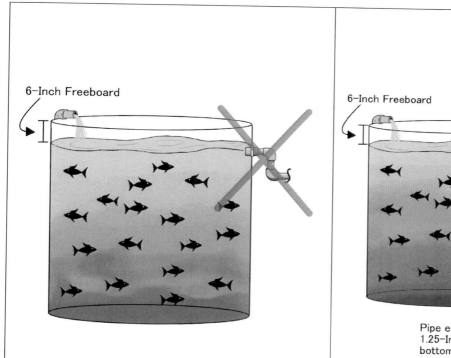

FIGURE 125. Draining from the surface will not remove the condensed fish waste water from the fish tank.

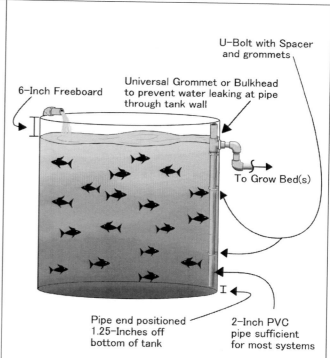

FIGURE 126. U-bolts with grommets for the vertical pipe may not be appropriate for all tank material types. Also, strategically placing a few bricks against the bottom of the pipe can help support it. Just make sure the pipe inlet is not obstructed. Also, placing a screen or net over the pipe inlet will prevent smaller fish from getting pulled into the pipe.

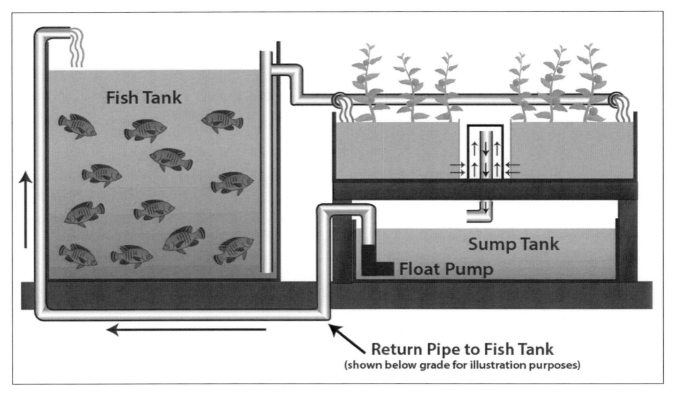

FIGURE 127. Media-Bed (Flood-and-Drain) Aquaponic System with a Sump Tank an Auto-Siphon Drain (i.e. Bell Siphon). See Chapter 26 for plans and instructions on how to build this unit. Pipe shown under floor for illustration purposes only.

and the solid waste from the bottom of the tank, as desired, thereby cleaning the fish tank and delivering the waste (nutrients) to the grow bed and plants where needed.

The SLO is typically made up of a 2-inch diameter pvc pipe and fittings. Ideally, it would be positioned at the center of the fish tank. However, it can be secured easier against the inside wall of the fish tank, so that is where it is mounted in most aquaponics systems using a SLO. Locating the SLO intake pipe approximately 1.25-inches off the bottom surface of the fish tank has proven to be most effective in removing the solids without running the risk of clogging the pipe. The vertical pipe is fitted with a T-connector at the best location within the top half of the fish tank, whereby the pipe then passes through the tank wall via a uniseal grommet or bulkhead fitting and then

on to the grow bed(s). Using a Tee fitting instead of a 90-degree elbow prevents a siphon from forming and ensures water never flows backward into the fish tank.

Operation Method Options (and Recommendation)

The next consideration is how you will flood and drain the grow beds. There are four main methods that are commonly used:

- Constant Flood
- Timed Flood-and-Drain
- Flood and Drain with Siphons
- Mechanical -Pump in grow bed. (This is a practical option if the fish tank is located at a higher elevation than the grow bed)

In order to make the best possible decision as to which one of the above methods is best for you, consider the following:

- **Simplicity** — The more complicated it is — the more likely it is to break!
- **Short** — Shorter pipe runs help reduce temperature variations, reduces friction loss, and is easier to maintain.
- **Cleanings** — Consider how you will clean your system.
- **Accessibility** — Plan a way to access all system infrastructure. It will be difficult to make repairs, clear possible clogs, and clean pipes if there is no access to them.
- **Redundancy** — Plan and build in redundancy where possible. Using a minimum of two fish tanks and two grow beds has many advantages. An overflow pipe from the grow bed to the fish tank is helpful in case there is ever a problem with any of the grow bed outlet infrastructure. Always keep fish health and security first.
- **Water Conveyance** — Ensure water can flow easily through the system. Complicated joints and connections or under-sized piping will slow your water down.
- **Solid Waste Management** — Consider how you will move and deal with solids.
- **Future Expansion and Upgrades** — Keep in mind the possibility of future expansion and system upgrades. In the future, you may want to add more fish tanks and/or grow beds or upgrade system components. Expansion and upgrades will go much smoother, take less time, and be less expensive if you plan for such in the beginning.

The most basic system will encompass a grow bed and fish tank. This type of system works well as a starter or introduction into aquaponics. However, considering the above, in most cases it makes a lot of sense to implement a system where the fish tank is the highest point in the system and water gravity flows down to the grow beds and then on to a sump from where it is returned to the fish tank (see figure 127).

This method has several benefits:

- **Safety:** The Fish tank will never be drained if there is a plumbing problem.
- **Solid Waste Management:** Solid waste is efficiently removed from the tank. Pumping is not impacted by solid waste.
- **Efficient:** This set-up uses only one pump (even with multiple fish tanks and grow beds) and can be arranged very efficiently.
- **Flexible:** More fish tanks and grow beds can be added relatively easily.
- **Water Back-Up:** The sump adds water capacity to the system.
- **Fish Comfort:** The fish are not negatively affected by the constant humming of a pump.

There is a slightly higher cost for the sump and additional plumbing. However, if your situation allows, I recommend this type of system.

NOTE: Design plans and assembly instructions for the above illustrated system are included in 'Chapter 26: Design Plans and Construction Details DIY Flood-and-Drain System'.

Sizing a Flood-and-Drain System

After identifying your specific goals for getting into aquaponics, you will have a better idea regarding the size of system needed. Since the grow bed takes up the most square area space, it is the best place to begin planning the layout of your aquaponic system.

A National Garden Association study found traditional gardening methods yield 0.9 pounds per square foot (0.9 lbs/SF or 4.4 kg/m²) on average. That accounts for one growing season. As discussed in earlier chapters, aquaponics plants grow much faster and produce greater yields than traditional farming methods. With the use of a greenhouse for year-round production, aquaponics produces yields of 7 pounds per square foot (7 lbs/SF or 34.18kg/m²).

A properly setup and maintained system with a grow bed of 25 square feet will produce enough vegetables and soft fruits (tomatoes, peppers, squash) to supply one adult throughout the year, which amounts to 175 lbs of produce annually. That figure is based upon year-round yields without seasonal interruptions, typically a greenhouse operation in areas that are not tropic or subtropical. A family of four would need approximately 100 square feet to produce around 700 lbs of vegetables and certain fruits annually. Using the number of people you want to feed times the 25 square feet required for each person will provide the size of grow bed needed to supply 100 percent of your produce. Of course, one can have a smaller aquaponic system to simply reduce the amount of vegetables needed from the grocery store.

For a "real-world" example using a family of four (assuming all family members are over the age of 12) a 100 square feet grow bed that measure 5-ft x 20-ft. or 6-ft x 16-ft would work perfectly. These sizes are easy to manage as one can easily reach to the center of the grow bed from both sides. It is difficult to maintain the center portion of the grow bed if it is wider than 6-ft. Also, the above referenced sizes will fit comfortably inside a 10-ft x 24 ft or a 12-ft x 20-ft size greenhouse, respectively.

A second example would be sizing the grow bed for a family of eight (8) or planning to have excess to sell and barter. Using 200 square feet as an example, one 6-ft x 33-ft grow bed would work, but such a long grow bed would make it difficult to get an even distribution of nutrients throughout the grow bed. Yes, it can work, but careful planning must be done prior to assembly to ensure there is a relatively even dispersion of nutrients throughout the grow bed. Also, such a long grow bed is typically not the ideal configuration for most people in regards to available space. A better approach would be the use of multiple grow beds instead of just one. Furthermore, since it is difficult to reach more than

three feet, walking or service aisles should be planned between and outside of any grow beds larger than three feet wide. This will allow easy planting, maintaining, and harvesting of plants. Two grow beds measuring 6-ft x 17-ft, three beds measuring 6-ft x 11-ft, or four beds measuring 6-ft x 8.5-ft would be a better option than one large bed.

For commercial installations a 1,000 square feet of grow bed area will produce enough product to provide 40 people all the vegetables they need for an entire year. Using the 25 square feet per person rule: 2,000 SF = 80 people; 3,000 SF = 120 people; 4,000 SF = 160 people; 5,000 SF = 200 people.

Grow Bed Size Parameters

The size of the grow bed(s) area was addressed above in regards to sizing the aquaponic system, because the grow bed takes up the most area. However, the size of the grow bed and the volume of the fish tank volume must be considered together, because the plants need the fish waste to thrive. The bigger the grow bed and plant mass, the more fish waste required; therefore, there has to be enough fish to support the plants.

Ideally, it is best to have at least two separate grow beds so when the roots in one bed are being harvested or cleaned out, there will be another grow bed working to clean the waters. This also provides longer harvest times throughout the year, as the crops in the separate grow beds are typically at different stages of growth (one young and the other closer to harvesting), if planned correctly.

For most hobbyists, beginners, and smaller aquaponic operators a width of about 30 inches is common and seems to work well. This allows one to easily reach across the grow bed.

The ideal grow bed is 12 inches deep to ensure root support for most plants and enough bio-filter volume for bacteria growth. This also gives the bacteria enough time to break down fish solid wastes as

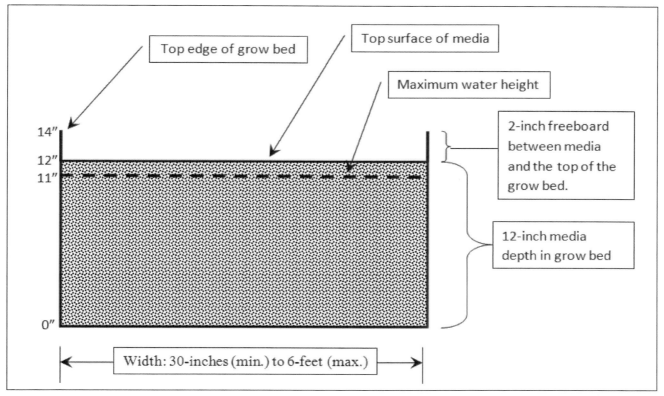

FIGURE 128. Recommended cross-section of grow bed. A grow bed can be up to 6-feet wide if it can be accessed on both sides.

they 'filter" through the media-filled beds, preventing them from over-accumulating. The area of grow bed is determined by your space constraints, desired crop production, and size of the fish tank.

Bed depth significantly greater than 12 inches is unnecessary, will be heavier, and will require more water to be pumped. The media-filled bed should not be flooded to the top. It works best if the water level is never allowed to exceed a height 1 inch below the top of the media surface. This prevents algae growth on the top surface of the media and helps keep mold from developing on the bottom leaves of the plants. It is also preferable to have 2 inches of freeboard. Freeboard is the distance between the top of the gravel surface and the lip of the grow bed. This will help keep the media in the tank during planting, plant care, grow bed maintenance, and harvesting of the plants. It also provides additional protection against significant water loss, if the grow bed drain system becomes clogged.

Grow Bed to Fish Tank Ratio

In general the recommended grow bed volume to fish tank volume ratio is 1:1. However, it can be 2:1, even as large as 3:1, if the fish tank remains densely stocked. However, a fish tank stocked dense enough to support a 3:1 grow bed configuration has to be closely monitored to ensure the fish are not overly stressed, and no detrimental water quality problems arise. In addition, as the fish are harvested in a 3:1 configuration equal replacements of fingerling fish must be added to the system replacing the harvested one, so as to maintain adequate flow of essential nutrients to the bacteria and plants. Technically a 3:1 configuration will work, but it takes a great deal of effort to ensure water quality is maintained, fish health is not compromised, and system balance is not disturbed during the harvesting of fish or if there is a disruption to grow bed(s) production for maintenance, etc. Therefore, with all of the potential problems that can occur, a 1:1 configuration (grow bed volume being in equal volume to fish tank) is ideal.

To compare the volume of the tank and media bed, convert both to cubic feet. To determine cubic feet of the grow beds and fish tank multiply the dimensions (length x width x depth of media). Only consider depth of media for the grow bed. For instance, a 14 inch deep grow bed would have media 12 inches deep. In this case, you would consider only the 12-inch dimension. Convert all dimensions to feet by dividing inches by 12. For example, to determine the size of a 48-inch grow bed in feet, divide 48 by 12 to determine it is 4 feet. To convert gallons to cubic feet, by multiply by 7.48; consequently, 1 cubic foot = 7.48 gallons.

Grow Bed Functions

An aquaponics media-filled grow bed is simply a suitable container filled with media such as gravel, hydroton, lava rock, any number of other substances, or a combination of materials (See Chapter 20: Growing Media for Plants). The grow bed performs four separate functions in aquaponics:

- **Support for Plants** — The grow bed with media provides a means for plants to use their roots to anchor themselves.
- **Water Filtration** — The media filters (removes) solid waste in the water. This waste gets trapped in the grow bed.
- **Mineralization** — This is the process whereby the solid waste breaks down so that the plants can use it. In more scientific terms, mineralization is the breakdown of organic matter into individual elements (macro nutrients like potassium, calcium, sulfate, phosphorous, magnesium and micro nutrients like iron, copper, molybdenum, zinc, etc) into plant-accessible forms.
- **Biological Filtration** — The media provides extensive surface area for the beneficial bacteria to colonize.

The media-filled grow bed performs all of these functions easily in a very space-efficient and cost-effective way.

Grow Bed Materials

In a flow-and-drain system plants are cultivated in the media-filled grow bed. There are a number of things to consider during the grow bed planning process. Obviously, a grow bed needs to be watertight. It also needs to be strong enough to hold the weight of the media, water, plants and potentially the weight of the operator leaning on or against it. Depending on the size of the grow bed this could equate to a fairly significant amount of pressure.

Grow beds can be purchased, or made from a number of different types of materials, such as plastic, fiberglass, concrete, bricks, etc. However, the most common and cost-effective is wood, lined with a water-proof plastic liner or thick epoxy compound. In cooler climates, depending upon the set up, adding insulation to the sides of the grow beds to keep them warm in the winter and cool in the summer is a good idea, especially if the aquaponics system is outdoors.

Some operators line their beds with plastic, while others use fiberglass they have mixed and prepared themselves. Both have advantages and disadvantages, and anyone can easily learn how to do both. YouTube videos, other internet resources, library books, and product vendors provide a great deal of "how to" information. A plastic liner is the least expensive and easiest to install; however, it is more susceptible to rips or puncture holes than a thicker alternative material. Creating your own fiberglass mix requires proper personal safety precautions. One can also purchase a fiberglass or plastic tank, although size options are limited, and they cost substantially more than a plastic liner.

Basically, any watertight, food-safe, fish-safe container can be used, depending on the size of the aquaponics system.

- Small systems can use food containers, plastic containers from the DIY store or wooden boxes with a suitable liner.
- Medium sized systems can use cut-up IBC totes, Rubbermaid-type water troughs, animal feed troughs, and concrete mixing troughs.
- Larger sized systems can use multiple units from above, hand built and lined wooden grow beds, and, of course, commercially available aquaponics grow beds.

A grow bed can be made from a wide variety of materials, but care should be taken to ensure it is made of materials that will not leak unwanted chemicals into the water or affect the pH of the water. If the grow bed is being used outside, it will also need to be UV stabilized to ensure it will not degrade in the sunlight and leach chemicals into the system.

Water Entry and Exit Placement in Grow Beds

There are a number of ways the inflow of water into the grow beds can be configured; however, the main objective is to ensure that waste from the fish tank is spread throughout the grow bed as uniformly as possible. A concentrated area of waste can form an anaerobic spot which will prohibit plant growth, deprive plants in other locations of obtaining

maximum nutrient benefits, and impede water quality process. Good relative placement of your inflow and outflow plumbing will allow for good water movement within the grow bed, provide an equal spread of nutrients, and help optimize water quality. The following are a few common ways of setting up a grow bed.

In figure 129, water enters the grow bed at one single point and exits via the outflow pipe in the opposite end of the grow bed. With this set up there is potential for solid waste to have limited movement within the grow bed. This is however a common setup in many

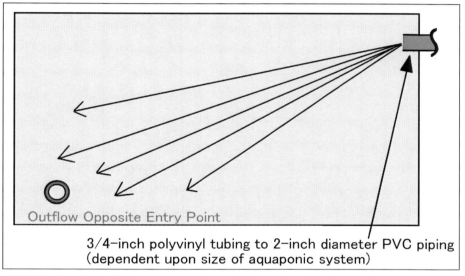

Outflow Opposite Entry Point

3/4-inch polyvinyl tubing to 2-inch diameter PVC piping (dependent upon size of aquaponic system)

FIGURE 129. Media filled grow bed with one inflow and outflow in opposite corner

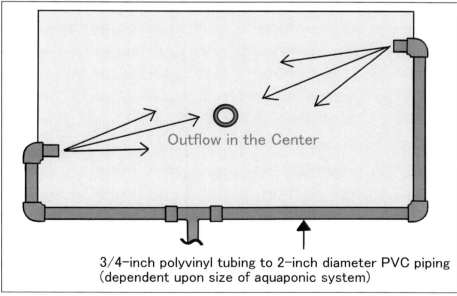

Outflow in the Center

3/4-inch polyvinyl tubing to 2-inch diameter PVC piping (dependent upon size of aquaponic system)

FIGURE 130. Media grow bed with two inflow feeds and outflow in the center

aquaponic systems and can still provide successful results. It is also very easy to set up.

In figure 130, the outflow is placed in the center of the grow bed with two intakes located at opposite ends of the bed. This allows for a more uniform dispersion of waste water throughout the grow bed. It is also a fairly easy set up that reduces the potential for waste build up and anaerobic (no oxygen) spots.

In figure 131, water enters the grow bed on all sides. This is accomplished by drilling evenly spaced holes in irrigation tubing or PVC piping. In this set up water is spread evenly around the entire grow bed and ensures maximum dispersal of waste water (nutrients). Although requiring slightly more work than the two previous methods discussed, it is still relatively simple to set up. Over time the holes can clog, so periodic inspection is needed. Clogs can easily be undone by poking the end of a Phillips screwdriver in the clogged hole.

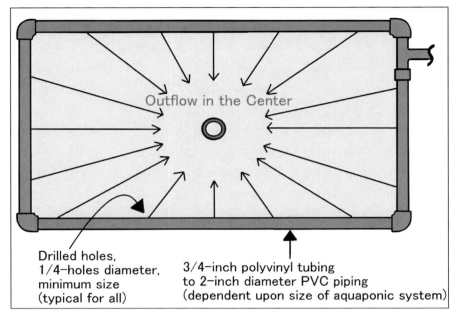

FIGURE 131. *Media grow bed with uniform inflow and centralized outflow*

Drilled holes, 1/4-holes diameter, minimum size (typical for all)

3/4-inch polyvinyl tubing to 2-inch diameter PVC piping (dependent upon size of aquaponic system)

Outflow in the Center

Emergency Overflow

When planning a system it is best to consider incorporating a back-up overflow pipe or hose as extra protection should something go wrong. This will simply be a hole strategically placed immediately below the top edge rim in the side of the grow bed and the fish tank. This hole will allow water to flow out of the media bed and into a safe drainage space (rather than all over the floor), should the media bed outlet ever become clogged. If the grow bed is placed above the fish tank then the water should flow back either to the sump or to the fish tank. If the fish tank is at the highest point, then the water should flow

either to the growbed or to the sump. The objective is to keep the water in the system, rather than have it spill out of the system. It is also prudent to place a screen at both ends of the overflow so that neither fish nor media can enter the overflow pipe or hose.

Natural, Mechanical and Bio Filtration

Some aquaponic operators prefer to integrate a filtration unit into their system. A biological filter is positioned between the fish tank and the grow bed. The water is routed from the fish tank into the biological filter then to the grow bed(s), NFT Channels, or DWC tank, and then back to the fish tank. Biofilters can be purchased or crafted by the DIY enthusiast and come in all types of configurations and sizes.

Biofilters, when used, are most often used in a Flood-and-Drain aquaponic system, where the fish waste production is more than the grow beds can process. Biofilters allow for more bacteria growth to ensure adequate conversion of the toxic ammonia fish waste and suspended solid waste into beneficial nitrates and dissolved solids for plants and to prevent toxicity to the fish.

In a balanced flood-and-drain system, the grow bed (with bacteria and plants) serve as the biofilter; therefore, additional filtration is typically not necessary. In other words, with a properly planned flood-and-drain aquaponics system additional or supplemental filtration (mechanical, natural, or bio-filtration) is not needed. To learn more about mechanical, natural, and bio filtration, refer to 'Chapter 19: Filtration (Mechanical, Biofiltration, Natural)'.

Pumping from the Fish Tank, Pond, or Sump

The pump is a critical component in a flood-and-drain aquaponics system. An entire chapter of this book is dedicated to pumps (Chapter 18: Pumps & Choosing the Right Pump). It is important that the chapter on pumps not be overlooked, or taken lightly, as it contains a vast amount of helpful information. For the purposes of addressing the pump in a flood-and-drain system, several issues will be reiterated in this chapter.

Two very important specifications must be considered when selecting a pump.

- **Flow rate** — tells how much water the pump can move per minute or per hour.
- **Working head specification** — the height at which the pump will pump the water.

The flow rate and working head are shown on the pump curve provided for most pumps. However, sometimes the manufacturer will just provide a range for both of these parameters rather than a pump curve. Typically, the greater the head (the higher the pump must push the water) the lower the flow rate.

When selecting a pump for your system, it is absolutely essential that you ensure both of these parameters (flow rate and working head) meet the operational needs of your system. Your pump needs to pump the entire volume of your fish tank every hour. If the elevation of your pump intake is 3.5 ft below the pump outlet elevation, then you will need a pump with a working head of 3.5 ft at your required flow rate. For instance, if you have a 500-gallon fish tank and must pump water up 3.5 ft in elevation, your pump must be able to pump 500 gallons per hour (gph), or otherwise stated as 8.3 gallons per minute (gpm), at 3.5 ft of head. To convert gph to gpm, divide by 60. Literature provided with most pumps has the flow rate stated in gph or gpm.

The pump works best when it is working at full capacity and not being throttled (restricted) between the pump and discharge outlet by a partially opened valve, undersized fitting, kink in a hose, undersized pipe or hose, etc. When the pump works without impediment there is less strain on the motor, pumping efficiency is optimized, and pump longevity is maximized.

If the pump is being used to draw solid waste from the fish tank, it is worth checking to ensure it can do this easily. Some pumps draw water from the sides, but not from underneath. Placing the pump on a paving stone slightly off the bottom of the tank (or pond) and/or installing a screen around the pump may be necessary.

One last point: always keep a backup pump in stock. If the pump breaks down it is important that you have the ability to promptly replace it. Even if several of your local home improvement stores usually have the pumps you need for your system in stock, it is still prudent to have your own backup pump on hand.

Plumbing / Piping / Hoses / Fittings

Piping is addressed comprehensively in 'Chapter 16: Plumbing'. It is highly recommended that you review Chapter 16 during the planning phase of your aquaponic system.

Steps for Planning and Building a Flood-and-Drain Aquaponic System

Following are step-by-step instructions for a re-circulating, media-filled aquaponic system after you have identified your specific goals for getting into aquaponics:

- Determine the area you have to work with, including space for storage of equipment and materials, walkways, and a harvesting area. Keep in mind future expansion.
- Determine your total desired grow bed area in square feet (or square meters).
- From grow bed area, determine the fish weight required (pounds or kg) using the ratio rule 1 lb (.5 kg) of fish for every 1 sq ft (.1 sq m) of grow bed surface area, assuming the beds are at least 12" (30 cm) deep.
- Determine fish tank volume from the stocking density rule above (1-pound fish per 5 — 7 gallons of fish tank volume or 1 kg per 40-80 liters).

Grow Bed and Fish Tank Relationship

- Start with a 1:1 ratio of grow bed volume to fish tank volume. The ratio can be increased after becoming confident in operating your system (e.g. proficient is managing water quality).
- Media bed supports must be strong enough to withstand the lateral and downward forces of the media, leaning (working) human body weight, water, and plants.
- The system needs to be made of only food-safe materials. They should also be safe for regular handling and not alter the pH of your system. Be wary of media or other items (tools, sharp gravel, etc.) that can rip liners or cut hands.

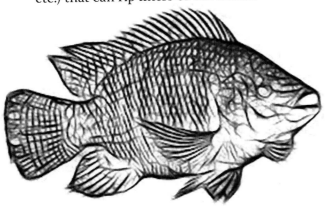

Grow Bed

The grow bed media should be 12 inches (30 cm) deep to allow for growing the widest variety of plants, to provide complete filtration, and to optimize bacterial colonization. A grow bed with a freeboard of 2 inches above the top of the media is helpful in terms of practical application. This allows the operator to work within the media bed without spilling media or water on the floor. Therefore, a grow bed 14 inches deep with 12 inches of media is recommended for optimal success.

Design the grow bed to be a working height that best suits the operator. An ergonomically correct height not only reduces strain on the back, arms and shoulders, but makes the aquaponics experience that much more enjoyable. Ergonomic studies show that the optimal standing work counter (surface of the grow bed) is about 4 inches (10 cm) below the operator's elbow.

Turning over or stirring the bulk of the media within the grow bed every 4 to 12 months is beneficial. If using a liner, be sure not to get too close with your shovel or do anything else that may risk puncturing or tearing the liner.

Use a media guard around all plumbing fixtures. A media guard can be made from a wide variety of common hardware supplies such as window screen material, larger pipes, wood, aluminum, plastic, paint strainers, etc. A media guard will greatly facilitate cleaning and repairing plumbing fittings.

Fish tank

A 250-gallon (1000 liters) or larger fish tank has been proven to create a more stable aquaponics system, where space allows. Larger volumes are better for beginners, because they allow more room for error. With larger volumes, changes to water quality happen more slowly than in smaller systems. Keep the optimal 1:1 size ratio in mind (volume of grow bed equal with fish tank volume). To raise a fish to a length of 12 inches or "plate size", a fish tank volume of at least 50 gallons is recommended

Plumbing and Pumping

Flooding and draining the grow bed works much better than continuous flow. The draining action allows more oxygen to infiltrate through the grow bed. The least complicated way to achieve a reliable flood-and-drain system is using a timer. Although more complex, using a siphon is also a viable option. Advantages and disadvantages of both methods are presented later in this book.

If using a timer, running it for 15 minutes on and 45 minutes off has provided excellent results for standardized setups (12-inch deep media, 1:1 fish tank to grow bed size ratio, and rightly sized pump).

The right size pump will move the entire volume of the fish tank through the grow bed(s) every hour. Therefore, if the pump is setup to run for 15 minutes every hour (see above), and you have a 100 gallon tank, you need at least a 400 gallon per hour (gph) pump. Larger tanks may require additional "on" time. Moving the entire fish tank volume every hour is possible with most small to medium size tanks, but much more challenging with large tanks or ponds. With these large tanks or ponds reasonable compromises need to be made to move the most realistic quantities of water without causing problems.

When choosing a pump, go by the height that you have to lift the water above the pump (head) and flow rate (gph). It is prudent to select a pump with a slightly larger head than the minimum needed in case you need to divert water elsewhere during repairs or while conducting a maintenance task. Do not get hung up on horsepower. All this is explained in much greater detail in 'Chapter 18: Pumps & Choosing the Right Pump'.

Media

- Try to select a media that is inert, i.e., will not alter the pH of the system.
- Avoid media materials that decompose.
- Try to select media that is of the preferred size (1/2" — 3/4" is optimal).

The most commonly used, and proven effective, media types are lightweight expanded clay aggregate, lava rock, expanded shale, and gravel. If gravel is your preference, avoid limestone and marble as they can alter system pH. It is prudent to rinse the media prior to adding it to your system. Refer to Chapter 20: Growing Media for Plants for a comprehensive understanding of media.

Be sure to use non-chlorinated water in your system. This can be achieved by using well water, capturing rain water, running tap water through a filter to remove chlorine, or allowing tap water to sit in a holding tank for several hours to "off gas" prior to adding it to your system.

Ideally, only non-fluoridated water will be added to the aquaponic system. See 'Chapter 31: Water Quality' of this book for information about water quality, the harmful effects of fluoride, and ways to remove it.

Temperature

- It is best to select fish that will thrive at the water temperature your system will naturally gravitate towards.
- It is easier and much less expensive to heat water than it is to cool it.
- Heat is attracted to the system when surfaces are black.
- It is much less costly to retain heat through good insulating techniques than to rely heavily on a heating system.

Oxygen

It is imperative that dissolved oxygen levels for fish be above 3 ppm and preferably above 6 ppm. Use an air pump if achieving these essential dissolved oxygen levels is a problem. The air pump can be set on a timer to supplement oxygen on occasion to maintain desired levels. It will take some trial and error to find the right"sweet spot" in regards to how frequently the air pump needs to be turned on. Running it all the time is more costly and usually not necessary. There are automated dissolved oxygen sensors that will turn the air pump on and off as necessary, but such systems are costly and usually only used in large commercial aquaculture applications or public aquariums.

pH

Generally, targeting a pH of about 6.8 to 7.0 works best. This is a good compromise between the optimal ranges of the fish, the plants, and the bacteria. pH must be tested at least once per week. It is optimal to test daily; however, 3 — 4 times per week is usually sufficient. Review 'Chapter 31: Water Quality' for a comprehensive understanding on pH.

During cycling there is usually a rise in pH. Be cautious about using aquarium industry products to lower pH, because they often contain sodium which is unhealthy for plants. The best methods for lowering pH, in order of preference, are as follows:

- Hydroponic acids (i.e. nitric or phosphoric acids). The nitrate or phosphate is also beneficial to most plants.
- Other acids, such as vinegar (weak), hydrochloric (strong), and sulphuric (strong). However, be very careful about adding these products. They should be used as a last resort since directly adding these acids to your system can be stressful for your fish.

Avoid adding anything to your system containing sodium as it is harmful to plants. Sodium can also build-up in system concentrations over time. Do not use citric acid, as this is anti-bacterial agent and will kill the beneficial bacteria in the media.

After cycling your system pH usually keeps dropping and requires the operator take measures to raise it to the desired range. High pH is generally due to the water source such as hard ground water, or because there is a base buffer in the system such as eggshells, oyster shell, shell grit, incorrect media, etc. The best method for raising (buffering) pH if it drops below 6.6 is calcium hydroxide — "hydrated lime" or "builder's lime", potassium carbonate (or bicarbonate) or potassium hydroxide ("pearlash" or "potash"). If possible, alternate between calcium hydroxide and potassium hydroxide each time you need to raise the pH in your system. These substances are also good for plants. Natural calcium carbonate products such as eggshells, snail shells, and sea shells will raise the pH, but they take a long time to work. The problem is most operators add these ingredients, check pH two, four, or even six hours later and nothing has changed, so they add more. Then suddenly, the pH spikes, because they have added too much.

Stocking Density

The recommended stocking density is 1 pound of fish per 5 to 7 gallons of tank water (.5 kg per 20-26 liters).

Fish selection should take into account the following:

- Edible (e.g. Bass, Tilapia, Trout, etc.) vs. Ornamental (e.g. Koi, goldfish, etc.).
- Water temperature based upon your climate (recommended).
- Diet of fish: Carnivore vs. omnivore vs. herbivore

In order to maintain the perfect balance between fish and plant population density, it is best to progressively harvest the fish as soon as they are big enough. Although the 1:1 fish tank to grow bed volume size ratio is optimal, it is better to have a larger grow bed to fish tank ratio than vice versa. Also, a lighter fish stock density has been found to be more forgiving if things go wrong.

However, bear in mind that there are other factors affecting the number of fish that can be grown in an aquaponic system, such as the species of fish and feed rates. The more the fish are fed, the more waste they produce. It is important to monitor system parameters such as water flow rates, oxygen levels, pump rates and water temperature, as they all play a critical role in the health of the system. All these issues are discussed in detail in their respective chapters of this book.

Plants

It is prudent to avoid plants that prefer an acidic or basic soil environment. Plants can be started for aquaponics the same way they would for a soil garden — by seed, cuttings or transplant.

If plants are not thriving, it is probably due to the pH being out of the 6.8 to 7.0 range or inadequate nutrient (fish waste) delivery to plants (very rare problem). Adding red worms to the grow bed once the system has been fully cycled can benefit plants and the system as a whole.

Introducing Fish into the System

Make sure your system is fully cycled before adding fish. Cycling is discussed in comprehensive detail within 'Chapter 30: Starting, Operating, and Troubleshooting Your Aquaponic System'. Ensure the pH is at the desired level for fish, plants, and bacteria. As a general rule of thumb a pH of 6.8 to 7.0 is typically ideal for most plants, fish and bacteria. Ensure the fish tank water temperature is within the recommended range for your fish.

FIGURE 132. *Step-by-step procedure of transferring a seedling into a media bed unit. Removing the seedling from the nursery tray (a); digging a small hole in the medium (b); planting the seedling (c); and backfilling the medium (d).*

Feeding Fish

A good rule of thumb is to feed your fish as much as they will eat in 5 minutes, 1 to 3 times per day. An adult fish will eat approximately 1 percent of its bodyweight per day. Fish fry (babies) will eat as much as 7 percent. Be sure your fish are being fed enough. However, be cognizant of the fact that over feeding fish will negatively affect water quality, is wasteful, and is an unnecessary increase in cost.

Fish not eating as they should, is a good indication they are stressed or unhealthy. Some factors that may result in fish not eating as they should include

- Living in conditions outside of their optimal temperature range
- Water quality issues: Improper pH range, too much ammonia in the system, inadequate dissolved oxygen
- Loud or irritating noises and vibrations
- Direct lighting upon the fish tank

Starting the System— "Cycling" with Fish

- Start out by adding only 1/2 as many fish as it would take for the fish tank to be fully stocked.
- Test daily for elevated ammonia and nitrite levels. If either becomes too high perform a partial water exchange.
- During the start-up cycling period, feeding the fish only once a day will help control ammonia levels.
- See 'Chapter 30: Starting, Operating, and Troubleshooting Your Aquaponic System'.

Fishless Cycling

There are several sources of ammonia including synthetic (pure ammonia and ammonium chloride) and organic (urine and animal flesh). Add the ammonia to the fish tank a little at a time until a reading from your ammonia kit of 5 ppm can be obtained. Record the amount of ammonia this took and add that amount daily until the nitrite appears (at least 0.5 ppm). If ammonia levels exceed 8 ppm, stop adding ammonia until the levels decrease back to 5 ppm. Once nitrites appear, cut back the daily dose of ammonia to half the original volume. If nitrite levels exceed 5 ppm stop adding ammonia until they decline to 2.0ppm. Once nitrates appear (5 to 10 ppm), and both the ammonia and the nitrites have dropped to zero, fish can be added to the system.

System Maintenance (after "cycling" is complete)

Ammonia and Nitrite levels should be less than 0.75 ppm. If ammonia levels rise suddenly, check to see if there is a dead fish in your tank. If Nitrite levels rise undesirably, something has likely occurred that has damaged the bacteria environment in the system. If either of these circumstances occur, stop feeding the fish until the levels stabilize, and, in extreme cases, do a 1/3 water exchange to dilute the existing solution. Nitrates can rise as high as 150 ppm without causing problems. If nitrates exceed 150 ppm, it would be prudent to harvest some fish, add additional plants or expand the system by adding another grow bed.

CHAPTER 22

Media Grow Bed Drain Options, Drawings, and Information

Media Guard

Regardless of what type of drain option is selected, they all need a media guard. The media guard can be a screen or a wide diameter piping with small holes or gaps drilled or cut into its sides. Its purpose is to allow the water to flow, but to block the media from getting into the plumbing. The media guard is very important as it performs a couple of functions. First, it allows you access to the outflow plumbing in case you should need to change anything, or access it for repairs or cleaning purposes. Secondly, it helps to stop roots and media from getting into the plumbing.

Some operators prefer to have the media guard securely fastened in place. Others prefer to have it sitting freely so that it can be rotated to break loose attached roots or removed easily for cleaning. Regardless of your preference, the media guard should be constructed in such a way as to allow air to enter at the top so that it does not form a siphon.

Drain System Options for a Flood-and-Drain System

There are two standard systems used to achieve the flood-and-drain effect. One or the other can be used, but not both within the same system. They are:

1. **An outlet drain located within the grow bed, with a timer based pump in the fish tank set on a defined periodic pumping schedule.**
2. **An auto siphon in the media grow bed with the pump in the fish tank or within a sump tank.** There are several types of auto siphons being used in aquaponic media bed systems. They are Bell, J-bend, loop, or pivot siphons.

These drain system options are explained in more detail below.

1. Outlet Drain with a Timer Based Pump System

A timer-based system is one common operational method as it is easy to setup and maintain. Basically, a timer is attached to the pump so that the pump is powered on for a specified time, depending on the media being used. A schedule of 15 minutes every 30-45 minutes tends to work well for most setups. During the pumping phase, the water is pumped into the grow bed until the water level reaches the level of the 'overflow drain'.

The overflow outlet drain high-point is set at 1-inch below the surface of the grow bed media. The

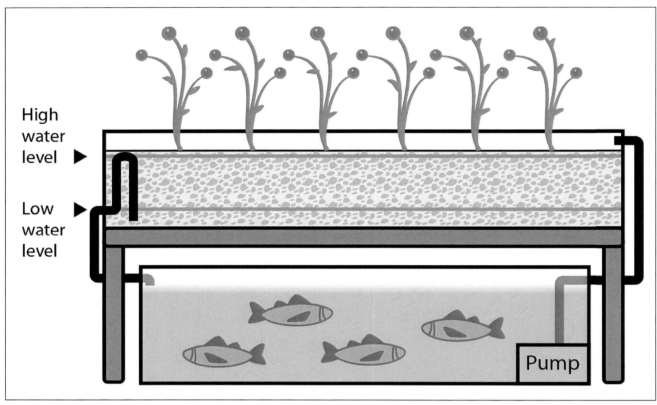

FIGURE 133. Flood and Drain Style Grow Bed

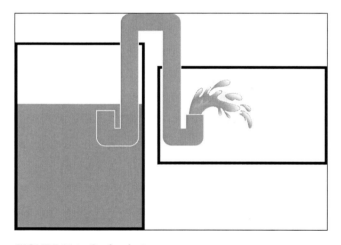

FIGURE 134. Outlet drain system concept

objective is to keep the top layer dry. This helps prevent the bottom leaves of the plants from becoming moldy, and to avoid an algae bloom from developing on the wet media surface.

After 15 minutes or so of flooding, the pump is switched off via of an automatic timer system. Water then drains back through the 'water-in-pipe' at the base of the grow bed and back to the fish tank.

J-Bend (Carlson Surge Device) / U-Bend System

A J-Bend is a tube bent like the letter "J" and used upside down. The long end is the drainage outlet. The short end is where the water will enter and seal off the opening. Once the water level is high enough to cover the top of the upside down "J", the siphon is started. These are used inside the container with the long end protruding through the container. A small U-Bend water trap at the bottom of the outlet pipe may be helpful if difficulties arise using this type of siphon.

U-Bend Siphon

Three U-Bends are assembled together to create a siphon-activated raised tank "no holes overflow" to transfer water outside a container without drilling holes through it and without spilling over the top of the container. It must be primed with water to remove all internal air and both ends at the same height to prevent air leaking inside. It is important that 'no holes overflows' be checked regularly to ensure that no air has accumulated inside the top, thus preventing normal operation. This is not usually visible when it occurs.

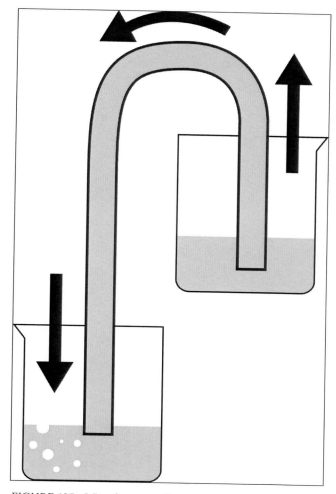

FIGURE 135. J-Bend concept illustration

FIGURE 136. U-Bend

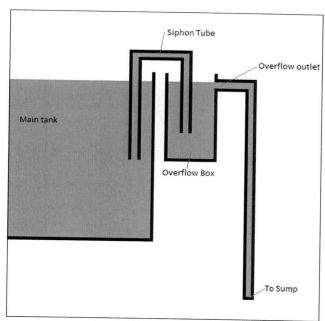

FIGURE 137. U-Bend concept illustration

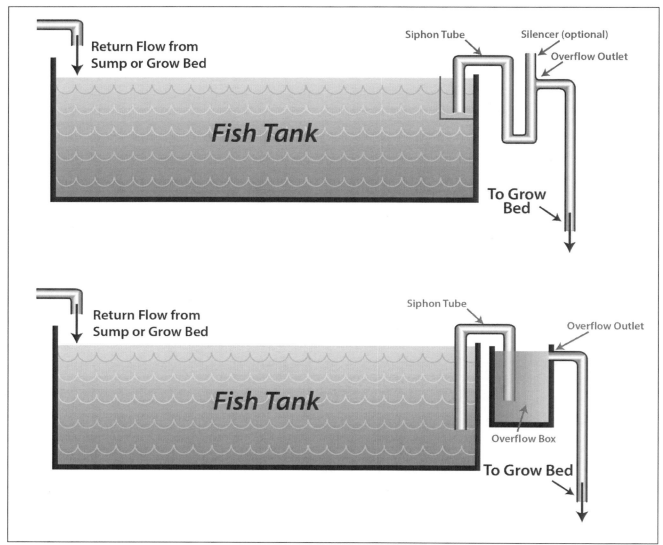

FIGURE 138. U-Bend examples

An "overflow box" is an upside down U-Bend/U-Tube with both ends in separate boxes, and works on the same principal. Figures 134-138, are examples. A clear hose facilitates visual inspection.

Loop Siphon System

NOTE OF CAUTION: It is with much reservation that a loop system is included within this book. The author has not had any success using a loop system. However, it is included as others claim it as a reliable tank draining option.

This system features a loop of tubing with the outlet end usually pointed down. The open input end is where the water will enter and seal off the opening. Once the water level reaches the height of the top of the loop, it starts to push air and water down the output side, which engages the siphon affect. It is supposed to work the same way as a J-Bend, but the tubing forms a complete circle. A loop siphon can be used inside or outside the container.

The tube diameter also needs to be varied according to the size of the grow bed and the volume of water that needs to be drained. As a rule of thumb,

FIGURE 139. *Loop Siphon System*

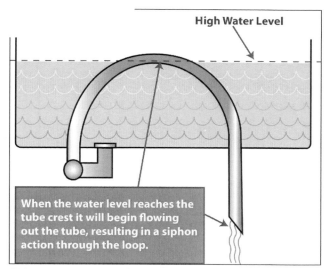

High Water Level

When the water level reaches the tube crest it will begin flowing out the tube, resulting in a siphon action through the loop.

FIGURE 140. *Loop Siphon System*

it should be larger than the piping that brings the water to the grow bed so that it can drain faster than the rate that the grow bed is being filled.

As mentioned above, clear tubing provides the operator with the joy and confidence of watching the system at work. If using clear tubing, makes sure it is not exposed to direct sunlight, otherwise algae will grow on the inside of the tube.

2. Auto Siphon in Media Grow Bed with Pump in the Fish Tank or a Sump Tank

The second drain option is to use an auto siphon in the media grow bed with a pump in the fish or sump tank. The drain line can be tubing, garden hose, or PVC piping. Preferably, this will be larger in diameter than the pump line. Although not necessary, using clear tubing on the siphon drain line (or on a segment of the drain line) will allow you to

observe water flowing through the tubing to ensure it is working properly. While a clear hose cost more, it also provides more confidence being able to watch the entire system at work.

The maximum height of water in siphons will match the maximum height of water in the container, so you need to adjust your siphon size and position it accordingly so it works at the proper water level, which is about 1-inch below the surface of the media. Another important item to note is that if siphons trap air at the top, they may not function properly, so it is best if they are tube shaped.

Aquaponic operators use all types of auto siphons, also referred to as bell siphons. With all siphon systems, typically the pump constantly propels water from the fish tank into the grow bed. As the water level in the grow bed rises, it fills the interior of the siphon, which is located within the grow bed. When the water level reaches a specific height, it overflows into a pipe within the siphon.

A low-pressure area is created within the siphon, triggering the drawing off of water from the grow bed, back to the fish tank. When the grow bed is almost completely drained, air enters the siphon and the draining action stops. The grow bed then begins to fill up slowly.

The design of the siphon is critical to the successful functioning of the siphon and its timely draining effect. The www.FarmYourSpace.com website has helpful instructional videos on these types of siphons, and well as other useful information.

NOTE: Some bell siphon setups have a funnel fitting at the top of the standpipe. Others have just a straight standpipe. Both configurations will work, therefore both types are shown within this book. The author favors a straight standpipe (without the funnel at the top), as it is easier to construct, and the funnel has not proven to provide any substantial claimed advantage.

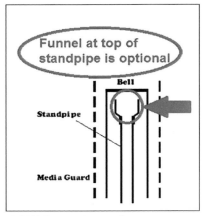

FIGURE 141. Auto siphon.

FIGURE 142. Top of an auto siphon.

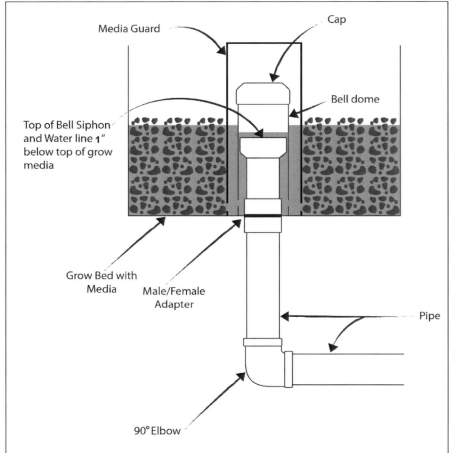

FIGURE 143. Auto siphon.

Be sure to read 'Chapter 25 How to Make a Auto Siphon (Bell Siphon)' for more information and DIY instructions on how to make an auto siphon.

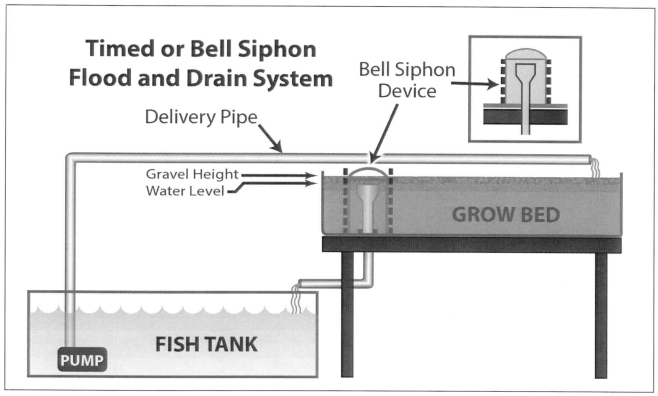

FIGURE 144. *Media-bed system without a sump.*

A sump system has several advantages over a non-sump system. Therefore, incorporating a sump is the better approach than the basic system shown in Figure 145..

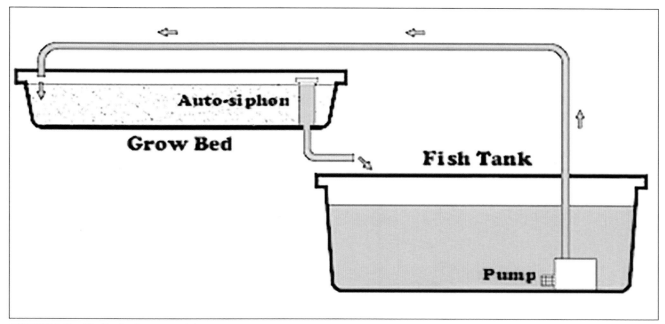

FIGURE 145. *Media-bed system without a sump.*

CHAPTER 23

How to Make a Auto Siphon (Bell Siphon)

Bell Siphon

A bell siphon is an ingenious way to drain the grow bed in a flood, and drain aquaponics system without using a timer to turn the pump on and off. Bell siphons enable you to effectively run a media filled aquaponics system by using the laws of gravity. To keep things simple, the bell siphon acts as a way to drain your system faster than it fills up. This process provides the plant roots with abundance of water, nutrients, and oxygen; thereby maximizing plant growth.

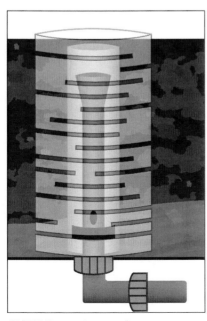

FIGURE 146. Auto-siphon

Bell Siphon Fundamentals

* As the water level rises in the grow-bed, water is forced through the teeth on the bottom of the bell and up between the walls of the standpipe and bell.
* As the water level exceeds the height of the standpipe and the drain begins to fill, a siphon is created.
* Most of the water in the grow-bed is then drained by the siphon until the water level reaches the height of the teeth and tip of the snorkel.
* Air is then forced through the snorkel and, as a result, the siphon is broken resulting in the grow-bed beginning to fill again; the cycle then repeats itself.

Benefits of Using a Bell Siphon:

* **No more timer** — This eliminates this cost of the timer and will lengthen the lifespan of your pump.
* **Pump runs continuously** — Pumps that run continuously suffer less wear and tear. This will result in a longer pump life.
* **More aeration** — If you are diverting part of your water stream back into your fish tank for aeration, using a siphon to drain your beds will increase the aeration you deliver to your fish tank (since

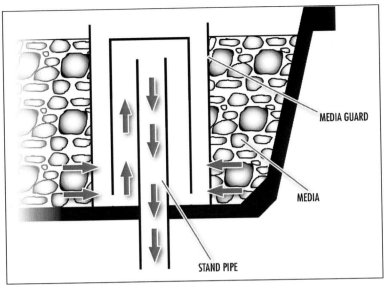

FIGURE 147. Auto-siphon illusrtation

pressure build up creates a vacuum and drains the grow bed faster than it fills.

Sizing Bell Siphons and Drains

Before constructing a bell siphon, you need to decide which size of drain is appropriate for your grow-bed. The appropriate size of the bell siphon depends on the size of the individual grow-bed. In general, the larger the grow-bed, the greater the volume of water it can hold, and a larger standpipe and bell siphon is necessary to drain it. The recommended ratio of bell siphon size to drain is 2:1; the diameter of the pipe used to build the bell siphon should be twice that of the standpipe (i.e., if the standpipe is 1-inch in diameter, the bell siphon should be made using a 2-inch diameter pipe). Table 16 below shows some general sizing parameters for square and rectangular grow beds.

Figure 148 shows four sizes of bell siphons with accompanying standpipe and drain assembly. From left to right: 1/2-inch standpipe with 1-inch bell pipe, 1-inch standpipe with 2-inch bell pipe, 1.5-inch standpipe with 3-inch bell pipe, 2-inch standpipe with 4-inch bell pipe. Note that the top of the standpipe should be positioned 1-inch lower than the media surface. This will be the media bed high water mark.

aeration based on diverting a portion of the water stream only works while your pump is running).

As mentioned above, with a bell siphon, the pump is working all the time so the grow bed is filling continuously, but at regular intervals the siphon is activated and pulls all the water from the grow bed. The bell siphons work constantly, day and night, powered by nothing but simple physics (otherwise known as hydrodynamic water head pressure).

As the grow bed fills up with water, it reaches the designated set point whereby the water will start to drain. With just a drainage pipe, the media grow bed would fill and drain at the same rate. The water

TABLE 16. **Measurements of Bell Siphon Components for Various Size Tanks**

Bell Pipe Diameter	2-inch	3-inch	4-inch
Standpipe/Drain Size (Diameter)	1-inch	1.5-inch	2-inch
Snorkel Tube Size (Dia.) and Material Type	7/16 OD × 5/16 ID Vinyl Tubing	5/8 OD × ½ ID Vinyl Tubing	7/8 OD × 1/2 ID Vinyl Tubing
Grow Bed Dimensions	1' x 4' x 4'	1' x 4' x 6'	1' x 4' x 8' to 1' x 6' x 10'
Volume of Grow Bed	16-ft³, 120-gallon	24-ft³, 180-gallon	32-ft³, 240-gallon to 60-ft³, 448-gallon

NOTE: Diameters(Inside Diameter = ID; Outside Diameter = OD) in inches

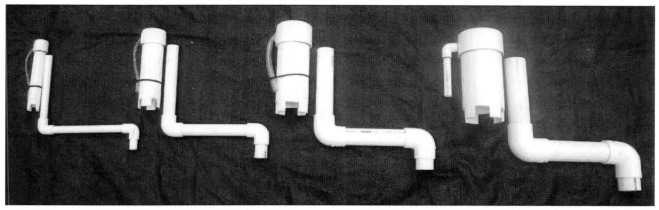

FIGURE 148. Auto siphons of different sizes.

How to Build a Bell Siphon

The height of the bell siphon needs to be appropriate for the size of your standpipe. Creating a space of about 1 to 2-inches between the top of the standpipe and the top of the standpipe works best. The bell siphon is connected to the bulkhead at the bottom of the grow bed.

Step 1

Install a bulkhead fitting that will hold the standpipe in the grow-bed and drain the water into the fish tank. Bulkhead and Uniseal fittings are addressed comprehensively in 'Chapter 16: Plumbing'. Some aquaponic operators also apply silicone caulking around their bulkheads as additional protection against leaks.

Step 2

Adjust the height of the standpipe to be 1-inch below the surface of the grow media. As discussed in the previous chapter, the grow-bed should be 14-inches deep with 12-inches of grow media. Therefore, the standpipe (where the water enters) would be 11-inches above the bottom surface of the grow bed. This keeps water from reaching the surface of the media where algae can grow.

NOTE: The top of the standpipe should be level. Coincidently, this is also 1-inch below the surface of the media. See figure 149.

Figure 149 shows the components of a bell siphon and companion standpipe with a bulkhead fitting. The dotted line (top large arrows) represents the maximum water level in the grow bed (located 1-inch below the surface of the media). Note that it is even with the top of the standpipe as well as the bottom of the bell cap. The lower dashed line and large arrows represents the minimum water level or the bottom of the grow bed. The dashed line is even with the top of the bulkhead fitting and the bottom of the teeth.

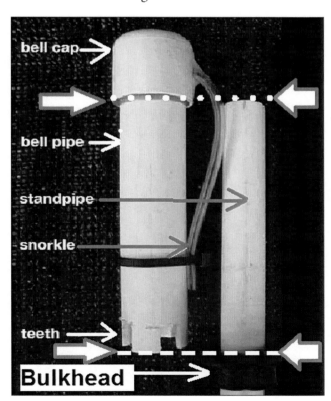

FIGURE 149.

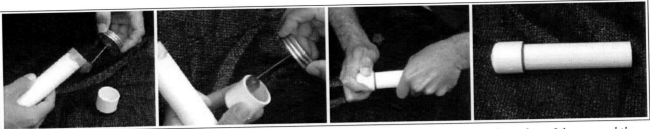

FIGURE 150. *Attach the bell cap to the bell pipe with PVC primer and glue. After priming the inside surface of the cap and the outside surface of the pipe, apply glue to the rim of the pipe and the inside of the cap, as shown. Then, push the cap onto the pipe and twist the cap a quarter turn to seal the joint. Make sure the seal connecting the cap to the bell tube is airtight.*

FIGURE 151. *Cut notches to make teeth on the bottom of the bell pipe. This can be done with various tools and methods.*

Step 3

Prime and glue a PVC cap onto the end of the bell pipe (see figure 150). Next, cut the standpipe to the appropriate length (1-inch below the media surface — be sure to allow for the bulkhead fitting), and cut notches (or "teeth") into the bottom of the bell pipe. This can be done by securing the capped end of the bell pipe in a vise, and making two sets of two straight cuts perpendicular to each other across the open end of the pipe using a saw (see figure 151). Additional cuts should then be made on the lateral surface of the bell pipe, at the apex of the first cuts, to loosen the teeth (see figure 152). Pliers can be used to gently break away the material between the teeth, revealing the spaces through which the water will flow (see figure 153).

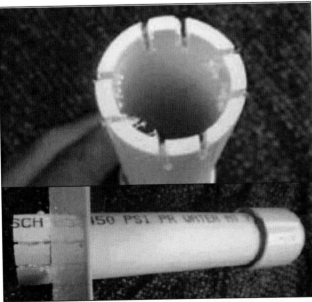

FIGURE 152. *Make lateral cuts to weaken the spacers between the teeth.*

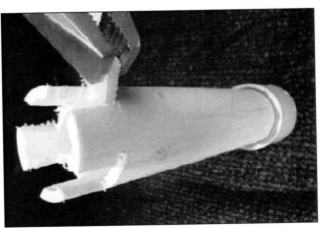

FIGURE 153. *Remove the spacers between the teeth with pliers. If cut properly, the spacers break off cleanly and with ease.*

Step 4

Once the teeth have been cut in the bottom of the bell pipe, the snorkel that will ultimately break the siphon must be made. Depending on the size of your bell siphon, use a drill bit or hole-saw with a diameter approximately the same size as the tubing or pipe (see figure 154), and drill a hole into the side of the cap that makes up the end of the bell (see figure 155).

Next, push the tubing or pipe through the hole so that the tubing penetrates the inside of both the cap and pipe wall of the bell and extends 1/4 inch inside the bell cap (figure 156). Using a bead of 100 percent silicone, seal the gap surrounding the tubing at the entrance to the bell and allow to dry completely. It is important to create an airtight seal, because if air enters the top of the bell through the space around the snorkel during use, the siphon will not start properly.

After the seal has dried, gently train the snorkel along the length of the bell pipe and secure the snorkel in place with a cable tie. Next, cut the free end of the snorkel so that it ends above the teeth. If the snorkel is cut too long (i.e., the open end of the snorkel is lower than or even with the height of the teeth), the siphon will not break properly.

An alternative approach to snorkel design is to drill a threaded "tap" hole in the bell pipe and screw a 90° hose barb fitting into place. This way, the snorkel tube can extend directly down along the bell pipe toward the teeth without having to make a sharp turn. The absence of a silicone seal and the lessened stress on the vinyl tubing should extend the life of the bell siphon. An example of this design can be found in figure 148 (the 4-inch bell siphon was built using a 1/2-inch, 90° PVC elbow and straight pipe).

Step 5

Once the bell siphon is completed, a "media guard" needs to be constructed. This is a porous tube placed around the standpipe and bell siphon before adding the media to the grow bed. The function of the media guard is to prevent clogs to the standpipe and bell

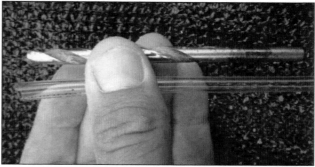

FIGURE 154. *Choose the appropriate size (diameter) drill bit or hole-saw for making the snorkel. The hole drilled in the bell pipe should be only slightly larger than the diameter of the tubing itself, to ensure a tight seal.*

FIGURE 155. *Drill a hole in the bell pipe for the snorkel tube.*

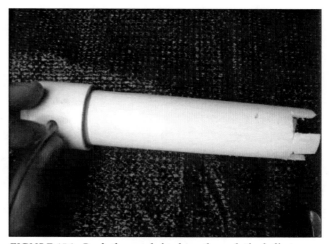

FIGURE 156. *Push the snorkel tubing through the bell pipe cap assembly.*

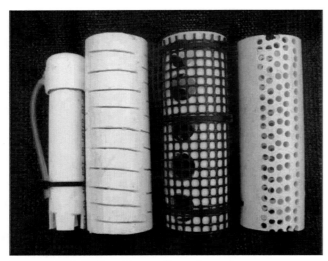

FIGURE 157. *Different types of gravel guards*

siphon while allowing water to easily flow through. The medial guard also allows easy access and maintenance to the bell without having to remove or dig through the media. Although a media guard is not necessary for bell siphon function, it is a prudent investment of time and materials for the added benefit of ease of maintenance and protection. Particles from the grow media can obstruct or constrict the flow to the bell siphon, so the media guard will allow the operator to easily access the bell siphon for maintenance, repairs, and cleaning (see figure 157).

Step 6

Following construction of the bell siphon and media guard, the completed auto siphon array can be assembled over the standpipe in the grow bed. Place the bell pipe over the standpipe so that the teeth rest evenly on the bulkhead or on the bottom of the grow bed. Next, place the media guard over the bell siphon. Refer to 'Chapter 20: Growing Media for Plants' for media options. If using cinder, gravel, or clay balls media, be sure to thoroughly rinse them before adding them to the grow bed. Carefully add the media around the base of the media guard so as not to disturb its placement. Once a firm base of medium has been added around the gravel guard, continue filling the rest of the grow-bed to a height of about 1-inch above the top of the bell siphon (a total of 12-inches of media depth). This added height of media ensures that the ebbing water in the grow-bed is not exposed to sunlight before the system flushes, which helps prevent algal growth in the grow-bed.

Step 7

The last step in the bell siphon assembly is the installation of the drain extending from the bottom of the standpipe on the underside of the bulkhead beneath the grow-bed (see figure 158 below). Add a 90° elbow to the bottom of the standpipe. Extend this elbow with a length of straight pipe and add an additional 90° elbow fitting. The bends in the drain created by the elbows assist the bell siphon in starting and stopping the flow of water by providing some resistance to the water exiting the grow bed.

FIGURE 158. *The drain assembly on the underside of the grow bed. Note the two sequential 90° elbow fittings, which directs the flow of water to the sump tank, located beneath the grow bed.*

Bell Siphon Assembly Summary

The height of the standpipe in the grow bed should be level with the bottom of the cap on the bell pipe. This relationship of standpipe to bell pipe height is important in ensuring that the volume of air resident in the top of the bell pipe is sufficient to start the siphon. The "double-double rule" is that the diameter of the media guard should be at least double the diameter of the bell pipe, which is double the diameter of the standpipe.

The drain assembly (consisting of the plumbing on the underside of the grow bed extending from the bottom of the standpipe) should contain two 90° elbow fittings in series connected by a length of straight pipe (see photo above). This arrangement is necessary to restrict the flow of water moving through the drain, and it assists both the starting and stopping of the siphon. An alternative approach is to add a reducer fitting to the bottom end of the standpipe, which acts in a similar way.

How fast water flows into the grow bed will determine the duration of cycling in the system. In other words, the faster water is added to the grow-bed, the faster it will fill up, and the shorter the duration between flushes. In general, flow-and-drain cycles should be about 15–20 minutes, regardless of the size or volume of the grow-bed. If possible for your size system, adjust the flow water into the grow bed (via proper pump size selection) so that the bell siphon starts, drains, and stops every 15–20 minutes. This also removes the fish tank volume once every hour. As a friendly reminder, the depth of the growth media should be around 12-inches for optimal filtration and plant growth.

CHAPTER 24

Design Plans and Construction Details DIY Flood-and-Drain System

Building Your Own Flood-and-Drain Aquaponic System

The aquaponic system design details provided in this chapter are for a system that can easily be constructed using common materials. If budget is an issue, these materials can gradually purchased over time. Perhaps used lumber can even be acquired at a lower price in your area. Craigslist can be a good resource for used building supplies, where applicable.

Another benefit to this system is that the sump tank is also located directly under the grow bed. Therefore, the sump tank does not take up any additional space. This configuration will allow for efficient drainage of the grow bed during operation, and if/when the grow bed ever needs to be emptied for

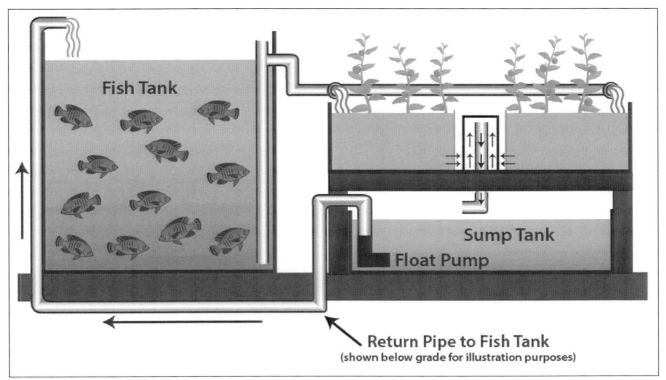

Fish Tank

Sump Tank

Float Pump

Return Pipe to Fish Tank
(shown below grade for illustration purposes)

FIGURE 159. Illustration of the aquaponic system referenced in this chapter.

maintenance, repairs, or for swapping out a different type of media. The sump tank size and location will also allow it to be utilized as a temporary back-up fish tank in case there is an emergency problem with, or the need to switch out, the main fish tank.

The size of this system is appropriate for beginners and can easily be enlarged over time. Furthermore, this system will easily fit in most backyards and still leave the home owner with space to spare. Best of all, this low-maintenance system will provide a substantial amount of healthy food at a very low operational cost. It will also serve as a wonderful conversation topic during social encounters, and is fun to show off to others. It can also be a very fun and educational family enterprise; providing bonding opportunities, and teaching youth many valuable lessons.

System Annual Production Output

Under normal operating conditions this system will produce an average of 77 lbs (35 kg) to Tilapia per year. This relatively small system will produce 144 lbs (65 kg) of vegetables annually. These figures are based upon proven values for tank space volume for Tilapia and grow bed square footage area of vegetables of typical flood-and-drain aquaponic system remaining in active operation throughout the year. Full year production is accomplished via location in a temperate climate or with the use of a greenhouse in colder climate regions and supplemental lighting up to a few hours each during winter months.

Construction Flexibility Options

Several fish tank options are provided in this design layout so as to give the end some end product and cost flexibility alternatives. Several options are also provided in regards to waterproofing the grow bed and sump tank. The hope and intention of these construction options will provide the end user some flexibility in constructing the level of quality aquaponic system that best fits his/her preferences and budget.

System Development Notes

1. **Fish Tank:** This system is based upon 300 gallons of water in the fish tank. The actual size of the fish tank will be listed greater than 300 gallons to accommodate freeboard (the vertical distance between the maximum water level and the top of the tank).
2. The **grow bed** and **sump** are each designed to hold 300 gallons of water.
3. **Ratio:** The volume of fish tank to grow bed volume has the desired 1:1 ratio (approx.) in order to provide optimal system operational conditions.

System Weight:

1. One (1) cubic foot of water = 7.48 gallons = 62.43 lbs.
2. One (1) gallon of water weighs 8.3 lbs.
3. The fish tank will have an approximate weight of 2,575 lbs.
4. The grow bed can weigh up to 3,100 lbs (water+media+plants+growbed+weight of operator leaning against the bed).
5. The sump tank can weigh up to approximately 3100 lbs.
6. The weight of the finished grow bed, sump, and appurtenances thereto could potentially weigh up to 6,500 lbs (approx. 136 lbs/SF).
7. The total weight if this operational aquaponic system is acceptable for most concrete slabs-on-grade floors. Further structural evaluation is needed if considering placement of this system on any ancillary structures (i.e. second floor, deck, etc.).

Material Notes:

1. **Bell Siphon:** Refer to Chapter 25 on 'How to Make a Bell Siphon' for making a Bell Siphon for this system.
2. Use **wood screws** for assembly.
3. **Adaptor:** Installing an adaptor at the ½-inch diameter pipe outlet to allow the return line to

be either 5/8-inch diameter irrigation tubing or a 1-inch diameter PVC pipe will help to reduce friction head on the return line.

4. **Growing Media:** Using a growing media of expanded clay pebbles (common trade name: Hydroton) would provide the best results, but is also the most costly option. Cost can be reduced by using a growing media mix of expanded clay pebbles and smooth pea gravel (no sharp edges on the gravel). Be sure to rinse the pea gravel thoroughly before placement. Other growing media options are available as well (refer to 'Chapter 20: Growing Media for Plants'). This system will need approximately 52 cubic feet of media.

5. **Lumber:** Treated lumber is more costly, but will provide the greatest longevity and is a wise choice given the ambient area moisture from the fish tank , sump, and grow bed. However, using treated lumber is not essential.

Material Information

The total material and supplies estimated cost to build this system is $1,000 (USA year 2022 prices). This cost includes all construction materials, pump, media, and plumbing costs. However, considerable savings of several hundred dollars can be achieved by purchasing a used fish tank, used and/or lumber that is not treated.

Only one pump is needed for this system. However, it is prudent to purchase two pumps so as to have a backup pump readily available in case the system goes out.

Plumbing Material Cost: 2-inch diameter PVC piping and fittings, auto siphon (Bell Siphon) parts, Return Line from sump pump to fish tank, plumber's tape (Teflon Tape), PVC cement (glue), and misc. items. Approximate Cost = $140 (USA 2022 prices).

TABLE 17. **Lumber Sizes Need**

NOMINAL SIZE	ACTUAL SIZE	QUANTITY
1" x 12" x 12'	¾" x 11¼" x 12'	4
1" x 12" x 4'	¾" x 11¼" x 4'	*4
1" x 3" x 12'	¾" x 2.5" x 12'	4
1" x 3" x 4'	¾" x 2.5" x 4'	*4
2" x 4" x 12'	1.5" x 3.5" x 12'	2
2" x 4" x 38"	1.5" x 3.5" x 38"	**9
4" x 4" x 37.25"	3.5" x 3.5" x 37.25"	***8
15/32" x 4-ft x 8-ft Plywood	—————	1
15/32" x 4-ft x 4-ft Plywood	—————	1

*The most practical and economical approach is to purchase two standard 8-ft long boards and cut them in half to obtain the required 4-ft long boards.

**The most practical and economical approach is to purchase five standard 8-ft long boards and cut them to obtain the required four 38-inch length 2"x4" boards.

***The most practical and economical approach is to purchase four standard 8-ft long boards and cut them to obtain the required four 37.25-inch long 4"x4" boards.

TABLE 18. Lumber Shopping List & Estimated Cost

(The below table is a summary of Table 17 to make your shopping easier)

LUMBER	QUANTITY	USA 2022 AVERAGE COST (EACH)	USA 2022 AVERAGE COST (TOTAL)
1" x 12" x 12'	4	$39.89	$159.56
1" x 12" x 8'	2	$27.36	$54.72
1" x 3" x 12'	4	$14.25	$57.00
1" x 3" x 8'	2	$10.98	$21.96
2" x 4" x 12'	2	$17.25	$34.50
2" x 4" x 8'	5	$8.25	$41.25
4" x 4" x 8'	4	$16.98	$67.92
15/32" x 4-ft x 8-ft Plywood	2	$63.78	$127.56
Box of 3-Inch Long Wood Screws	1	$7.72	$7.72
Box of 2-Inch Long Wood Screws	1	$7.47	$7.47
Box of Staples for Staple Gun —Used to Staple Liner (Not Needed if Using the DIY Fiberglass Option for Sump Tank and Grow Bed)	1	$4.29	$4.29
		Subtotal	$583.77
		Estimated Sales Tax (various per location)	$46.70
		Total Estimated Lumber Cost	**$630.47**

TABLE 19. Fish Tank Options

OPTIONS	TANK TYPE	APPROX. COST (USA, YR 2022)
Option #1	330 gallon IBC Tank	$150 (used)
Option #2	48" diameter x 44" deep Fiberglass Tank	$483

TABLE 20. Sump Tank & Grow Bed Waterproof Options

OPTIONS	TANK TYPE	APPROX. COST (USA, YR 2022)
Option #1	20 to 40 mil HDPE Liner — 6.5-ft x 14.5-ft for Grow Bed — 6.5-ft x 14.5-ft for Sump Tank	$85–$153
Option #2	Fiberglass (DIY Inside Boards)	$83–$133

TABLE 21. **Plumbing List**

(Summarized for User-Friendly Shopping Purposes)

ITEM	QUANTITY
2-Inch Dia. PVC Pipe (Schedule 40) typically sold in 10-ft lengths	Purchase two 10-ft pipes.
2-Inch Dia. PVC Tee-Fitting	2
2-Inch Dia. PVC 90-Degree Bend Fitting	4
2-Inch Dia. PVC 30-Degree Bend Fitting	1
PVC Cement (Glue), 8-Ounce Can	1
Plumber's Tape (Teflon Tape), Roll of Tape	1
Sump to Fish Tank Return Line: 5/8-Inch Dia. Polyvinyl Tubing (Irrigation Tubing), or 1-Inch Dia. PVC pipe. Be sure to purchase fittings (Adapter from pump outlet to tube or pipe, and 90-Degree Bends).	Approximately 20-ft of 5/8-Inch Dia. Irrigation Tubing or 1-Inch Dia. PVC Pipe needed (plus associated fittings)
Pump (Brand: United Pump UP-580 Submersible (or equal), 580 GPH. Only one pump is needed, but it is prudent to have a back-up readily available; therefore two pumps are recommended ($65 each at USA 2020 prices)	1
2" x 12" x 12" Concrete Block	1
U-Bolts to secure SLO 2-Inch Dia. Pipe within Fish Tank (2.5" x 3" U-Bolt)	2
Grommet for U-Bolts (Size to Fit Thread Dia. Of U-Bolt)	4
Grommet for SLO 2-Inch Dia. PVC Pipe Protrusion through Fish Tank (2-Inch Dia.)	1
Silicon Caulking, Tube	1
Pipe Clamp to Secure 2-Inch Dia. PVC Pipe to Top Edge of Grow Bed	6
Pipe Clamp to Secure 5/8-Inch Dia. Irrigation Tubing or 1-Inch Dia. PVC Piping to Wood Frame	4
Bell Siphon Assembly (Refer to Chapter 25 on How to Make a Bell Siphon for Details)	1
Grow Media (refer to note #14 above regarding the grow media)	52 cubic feet

Safety Precautions

- A simple tank leak or plumbing problem could be deadly situation if the water comes into contact with electricity. Secure all electrical conduits. Do not leave extension cords on the ground.
- Ensure all electrical outlets in the area are of the GFCI type, or replace them with such if they are not.
- If the aquaponic system is to be constructed on a concrete slab, then it is recommended that a non-slip epoxy coating be applied on walking paths near the system.
- Be sure that remove all tripping hazards from the area.
- If applicable to your situation, be sure to child proof the fish tank and any other potential hazards.

Design Plans

Build according to the following drawings.

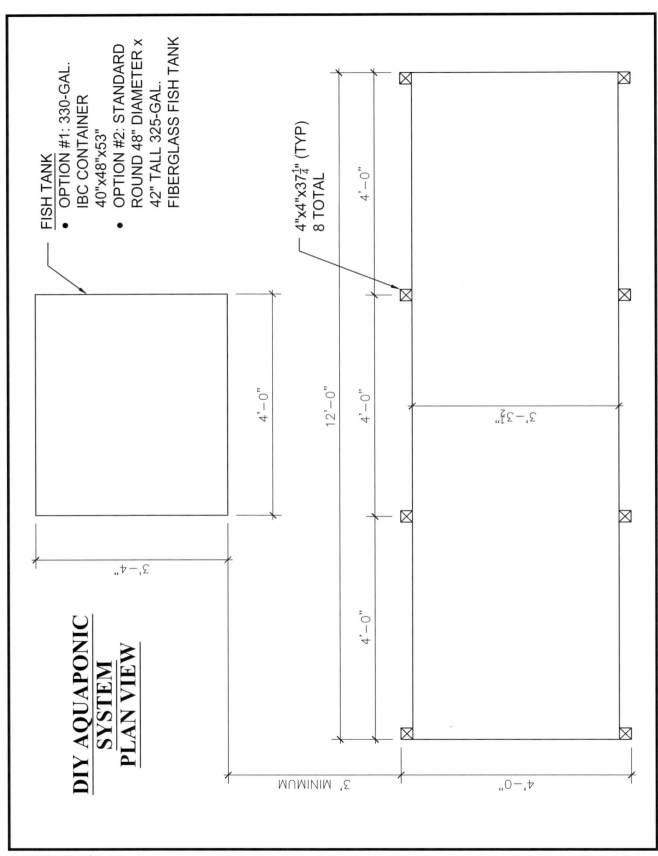

FIGURE 160. Plan View.

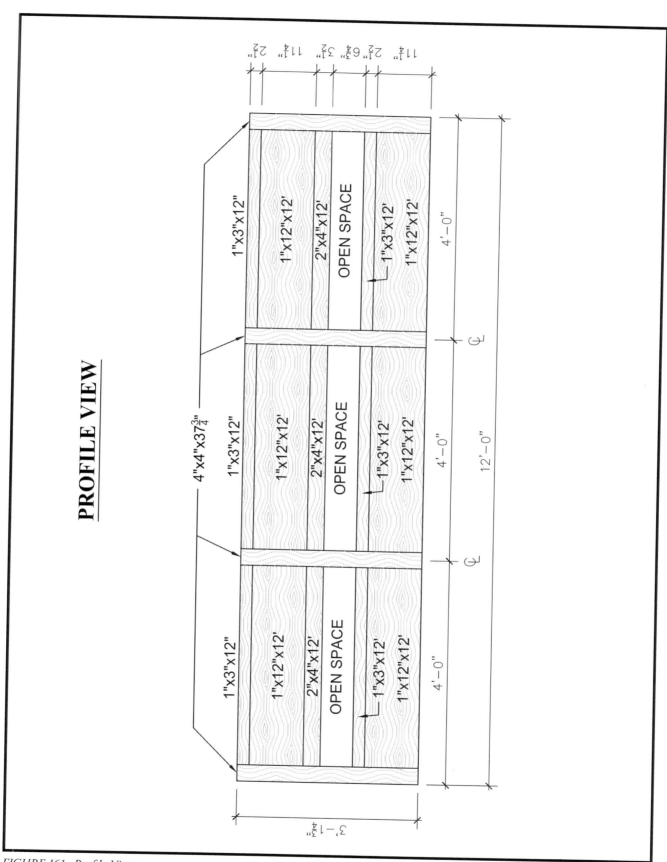

FIGURE 161. Profile View.

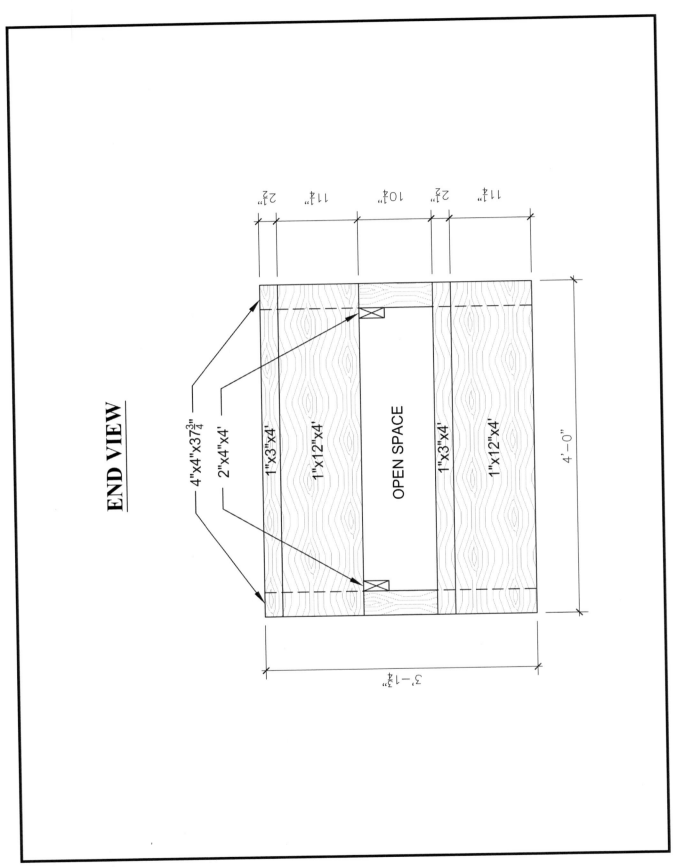

FIGURE 162. End View.

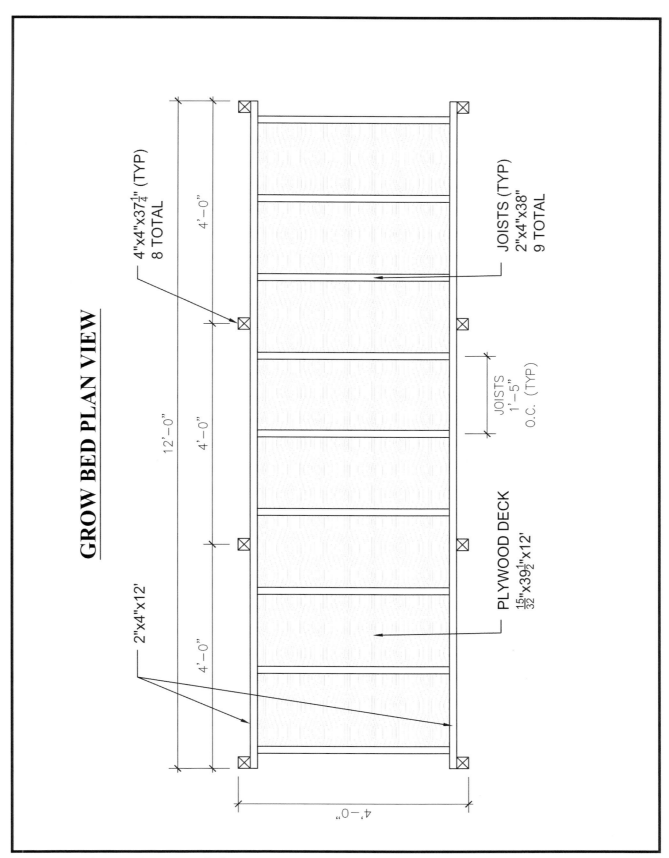

FIGURE 163. *Plan view showing grow bed supports.*

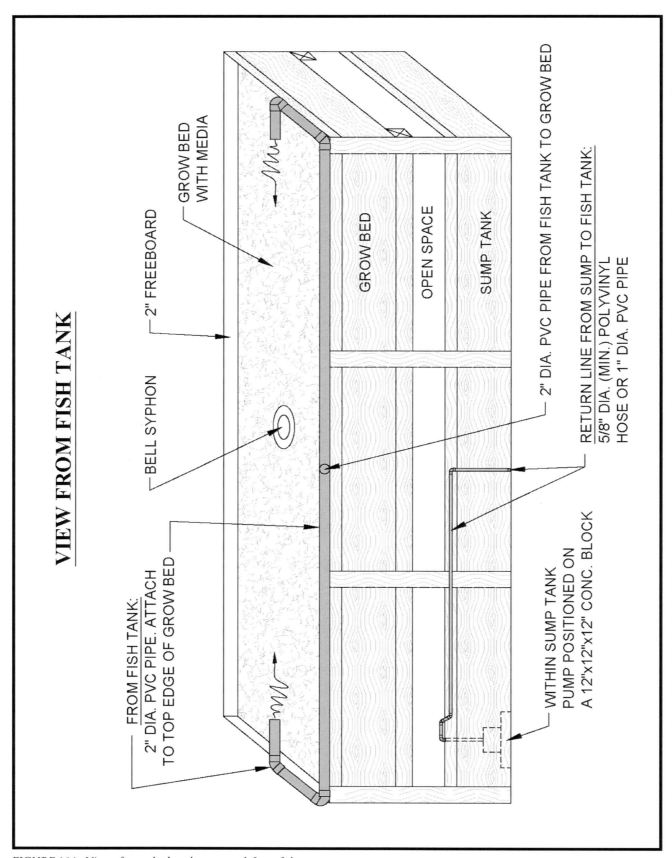

FIGURE 164. View of grow bed and sump tank from fish.

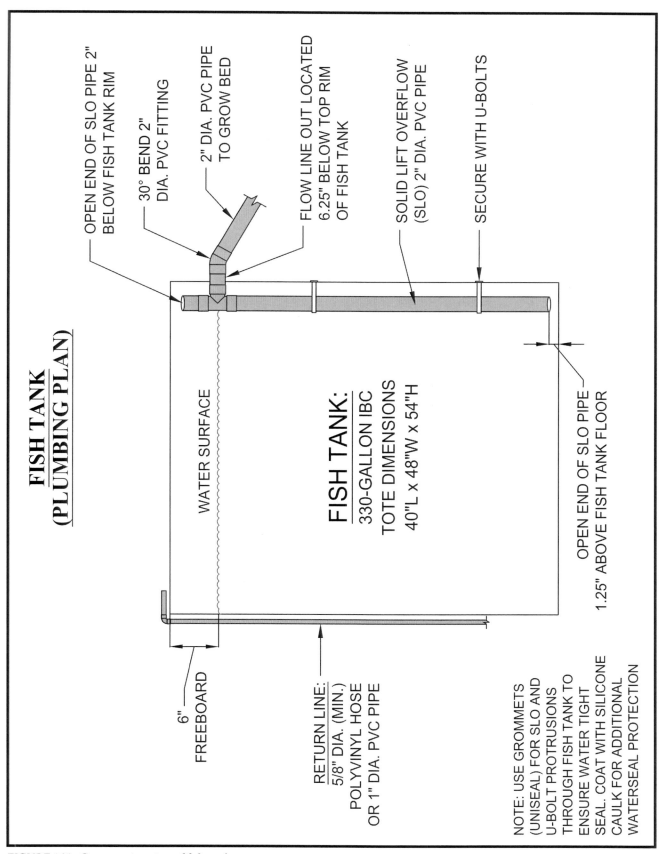

FIGURE 165. Cross-section view of fish tank.

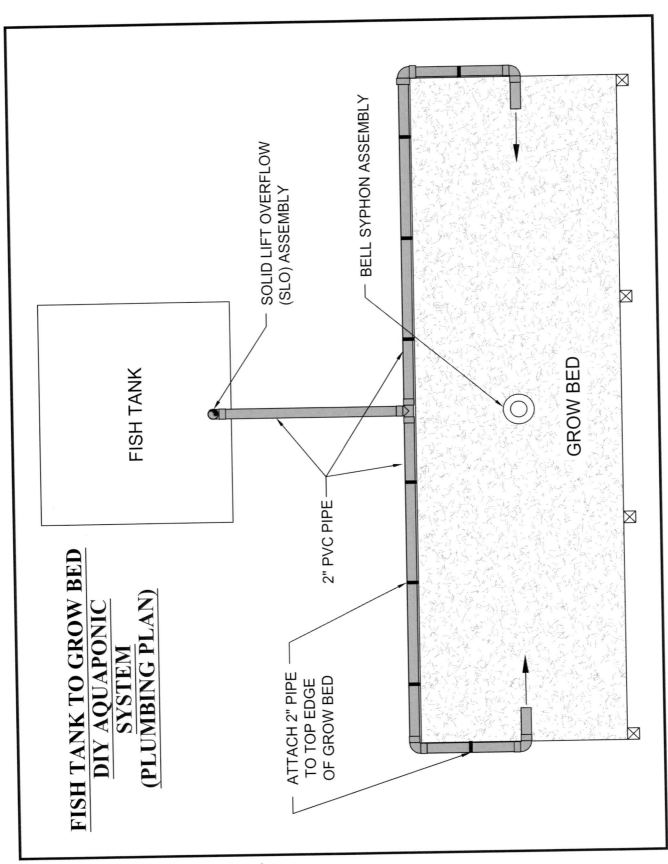

FIGURE 166. *Fish tank to grow bed plumbing plan.*

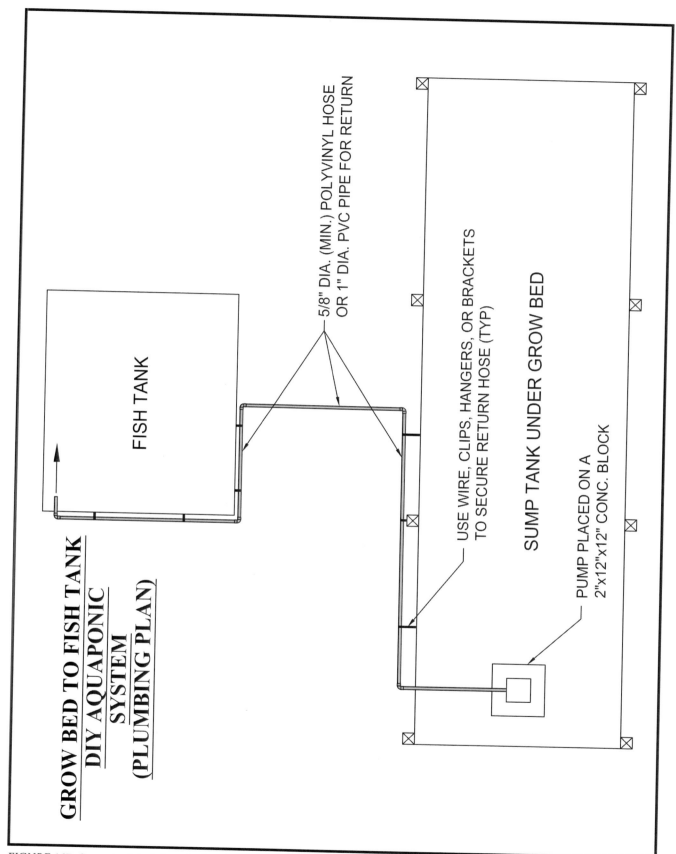

FIGURE 167. Sump tank to fish tank plumbing plan.

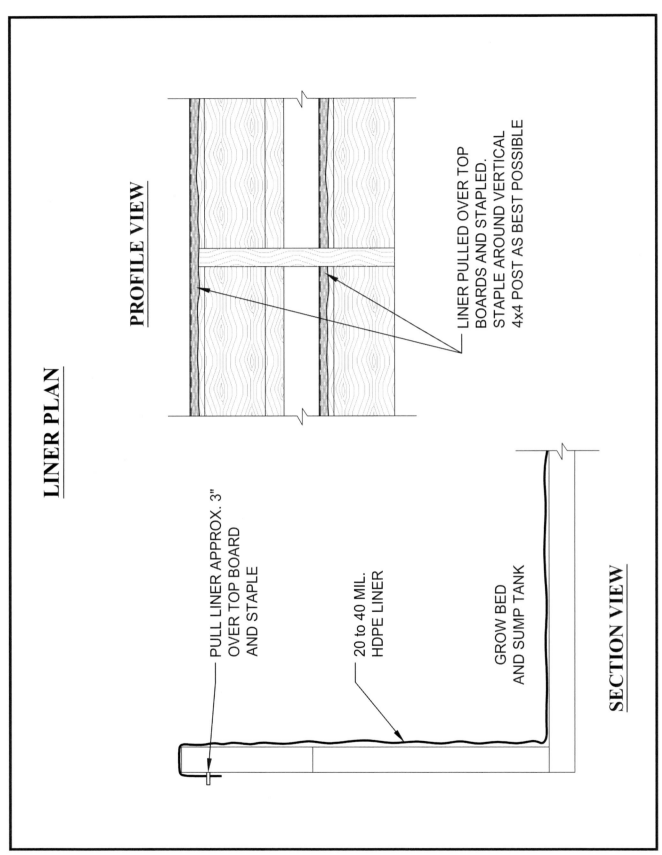

FIGURE 168. Liner plan.

CHAPTER 25

Design Plans and Construction Details Using IBC Containers Flood-and-Drain System

This chapter will provide step-by-step guide instructions and design details on how to build the media bed aquaponic system, shown below, using Intermediate Bulk Carrier (IBC). **For a Cost-Benefit Analysis** **(Aquaponic Economics) for this system, please refer to any of the author's *'Aquaponics for Profit'* book which address the aquaponics.**

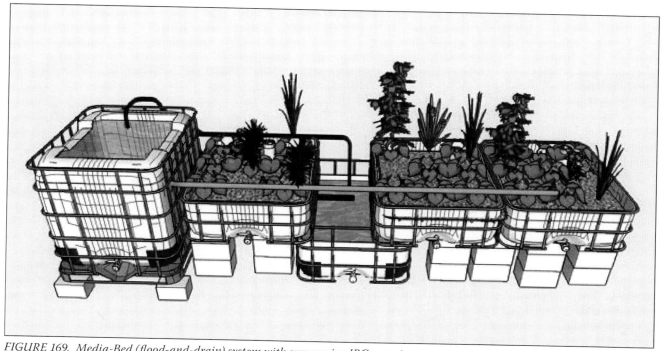

FIGURE 169. Media-Bed (flood-and-drain) system with sump using IBC containers.

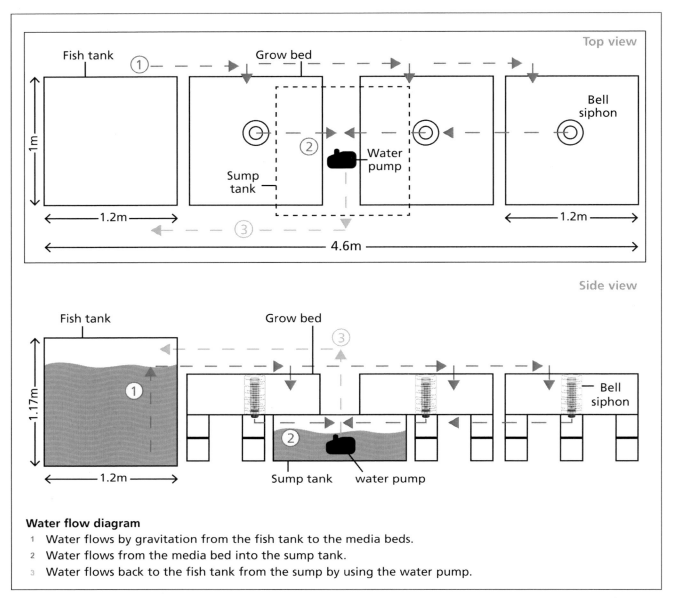

FIGURE 170. *Overall dimensions and schematic views.*

Tools Needed

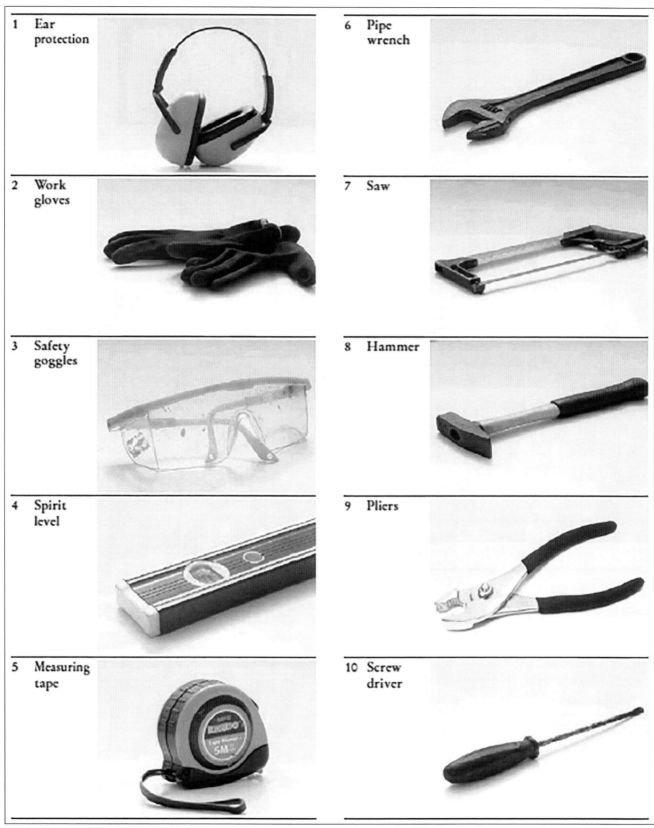

1 Ear protection

2 Work gloves

3 Safety goggles

4 Spirit level

5 Measuring tape

6 Pipe wrench

7 Saw

8 Hammer

9 Pliers

10 Screw driver

FIGURE 171.

11 Electric drill

12 Conical drill (0–1 in)

13 Jigsaw

14 Knife

15 Marker

16 Circular drill bit (hole saw)

17 Angle grinder

18 Star-headed key

FIGURE 172.

TABLE 22. **List of Material Items Needed**

NO.	ITEM DESCRIPTION	QUANTITY
1	IBC Tank (275 gallon or 1000 liter)	3
2	Concrete Blocks (6"x8"x16")	48
3	Lumber, 1"x4" x8' (1cm x 8cm x 2.4m)	3
4	Pea Gravel Media	13-Cubic Feet (375 liters)
5	Expanded Clay Media	13-Cubic Feet (375 liters)
6	Shade Material for Fish Tank	10 Square Feet (2 Square meters)
7	Teflon Tape (Plumber's Tape)	2 Rolls
8	Cable Ties	15
9	*Electric Box Upgrade	1
10	*Residual-Current Device (RCD)	1
11	Ecological Soap or Lubricant to slide pipe through Uniseal°	1
PVC PIPE AND FITTINGS		
12	PVC Pipe; 2-inch or 50mm Diameter	25-Feet (7.5 Meters)
13	PVC Elbow; 2-inch or 50mm Diameter	5
14	PVC Coupler, Straight; 2-inch or 50mm Diameter (if using male to female slide over fittings, couplers will not be needed)	6
15	PVC Connector (T-Connector); 2-inch or 50mm Diameter	2
16	PVC Endcap/Stopper; 2-inch or 50mm Diameter	4
17	PVC or Metal Tap (1-inch or 25 mm); Male to Female Fitting	3
18	Rubber Grommet (Uniseal°; 2-inch or 50mm Diameter	1
BELL SIPHON		
19	PVC Pipe; 4-inch or 110mm Diameter	1-Foot (0.9 Meters)
20	PVC Pipe (3-inch or 75mm) with Flared End + PVC Endcap (3-inch or 75mm) + Rubber Washer (3-inch or 75mm)	3
21	PVC Pipe; 1-inch or 25mm Diameter	2-Feet, 7.5-Inches (0.8 Meters)
22	PVC Bulkhead (Barrel Connector); B-Type; 1-inch or 25mm Diameter	3
23	PVC Adapter (Reducer); (1-1.5 inch or 25-40 mm)	3
24	PVC Female Fitting; 1-inch or 25mm Diameter	3
25	PVC Elbow, Female; 1-inch or 25mm Diameter	3
26	Polyethylene Hose or Tubing; 1-inch or 25mm Diameter	30-Feet (9 Meters)

***NOTE:** Replace existing electrical box with a residual-current device (RCD). This is a type of circuit breaker that will cut the power to the system if electricity grounds into the water. The best option is to have an electrician install one at the main electric junction. Alternatively, RCD adaptors are inexpensive and readily available at most hardware or home improvement stores. Also, replace current electrical junction box with an outdoor junction box. One each is listed in the above table, but use as many RCDs and outdoor junction boxes as needed in the aquaponic area. These simple precautions can save lives and protects fish.

TABLE 23. *Images of Material Items Needed*

ITEM DESCRIPTION	PHOTOGRAPH
IBC Tank	
Shade Cloth for Fish Tank	
Plastic Netting; Prevents Fish from Jumping Out	
Concrete Block	

ITEM DESCRIPTION	PHOTOGRAPH
Lumber	
Active Aqua, AAPW550 550-GPH (2000 LPH) Submersible, Pump — 6 Foot Cord (Cost: $25 USD, year 2020); or different brand pump with equal specifications. NOTE: Due to variations in plumbing, media, or other conditions between the directions provided in this chapter and your system, should you find that the grow beds are not going through the 'flood-and-drain' cycle, then install a timer or float switch on this sump pump.	
Teflon Tape (Plumber's Tape)	
Cable Ties	

ITEM DESCRIPTION	PHOTOGRAPH
PVC Pipe	
PVC Pipe (3-inch or 75 mm) with Flared End + PVC Endcap (3-inch or 75 mm) + Rubber Washer (3-inch or 75 mm)	
Polyethylene Hose or Tubing (1-inch or 25 mm Diameter)	
Rubber Grommet (Uniseal® (2-inch or 50 mm)	
PVC Adapter (Reducer) (1-1.5 inch or 25-40 mm) Examples of two different types of reducers/adapters shown.	

ITEM DESCRIPTION	PHOTOGRAPH
PVC Female Fitting (1- inch or 25 mm Diameter)	
PVC Elbow (1-inch or 25mm Diameter)	
PVC Elbow (2-inch or 50 mm Diameter)	
PVC Coupler, Straight (2-inch or 50 mm Diameter)	

ITEM DESCRIPTION	PHOTOGRAPH
PVC T-Connector Fitting (2-inch or 50 mm Diameter)	
PVC Endcap/Stopper (2-inch or 50 mm Diameter)	
PVC Bulkhead (Barrel Connector); B-Type 1-inch or 25mm Diameter	
PVC or Metal Tap (1-inch or 25 mm Diameter) Male to Female Fitting	

Construction Instructions (Step-By-Step Details)

1. Preparing the Fish Tank

1.1 — Remove the two horizontal steel lengths attached to the top surface of the IBC tank holding the inner plastic container in place. The steel lengths are fixed with 4 star-headed screws. Remove these four screws (figure 173, photo-1) using a star headed screwdriver (figure 173, photo-2) or star-headed key (figure 173, photo-3). Once the steel lengths are removed, pull out the inner plastic tank. If there is no star key, cut the screws with an angle grinder.

FIGURE 173.

1.2 — After pulling out the tank, draw a rough square shape on the top surface of the tank, 2-inches (5 cm) from, parallel along each of the 4 sides of the tank (figure 174, photo-4). Then, using the angle grinder (figure 174, photo-5), cut along the square shape and remove the cut piece from the top (figure 174, photo-6). Once removed, wash the inside of the container thoroughly with soap and warm water and leave to dry for 24 hours (figure 174, photo-7). The cut out top piece removed can be used as a fish tank cover.

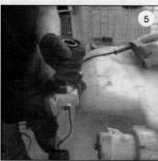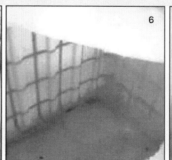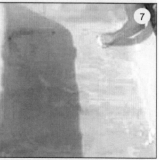

FIGURE 174.

2. Installing the Fish Tank Exit Pipe

2.1 — On one side of the IBC tank, mark a point 4.75-inches (12 cm) from the top and 4.75-inches (12 cm) from the side of the tank (figure 175, photo-8), and drill a hole at that point using the 57 mm circular drill bit (figure 175, photo-9). Insert a 2-inch (50 mm) uniseal (figure 175, photo-10) inside this hole. NOTE: The circular drill bit size should be 2 ¼ -inches (57 mm) and not 2-inches (50 mm).

FIGURE 175.

2.2 — The fish tank exit pipe is made of 2 lengths of PVC pipe 2-inch (50 mm) combined using a PVC elbow 2-inch (50 mm) and PVC coupler/straight connector 2-inch (50 mm) (figure 176, photo-11). The length of PVC 2-inch (50 mm) along the bottom surface of the tank is cut with horizontal slits 2–3 mm wide by using the angle grinder (figure 176, photo-12) to allow solid waste to enter the pipe but to prevent fish from doing so. The open end of the PVC length along the bottom surface of the fish tank is sealed with a PVC endcap/stopper 2-inch (50 mm). Slot a short length of PVC (50 mm) through the uniseal 2-inch (50 mm) and attach to a PVC elbow 2-inch (50 mm) on the inside end (figure 176, photo-11) and then attach the other (vertical) pipe length to the elbow that is now connected to the uniseal 2-inch (50 mm). Finally, drill a ¾ to 1-inch (2–3 cm) diameter hole into the PVC elbow 2-inch (50 mm) attached to the uniseal 2-inch (50 mm) (figure 176, photo-13). This small hole prevents any air seal forming inside the pipe, which would drain all the water out of the fish tank in the event of power cut or if the pump stopped working. This is also called an accidental siphon. This step is not optional.

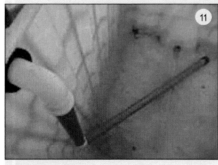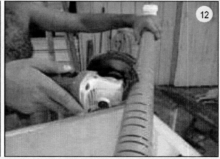

FIGURE 176.

3. Preparing the Media Beds and Sump Tank

3.1 — To make the 3 media beds and 1 sump tank, the 2 other IBC tanks are needed: the first to make the sump tank and 1 media bed, and the second to make the two remaining media beds. Take the 2 IBC tanks and remove the 4 steel profiles and pull out the plastic containers as shown before in figures 173, photos-1–3.

4. Making Two Media Beds From One IBC

4.1 — First, stand the plastic inner container upright (figure 177, photo-14) and mark, using a metre stick and pencil, two bisecting lines 12-inches (30 cm) from both sides of the tank (as seen in figure 177, photo-15). Make sure to mark the exact lines (shown in the figure 177, photo-15). Take the angle grinder and carefully cut along both bisecting lines marked out to create two uniform containers with a depth of 12-inches (30 cm) (figure 177, photo-16). Then, take both containers and wash them thoroughly using natural soap and warm water and leave them out to dry in the sun for 24 hours.

  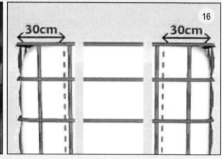

FIGURE 177.

5. Metal Supports For Both Media Beds

5.1 — Take the IBC metal support frame and cut out two support frames by following the same bisecting lines shown in figure 177, photo-14 using the angle grinder (figure 178, photo-17). When cutting the two 12-inches (30 cm) sides of the support frame, make sure to keep the two horizontal steel profiles intact as they will provide excellent support to the sides of the beds once they are full of water and medium (figure 178, photo-18).

FIGURE 178.

5.2 — Then, take both support frames and lay them out on the floor. Take the wood lengths (4 lengths of 41-inches (104 cm), 1 length of 16 ½–inches (42 cm) and 1 length of 19–inches (48 cm) and place them on top of the support frame as shown in figure 179, photo-19. These wood lengths keep the media bed horizontal, which is vital for the functioning of the bell siphons. Next, take the washed media beds and place them on top of the support frame and wood lengths (figure 179, photo-20). Finally slot in the remaining wood lengths in between the plastic media bed and support frame on both sides of each bed to provide further support (figure 179, photo-21).

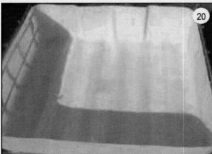

FIGURE 179.

6. Making A Sump Tank and One Media Bed From an IBC

6.1 — Take the remaining IBC, place it upright and mark out, using a metre stick and pencil, only one 12-inches (30 cm) bisecting line as seen in figure 180, photo-22. Then, take the angle grinder and cut the inner plastic container and metal support frame at once by following the bisecting line (see figure 180, photo-22). Remove the 12-inches (30 cm) container (third media bed) from the remaining 27 ½–inches (70 cm) container (sump tank) (figure 180, photo-23). Wash out both containers thoroughly with natural soap and warm water and leave in the sun for 24 hours.

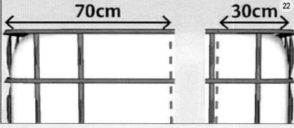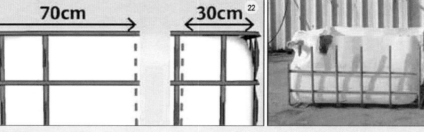

FIGURE 180.

6.2 — For the third media bed, follow the same steps regarding the wood lengths as detailed above for the first two. Finally, take the

FIGURE 181.

sump tank container and drill two holes 1-inch (25 mm) diameter) using the conical drill bit as shown in (figure 181, photo-25) where the 1-inch (25 mm) pipes will be inserted into both of these holes later, the pipes will drain water from each media bed.

7. Preparing the Bell Siphons

As explained elsewhere in this book, bell siphons are simple mechanisms used to automatically flood and drain each media bed. Refer to Chapter 25 and/or this section for information on how to make a bell siphon. The following materials are needed to make one siphon. Multiple by three, since a total of three bell siphons will be needed for this IBC aquaponic media bed system.

- 14-inch (35 cm) media guard using 4-inch (110 mm) diameter PVC pipe
- 10 ½-inch (27 cm) bell using [PVC pipe 3-inch (75 mm) with flared end + endcap/stopper 3-inch (75 mm) + rubber washer 3-inch (75 mm)]
- 6-inch (16 cm) standpipe (using a 1-inch or 25 mm PVC pipe)

- Bulkhead Fitting (Barrel Connector) (1-inch or 25 mm)
- PVC Adapter (Reducer) 1 ½ — 1-inch (40–25 mm)
- PVC Female Fitting; 1-inch (25mm) Diameter
- PVC Elbow, Female; 1-inch (25mm) Diameter

7.1 — First, create the bell. Take a 10 ½- inch (27 cm) section of 3-inch (75 mm) diameter PVC pipe and cut out 2 pieces as shown in figure 182, photo-26 using the angle grinder. Then, drill a hole with a 25/64 (10 mm) drill bit about 5/8-inch (1.5 cm) from the two cut pieces as shown in figure 182, photo-26. Finally, seal one end of the bell using the PVC endcap/stopper 3—inch (75 mm) and rubber washer 3-inch (75 mm).

7.2 — Next, make the media guards from the 14-inch (35 cm) length of PVC pipe 4-inch (110 mm) and cut 5 mm slots along their entire length using the angle grinder (figure 182, photo-27).

7.3 — Now, take each media bed and mark their centre points in-between the two wooden lengths below as shown in figure 182, photo-28. Drill a hole 1-inch (25 mm) in diameter at each center point

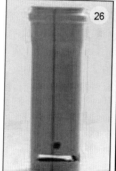
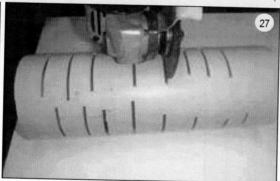
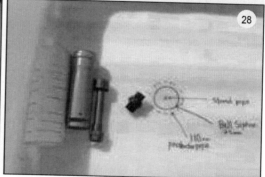
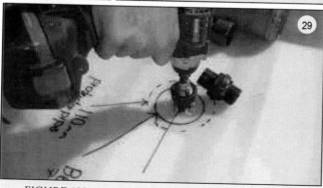

FIGURE 182.

(figure 182 photo-29) and insert the bulkhead fitting (barrel connector) 1-inch (25 mm) with the rubber washer placed inside the media bed. Tighten both sides of the bulkhead (barrel connector) using a wrench (figure 182, photo-30).

7.4 — Screw the PVC adaptor 1–inch (25 mm) onto the bulkhead fitting (barrel connector) 1–inch (25 mm) inside the media bed and then slot the standpipe into the PVC adaptor 1–inch (25 mm). After, attach the second PVC Adaptor (Reducer) 1½ — 1-inch (40–25 mm) to the top of the standpipe (figures 183, photos-31–33). The purpose of this adapter is to allow a larger volume of water to initially flow down the standpipe when the water has reached the top. This helps the siphon mechanism to begin draining the water out into the sump tank.

7.5 — Place the bell siphons and the media guards over the standpipes (figures 184, photos-34–36).

7.6 — Finally, connect the PVC elbow 1 inch (25 mm) to the other end of the bulkead fitting (barrel connector) underneath the media bed, which allows the water to flow out of the media bed (figures 185, photos-37–39).

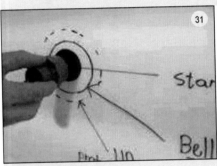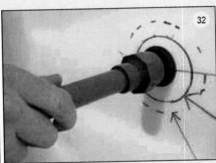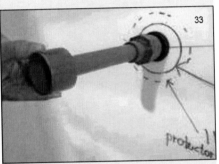

FIGURE 183.

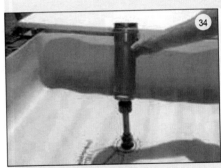

FIGURE 184.

8. Assembling the Media Beds and Sump Tank

8.1 — First, place the sump tank and brace it with six concrete blocks from each side (12 blocks in total) as shown in figures 186, photos-40 and 41. Make sure the blocks do not cover the holes already drilled into the sump tank (figure 186, photo-42).

8.2 — Place the remaining blocks and the fish tank according to the distances described in figure 187, photo-43. The fish tank should be raised up about 6-inches (15 cm) from the ground. This can be done by using concrete blocks as shown in figure 187, photo-43. Place the three media beds

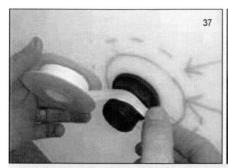
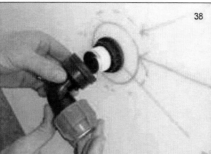
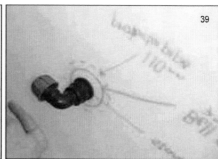

FIGURE 185.

(including the metal support frames and wood lengths) on top of the blocks (as shown in figure 187, photo-44). Make sure the grow beds are secured on top of the blocks and horizontal by verifying with a spirit level. If not, slightly adjust the layout of the blocks underneath.

9. Plumbing the System: Fish Tank to the Media

FIGURE 186.

Beds (Distribution Manifold)

9.1 — The plumbing parts needed for this section are as follows:

- Bulkhead Fitting (Barrel Connector), B-type (1-inch or 25 mm) × 3
- PVC Tap (1-inch or 25 mm) × 3
- PVC Endcap/stopper (Diameter: 2-inch or 50 mm) × 3
- PVC Elbow (Diameter: 2-inch or 50 mm) × 2
- PVC T-Connector (Diameter: 2-inch or 50 mm) × 2
- PVC Coupler (Diameter: 2-inch or 50 mm) × 3

FIGURE 187.

303

- 60-inches (150 cm) of PVC Pipe (Diameter: 2-inch or 50 mm) × 1
- 34-inches (85 cm) of PVC pipe (Diameter: 2-inch or 50 mm) × 1

9.2 — Go back to the "preparing the fish tank" (2.2) instructions. The last instruction shows a length of PVC (50 mm) slotted through the uniseal 2-inch (50 mm) diameter and exiting the fish tank. Take another PVC elbow 2-inch (50 mm) and connect it to the pipe slotted through the uniseal (figure 188, photo-45). Then, using a PVC straight coupler 2-inch (50 mm) and another PVC elbow 2-inch (50 mm), connect the fish exit pipe to the distribution pipe 2-inch (50 mm) at the same height as the top of the media bed (figure 188, photo-46).

9.3 — On each media bed, a valve is used to control the water flow entering the bed. To include a valve, first take a PVC endcap/stopper 2-inch (50 mm) and drill a hole (25 mm diameter). Insert a bulkhead fitting (barrel connector) 1-inch (25 mm) into the hole and tighten both ends using a wrench. Then, wrap Teflon tape around the threads of the male end of the barrel connector and screw the tap valve 1-inch (25 mm) onto the bulkhead (barrel connector) (figures 189, photos-47–50). There is one valve for each media bed for a total of three valves.

9.4 — From the PVC elbow 2-inch (50 mm) attached to the fish tank exit pipe, follow the pipe layout shown in figure 190-51 that allows water to flow into each media bed. Materials include: PVC

FIGURE 188.

pipe 2-inch (50 mm), PVC elbow 2-inch (50 mm) and PVC T-connector 2-inch (50 mm). Next, attach the pipe caps fitted with the valves to the PVC T connectors and PVC elbow connectors from the distribution pipe as in figure 190, photo-51, using one for each media bed. Use a PVC straight coupler 2-inch (50 mm), if necessary.

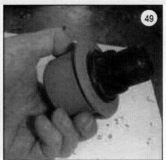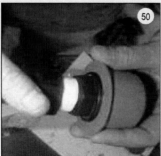

FIGURE 189.

10. Plumbing the Unit: Media Beds to the Sump Tank (Drain Pipe)

10.1 — Figures 191, photos-52 and 53 show the media beds marked as A, B and C. For media bed A, attach a drain pipe of 24-inch (60 cm) length of PVC pipe 1-inch (25 mm) to the elbow connection underneath the media bed (figure 192, photo-54), which exits from the bottom of the bell siphon standpipe. Next, slot the 24-inch (60 cm) length of pipe into the closest drilled hole on the side of the sump tank allowing the water to flow directly into the sump.

FIGURE 190.

10.2 — Attaching media beds B and C (figure 191, photo-53): Under media bed C: attach a PVC elbow connector (25 mm to 1 inch) to the end of the bulkhead (barrel connector) (figure 192, photo-54). Then, take a 80-inch (2 meter) length of polyethylene pipe 1-inch (25 mm) diameter and attach it to the drilled holes at the side of the sump tank (figure 191, photo-53 and figure 192, photo-55).

10.3 — Do the same with media bed B using 40-inch (1 meter) length of polyethylene pipe 1-inch (25 mm) diameter (figure 192, photo-55). Now, the water exiting media beds B and C will flow through separate polyethylene pipes 1-inch (25 mm) into the sump tank.

Finally, it is advisable to fix the pipes underneath the beds to the metal frame using cable ties to relieve any pressure on the pipe fittings (figure 192-54).

FIGURE 191.

11. Plumbing the Unit: Sump Tank to the Fish Tank

11.1 — Take the submersible pump and attach a polyethylene pipe 1-inch (25 mm) diameter using a

FIGURE 192.

PVC straight connector 1-inch (25 mm) diameter, or any other connector that can attach the specific pump to the 1-inch (25 mm) diameter pipe (figure 193-56). Take a length of the polyethylene pipe 1-inch (25 mm) diameter that is long enough to reach the inside of the fish tank from the submersible pump (figure 193-57). Attach one end to the submersible pump and the other into the top of the fish tank (see figure 193-57–60). It is recommended to use the fewest connectors, especially elbows, between the pump and fish tank which will decrease pumping capacity.

11.2 — Place the electric box in a safe place higher than the water level and shaded from direct sunlight. Make sure it is still waterproof after plugging in the water and air pump plugs (figure 193-61).

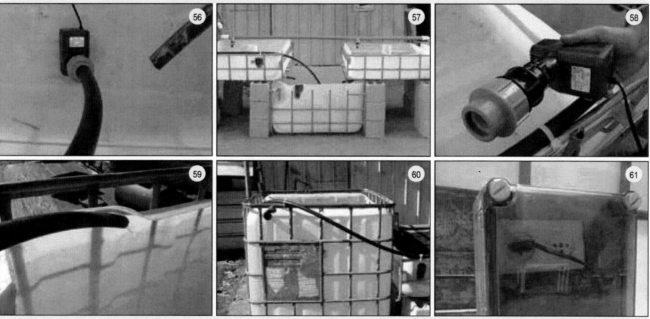

FIGURE 193.

12. Adding the Medium and Running the Unit

12.1 — All parts of the system are now in place. Before adding the media fill the fish tank and sump tank with water and run the pump to check for any leaks in the system. While checking for leaks, remove the standpipe and bell siphon so the water flows straight into the sump tank. If leaks appear, repair them where they arise by tightening the plumbing connections, re-applying Teflon to the treaded connections and making sure all taps are in their ideal position (figures 194-62–67).

12.2 — Once the water is flowing smoothly through all components of the unit, re-assemble the siphon bell and standpipes. Now mix and rinse the growing media outside the system. Flowing the rinsing of the media, fill the media beds to a depth of 12-inches (30 cm) (figures 194-68–69).

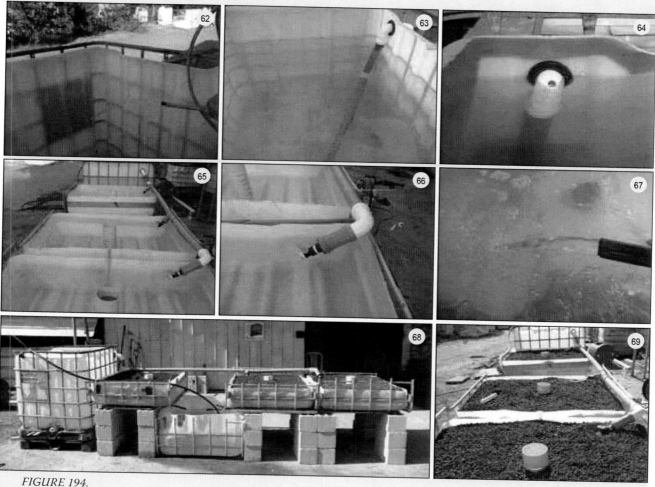

FIGURE 194.

12.3 — Verify that the grow beds are filling and draining appropriately (a thin layer of water in the grow bed is acceptable). Due to variations in plumbing, media, or other conditions associated with the system provided in this example and your system, should you find that the grow beds are not going through the 'flood-and-drain' cycle, then install a timer or float switch on the sump pump. A timer or float switch can easily be purchased at a well equipped hardware store, home improvement center, or online for less than $30 (USD, year 2022).

12.4 — Following successful construction of the system refer to 'Chapter 30 Starting, Operating, and Troubleshooting Your Aquaponic System', of this book. Enjoy an abundance of healthy organic food.

PART VI

Operation and Maintenance

CHAPTER 26

Starting, Operating, and Troubleshooting Your Aquaponic System

Successfully Activating Your Aquaponic System

When starting the system, you must be very patient. Don't expect your system to be running smoothly immediately. It can take up to five weeks, or even longer in some cases, before all living components of your system are in a thriving state of development. This is a good time to gain experience in testing the water and getting familiar with your automatic monitoring systems (should you elect to install such). Practice testing the tap water immediately out of the faucet (if you are using a public water source) and test it again after it has been in the system every couple of days. Also, practice recording the water quality readings, adjustments to your system that you have made, and organizing everything associated with your system (e.g. supplies, paperwork, tools, etc.). This will make things go much more smoothly over the long run, saving you time and trouble in the future. Most municipal tap water has chlorine added. This water needs to be dechlorinated. When starting, the water can be dechlorinated in the system over a few days. After your system it running, it is important to dechlorinate the water before adding fish to your system by letting it sit in another container for a day or two (if you have another container available). The more water, the longer it will take it to dechlorinate. If your tap water contains chloramines, it will be necessary to obtain a chemical neutralizer, available in most fish shops or online, to properly address this issue (just follow the directions on the container).

After you put your system together (pipes, water containers, media) and fill it with water, add some quick growing plants (such as beans), and run the system for a few weeks as if it were fully stocked. This will provide you with an opportunity to troubleshoot any problems, and should be enough time to let chlorine dissipate from the system. It will also allow you time to evaluate whether or not you need to rearrange your system for more optimal plant growth in regards to lighting, etc. Ensure all equipment (e.g., timers, backup power system, pumps, etc.) and piping is functioning properly. By the way, you can always replace the trial-and-error, fast growing plants (e.g., beans) with more desirable plants once you are comfortable the system is running smoothly.

Starting the 'Cycling' Process

After the system has been setup, it is important that it is 'cycled' properly. Just planting the seeds in the pots the moment you place the fish in the tanks will result in poor, if not fatal, results. The bacteria that is essential in establishing the balanced ecosystem and synergy between the fish and plants are lacking at the beginning stage. 'Cycling' is the term used to describe the process of establishing the vital system bacteria.

Without the establishment of these bacteria, the ammonia-rich fish wastes cannot be broken down and transformed into soluble nutrients (nitrates) that can be absorbed by plants for growth. As a result, the fish wastes will build up to toxic levels, and the fish will perish. The plants are also unable to grow adequately due to the lack of nutrients. Therefore, bacterial populations need to be established within the aquaponics system so that plant growth and fish life can be supported.

The two main methods for cycling (or establishing the bacteria) is by raising fingerlings (feeder fish) and fishless cycling. However, the first thing needed is a freshwater test kit to monitor the ammonia, nitrite, and nitrate levels as well as pH throughout the cycling process. This is the only way to identify problems, determine if corrective action is needed if any of these elements get out of range, and to know when the system is fully cycled.

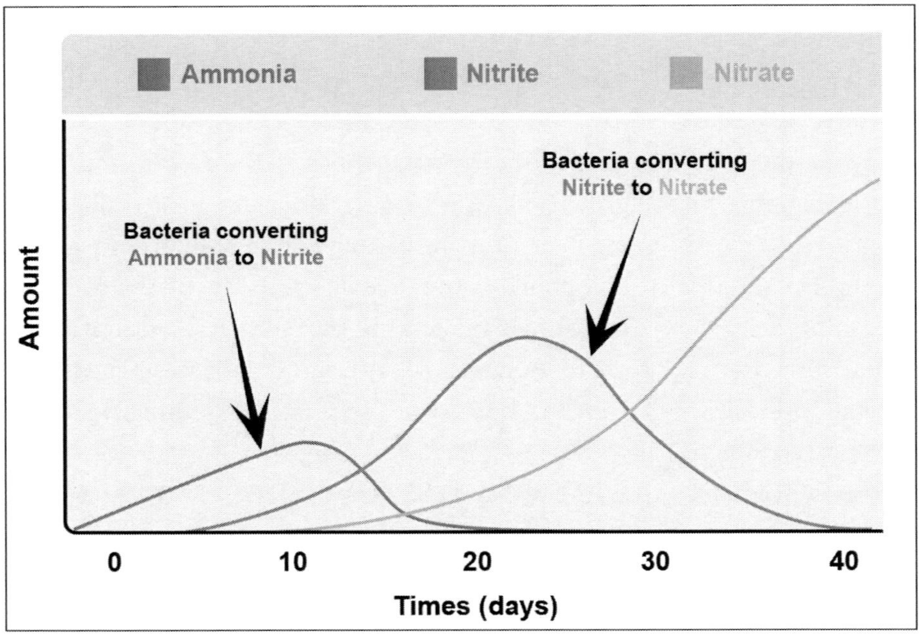

'Cycling' with Fingerlings

Using fingerlings is a traditional method to establish bacteria populations naturally. It can take up to two months. You can start up your system by using either the fingerling of your intended fish species or cheap feeder fish such as goldfish or minnows.

The fish in the tanks start producing ammonia-rich waste, which in turn attracts the air-borne nitrosomonas bacteria to populate the surface of the water. These bacteria convert the toxic ammonia into nitrites, which are still toxic to fish. However, the presence of nitrites will attract the nitrobacter bacteria. The nitrobacter bacteria then convert the nitrites to nitrates, which are harmless to the fish but are essential nutrients for the plants.

During this process it is important to monitor the water quality closely, as well as the state of health of the fish. At this initial stage of getting your system cycled, toxic ammonia and nitrites are accumulating in the tanks. This can be very stressful to the fish, and even be toxic if not maintained properly.

When cycling the system it is best to feed the fish small amounts of food to avoid ammonia spike and algal bloom. Cease feeding the fish if you observe an algae bloom or the ammonia/nitrites levels increasing to a high level of 1 ppm; as this signals that the bacterial population is insufficient to transform the wastes. Only resume feeding when the ammonia and nitrite levels return to 0.5 ppm and below. Start increasing the feeding rates after two months, when a thriving bacterial base has been established.

FIGURE 195. Cycle process.

Fishless 'Cycling'

Fishless cycling makes use of other sources of ammonia instead of fish. Compared to the traditional method of cycling described above, fishless cycling is faster as higher doses of ammonia can be generated in a shorter period of time. You can also control precisely how much ammonia to add without being concerned about fish survival.

Fishless cycling can be accomplished within 10 days. You can then fully stock your fish tank.

Two Primary Methods to Add Ammonia to the System:

1. **Pure Liquid Ammonia:** It is relatively inexpensive and can be found in most home improvement and cleaning supply stores. It is also available online.

2. **Ammonium Chloride:** Also known as Sal ammoniac. Sold in some hardware stores, but most commonly purchased online. It is more costly than liquid ammonia.

Once you have decided which source of ammonia to use, simply add it to the water in incremental doses to start the cycling process; and then monitor the ammonia, nitrites and nitrate levels over time until the parameters within the water reach the desired quality.

Knowing When to Start Plants

Check temperature, pH, ammonia, nitrite, and nitrate levels, with a water test kit (available online, at most local aquarium and pet stores). Keep a log of date, reading levels, and any changes made to the system, including anything added, removing fish, plants, grow bed adjustments, equipment changes, modifications to lighting, and feed data. Without a proper recording everything it is extremely difficult, if not impossible, to operate the system at optimal efficiency. Keeping accurate records will also provide you with the information needed to quickly troubleshoot system problems. The more data recorded, the higher the success rate.

Each aquaponics system will level out at a different pH reading. This is determined by water source and constituents within the water, and media type; as well as system configuration.

If nitrite level is not zero, run the system another week and recheck. If the readings remain unsuitable for over a week with no changes to the system, the system may be imbalanced or materials used may be negatively affecting it (e.g. media impacting the pH).

When reading levels are good, add plants if you have not already done so. Many operators proclaim to have greater success when they gradually add more fish over time, rather than all at once. It is prudent to add plants and fish at a slow rate to make sure that the water nutrient levels are stable and to give the system time to adjust. Always be sure to temperature match the water before releasing fish into the tank. Once the system has "cycled", the water should be clear. Larger systems can adapt and absorb changes easier than a smaller system.

The only way to determine when is the cycling process has reach the desired outcome is to monitor the water quality daily with the water test kit. Cycling is completed when the ammonia and nitrite levels drop to zero and the nitrate levels increase to 5-10 ppm. Once theses readings are achieved fish can be added to the tank (if done via fishless cycling) and plants can be planted.

The cycling process can also be sped up by 'seeding' the system (i.e. adding bacteria) from existing colonies. Sources of bacterial include nitrifying bacteria product found in commercially available cycling kits and disease-free aquaponics filters.

System Startup Checklist

1. Define your short-term and long term goals. What is your objective for getting into aquaponics? Where would you like to be with your aquaponics endeavor in five years?

2. What type of plants and fish do you want to raise? Are they compatible with your proposed aquaponic system environment/climate? Is the demand/need for the plants & fish you have in mind worth your effort or would it make more sense to raise produce that has a higher profit margin, is expensive to purchase at the store, and/or difficult to obtain organically in your area?

3. Decide on type and size of system to build.

4. Draw design plans. Take into consideration a plan for future potential expansion.

5. Research where to get parts, equipment, and fish.

6. Buy and assemble components.

7. Start plants from seed or find a reliable source for seedlings. Be sure to obtain organic (non-GMO seeds).

8. Fill system with water and circulate (at least a week).

9. Add plants to the system and enjoy their growth.

10. If using a fishless cycle, begin the nitrification process.

11. Add fish to the system. Start out with about 20 percent of the final maximum capacity stocking density.

12. Monitor water quality, and perform partial water changes as needed.

13. Rinse media well before putting in the system, otherwise it can produce very cloudy dirty water introduce pathogens.

How to Introduce New Fish into Your Tank

Moving into a new home can be a shock for any creature, but for fish it is particularly stressful. Not only will a new tank be completely unfamiliar for your new fish, but the water will likely be of a different quality. Subtle changes in water temperature, pH, and other factors make a big difference in a fish's life. To keep your fish safe and healthy, there are certain measures you should take when introducing fish to a new tank. Following are some tips on how to make an easy transition:

1. Test your water quality before adding your new fish. Your chlorine level should be at zero, and your pH should match that of where the fish is coming from.

2. Gradually add your system water to the transport tank to equalize the temperature.

3. Feed the fish in your system before adding any new fish. This will make the existing fish less aggressive.

4. Before adding your new fish, dim the lights. This will create a less stressful environment.

5. When the transport tank water has relatively the same water parameters (e.g., temperature, pH, dissolved oxygen) as your fish tank, then relocate the fish to the new fish tank. Only relocate the fish. Do not relocate the transport water into your system. Dispose of the transport water.

6. If possible, add more than one fish at a time, as this reduces the chance of one fish being picked on and harassed.

Tips and Tricks for Aquaponics

1. Main tain system. Stay organized. Keep good records.

2. If using gravel media, always test the pH of the gravel media before adding it to your system. This will let you know if your system will have a tendency to be more on the acid or base side, so that you can be better prepared in regards to taking appropriate measures in maintaining the ideal pH.

3. For smaller systems vitamin C and an air pump can be used to more quickly bubble out chlorine and chloramine from tap water.

5. Never use cleaning products, pesticides, algae-cides, fertilizers or like substances in fish tanks or grow beds.

6. Spray plants with diluted vinegar and water solution if you discover aphides.

7. Avoid direct sunlight on fish tanks. You can limit light on the fish tank to avoid algae growth. Although tilapia will eat algae.

8. Never change more than ⅓ of water at a time. More than that will destroy the good bacteria in the system.

9. Cover outdoor plants during a frost, and shade sensitive plants from the scorching summer sun.

10. Make sure you have backup power available for pumps and aerators. Purchasing an inverter box (approx. $25 USD from an automotive store) and connecting it to an automobile battery when the power is out is the least expensive way to have a backup power. supply.

11. Prepare for system failure. Be proactive by having at least one spare pump and battery backup system on hand.

12. It is prudent to keep spare dechlorinated water readily on hand. It is recommended that you store at least 10 percent of your system water volume in a separate container. If using municipal water be sure to let it sit for a minimum of 24 hours before adding to your system so it can properly dechlorinate. Water will need to be added to the system on a regular basis to offset evaporation. Adding chlorinated water directly to your system will kill off the beneficial bacteria.

Aquaponic System Operation and Maintenance

Following is a preview of the tasks that can be expected in aquaponics gardening. It may seem like a lot of information to keep up with, but really, once the system has been established and you learn what to do, it only takes a small amount of your time.

Furthermore, there are automated monitors and controls that you can integrate into your system which will simplify the process even more.

Visual Inspection

A daily visual inspection is necessary to ensure that the system is operating as it should. A walkthrough inspection would consist of observing the filters, water clarity, pumps, aerators, and plants for any problems. The water circulation between the grow beds and fish tanks should be flowing normally. Water levels should be adequate, and topped off if necessary, especially during the summer.

Water Quality and Temperature Monitoring

An entire chapter in this book is dedicated to water quality (Chapter 31). The Water Quality chapter provides more detail than what is covered in this section. However, this section will provide a brief overview on water quality and temperature.

Maintaining water quality is essential to the success your aquaponics operation. Water pH should be checked at least 3–4 times a week. Generally speaking, the pH levels should be maintained as close to neutral as possible, preferably in the range of pH 6.8–7. This pH range is a compromise to the optimal range for most plants, fish and bacteria. However, this range may need to be adjusted to suit plants and fish that do not fit this norm.

If the pH falls below the optimal range, you can alternate between using calcium hydroxide and potassium carbonate or potassium hydroxide. Both calcium and potassium are important minerals for healthy plant growth. To bring down the pH levels, you can use some of the same pH regulators that are used in hydroponics. Be sure to avoid using pH regulators that contain sodium, as they are detrimental to the life within your system. In addition, do not use products containing citrus to adjust pH.

The water introduced into the system should be free of chlorine and chemicals. Bacteria colonies will be killed off by chlorine, chemicals can be harmful to all life within the system and enter into your food chain. If using municipal water, it is important to let it stand in a separate tank for 2 to 3 days so the chlorine can vaporize off before being added to your system. Aerating the water in the tank can speed up the process.

Also, monitor the water temperature using a submersible thermometer to ensure that water in the fish tank is kept stable and within the optimal range of your fish. Depending on your location, and the particular species of fish you are raising, you may need additional heating and insulation to help maintain temperatures.

Feeding of Fish

Feeding your fish is often viewed as one of the most enjoyable daily tasks by aquaponic operators. Fish need to be fed 1-2 times a day, but they don't necessarily have to be fed at regular timings. The process can even be automated with the use of auto-feeders. Some of these feeders can be acquired fairly inexpensively.

Most fish used in aquaponics can be fed with commercial feeds, worms (you can even grow your own worms), or with another species, scraps of food. Some operators have separate tanks that they use to grow algae or duckweed in which they net out periodically to feed their tilapia. Beware of commercial fish feed that is not organic if you are desiring to maintain a food supply that is completely free of heavy metals and other chemicals used on crops, as GMO feed will be a gateway of such into your food chain.

When fish are not eating, it typically signifies that they are stressed. It could be that they are too cold, too hot, there is too much direct lighting, oxygen is lacking, and/or there are water quality problems. If this happens, it is important to check all system parameters to identify the problem, and correct it right away.

Routine Aquaponic System Management Practices

Below are daily, weekly and monthly activities to perform to ensure that the aquaponic system is running well. These lists should be made into checklists and recorded. That way, multiple operators always know exactly what to do, and checklists prevent carelessness that can occur with routine activities. These lists are not meant to be exhaustive, but merely a guideline for management activities based upon a typical aquaponic system. Following this section are two 'go-by' checklist forms which will hopefully be helpful.

Daily Activities

Check that the water and air pumps are working well, and clean their inlets from obstructions.

- Check that water is flowing.
- Check the water level, and add additional water to compensate for evaporation, as necessary.
- Check for leaks.
- Check water temperature.
- Feed the fish (2–3 times a day if possible), remove uneaten feed and adjust feeding rates.
- At each feeding, check the behaviour and appearance of the fish.
- Check the plants for pests. Manage pests, as necessary.
- Remove any dead fish. Remove any plants/branches.
- Remove solids from the fish tank and sump; and rinse any filters being used.

Weekly Activities

- Perform water quality tests for pH, ammonia, nitrite and nitrate before feeding the fish.
- Adjust the pH, as necessary.
- Check the plants looking for problems. Address, as necessary.
- Check the fish tank from the bottom up.

- If using a biofilter, check it.
- Plant and harvest the vegetables, as required.
- Harvest fish, if required.
- Check that plant roots are not obstructing pipes or water flow.

Monthly Activities

- Stock new fish in the tanks, if required.
- Clean out the biofilter, or other filters, if not operating efficiently.
- Clean the bottom of the fish tank using fish nets.
- Weigh a sample of fish and check thoroughly for any disease.

System Maintenance Overview

1. Feed the fish daily, monitor fish health.
2. Test water quality (every other day for the first month, then about once a week, and when you suspect problems).

3. As needed, clean out filter screens, filter tanks (if using), tubing, water pump, growbed media, etc.
4. Check plant health, trim back, harvest or take cuttings.
5. Check plants for bugs or nutrient deficiencies.

Aquaponic Work Tools

Following are two very helpful tools for the aquaponic system operator:

1. Aquaponic System Data Tracking Worksheet (table 24)
2. Daily/Weekly/Monthly Maintenance Checklist (table 25)

Plant Care

To be a committed aquaponics operator, it is important to check on the plants regularly (preferably daily). Attention to pruning, plant structural support, and harvesting, when necessary, will provide optimal results. With aquaponics, gardening chores are much simpler as they are confined to waist-level activities, require no weeding, watering, or compost compared to soil-based traditional gardening chores.

TABLE 24. **Aquaponic System Data Tracking Sheet**

DATE	pH	AMMONIA	NITRATE	NITRITE	NOTES

TABLE 25. **Aquaponics System Maintenance Checklist**

Month_____

	MONDAY	TUESDAY	WEDNESDAY	THURSDAY	FRIDAY	SATURDAY	SUNDAY
Week 1							
Week 2							
Week 3							
Week 4							
Week 5							

Weekly Tasks

	WEEK 1	WEEK 2	WEEK 3	WEEK 4
Check pH				
Check Ammonia				
Add Water				
Check for Insects				

Monthly Tasks

	MONTH
Clean Out Pumps and Plumbing	
Check Nitrate Levels	

Harvesting of Fish and Stocking of New Fish

With the right set-up, and when done correctly, aquaponics allows for the regular harvesting of fish. You do not have to harvest the entire tank of fish at the same time. In fact, it is not advisable to do so. As a matter of fact, the closer you keep the system operating at optimal stocking density, the better the plants will do. If growing t ilapia or another species that does not typically eat the young, you can stock the tank with new fingerlings when the fish population has gone below the optimal stocking density.

Fish Health Check and Addressing Fish Illness

It is prudent to regularly net some fish to check on their state of health. Also, consider having a separate tank to isolate fish that appear to be sick, so as to prevent the spread diseases among the fish population.

Some aquaponic operators maintain a separate quarantine fish tank for sick fish. They will pull sick fish from their aquaponics system and put them in the quarantine tank. They then add salt to the quarantine tank periodically for disease control. Salt acts as a natural anti-bacterial agent on the fish body. Due to various risk to the overall fish health, this practice needs to be done slowly over time, with water quality and fish health closely monitored throughout and following the process. Only pure sea salt or swimming pool salt should be used. Table salt should never be used.

It is important to add only predetermined calculated amounts of salt as different fish species have varying levels of tolerance. Too much salt can be fatal to the fish. Whenever salt is added, it is important that a refractometer be used throughout the process so salt concentration can be properly monitored. Do not add salt to the aquaponic system (only add salt to a separate quarantine tank).

Addressing Emergencies

Emergency Response Processes to Have In Place

- Ready Phone List
  - » Plumbers
  - » Electricians
  - » Staff
  - » Fire/Emergency

- Trained Staff
  - » Logical Troubleshooting Procedures
  - » Triage
  - » Know when and who to call for addition help.
  - » Safety

- System Designed to Fail Reliably

Necessary Response Times for Emergencies

- **High** (fast response time — minutes)
  - » electrical power
  - » water level in tank
  - » dissolved oxygen — aeration system/ oxygen system

- **Medium** (moderate response time — hours)
  - » temperature
  - » carbon dioxide

- **Low** (normally slowly changing — days)
  - » pH
  - » alkalinity
  - » ammonia-nitrogen
  - » nitrite-nitrogen
  - » nitrate-nitrogen

TABLE 26. *Potential Emergencies*

NOTE: Not all below situations are applicable to all the different types of aquaponic systems

TYPE OF PROBLEM	CAUSES
Beyond your control	Flood, tornadoes, wind, snow, ice, storms, electrical outages, vandalism/theft
Staff error, diffusers plugged	Operator "errors", overlooked maintenance causing failure of back-up systems or systems components, alarms deactivated.
Tank water level	Drain valve opened, standpipe fallen or removed, leak in system, overflowing tank.
Water flow	Valve shut or opened too far, pump failure, loss of suction head, intake screen plugged, pipe plugged.
Water quality	Low dissolved oxygen, high CO_2, supersaturated water supply, high or low temperature, high ammonia, nitrite, or nitrate, low alkalinity.
Filters	Channeling/plugged filters, excessive head loss
Aeration system	Blower motor overheating because of excessive back-pressure, drive belt loose or broken or disconnected, leaks in supply lines.

Aquaponic Safety

Safety is important for both the operator and the system itself. The most dangerous aspect of aquaponics is the proximity of electricity and water, so proper precautions need to be taken. Food safety is important to ensure that no pathogens, chemicals, or heavy metals are introduced into the system, whereby they are then transferred to human food.

Electrical Safety

Always use a residual-current device (RCD). This is a type of circuit breaker that will cut the power to the system if electricity grounds into the water. The best option is to have an electrician install one at the main electric junction. Alternatively, RCD adaptors are available, and inexpensive, at any hardware or home improvement store. An example of an RCD can be found on most hairdryers. This simple precaution can save lives. Moreover, never hang wires over the fish tanks or filters. Protect cables, sockets, and plugs from the elements, especially rain, splashing water, and humidity. There are outdoor junction boxes available for these purposes. Check often for exposed wires, frayed cables, or faulty equipment and replace accordingly. Utilize "drip loops" where appropriate to prevent water from running down a wire into the junction. Never leave extension cords on the ground where water escaping the system can come into contact with it (such can be fatal to human life).

Food Safety

Good agricultural practices (GAPs), should be adopted to reduce, as much as possible, any food-borne illnesses. The first and most important is simple: always be clean. Most diseases that affect humans would be introduced into the system by the operators. Use proper hand-washing techniques and always sanitize harvesting equipment. When harvesting, do not let the water touch the produce; do not let wet hands or wet gloves touch the produce either. If present, most pathogens are in the system water and not on the produce. Always wash produce after harvesting, and again before consumption.

Second, keep soil, weeds, and pests from entering the system. Do not place harvesting equipment on the ground. Prevent vermin, such as rats, from entering the system, and keep pets and livestock away from the area. Warm-blooded animals often carry diseases that can be transferred to humans. Prevent birds from contaminating the system however possible, through the use of exclusion netting and deterrents (e.g., scarecrow, fake owl, plastic snake, etc.). If using rainwater collection, ensure that birds are not roosting on the collection area, or consider treating the water before adding it to the system. Preferably, do not handle the fish, plants, or media with bare hands; disposable gloves are always the safest bet.

General Safety

Often aquaponic systems, farms, and gardens in general, have other general hazards that can be avoided with simple precautions. Avoid leaving power cords, air lines, or pipes in walkways as they can pose a trip hazard. Water and media are heavy, so use proper lifting techniques. Wear protective gloves when working with the fish and avoid the spines. Treat any scrapes and punctures immediately with standard first-aid procedures — washing, disinfecting, and bandaging the wound. Seek medical attention, if necessary. Do not let blood or body fluids enter the system, and do not work with open wounds. When constructing the system, be aware of saws, drills, and other tools.

Keep acids and bases in safe storage areas, and use proper safety gear when handling these chemicals. Always keep all dangerous chemicals and objects properly stored and away from children. Ensure that children cannot fall into fish tanks.

Safety Summary Overview

- Take all necessary safety precautions where electricity and water combinations occur.
- Follow all National Electric Codes.
- Use RCD on electric components to avoid electrocution.
- Use only low voltage equipment and sources 24 VAC or 12 or 24 VDC.
- Shelter any electric connections from rain, splashes, and humidity using correct equipment.
- Implement a maintenance schedule & regular system checks.
- Ensure that everyone working with the aquaponics system is properly trained.
- Have strict policies, procedures, and supervision involved for all working with the system; especially for entry level staff and visitors.
- Follow OSHA guidelines for all aspects of the operation.
- Do not contaminate the system by using bare hands in the water.
- Avoid trip hazards by keeping a neat workstation.
- Wear gloves when handling fish and avoid spines.
- Wash and disinfect wounds immediately. Do not work with open wounds. Do not let blood enter the system.
- Be careful with power tools and dangerous chemicals; wear protective gear.
- Adopt GAPs to prevent contamination of produce. Always keep harvesting tools clean, wash hands often, and wear gloves. Do not let animal faeces contaminate the system.

Troubleshooting: Problems and Solutions

Plants Troubleshooting: Potential Problems & Solutions

Problem: *Plants are Dying*

Reason: Potentially due to any number of reasons such as: fish/plant ammonia ratio out of balance, not enough food for plants, oxygen deficiency, water quality, minerals, temperature, pH, bugs, lighting, fungus, etc.

Solution: Perform an internet search by typing in plant symptoms, and/or consult plant expert. Check all system parameters (pH, dissolved oxygen levels, etc.).

Problem: *Aphids Eating Plants*

Reason: Natural phenomenon in the real world. Not as common in greenhouses.

Solution: Spray the plants with water and/or buy a bag of ladybugs from local nursery. Ladybugs eat aphids. Release the ladybugs at night, when they are not active and can easily be handled.

Problem: *Caterpillars Eating Plants*

Reason: Natural phenomenon in the real world. Less common in greenhouses.

Solution: Use garlic spray on plants. Put caterpillars into the fish tank as free fish food.

Problem: *Plants are Discolored*

Reason: Typically, it is a sign of a mineral deficiency.

Solution: Perform an internet search by typing in plant symptoms, and/or consult a plant expert.

Problem: *Plants Not Growing or Have an Extremely Slow Growth Rate*

Reason: The pH may be too high. Inadequate nutrients in water.

Solution: Check pH, increase feed if fish eat it all too quickly or reduce number of plants in system.

Water Quality Troubleshooting: Potential Problems & Solutions

Problem: *The pH over 7.5 or pH is less than 6.5 (or out of your systems optimal range)*

Reason: Acidity of water is too low or too high.

Solution: Refer to section in this book regarding pH and how to adjust it. Remember though, quick pH level changes are hazardous to fish. Since most systems naturally settle into their own operating pH level over time, adjusting and maintain pH beyond this natural range can be an ongoing challenge. If a system component (like media, water content) is already buffering the system, additives will only change pH temporarily. It is best to find long-term solutions such as adjusting the media type, or go with plants and fish that best suit your natural pH parameters.

Problem: *Low Water Level*

Reason: Surface evaporation and plant transpiration reduce water in system. The larger the plant, the more water they absorb and transpire. Warmer temperatures, low humidity, and turbulent water will result in greater evaporation.

Solution: Top off system with dechlorinated water. Ensure there are no water leaks.

Problem: *Water is Green*

Reason: Too much algae. May be due to water having too many nutrients and/or too much light hitting the water surface.

Solution: Make sure you have the correct tank to grow bed volume ratio, you are not over feeding the fish, and the fish tank is properly shaded. Also note that some algae eating fish will only eat certain types of algae.

Problem: *Water is Dirty*

Reason: Usually a result of fish not eating all of their food, and/or the system is under-filtered.

Solution: Ensure that you are not over feeding. Use a towel or sock as a filter on the return water to help filter out sediment that is not captured in the grow bed.

Problem: *Water is Cloudy*

Reason: Overfeeding, system is out of balance, algae growth, and/or the system is under-filtered.

Solution: Ensure that you are not over feeding. Also make sure that all water parameters (i.e. temperature, pH, dissolved oxygen, etc.) are in the desired range.

Problem: *Top of Tank Has Iced Over*

Reason: Conditions are too cold.

Solution: Adjust temperature of water and/or room temperature. If fish are still alive, add air bubbles to fish tank to maintain oxygen levels.

Problem: *Water is Foaming*

Reason: Detergents or other chemicals may have been introduced into the system.

Solution: Perform 50 percent dechlorinated water changes every day until the foaming is gone. It is important to prevent fish shock as much as possible in this situation, but it is also critical to eliminate the contaminants. Be careful not to eliminate most of your beneficial bacteria, as they keep the system cycling properly Refrain from cleaning media.

Fish Troubleshooting: Potential Problems & Solutions

Primary Ingredients for Fish Health:

1. Know and maintain the optimal water parameters for your fish species (i.e. temperature, pH, dissolved oxygen, etc.).

2. Feed fish at a rate appropriate to the biomass of your fish and stage of growth. Observe feedings to ensure fish are being fed enough or that there is not a lot of waste. Adjust feedings appropriate with growth rate and with changes of stocked density.

3. Shade fish tank as appropriate. No direct lighting on fish tank.

4. Remove or minimize stress (i.e. vibration, loud noises, banging, etc.). The author prefers aquaponic system designs that do not have the pump inside the fish tank.

Problem: *Dead Fish*

Reason: Unknown.

Solution: Remove dead fish from the tank immediately to prevent decaying ammonia buildup. Try to identify the reason for death. Observe other fish to ensure there is not major problem with the system.

Problem: *Fish Seriously Sick, Almost Dead, No Hope of Recovery*

Reason: Unknown.

Solution: Euthanasia. Don't flush, suffocate (by allowing fish to die out of water), freeze, or use antacid. These methods are forms of extended torture and inhumane is to remove the fish from the tank and flatten fish's head hard and fast with a brick.

Problem: *Fish Swimming at Surface of Water Unusually or Gulping Air at Surface ('piping')*

Reason: Lack of dissolved oxygen. However, piping can also be a symptom of fish being infected with gill parasites.

Solution: Immediately add an air bubbler. Manually splash water but try not to stress fish.

Water/air exchange introduces oxygen into the water. Test to see if pH levels are low and increase slowly if necessary. Remember, changing pH as little as 0.2 quickly can be dangerous to the fish.

Problem: *Fish Acting Unusual, (i.e. not behaving normally, swimming sideways, floating upside down, etc.)*

Reason: Possibly a problem with the feed you are using. Could be the result of a disease, injury, or poor water quality. Odd behaviors could indicate breeding activity.

Solution: Monitor activity. Try a different feed. Do an internet search with the specific symptoms and type of fish. Consult a fish expert.

Problem: *Fish Jumping Out of Tank*

Reason: It could be that the water level is too high, they are trying to catch insects, a result of poor water quality, or water parameters are not within the proper range for your fish species.

Solution: Reduce water level if necessary, cover tank with wire mesh/netting, test water parameter conditions, test water quality, and/or filter water intake with a rag or sock to catch sediment if water is not clear.

Problem: *Fish Has Creamy White Film Slime*

Reason: Could be the result of low pH level, breeding behavior, or disease.

Solution: Check pH level, try to determine if it is potentially disease related (fish not acting healthy), and do an internet search with the specific symptoms.

Problem: *Fish has been determined to have Ich, Ick, or White Spot Disease*

Reason: A protozoa (one-cell animal parasite) called Ichthyophthirius multifiliis. Typically takes hold as a result of stress (environment change/fighting) which often negatively impacts the immune system of the fish making it more susceptible to such problems.

Solution: Easily treated if caught in time. It is best to treat the fish in a separate quarantine tank. Other solutions include:

Adding one-tablespoon sea salt (non-iodized salt) per 1-gallon water in the system. In addition, gradually raise water temperature to the upper limits of your fish species optimal temperature range.

Purchase one of the following products online, or from your local aquarium or pet shop: Coppersafe, Quick-Cure Ich-Ease, Aquari-sol, Cure-Ick, or Super Ick Cure. Follow directions.

Problem: *Fish Disappeared*

Reason: Critter, thief, or the fish flopped out of tank.

Solution: Cover tank with wire netting and secure it, erect a scarecrow to the tank, close and lock greenhouse at night, and/or monitor aggressive fish.

Problem: *Algae on Fish*

Reason: Algae does not grow on fish; it grows on fungus on your fish. It can also be the result of cyanobacteria and/or high nitrates in the tank. Too much light on the fish tank can exacerbate this problem.

Solution: Ensure tank conditions are in the optimal range. Filter the intake coming from your grow bed with a towel or sock (something extra to filter the water before if enters back into the fish tank).

Problem: *Fish Are Not Eating in Colder Weather*

Reason: Fish eat less the colder the water temperature. Water temperature impacts fish metabolism. Fish digestive enzymes are also not as active when temperature drops.

Solution: Feed less and/or raise the temperature (depending upon the circumstances and species). Every situation is unique.

Problem: *Power Outage*

Reason: Power grid is unreliable.

Solution: Always have a backup system readily available.

Problem: *Water Pump Stops*

Reasons: Lack of electricity, defective or clogged pump.

Solution: A system crash can occur in less than 24 hours. Switch to backup power system (if power outage). Replace pump right away. It is prudent to have at least one back-up pump readily available.

Problem: *System is Leaking Water*

Reason: Parts are old and cracking, sealants/tape defective.

Solution: Temporarily seal holes in pipes with plumbers tape (e.g., Teflon tape), replace worn parts, shutoff water flow to parts of system that are leaking and repair, use a silicon product to seal leaks.

Problem: *Red Worms Appeared*

Reason: Probably introduced by natural elements, feed, or someone else.

Solution: Do nothing, as red worms provide additional benefit, and can be good free fish food.

Bell Siphon Troubleshooting: Potential Problems & Solutions

NOTE: The vast majority of bell siphon problems can be solved by using a wider and taller siphon pipe. Others can be solved with a cheater air break tube, cheater bottom bends, or larger crenellations. A few problems are because the siphon pipe is too large in diameter, have extra holes where they do not belong, the airtight siphon pipe cap was not installed (or is not airtight), the cheater air break tube needs to be shortened, or it has too many bottom bends. Refer to Chapter 25: "How to Make an Auto Siphon (Bell Siphon)" for additional information.

Semantics: The standpipe is the inner drain pipe. The siphon pipe is the outer pipe with top cap. A shroud is the protective pipe with many holes (or other permeable material) that is around the unit to allow maintenance while preventing media from smothering it.

Problem: *Bell Siphon is Not Working Properly*

Reason: Poor design.

Solution: Most bell siphon issues can be solved with a wider and/or taller siphon pipe.

Problem: *Bell Siphon Will Not Start*

Reason: Standpipe is not level; water flows over one edge instead of entire edge surface.

Solution: Cut the top of the standpipe so it is level.

Problem: *Bell Siphon Does Not Stop Draining*

Reason: Siphon is not strong enough to break water tension at bottom of siphon pipe.

Solution: Make one crenellation/hole at bottom of siphon pipe higher for an air break. Make siphon pipe taller if it is too close to the top of the standpipe to increase vortex area. If this approach does not work, try using a wider siphon pipe.

Problem: *Bell Siphon Never Engages; Standpipe Only Drains Water Output to Equal Water Input*

Reason: Siphon pipe cap is not airtight or cap is missing. Another reason for this problem may be that the standpipe (output pipe) is too wide to create a water lock and begin the siphon action.

Solution: For the first reason, seal the cap on top of siphon pipe. For the second reason reduce width of standpipe or add an adapter to the top of it that reduces the opening. Some operators install a bend at the bottom (just outside the media bed) of the standpipe to resolve the problem.

Problem: *Bell Siphon Takes a Long Time from Dribble to Fully Starting the Siphon*

Reason: Siphon pipe does not have enough headroom to initiate a vortex over the standpipe

Solution: Make siphon pipe taller.

Problem: *Bell Siphon Does Not Drain Fast Enough*

Reason: Bell siphon was improperly designed and is thus too small for the amount of water it needs to address.

Solution: Reduce incoming water flow with ball valve in or use a larger bell siphon.

Problem: *Bell Siphon Stops Draining Midway*

Reason: Water pressure has equalized inside and outside the siphon at the standpipe height.

Solution: Use fewer crenellations in siphon pipe or use smaller diameter siphon pipe.

CHAPTER 27

Water Quality

Fish Life Support

As already addressed in previous chapters of this book, growing organic vegetables and fresh fish from your own aquaponic system has many advantages. These benefits come with lower costs and less maintenance compared to hydroponics and traditional agricultural methods. Expensive hydroponic nutrient solution for the plants and expensive aquaculture filtering equipment to clean the water for the fish are NOT needed with aquaponics.

To summarize key points of these previous chapters, even small systems can produce such high production yields that excess vegetables and fish can be given as gifts, bartered, and/or sold for a profit. Most importantly, you can rest assured that the fish that you are eating is free of mercury and other toxins, unlike the fish typically sold in grocery stores and served at restaurants, The produce cultivated will be 100 percent organic and free of harmful pesticides, herbicides, and fungicides widely used on conventional crops, if you feed your fish a high quality fish feed.

Because fish, bacteria, and plants are totally dependent upon the water surrounding them and are unable to escape this environment, the quality of the water is of great importance. Several water quality parameters are important in fish culture,

including dissolved oxygen (DO), temperature, mineral content, and the concentrations of several waste products excreted by the organisms. The mere presence of fish has a direct impact water chemistry. For example, fish excrete waste products that are high in ammonia and other nitrogen compounds, which tend to pollute the water. Likewise, plants favorably influence water chemistry by adding oxygen and by removing nitrogen compounds. Consequently, the relationship between the species in your aquaponic system and the surrounding water is a dynamic and crucially important one.

As emphasized early in this book, an aquaponic system operating at an optimal level is only achieved when there is harmonious balance of all the life support components of three groups of organisms: fish, plants and bacteria. Each organism has a specific tolerance range, and optimal point, for each water quality parameter (DO, pH, temperature, nitrate, nitrite, ammonia). These primary water quality components' tolerance ranges are relatively similar for all aquaponic aquatic species, but there are differences from species to species. Therefore, a compromise is necessary. Studies have shown that the best balance is achieved when water quality parameters are maintained, as shown in tables 39-40 on the following page.

TABLE 27. *General Water Quality Tolerances for Fish, Aquaponic Plants, and Nitrifying Bacteria*

ORGANISM TYPE	TEMP (°C)	pH	AMMONIA (mg/liter)	NITRITE (mg/liter)	NITRATE (mg/liter)	DO (mg/liter)
Warm water fish	22–32	6–8.5	< 3	< 1	< 400	4–6
Cold water fish	10–18	6–8.5	< 1	< 0.1	< 400	6–8
Plants	16–30	5.5–7.5	< 30	< 1	-	> 3
Bacteria	14–34	6–8.5	< 3	<1	-	4–8

TABLE 28. *Compromise of Ideal Water Quality Parameters for Fish, Plants, and Bacteria*

	TEMPERATURE	pH	AMMONIA	NITRITE	NITRATE	DO
Tolerance Range	18–30 °C	6–7	< 1 mg/L	< 1 mg/L	< 5-150 mg/L	> 5 mg/L
	64–86 °F		< 1 ppm	< 1 ppm	< 5-150 ppm	> 5 ppm

NOTE: It is important that the beginner not be intimidated or overwhelmed by the thought of maintaining a balanced aquaponic system. If constructed and maintained according to the basic principles and parameters stated in this book, operating a successful aquaponic system is a relatively simple and very enjoyable endeavor.

Fish Population Density

Aquaponics stocking density is usually defined as the weight of fish held in regards to the volume of water. The accepted approach for stating fish stocking density is the kilograms (weight) of fish per liters (volume) of water.

The more fish, the greater yield and the higher profit. However stocking too many fish will lead to ill health of the fish, and can also be detrimental to the plants. The fish will not grow as well and will start dying, and there will be a buildup of wastes which will be toxic to both fish and plants. Finding the perfect balance of stocking as many fish as possible without adverse impacts is key.

Some species are able thrive in a denser population while others require considerably more space. Some species are territorial and expend a lot of energy fighting if packed too close together. Whereas others prefer to be in a denser pack, shoaling, and schooling. It is important to select a fish species that is not territorial. Territorial fish forced to live close together expend a great deal of energy, have high stress levels, and lower survival rates. In addition, it is not ethical to raise animals under stressful conditions. As a rule, smaller fish are more likely to live out their lives in schools, although some large fish will school together. The fish described in this book are species common to aquaponics and do fine when stocked at the recommended densities. However, if you are thinking about raising fish that are not listed in this book, it would be prudent to ensure that they are not a territorial species.

What is the recommended stocking density? It will depend upon your bio-filter (grow bed) capacity, the feeding rate, ammonia production rate, oxygen consumption rate, and aeration rate. Either gas exchange or ammonia toxicity are what will most likely be the limiting factor that will determine your stocking density. **An experienced operator is usually able to stock a tank at 1 lb of fish per 5 -10 gallons of water, or one to two fish per 10 gallons of water (38 liters). Inexperienced operators are better off following a stocking density of one fish per 22.5 gallons (85 liters) of water.**

However, it is more accurate to talk about stocking densities in terms of kilograms of fish per cubic meter or liters of waters, as this is the industry standard and doing math via the metric system is a much easier process. For most aquaponics set-ups, using 66 to 88 pounds of fish to 264 gallons (30 to 40 kg of fish per 1000 liters) will work fine.

Large, commercial recirculating fish growing facilities will keep fish at densities up to approximately 3-lbs/ft^3 (50 kg/m^3) in aerated systems and up to 9.5-lbs/ft^3 (150 kg/m^3) or higher in direct oxygen injected systems. Aquaponic hobbyists rarely approach these high fish densities in their smaller-scale systems.

In order to ensure fish health and well-being via water quality optimization, most hobby aquaponics practitioners keep fish at densities well below 1.5-lbs/ft^3 (20 kg/m^3). Commercial aquaponic operators will often reach higher aerated fish stocking densities as this is required to recover capital and operating costs, and so the design and efficient operational characteristics of the system are critical.

Lower stocking densities are much more manageable and have higher success rates as there is more room for error. Lower stocking densities are recommended for those that are new to aquaponics. The amount of food you put into the tanks will also dictate how well the system runs. If you feed too much, there will be an accumulation of waste that the bacteria may not be able to handle.

Ideally, you will harvest the fish as soon as they're big enough. This avoids ending up with a stocking density which otherwise strains the system. Since individual fish grow at different rates, you should start taking out the bigger ones as soon as they are large enough to eat, rather than waiting until you can harvest all the fish at one time. This approach works best for smaller operations, as you will have an ongoing manageable harvest rate where you can eat and/or sell them without having to freeze storage a large quantity of fish at one time.

Temperature Range

What is the temperature range of your aquaponics location? Ideally, it should match the optimal temperature of your aquaponics fish. If not, you will incur higher upfront capital cost and more expensive ongoing operational cost maintaining the temperature at the preferred range of the fish, via heating, cooling, and insulation adjustments. Also, a temporary power failure can end up being fatal to your system if it has to be kept at a significant different temperature than the exterior environment.

Fish prefer a specific temperature range, and do best when raised at their optimal temperature. As mentioned above, the easiest, most energy efficient and cost effective option is to select a fish species that has an optimal temperature range that matches your location's natural temperature. However, the ultimate decision comes down to your personal preference and if you are willing to incur the cost of additional cooling, heating, and insulation. This is essential if your environment has widely fluctuating temperatures. Placing a fish tank in the garage, a shop, or green house will help maintain a stable water temperature.

Fish cannot regulate their body temperature like humans do. They are dependent on the water temperature for their body temperature. **To maintain fish health the water temperature should never be adjusted, or allowed to fluctuate, more than 3°F per day.**

Rates of Growth

Obviously, fast growing fish provide food and revenue quicker than slow growing fish. However, fast growing fish have higher metabolic rates, consume more food, and produce more wastes. This is not necessarily a bad thing. It just means that growing conditions need to be monitored more closely, and adjustments made to accommodate these higher growth rates. Higher waste production can be beneficial if the plants being grown require higher levels of nutrients (such as tomatoes).

Balance of Water Constituents

One also needs to be careful not to assume that fish data that is based upon a particular species is applicable to all fish species. Each species, and even varieties of certain species, will have unique characteristics, growth rates, and require specific growing conditions.

The fish tank encompasses a direct relationship between ammonia levels, water temperature, and pH, and if their inter-relationships are not understood it can lead to impending disaster. Just as dissolved oxygen is crucial to fish health, the following constituents also need to be well understood by the aquaponics operator:

Ammonia

All fish give off ammonia. Ammonia is generated from their gills and waste. Uneaten fish food also is converted into ammonia as it breaks down. If not properly addressed, the buildup of ammonia becomes toxic to fish. Ammonia levels as small as 5 ppm is typically deadly to fish. Fortunately, beneficial bacteria within the grow beds converts ammonia into nitrates that the plants ingest, thus addressing the problem. This is known as the Nitrogen Cycle. When first starting up, it can take a new aquaponics system some time to fully cycle or balance. It can take as long as six to eight weeks in winter months or just a few weeks in the summer (or warmer conditions) before the system is said to have "cycled" and all is in balance.

The Nitrogen Cycle is addressed in more detail elsewhere within this book. For now, know that nitrite is the product of ammonia being digested by bacteria in the water, on the skin of the fish, and in the bio-filter (if the system has one). Nitrite is poisonous to fish at 225 ppm. Nitrite is broken down by bacteria to form nitrate. Nitrate is a natural fertilizer, used by plants.

An overstocked tank with fish is much more susceptible to fatal flaws if any of these parameters are pushed beyond their tolerable limits. Ammonia levels will depend greatly on the temperature of the fish tank water and the pH of the water, fish density, and how much uneaten fish food remains floating in the system. It gets more complicated with warmer water and a pH that is out of balance. Nevertheless, it is easy to monitor these conditions, and there are a number of things that can be done to ensure the system remains healthy and successful. Ideally your ammonia level should be near zero but there will always be traceable amounts being emitted constantly by your fish. It gets more complicated if you stock your system with a heavy fish load.

Fish can tolerate higher levels of ammonia the cooler the water. The same goes for dissolved oxygen. Cold water can store more dissolved oxygen than the same volume of warm water.

Understanding the relationship between ammonia and water temperature provides you with the ability to better manage your aquaponic system and avert catastrophic danger.

pH Range

The pH is the measure of the hydrogen ion (H+) concentration in the water. The pH scale ranges from 0-14 with a pH of 7 being neutral. Pure water has a pH of 7, but additives (i.e. chlorine, fluoride, etc.) can alter the pH. A pH below 7 is acidic and a pH of above 7 as basic. Different species of fish have

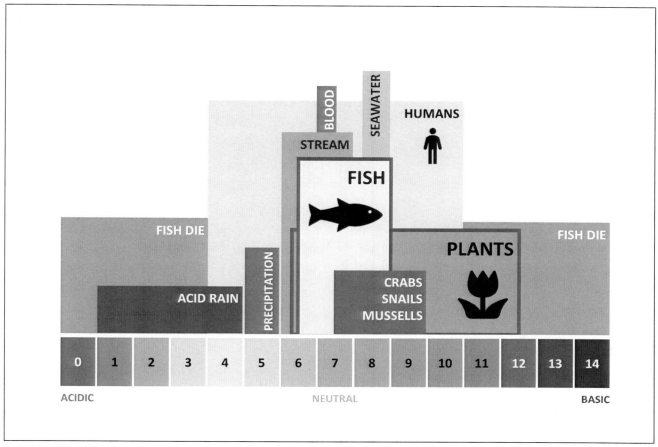

FIGURE 196. *Typical pH range of various living organisms.*

varying pH requirements. However, the typical pH range for aquaponics is between 6 and 7.2. **A pH of 6.8 to 7 is usually a happy compromise for most fish, plants, and the good bacteria;** but again the pH can be slightly more or less depending upon the fish species.

The pH levels of tap water can significantly exceed the required pH range required. As a matter of fact, such detrimental differences are fairly common. Therefore, the pH of tap water needs to be properly adjusted before adding the fish.

Adjusting pH: Adjust pH Slowly After Fish are Present

When fish are already in the tank, it is important to adjust the pH slowly. If pH is lowered too much too fast, it will stress the fish, possibly the plants, and can even be fatal. Therefore, pH should be lowered over the span of a week or more when fish are present.

pH Fluctuations

The pH will change in response to system input (rain, fish, plants, topping off the tank periodically). Temperature will also cause your pH to vary. When testing pH, measure at several points in the day for an average, or measure at the same time and temperature each day in order to obtain reliable data.

In the beginning, when you have water without a bacteria colony, pH will fluctuate significantly. This is normal. Adding water directly from public water sources is not a good idea because most municipal water has chlorine, which is toxic to the fish and bacteria. It will cause the pH to change. Store municipal water in a separate container (e.g. 55 gallon drum, etc) for a few days, which will allow the chlorine to 'gas off', before adding the water to your system.

Lowering pH

Again, the lower the pH, the more acidic the water. The following are some safe additives that can be implemented to lower the pH in an aquaponics system.

- Hydrochloric Acid one or two caps per 250 gallons
- Acetic Acid (Vinegar)
- Sulphuric Acid
- Maidenwell media or Diatomite
- Iron sulfate fertilizer

Hydrochloric acid (swimming pool acid) is most frequently used to lower pH to the optimal level. Some gravel, such as limestone, will lower pH. Injecting CO_2 directly into the water has also been reported to lower pH.

Citric acid should never be used. Citric acid is an antibacterial agent that can be fatal to the good bacteria living within the media.

Raising pH

Higher pH readings are called "base". The following are some additives that can safely be used in an aquaponic system to raise the pH:

- Dolomite Lime — Calcium Magnesium Carbonate
- Calcium Hydroxide (hydrated/builder's/slaked/ hydrated limes)
- Potassium Carbonate (bicarbonate)
- Potassium Hydroxide (pearl ash/potash)
- Snail Shells
- Sea Shells
- Egg Shells

If using shells, it is best practice to boil, bleach, or use hydrogen peroxide on them first in order to kill all bacteria. Containing these chemicals or ingredients in a nylon stocking, paint strainer sack, or other breathable bag will allow for easy removal once the desired pH range is achieved.

pH Cycling

When the term 'cycling the aquaponic system' is used, it simply means that the nitrifying bacteria (good bacteria) are present and the system is stable. Regular monitoring and recording pH enables one to not only evaluate the current status of the system at a specific point in time, but shows any pH trends in one direction or another. Keeping pH within the desired range also prevents "nutrient lockout" enabling plants to readily take up the right nutrients and grow properly.

pH Adjustment Notes:

1. Adjusting pH fast can be hazardous to fish. A matter of fact, changing pH by only 0.2 too quickly can be dangerous.

2. If your system has a pH crash, identify the problem and remedy what caused it rather than just trying to adjust the pH when starting over.

3. Small crushed particles work faster while larger particles work slower to maintain system pH.

4. Keep "pH increase" equivalents on hand: sodium bicarbonate (baking soda), limestone, and calcium carbonate (egg shells, snail shells, sea shells).

5. It is easier to increase pH than it is to decrease.

6. Keep "pH decrease" equivalents on hand: vinegar, Hydrochloric Acid (one or two caps per 250 gallons), Acetic Acid (Vinegar), Sulphuric Acid, Maidenwell media, Diatomite, or Iron sulfate fertilizer.

7. If possible, keep a back up water tank (or barrel) nearby filled with dechlorinated water bucket for topping off the tank periodically as water is lost through evaporation and plant transpiration, or even in an emergency (i.e. pipe leak, etc.). Preferably, this back up supply will hold at least 10 percent of the fish tank volume.

8. Use a mixture of plant ages and/or types so they do not all die off at the same time, causing the system to crash.

pH Impacts Upon Fish Breeding

There is a relationship between pH and aquatic life breeding cycles. As pH changes, so will the number of fish eggs that are produced, if they can be produced at all. Keep this in mind if you desire to reproduce your fish.

Calcium Carbonate

What is calcium carbonate? Calcium is a mineral that is found naturally in foods. Calcium is necessary for many normal functions of the body, especially bone formation and maintenance. Calcium can also bind to other minerals (such as phosphate) and aid in their removal from the body. Calcium carbonate supplements are used to prevent and to treat calcium deficiencies. Natural forms of calcium carbonate are eggshells, snail shells, and seashells.

Even though calcium carbonate works to lower pH and natural forms don't do any harm, be cautious in using it. It can take a long time to dissolve and affect the pH. Therefore, after adding a little, wait and check pH after two hours before adding any more. Adding too much at one time or over a short period can cause the pH to spike, and could result in doing more harm than good.

How much should you add to your system to raise the pH? That question does not have a specific answer. It all depends on the type of calcium carbonate you are using and its form (i.e. natural egg shells, bag of ground powder, etc.), the size of your system, fish density, the type of media you are using, temperature, and how far your pH is off the optimal range. It is always better to be safe than sorry. Raise the pH using small amounts of calcium carbonate over time, little by little every two hours. With some experience, you will come to know your system, and have a better understanding of how much to add whenever the pH needs to be adjusted.

Dissolved Oxygen (DO)

The limit of dissolved oxygen in fish tank water is termed "saturation level" and the level is measured in parts per million (ppm). DO is essential to the health of your fish, and can be impacted by the temperature of your water. Beneficial nitrifying bacteria, which break down the metabolic waste of aquatic creatures, are equally dependent on oxygen.

Oxygen is introduced into the aquaponics system naturally through the plant life, waves, cascades, and turbulence. If these natural methods are not sufficient, then an aeration device is necessary. Poor aeration your tank, and/or an extremely high density of fish in your tank can lead to inadequate DO.

The amount of oxygen that water can hold is temperature dependent. Warm water holds less oxygen than colder water. In other words, the colder the water, the more oxygen the water can hold.

Water is 800 times denser than air and contains 95 percent less oxygen. Fish expend a considerable amount of energy breathing but are able to extract 80 percent of the available oxygen from water, as opposed to humans, who extract only 25 percent of the oxygen they breathe in from the atmosphere. The saturation level of oxygen in water is in the region of seven to eight parts per million.

Under normal conditions, there is never too much oxygen in a fish tank, unless the operator purposely attempts to super saturate the water. Operators can super saturate aquarium water by diffusing 100 percent liquid oxygen into the water, but there is no real value to doing so. Too much oxygen is harmful to fish.

Hyperoxia is the state of water when it holds a very high amount of oxygen. At this state, water is described as having a dissolved oxygen saturation of greater than 100 percent. This percent can be 140-300 percent. If fish are exposed to such water, their blood equilibrates, bubbles form in the blood, and can block the capillaries. In severe cases, death occurs rapidly as a result of blockage of the major arteries. The remedy is either to remove the fish to normally equilibrated water or to provide vigorous aeration to strip out the excess gas.

Most aquaponic fish, including Tilapia, prefer dissolved oxygen levels above 6 ppm. Dissolved oxygen levels should never drop below 3 ppm.

The fish will suffocate from low DO. Symptoms of low DO include fish swimming close to the water surface grasping for air, fish lying on the bottom of the tank, and red gills. However, waiting till then is not a great idea. Preventative measures should be taken before the health of your fish is jeopardized. Most importantly, be sure you have operational features built into your system so that there is always adequate dissolved oxygen present should your system setup be inadequate. If your system does not naturally generate enough DO, then simply adding an aeration device or air pump will ensure that there is sufficient supply for the fish to thrive.

To measure DO, use a DO meter. This is typically the most expensive piece of measuring equipment used in aquaponics. Although many operators get by without them, they do so at a risk. If you have the money to spend, they are nice to have on hand. "Dissolved oxygen meters range in price from about $150 to $600 (USD, 2022).

It is important to have a backup aerator (battery or generator operated) that is independent of the main power supply. This ensures that air can be continually pumped into the water to keep the fish alive, in case of a power failure.

Temperature has a very important effect to dissolved oxygen. As the temperature of the water goes up, the water loses the ability to hold the dissolved oxygen and the concentration goes down. When the water cools, it regains the ability to hold higher amounts of oxygen. Figure 197 below simplifies this rule. Knowing this relationship, one can deduce that hypoxia tends to occur in the warmer months of the year, namely during the summer.

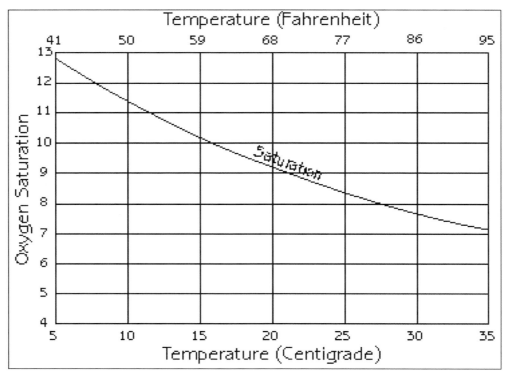

FIGURE 197. Oxygen and temperature relationship.

TABLE 29.

BENCHMARK	OXYGEN DEFICIENCY	ALGAE BLOOM	DISEASE
Fish Behavior	Swimming Near Surface Gasping for Air	Abnormal Swimming	Abonorma Swimming
Time of Fish Kill	Nighttime into Morning	Brightest Part of Day	Anytime
Size of Dead Fish	Large Fish Die First	Small Fish Die First	Small Fish Die First
Microscopic Algae Abundance	Algae Dying	One Dominant Algal Species	No Effect
Dissolved Oxygen Concentration	Less than 3 ppm Oxygen	Supersaturated Oxygen Concentrations	No Effect
Water Color	Brown or Gray or Black	Dark Green or Brown or Golden	No Effect

Aeration Sizing

The aeration rate is measured in cubic feet per minute (CFM). CFM is the measurement of the volume of air flow being introduced into the system.

Air pressure is the pressure required to deliver the correct amount of air flow for proper aeration. Air pressure is measured in terms of pounds per square inch. Professional aquaponic and aquaculture operators strive to ensure that 1 cfm per 300 gallons is being achieved. This is typically not a problem when the system is being properly circulated. However, aeration devices, oxygen injectors, or oxygen diffusers are necessary if the fish tank does not have adequate circulation (dead spaces), and/or there are high stocking densities.

As figure 198 illustrates below, dissolved oxygen increases throughout the day and decreases throughout the night. The most critical time to aerate is just before dawn.

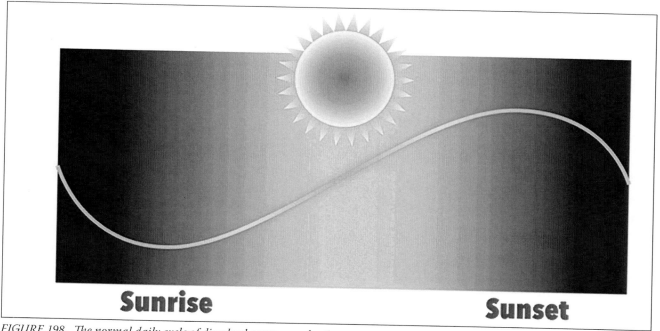

FIGURE 198. The normal daily cycle of dissolved oxygen production.

Nitrogen, Potassium, and Phosphorous (NPK)

NPK are the base nutrients your plants will need to thrive. If your system is low in one of these nutrients, the whole system will suffer. To monitor NPK the best thing you can do is watch your plants — they will tell you what they need. A plant chart, such as the figure 199 below, is most useful for diagnosing NPK problems.

Pump Size

The pump(s) should cycle the total volume of fish tank water once every two hours, but ideally once every hour. If the pump is on a timer, then the 'on' and 'off' phases need to be considered, so that the tank volume can still be pumped within an hour.

Clean Water

Don't be fooled by looks. Clean water is not always necessarily clear. Harmful substances such as nitrite, carbon dioxide, as well as other pollutants, do not discolor water. Low DO levels also do not necessarily alter water color. Therefore, monitoring water quality on a regular basis is critical.

Chlorine

Chlorine kills fish, and is also harmful to humans. If water must be added directly to the tank it, is best to use non-chlorinated well water or run water through a filter that removes chlorine prior to adding it to tank. Otherwise, set up a temporary holding tank, such as a 55-gallon drum, where the chlorinated water can be stored for a few hours in advance of adding it to the aquaponic system. This will provide an opportunity for the chlorine to dissipate from the water before becoming part of the system (this process is also referred to as 'off gas').

It is prudent to keep spare dechlorinated water readily on hand. It is recommended that you store at least 10 percent of your system water volume in a separate container. If using municipal water, be sure to let it sit for a minimum of 24 hours before adding it to your system so it can properly dechlorinate. Water will need to be added to the system on a regular basis to offset evaporation. Adding chlorinated water directly to your system will also kill off much, if not all of, the beneficial bacteria.

New Growth

1 Calcium/Traces Deficiency (or might be K, Mg overdose) twisted pale new growth

2 Severe Nitrogen Deficiency (white/yellow tiny leaves)

Old Growth

3 Normal leaf growth

4 Iron Deficiency (yellowing of entire plant)

5 Early Signs of Nitrogen Deficiency (old leaves are reabsorbed from tip to stem)

6 Phosphate Deficiency (older leaves yellow, and parts of the leaf are reabsorbed leading to dead patches, the leaf falls off rather quickly, looks similar to early nitrogen deficiency; green spot algae on older leafs)

7 Magnesium Deficiency (dark veins lighter leaf tissue)

8 Potassium Deficiency (pin-holes form in leaf that enlarge with a yellowing edge, leaf is otherwise normal looking)

FIGURE 199. Plant Chart

Light

Fish are sensitive to light, and some much more than others (e.g. largemouth bass). Avoid any direct lighting to the fish tank. Even a fish tank positioned under a typical room light can stress the fish. Therefore, it is prudent to ensure that the only lighting of the fish tank, or fish tank area, be that of the ambient lighting type. Ambient lighting is a general illumination that comes from all directions in a room that has no visible source. This type of lighting is in contrast to directional lighting. Even so, the ambient light should not be too bright.

Water Hardness

Aquarium water hardness is a part of water chemistry that is often not fully understood. However, don't let the subject intimidate you, it is not that complicated. Fish tank water hardness is measured in degrees of hardness. Many home aquarium water test kits will give you measurements in either degrees of hardness (dh) or in parts per million (ppm).

When we discuss water hardness, we are simply looking at the amount of dissolved minerals in our water. There are two distinct measurements of water hardness. When you test your water, you will test for general hardness (GH) and carbonate hardness (KH).

General Hardness (GH)

The general hardness (GH) of your aquaponics water is a measurement of dissolved magnesium and calcium. The (GH) of aquaponics water can have great effects on your fish, so it is very important to ensure that the fish you choose to keep will thrive in your water or adjust the water accordingly.

There are species of fish that live in soft water and others that live in hard water. Like with many other aspects of raising fish, it is important to do your research in advance. You need to know your water quality, pretences of the fish you desire to raise, and

what would need to be done to the water to accommodate the fish. This will minimize losses. You can also keep water treatment cost down by going with a species that is most closely compatible to your water supply.

Most fish will survive in the a water obtained from our tap following removal of chlorine, chloramines, and other contaminates. Unless tests reveal unusually hard or extremely soft water, there should not be a problem. Most fish will adapt just fine. However, successful breeding and the overall coloration of the fish can be directly linked to the water hardness.

Carbonate Hardness (KH)

The second component of water hardness is the carbonate hardness (KH). (KH) is the measurement of carbonate and bicarbonate ions in your water. In simple terms, the (KH) of water is a measurement of the buffering capacity of your water. The (KH) of water will determine how much your pH will fluctuate. The higher the (KH) is in your water, the more stable your pH will remain. When (KH) drops, so too will your pH. There is a distinct relationship between (KH) and pH. If you have ongoing problems with the pH dropping, check the (KH) levels in the tank water.

TABLE 30. **General Hardness Chart**

DEGREE OF HARDNESS (DH)	ppm	HARDNESS
0–3	0–50	Very Soft
6–Mar	51–100	Soft
12–Jun	101–200	Slightly Hard
18–Dec	201–300	Moderately Hard
18–30	301–450	Hard
30+	450+	Very Hard

How to Soften Aquaponics Water

There are several ways to soften your aquaponics water if your your tap is too hard for your fish. However, if you do need to soften your aquaponics water, do so slowly. Any drastic changes can shock the fish, cause injury, or even result in death.

Reverse Osmosis

The most economical and popular method to soften your aquaponics water is to use a Reverse Osmosis (RO) system. These units remove heavy metals, minerals, and contaminants from your water source.

Water Softening Pillows

Water softening pillows can be used on very small systems. There are several different manufactures of water softening pillows. These pillows work well for aquaponics systems that are less than 50 gallons. You simply channel the water through the pillow material. It softens the water through ion-exchange. Many pillow softeners can be recharged and reused by soaking the pillow in a salt water solution. It is then placed in the tank where the sodium ions are released into the water and replaced by calcium and magnesium ions. After a few hours or days, the pillow (along with the calcium and magnesium) is removed, and the pillow recharged again.

How to Increase Aquaponics Water Hardness

If you find that your water source is too soft, you may need to harden your aquaponics water. There are several things you can do to harden your aquaponics water.

Crushed Coral

Adding crushed coral to your tank can help increase the water hardness. Some operators burdened with a hard water sources, choose to use crushed coral as their substrate media or integrate it into other media types creating a media mix that resolves the problem.

Limestone

Using limestone allows for calcium and other minerals to leach out into the water column. The most popular limestone used is Texas Holey Rock Limestone.

Buffer Additives

There are several buffers on the market that will help raise GH and KH while maintaining the pH of the water. Most use a combination of different salts including carbonate salts to increase water hardness. Be sure to closely follow the directions on the manufacture's label.

Aquaponics Water Hardness Tips

- Maintaining a regular schedule of water changes to ensure high water quality will typically prevent your pH, GH, and KH from swinging back and forth so much.
- If you decide to dose additives, be sure they are safe to enter your food chain, and follow the directions on the manufacturer's label.
- When you use limestone or crushed coral, ensure that you clean it thoroughly.
- When adjusting any water parameters, such as aquaponics water hardness, adjust slowly. You can kill your fish with extreme changes.
- Purchase a high quality aquaponics water test kit.

Algae

Photosynthetic growth and activity by algae in aquaponic systems affect the water quality parameters of pH, DO, and nitrogen levels. Algae are a class of photosynthetic organisms that will readily grow in any body of water that is rich in nutrients and exposed to sunlight. Some algae are microscopic, single-celled organisms called phytoplankton, which can color the water green. Macroalgae are much larger, commonly forming filamentous mats attached to the bottoms and sides of tanks.

It is important to prevent algae growing in an aquaponic system because they are problematic for several reasons. First, they will consume the nutrients in the water and compete with the target vegetables. In addition, algae act as both a source and sink of DO, producing oxygen during the day through photosynthesis and consuming oxygen at night during respiration. They can dramatically reduce the DO levels in water at night to the point of even being fatal to fish. This production and consumption of oxygen is related to the production and consumption of carbon dioxide, which causes daily shifts in pH as carbonic acid is either removed (daytime — higher water pH) from or returned (night time — lower water pH) to the system. Finally, filamentous algae can clog drains and block filters within the unit, leading to problems with water circulation. Brown filamentous algae can also grow on the roots of the plants, especially in deep water culture, and negatively affects plant growth. It should be noted that some aquaculture operations benefit greatly from culturing algae for feed, referred to as green-water culture, including tilapia breeding, shrimp culture, and biodiesel production; these activities should never be conducted within an aquaponic system.

Algae Control

Algae are unsightly and, on drying, it can emit a foul odor. As mentioned above they will also rob the water of minute elements, including oxygen. Algae are not harmful to plants, except on rare occasions where there is stagnant water when it can harbor insects and diseases. Some people will even argue that algae gives off certain enzymes which are beneficial to your plants, and they openly encourage its growth. The main problem with algae is that it pulls oxygen out of the water and, as a result, can be harmful and even deadly to fish.

Again, algae require two things to flourish: light and oxygen. If one or the other is not present, algae will not grow. In aquaponics, algae growth can be limited or excluded by minimizing light. Do not let any direct light shine on the fish tank (only ambient lighting).

For open aquaponic systems that use a growing substrate (i.e. grow bed surface of the flood-and-drain system), black/white plastic film can be cut to size and placed over the grow bed so that light cannot reach the medium (have holes where the plants can grow through). Fish tanks should be shaded. Outdoor fish ponds can have a shade cover or D.W.C. raft(s) floating on the surface of the water to provide shade.

Nitrite

Nitrite enters a fish culture system after fish digest feed and the excess nitrogen is converted into ammonia, which is then excreted as waste into the water. Total ammonia nitrogen (TAN; NH_3 and NH_4+) is then converted to nitrite (NO_2) which, under normal conditions, is quickly converted to non-toxic nitrate (NO_3) by naturally occurring bacteria. Uneaten (wasted) feed and other organic material also break down into ammonia, nitrite, and nitrate in a similar manner.

Brown blood disease occurs in fish when water contains high nitrite concentrations. Nitrite enters the bloodstream through the gills and turns the blood to a chocolate-brown color. Hemoglobin, which transports oxygen in the blood, combines with nitrite to form methemoglobin, which is incapable of oxygen transport. Brown blood cannot carry sufficient amounts of oxygen, and affected fish can suffocate despite adequate oxygen concentration in the water. This accounts for the gasping behavior often observed in fish with brown blood disease, even when oxygen levels are relatively high.

Nitrite problems are typically more likely in closed, intensive culture systems due to insufficient, inefficient, or malfunctioning filtration systems. High nitrite concentrations in ponds occur more frequently in the fall and spring when temperatures are fluctuating, resulting in the breakdown of the nitrogen cycle due to decreased plankton and/or bacterial activity.

A reduction in plankton activity in ponds (due to lower temperatures, nutrient depletion, cloudy weather, herbicide treatments, etc.) can result in less ammonia assimilated by the algae, thus increasing the load on the nitrifying bacteria. If nitrite levels exceed that which resident bacteria can rapidly convert to nitrate, a buildup of nitrite occurs, and brown blood disease is a risk. Although nitrite is seldom a problem in systems with high water exchange rates or good filtration, systems should be monitored year-round and managed when necessary, to prevent severe economic loss from brown blood in any fish culture facility.

Nitrite — Susceptibility of Fish Species to Brown Blood Disease

Largemouth and smallmouth bass, as well as bluegill and green sunfish, are resistant to high nitrite concentrations. Catfish and tilapia, are fairly sensitive to nitrite, while trout and other cool water fish are sensitive to extremely small amounts of nitrite. Goldfish and fathead minnows fall in between catfish and bass in their susceptibility to brown blood disease resulting from high nitrite levels. Striped bass and its hybrids appear sensitive to nitrite, but little is known about the relative sensitivity compared to other species.

Fluoride

Water fluoridation is the practice of adding industrial-grade fluoride chemicals to water for the purpose of preventing tooth decay. The fluoride being added to public drinking water is actually an industrial waste product. One of the little known facts about this practice is that the United States, which fluoridates over 70 percent of its water supplies, has more people drinking fluoridated water than the rest of the world combined. Most developed nations, including all of Japan and 97 percent of western Europe, do not fluoridate their water.

Harmful Effects of Fluoride

Contrary to popular belief and despite US government propaganda, comprehensive data from many unbiased scientific studies (as well as the World Health Organization) have proven that there is no discernible difference in tooth decay between the minority of western nations that fluoridate water, and the majority of nations who don't fluoridate their water. In fact, the tooth decay rates in many non-fluoridated countries are lower than the tooth decay rates in fluoridated ones.

Fluoride is extremely toxic to fish, plants, and humans. Check out the warning label on the back of your toothpaste, then immediately throw it in the trash, and start using non-fluoridated toothpaste from now on.

Most fluoride that is added to municipal water is an unnatural form of fluoride that contains sodium. It is over 80 times more toxic than naturally-occurring calcium fluoride.

The fluoride ion (F-) is extremely reactive and strongly attracted to calcium. Its preference for calcium overrides its attraction to other ions. In nature, fluoride is most often bound to calcium. When sodium fluoride is ingested, it rapidly robs the body of calcium. In fact, sodium fluoride poisoning results when calcium is stolen from the blood.

Fluoride has the ability to affect other chemicals and heavy metals, in some cases making them even more harmful than they would be on their own. For example, when you combine chloramines with the hydrofluorosilicic acid added to the water supply, they become very effective at extracting lead from old plumbing systems, promoting the accumulation of lead in the water supply.

Studies have shown that hydrofluorosilicic acid increases lead accumulation in bone, teeth, and other calcium-rich tissues. This is because the free fluoride ion acts as a transport of heavy metals, allowing them to enter into areas of your body they normally would not be able to go, such as into your brain.

Fluoride has long been known to be a very toxic substance. This is why, like arsenic, fluoride has been used in pesticides and rodenticides (to kill rats, insects, etc). It is also why the Food and Drug Administration (FDA) now requires that all fluoride toothpaste sold in the U.S. carry a poison warning that instructs users to contact the poison control center if they swallow more than used for brushing.

Excessive fluoride exposure is well known to cause a painful bone disease (skeletal fluorosis), as well as a discoloration of the teeth known as dental fluorosis. Excessive fluoride exposure has also been linked to a range of other chronic ailments including arthritis, bone fragility, dental fluorosis, glucose intolerance, gastrointestinal distress, thyroid disease, possibly cardiovascular disease, and certain types of cancer.

Certain subsets of the population are particularly vulnerable to fluoride's toxicity. Populations that have heightened susceptibility to fluoride include infants, individuals with kidney disease, individuals with nutrient deficiencies (particularly calcium and iodine), and individuals with medical conditions that cause excessive thirst.

For a complete breakdown of all the harmful effects of fluoride, please refer to the Fluoride Action Network (FAN). FAN's work has been cited by national and international media outlets including the *New York Times*, *Wall Street Journal*, *TIME Magazine*, *National Public Radio*, *Scientific American*, and *Prevention Magazine* among others. *FAN is an official project of the American Environmental Health Studies Project (AEHSP) — a registered non-profit (501c3) organization. FAN's website address is: http://fluoridealert.org/faq*

Fluoride negatively impacts health and it is prudent to avoid it. The following is a brief list of some of the detrimental health consequences of ingesting fluoride:

- Gastrointestinal Effects
- Bone Fractures
- Brain Effects
- Cancer
- Cardiovascular Disease
- Diabetes
- Endocrine Disruption
- Acute Toxicity
- Hypersensitivity
- Kidney Disease
- Male infertility
- Pineal Gland
- Skeletal Fluorosis
- Thyroid Disease

Fluoride Side Note

We all need to beware of other ways we are constantly exposed to fluoride. Not only is one source bad enough (e.g. drinking water, toothpaste, etc.), but the accumulation from multiple sources is especially harmful.

One of the primary sources of fluoride exposure is non-organic foods, due to the high amounts of fluoride-based pesticide residues on these foods. Non-organic foods may account for as much as one-third of the average person's fluoride exposure. Foods particularly high in fluoride include non-organic fresh produce, breakfast cereals, juices (particularly grape juice), deboned meats such as lunch meats, other meats through food chain accumulation, and black or green tea (even if organic).

How to Remove Fluoride from Water

Unfortunately, water filtration does not remove fluoride. Many water filters (e.g., Brita & Pur) use an "activated carbon" filter that does not remove fluoride. The fluoride molecule is smaller than the water molecule, therefore it cannot be removed by filtration.

If you live in a community that fluoridates its water supply, there are several options to avoid drinking the fluoride that is added. Unfortunately, each of these options will cost money (unless you happen to have access to a free source of spring water). These options include:

- **Spring water:** Most spring water contains very low levels of fluoride (generally less than 0.1 ppm).
- **Reverse Osmosis:** Reverse Osmosis removes between 90 and 95 percent of fluoride. Contaminants are trapped by the RO membrane and flushed away in the waste water. The process requires between two and four gallons of water to produce one gallon of RO water (depending on the quality of the water and the efficiency of the RO unit).
- **Water Distillation**: Distillation is capable of removing just about anything (except volatile compounds) from water. Distilling water is an effective way of removing fluoride from water. The drawback to distillation is that the process is time and energy consumptive. Distillation also leaves the resulting water empty and lifeless. If you use distilled water, you need to do research on how to add minerals back to the water following the distillation process, often referred to as the 'full-spectrum living water'.

Sources of Water for Aquaponics

On average, an aquaponic system uses 1–3 percent of its total water volume per day, depending on the type of plants being grown and the location. Water is used by the plants through natural evapotranspiration as well as being retained within the plant tissues. Additional water is lost from direct evaporation and splashing. As such, this water loss will need to be replenished periodically. The water source used will have an impact on the water chemistry of the unit. This section will review some common water sources and the common chemical composition of that water. New water sources should always be tested for pH, hardness, salinity, chlorine, and for any pollutants in order to ensure the water is safe to use.

Salinity

Now is a good place to discuss a water parameter not yet addressed in detail — salinity. Salinity indicates the concentration of salts in water, which include

 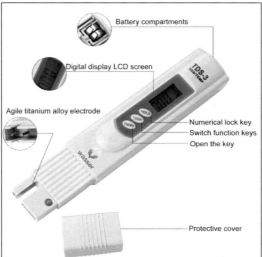  

FIGURE 200. (Left to Right): EC meter, TDS meter, Refractometer, Hydrometer

NOTE: All above meters, or an equal, can be acquired for less than $30 each (USD, 2022). Several of these meters measure multiple water constituents.

table salt (sodium chloride — NaCl), as well as plant nutrients, which are in fact salts. Salinity levels will have a large bearing when deciding which water to use because high salinity can negatively affect vegetable production, especially if it is of sodium chloride origin, as sodium is toxic for plants. Water salinity can be measured with an electrical conductivity (EC) meter, a total dissolved solids (TDS) meter, a refractometer, or a hydrometer or operators can refer to local government reports on water quality.

Salinity is measured either as conductivity, or how much electricity will pass through the water, in units of microsiemens per centimetre (μS/cm), or in TDS as parts per thousand (ppt) or parts per million (ppm or mg/liter). For reference, seawater has a conductivity of 50,000 μS/ cm and TDS of 35 ppt (35 000 ppm). Although the impact of salinity on plant growth varies greatly between plants, it is recommended that low salinity water sources be used. Salinity, generally, is too high if sourcing water has a conductivity more than 1 500 μS/cm or a TDS concentration of more than 800 ppm. Although EC and TDS meters are commonly used for hydroponics to measure the total amount of nutrient salts in the water, these meters do not provide a precise reading of the nitrate levels, which can be better monitored with nitrogen test kits.

Rainwater

Collected rainwater is an excellent source of water for aquaponics. The water will usually have a neutral pH and very low concentrations of both types of hardness (KH and GH) and almost zero salinity, which is optimal to replenish the system and avoid long-term salinity buildups. However, in some areas affected by acid rain, as recorded in a number of localities in eastern Europe, eastern United States of America, and areas of southeast Asia, rainwater will have an acidic pH. If this is the case in your location, it is good practice to buffer rainwater and increase the KH.

If you desire to catch rain water for aquaponics use, make sure that the gutters and roof do not contain any chemicals that may leach into your water from roofing materiels. Also, depending upon your location, you made need to beware of the potential for harmful concentrations of air pollution residue on the roof, which would also negatively impact your system. Lastly, in some jurisdictions it is illegal to catch rainwater. These government jurisdictions have decided that homeowners don't own the rain that falls on their property.

A well-designed system includes an overflow pipe to protect against damage caused by the tank overflowing during periods of heavy rains or low usage. All overflow water should be discharged away from foundations and other structures.

- One inch of rain falling on a square foot of surface yields approximately 0.6 gallons of water.

Using the following equation, it is easy to determine how much rainwater can be collected.

- Rain caught (gallons) = (inches of rain) x 0.6 x (portion of building footprint)

For example, if your home's footprint is 1,400 square feet and you want to know the amount of water that comes from a ¼ inch (.25") rain event:

- Rain caught (gallons) = (.25) x (.6) x (1,400) = 210 gallons.

Rainwater collection can be easily achieved by connecting a large clean container to water drainage pipes surrounding a building or house (see figure 201).

Collecting rainwater is relatively easy, but storing rainwater can be a bit more challenging. The water has to be retained until needed, and the water has to be kept clean. The storage container(s) should be covered with a screen to prevent mosquitoes and plant

FIGURE 201.   *Rainwater collection examples*

debris from entering. Depending on the intended uses of your collected rainwater, some form of filtration and/or disinfection of the water that comes from the storage tank may be necessary. Do your research and take the necessary protection measures.

Cistern or Aquifer Water

The quality of water taken from wells or cisterns will largely depend on the material of the cistern and bedrock of the aquifer. If the bedrock is limestone, then the water will probably have quite high concentrations of hardness, which may have an impact on the pH of the water. Water hardness is not a major problem in aquaponics, because the alkalinity is naturally consumed by the nitric acid produced by the nitrifying bacteria. However, if the hardness levels are very high and the nitrification is minimal because of small fish biomass, then the water may remain slightly basic (pH seven to eight) and resist the natural tendency of aquaponic systems to become acidic through the nitrification cycle and fish respiration. In this case, it may be necessary to use very small amounts of acid to reduce the alkalinity before adding the water to the system in order to prevent pH swings within the system. Aquifers on coral islands often have saltwater intrusion into the freshwater lens, and can have salinity levels too high for aquaponics, so monitoring is

necessary, and rainwater collection or reverse osmosis filtration may be better options.

Tap or Municipal Water

Water from the municipal supplies is often treated with different chemicals to remove pathogens. The most common chemicals used for water treatment are chlorine and chloramines. These chemicals are toxic to fish, plants and bacteria; they are often used to kill bacteria in water and as, such are detrimental to the health of the overall aquaponic ecosystem. Chlorine test kits are available, and if high levels of chlorine are detected, the water needs to be treated before being used.

The simplest method is to store the water before use, thereby allowing all the chlorine to dissipate into the atmosphere. This can take upwards of 48 hours, but can occur faster if the water is heavily aerated with air stones. Chloramines are more stable and do not off-gas as readily. If the municipality uses chloramines, it may be necessary to use chemical treatment techniques such as charcoal filtration or other dechlorinating chemicals. Even so, off-gassing is usually enough in small-scale units using municipal water. A good guideline is to never replace more than 10 percent of the water without testing and removing the chlorine first. Moreover, the quality of the water will depend on the bedrock were the initial water is sourced. Always check new sources of water for hardness levels and pH, and use acid if appropriate and necessary to maintain the pH within the optimum levels indicated above.

Filtered Water

Depending on the type of filtration (i.e. reverse osmosis or carbon filtering), filtered water will have most of the metals and ions removed, making the water very safe to use and relatively easy to manipulate. However, like rainwater, deionized water from reverse osmosis will have low hardness levels and may need to be buffered.

Water Testing

In order to maintain good water quality in aquaponic units, it is prudent to perform water tests once per week to make sure all the parameters are within the optimum levels. However, mature and seasoned aquaponic systems will have consistent water chemistry and do not need to test as often. In these cases, water testing is only needed if a problem is suspected. In addition, daily health monitoring of the fish and the plants growing in the unit will indicate if something is wrong, although this method should not be a substitution for testing the water.

Access to simple water tests are strongly recommended for every aquaponic unit. Color-coded freshwater test kits are readily available and easy to use. These kits include tests for pH, ammonia, nitrite, nitrate, GH, and KH. Each test involves adding five to ten drops of a reagent into 5 milliliters of aquaponic water; each test takes no more than five minutes to complete. Other methods include some of the meters and water testing tools referenced in the sections above or water test strips, which are inexpensive and moderately accurate (see figure 203).

The most important tests to perform weekly are pH, nitrate, carbonate hardness and water temperature, because these results will indicate whether the system is in balance. The results should be recorded

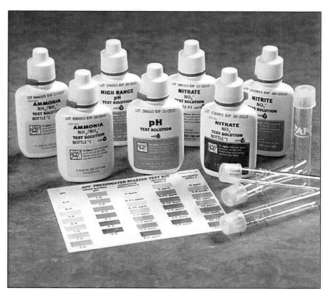

FIGURE 202.   *Rainwater Collection*

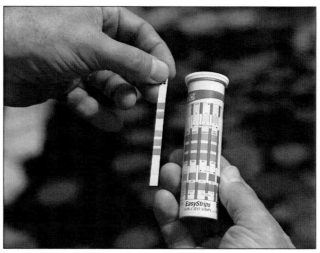

FIGURE 203.   *Water test strip kit.*

each week in a dedicated logbook so trends and changes can be monitored. Testing for ammonia and nitrite is also extremely helpful in order to diagnose problems in the system, especially in new systems or when significant changes occur, such as with a major fish harvest, or if there is increase in fish mortality. Although weekly monitoring may not be necessary in established systems, the testing can provide very strong indicators of how well the bacteria are converting the fish waste and provide feedback as the overall health of the system. Testing for ammonia and nitrate should be the first priority if any problems are observed with the fish or plants.

Summary

- Water is the life-blood of an aquaponic system. It is the medium through which plants receive their nutrients and the fish receive their oxygen. It is very important to understand water quality and basic water chemistry in order to properly manage aquaponics.

- There are five key water quality parameters for aquaponics: dissolved oxygen (DO), pH, water temperature, total nitrogen concentrations and hardness (KH). Knowing the effects of each parameter on fish, plants and bacteria is essential.

- Compromises are made for some water quality parameters to meet the needs of each organism in aquaponics.

- The target ranges for each parameter are shown in table 31.

- There are simple ways to adjust pH. Bases, and less often acids, can be added in small amounts to the water in order to increase or lower the pH, respectively. Acids and bases should always be added slowly, deliberately, and carefully. Rainwater can be alternatively used to let the system naturally lower the pH through nitrifying bacteria consuming the system's alkalinity. Calcium carbonate from limestone, seashells, or egg shells increases KH and buffers pH against the natural acidification.

- Some aspects of the water quality and water chemistry knowledge needed for aquaponics can be complicated, in particular the relationship between pH and hardness, but basic water tests are used to simplify water quality management.

- Water testing is essential to maintaining good water quality in the system. Test and record the following water quality parameters each week: pH, water temperature, nitrate and carbonate hardness. Ammonia and nitrite tests should be used especially at system start-up and if abnormal fish mortality raises toxicity concerns.

- It is important that the beginner not be intimidated or overwhelmed by the water testing and water quality management process. Everything discussed in this chapter can be easily learned. Furthermore, experience is an excellent teacher.

- A pH of 6.8 to 7 is usually a happy compromise for most fish, plants, and the good bacteria.

- Most aquaponic fish, including Tilapia, prefer dissolved oxygen levels above 6 ppm.

- All water testing results should be recorded in a dedicated logbook so trends and changes can be monitored.

TABLE 31. **Compromise of Ideal Water Quality Parameters for Fish, Plants, and Bacteria**

	TEMPERATURE	pH	AMMONIA	NITRITE	NITRATE	DO	KH
Tolerance Range	18–30 °C	6–7	< 1 mg/L	< 1 mg/L	< 5-150 mg/L	> 5 mg/L	60–140 mg/L
	64–86 °F		< 1 ppm	< 1 ppm	< 5-150 ppm	> 5 ppm	60–140 ppm

CHAPTER 28

Fish Breeding, Fish Reproduction, and Raising Your Own Crop of Fish

Breeding and Raising Fish Overview

Breeding fish successfully requires knowledge, effort, and attention to details, but it also provides many rewards. Besides the personal gratification one acquires through the process, a great deal of money can be saved, and gained, as a result. The increasing demand for fish and fish protein has resulted in widespread overfishing, increased prices, and diminishing supply. Throw in the fact that the general public is becoming more knowledgeable about our fish food supply being heavily contaminated with heavy metals (including mercury) and radioactive isotopes, it makes raising your own fish a very lucrative endeavor. Also, replenishing your aquaponic fish tank with your own bred fish, rather incurring the cost of another supply of fingerings (as well as taxes, shipping, and handling fees) can greatly reduce your operational expenses.

It is difficult to raise fish from young in an aquaponic fish tank. Using separate tanks for breeding and raising the fry is the best approach. The more conditions that are right within the tank, the greater your fish breeding success rate, although some species, such as tilapia, are quite forgiving and make fish breeding a relatively easy process.

Many fish will spawn if you place a male and female in their own tank and give them a green "spawning mop" or create a dark "pot cave". To make a pot cave, simply place a terracotta pot on its side, and then fill it approximately ¼ full with sand. This setup will work for many different species. Most will use the sand, some will use the hard, under-surface, while others will use the crevice created on the outside of the pot. Some fish require a certain speed of water current. Temperature, pH, and overall water quality are also important. For some species, the male and/or mother will need to be removed at some point in the process. Generally, fry can be fed small pieces of flakes, brine shrimp, small worms, and soaked oatmeal. Do your research and know your fish species to understand their natural habitats for determining which methods and food options best suit them.

There are already many resources readily available which provide detailed, systematic instructions on breeding and raising all aquaponic friendly fish. This book will not attempt to address all the specifics of breeding for each species. Rather, this chapter will provide an overview of what it takes to successfully breed tilapia, the most common aquaponic species. For a comprehensive understanding, and to opbtain specific instructions, along with many great ideas, I recommend that you obtain the book "Tilapia Farming" (2021, Author: David Dudley).

Although most of what is being described in this chapter, will also apply to other species, it would be prudent for you to investigate the reproduction needs of your fish species if you are not raising tilapia.

Breeding Tilapia

Tilapia are classified as either mouth brooders or substrate spawners. All tilapia are prolific breeders. With the proper environmental conditions, tilapia can easily reproduce and provide an ample fish supply for consumption and commercial success.

Mouth Brooders

Members of the Oreochromis genus are maternal mouth brooders and are a common choice for aquaponics or aquaculture. In terms of popularity, the Nile Tilapia (*O. niloticus*) is the most widely cultured tilapia, followed by Blue Tilapia (*O. aureus*), and Mozambique Tilapia (*O. mossambicus*).

The *Oreochromis* display an elaborate courtship behavior. After building a nest, the male aggressively repels other males that enter into proximity of the nest. When ready to spawn, the male displays a darkened color and leads a female to the nesting area. The fish then swim around the nest and the male will butt against the female genital area to induce egg laying. The courtship is often brief, lasting only a few minutes in many cases and seldom more than a few hours.

The female tilapia lays her eggs in pits (nests) and after fertilization by the male, the female collects the eggs in her mouth (buccal cavity) to maintain them until hatching.

Other tilapia display different mouth brooding behavior. *Sarotherodon galilaeus* are bi-parental, with both parents brooding the eggs and defending the newly hatched fish.

The male *Sarotherodon melanotheron* is the parent that performs the mouth brooding, while the female leaves the nest.

Substrate Spawners

Tilapia rendalli and *Tilapia zillii* are two popular, commercially-raised species that are substrate spawners. The male and females will build a nest and defend it together. A male and female will typically form a

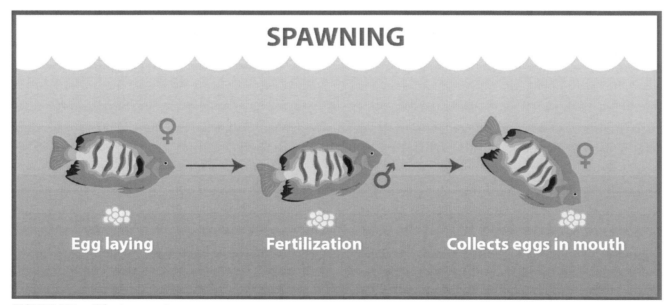

FIGURE 204.   Tilapia spawning process.

bonded-mating-pair and courtship can last up to a week, but usually takes place over several days.

Females will first lay their eggs in pits (nesting area) dug in the bottom of a lake or pond. You can simulate this condition in a tank by adding some substrate (e.g. gravel) which allows the tilapia to evacuate a nesting area. The male will then spawn and fertilize the eggs. After fertilization, the parents guard the eggs, chasing away predators and making sure proper aeration is maintained for hatching.

Frequent Breeding and Mouth Brooding

With the proper set up, at temperatures of 85°F (29°C), they can produce baby tilapia (fry) almost every week, year round. The mouth brooding and maternal protection of the fry helps to create a high survival rate. This combination of continuous production and high survival rate allows the tilapia aquaponics operator to have a constant supply of fingerlings to replace those that get big enough to eat.

Tilapia Fish Farming Stages

The process for farming tilapia includes the following stages:

(1st) Breeding, (2nd) Fry sizing, (3rd) Fingerling production, (4th) Grow-out to plate/market size, (5th) Purging, (6th) Harvesting, (7th) Processing, (8th) Packaging, (9th) Marketing, (10th) Cooking, (11th) Eating

Tilapia Breeding Fundamentals

Tilapia will reproduce profusely if adults are well fed and the young can find refuge in the tank. If hungry, the adults will cannibalize their young to some degree, but rarely will they control their own population. They prefer many other food items instead of their own young. However, non-spawning adults do have a seemingly insatiable appetite for eggs. Juveniles from previous spawns will actually be the

most cannibalistic fish in the tank. They will eat any sibling they can fit in their mouth.

One female will typically produce about 200-1,000 eggs per spawn, and she will spawn every four to five weeks or so if conditions are right. Even with low survival, that is still a lot of tilapia recruitment. In an average small system, a single female could have a tank filled to the brim with young tilapia in a relatively short period.

In large-scale tilapia farming operations, only the male population is raised, to avoid wild-spawning and eliminate the small size of females. These commercial growers use hormones to convert female fry to male fry. This practice is rarely done in most aquaponic operations, especially those that are on the small to mid-size scale.

Tilapia Breeding Made Easy

Breeding tilapias is relatively easy once you have a pair. The natural way to find a breeding pair is to raise several young tilapias together and observe them as they pair up. Feed them well, maintain water quality, provide the right conditions, and they will spawn readily.

Most tilapias are open substrate spawners who dig large pits in which the male and female will clean and prepare before laying their eggs. The female will select her spot to lay her eggs and the male will follow behind to fertilize them. The female will use her ovipositor, which is a short, wide tube that dispenses her eggs. The male uses his own ovipositor, which is longer and thinner than the female's. He uses this ovipositor to fertilize the eggs with his sperm.

Tilapia parents have the tendency to be extremely aggressive toward all other fish when spawning. If spawning several pairs in the same tank, be sure to add plenty of hiding places.

Large quantities of fry are produced in each brood. Much like many other cichlids, tilapias use their great parenting skills to protect and provide for their young. Tilapia fry grow quickly and can begin eating as soon as their egg sacs are absorbed. In just a few months, these fry will be able to produce their own young.

Tilapia Breeding Methods

A male and female tilapia pair can be separated out to have their own tank, or several pairs can be bred in the same tank, so long as there is an abundance of space for each pair to have their own territorial area.

Place a flowerpot (laying on its side) into the tank with the open end of the flowerpot facing the tank wall, about 8-inches away from the tank wall. The male will make his territory between the open end of the pot and the tank wall. This allows females who are on the other side of the flowerpot to be out of site when he is in his territory. The male tilapia claims a territory usually 2.5 times his body length in all directions that he can see from the center of his arena.

Place some pea size gravel in and around the flowerpot before adding the fish to the tank. Be sure to rinse the gravel before adding it to the tank. Make sure the tank also has the preferred water quality before adding the fish. The temperature of the water needs to be within the desired range and similar to the tank temperature where the fish are being removed from.

Tips from Commercial Tilapia Breeding Professionals

If breeding several pairs of tilapia within the same tank, it is wise to take a page out of the professional breeders playbook. Professional tilapia breeders cut the upper lip off the male with a sharp pair of scissors before adding them to the breeding tank. Pulling the upper lip out will reveal the articulation between the edge of the lip and the front area of the tilapia.

The reason for trimming his lip is that the male is very aggressive with any fish that is within the area he claims as his territory. Breeding multiple pairs of tilapia in a tank often leaves the females with nowhere to get away from the breeding efforts of the males. The constant harassment from the males can be fatal to other fish.

The flowerpot and anything else that you can add to help define his area, such as a small piece of plywood standing vertically near the base of the pot, is helpful, but it typically does not completely prevent the male tilapia from continuously chasing the females, even if they are not ready to breed. The male bites them and after so much of this, he ends up scraping a lot of skin and scales off of them. Removing the male tilapia's upper lip prevents him from causing injury to other fish, but does not interfere with his ability to breed with the females that are ready.

To perform this procedure, take the scissors while holding the male firmly (with a towel or wash cloth), then cut a line across the hinge of the upper lip through the thin membrane and the center cartilage over to the opposite hinge, making a clean cut. This cut heals quickly and the male is capable of breeding within a few minutes of being placed with the females. Once the males are trimmed, they can be placed in the tank with the females.

Breeding Tank Conditions

Automatic controls need to be set up for the breeding tank that maintains the optimal conditions for successful breeding.

1. **Lighting:** If your breeding tank is in a closed room, rather than outdoors or in a greenhouse, the lights should come on at 6 a.m. and go off at midnight. If you place the tank in a greenhouse or near a brightly lit window, then the lights should come on at 6 p.m. and go off at midnight.

2. **Heating:** Plug in an aquarium heater with a thermostat. Set the thermostat 85 to 88 degrees °F (29 to 31 degrees Celsius).

3. **Thermometer:** A thermometer needs to be installed so that the temperature of the tank water can be checked at least once a day.

4. **Oxygenation:** Plug in an air pump and attach a line to the filter and air stones, which are located

in the tank as far away as possible from where the flowerpot(s) is placed. Once a day, the air pump should be checked to ensure the bubbles are being delivered out of the top of each filter and that the air stone is properly connected to it. If the oxygen level is low, the tilapia will usually warn you in advance by rising to the surface and skittering. The filter should be taken out of the tank about every three days and washed out under running water and then put back into the tank and hooked up to the air.

Feed for Breeders

Professional tilapia breeders claim that they have better success using a type of feed for breeding that is different from that used to grow or maintain tilapia. The feed used by commercial tilapia breeders has a higher concentration of protein and vitamins, which better meets the needs of the breeders for producing healthy eggs and sperm. The feed also needs to have a higher utilization rate to reduce the amount of waste so that cleaning up after the breeders is not a constant chore.

Commercial tilapia breeders usually use a good quality salmon or trout breeder chow booster. Other commercial breeders use *Tuna Tender Vittles* cat food from *Purina*.

Feeding Process for Breeders

Feeding should be done two or three times a day. Start off using a teaspoon of feed for every ten tilapia each feed session. If all the feed is being consumed, then add a little more each feed session until you observe that there is left-over feed. This will be the threshold and the point in which you will know the correct amount of feed to use each feed session.

Breeder Transfer

As the male dances around a female and she joins in the dance, it is a good indication that they will breed soon. Once they have bred, the female will have a mouthful of eggs and will not show much interest in eating. When a female is observed in this state, take note and then in three or four days, gently remove her from the breed tank and place her in a separate tank until her eggs have developed into free-swimming fry. The best way to do this is to take two 6 by 6 inch nets and very slowly herd her into one. Gently hold the net against the side of the tank wall and bring it up over the side, transfering her immediately into a bucket with water that was taken directly from the breeder tank. Quickly and gently, transport the female into the tank exclusively for her. This is referred to as the nursery tank. The nursery tank needs to have the water at the same temperature as the breeding tank.

Leaving a female in the tank after she has bred will result in fewer eggs reaching the hatching stage. Other female adults will eat many free-swimming fry that do develop from the remaining eggs. Therefore, to obtain maximum breeding results, having a separate nursery tank very important.

If the female spills her eggs during the transfer, don't fret. Although this is not ideal, all is not lost. Catch the female, preferably with two nets, and transfer her and her eggs to the nursing tank. If she has eggs in her mouth and spits them out, simply pick them up with the net and transfer those eggs as well. Once the female and her eggs are moved, she will usually pick them up relatively soon and continue the incubation process.

Sometimes, especially with young females, the male does not properly fertilize the first brood, and the female will not swallow them because she instinctively knows that they are not developing properly. Each female incubates her eggs by slowly and continuously rolling them gently in her mouth. She can tell whether each egg is sick or dead, and then separate those eggs from healthy live eggs while swallowing any that are not right. The eggs begin development almost immediately after the female picks them up in her mouth and within 48 hours, the beginnings of eyes and tails can be seen on the eggs. By the fourth day the fry begin to resemble small fish attached to little yellow balls, which are the egg sacks.

Post-Breeding Behavior

Tilapia males in general are aggressive and territorial. To a certain extent, the female tilapia also becomes territorial for a period after breeding. Besides the obvious full mouth, the female develops a dark marking on her forehead and the vertical stripes on her body become darker when brooding eggs. She also becomes more sensitive to many things and can be upset rather easily.

Nursery Tank Management

When a female is stressed in the nursery tank, she may get overly excited and try to escape. This may cause her to spit all or part of her eggs out. The best thing, of course, is to move very slowly and gently when near the tank. The more you can do to minimize unnecessary disturbances, the better. For instance, don't play music, slam doors, clang pipes and avoid turning lights off and on unnecessarily. This is being a responsible, animal friendly operator.

Tilapia Motherly Behavior

The mother tilapia behavior changes as the young eggs develop into fry (baby fish). During the first two or three days, she simply swims around in a group with the rest of the females and young males. By the fourth or fifth day, she begins to look for a place that she can claim as her home area. During this time, she turns a darker shade on the front of her head and sometimes develops darker bands running vertically (kind of like a zebra). Scientist believe that this darker forehead is a warning signal to other tilapia and fish to stay away. It signals to other fiah that if they make the mistake of coming too close to her, she will dart at them and even bite them if she can. As the ole saying goes 'there Is nothing more dangerous than a mother protecting her young'.

By the fifth to ninth day, the fry can navigate well enough on their own to be released by the mother for brief excursions out of her territorial area. At first she lets them out for a brief swim and sucks them back into her mouth within a few minutes. By the sixth day, she allows them to feed on zooplankton, bacteria, algae, and fungal growths on the surface of plants, rocks, or tank walls. While the fry are free swimming, the mother keeps a sharp eye out for any intruders such as other fish and will aggressively chase them away if they approach the area where the fry are feeding.

If the mother perceives any danger to the fry that she cannot chase away, she will signal the fry by with a sideways wriggle of her body and an open mouth. The fry will immediately swim towards and into her mouth.

The older the fry get, the more time the mother allows them to spend outside. By the tenth day, she will no longer tend them or allow them oral sanctuary. It is also true that the older the fry are, when the mother is disturbed, the more likely she is to spit them out to fend for themselves if she feels her life is in danger.

Tilapia Mother Post Nursing Phases

Once the mother tilapia begins to allow the fry out to browse on microscopic plankton, the mother can be caught and put back into the breeder tank to breed again. However, for ethical reasons, I believe it is more appropriate to wait unto the mother and fry are more comfortable about being on their own, generally two to three weeks after birth. It is best to catch her with a net with at least 1/4-inch holes in it so as to allow any fry to escape. When picking up the mother tilapia, hold her gently and firmly with a wet towel or a cloth glove. It is also advisable to place your fingertip on her lower lip and pull downward to open her mouth to ensure she is not harboring any fry in her mouth.

If she is holding fry, continue holding her mouth open and place her back into the tank or into a large shallow pan with water from the tank and swish her forward and backward until all of the fry are washed out. You may then place her back into the breeding tank and return to the fry.

Tilapia Fry to Fingerlings

Immediately after the mother is removed from the nursing tank, fry frantically search for a hole or nook that will take the place of their mother's mouth. This behavior typically last a few hours. To be kind to your animals, and reduce their stress, place something in the nursing tank (i.e. rinsed concrete blocks with holes, thick leafless branches, etc.) a couple of days in advance of taking the mother out so that the fry can take refuge and feel secure.

Feeding can begin on their first day, but keep in mind that they will not consume large quantities of food, or some may not eat at all. Some tilapia fry may not eat the first day or two because the yolk sac egg is still showing in their own stomachs. Any feed that is not eaten by the second feeding should be taken out of the tank and disposed of. After day four, for best results, feed the fry three times a day. Continue to keep the tank as clean as possible. A tank cleaning suction device works great for cleaning the tank.

By the second or third day, the fry will swarm around the feed and gobble it up with astonishing tenacity. Feed them as much as they will eat within a fifteen-minute period. Once you know about how much they eat on an individual feeding, try to give them that much for the next two feedings that day. Each day they will eat a little more as long as the oxygen levels, temperature, pH, and water quality parameters remain within the tilapia's desirable range.

Tilapia Fry Food

The food for the fry needs to be either live food like zooplankton, brine shrimp or high protein powder of flake food such as is used for trout or salmon fry. Obviously, the closer one can stay to a healthy and organic food source, the better.

Many operators claim that the best food they have found is a diet consisting of a mixture of dried spirulina and artificial zooplankton. This type of feed can be purchased online or from most local tropical fish stores. If your local store does not carry it, you can ask them to order it for you. This approach will often enable you to acquire the feed you are after without having to incur the shipping cost.

There are also a number of other ways to feed tilapia fry. One method is to take a quart of the same food that you use for the larger tilapia and soften it in water. Next, add two eggs and blend it until it becomes soupy. Mix it with two cups of boiled water and stir-in one ounce of knox gelatin. Place the mixture into a bucket, pan, or bowl and refrigerate it until needed. When feeding it to the fry, drop a half-teaspoon into the tank for each feeding.

Moving the Fry out of the Nursing Tank

When the fry reach about 1-inch (2.54 centimeters) in length or more they can be moved into a larger growing area, such as a pond, a larger tank, or into the aquaponics fish tank.

Tilapia Production Goal

How many pounds of fish do you want to have each week? The amount of tank space you can provide for growing fish can then be designed to produce the amount of fish that you wish to harvest or eat each week. The production per week goal is usually measured by the cubic foot of growing space—defined by the size of the tank—and the type of system being used. These factors determine how many fish can be stocked.

For instance, in a small tank or a tank with a negligible water exchange, the weight of fish that can be maintained is very small (around one to two ounces of fish per cubic foot). This type of set up is precarious because the amount of delicate balance of life supporting parameters. A minor disruption of dissolved oxygen levels, a little left over feed, and/or waste generated can easily upset the water quality conditions. Therefore, fish density must be kept to a minimum to ensure life support conditions are not compromised.

If an aeration device is added, or the water can be aerated via an aquaponics media bed, a much higher density of fish can be achieved. This will enable production to be increased substantially, with up to a half pound of fish per cubic of foot water being possible.

For example, considering a tank that is 10 feet by 10 feet with 3 feet of depth is 300 cubic feet. A tank with limited aeration can only hold one ounce per cubic foot of water and would only achieve a production amount of 300 total ounces (18.75 lbs) of fish in the tank at any one time. Having this same tank integrated into an aquaponics system, producing a half-pound of fish per cubic of foot water, would result in a total tank production of 150 pounds at any one time. That is a significant difference of 131.25 lbs (59.5 kg). In a well-designed aquaponic system, the media bed serves as an effective means of eliminating waste and increasing dissolved oxygen.

Tilapia Weight Gain and Measurement

Per industry nomenclature, a standing crop is the total weight of all of the fish in a tank or pond at any chosen moment of time. This number is generally expressed in pounds per cubic foot.

It is important to note that most literature discussing the rearing, breeding, and harvesting of tilapia is based upon large commercial scale operations. These operations typically discuss tilapia in regards to larger scale measurements pertaining to ponds referenced in acre-feet or hectors. Fret not, for the oxygen required per cubic foot, the pH, dissolved oxygen parameters, temperature, feed required per cubic foot, feed conversion rates, as well as other life sustaining parameters referenced will be the same for a tank as it is for a pond. The numbers simply have to be adjusted for your tank size via of some basic arithmetic.

The growth rate of tilapia is determined by several factors. It is affected by water quality, temperature, oxygen levels, and the general health of your fish. The type of food, along with the quantities provided, is also of imperative importance. Ensuring stocking density does not exceed the optimal range is a critical factor as well.

Furthermore, it is important to choose a species, hybrid or strain, that is a good 'fit' for your particular operation and goals. Many tilapia vendors advertise strains with a super-fast growth rate. However, the purported growth rate will not be attained unless the living environment is ideal and suitable for their particular needs. The tank environment *must* be taken into account.

Mixed-Sex versus Mono-Sex Culture

When male and female tilapias are kept together, they will readily breed and produce a lot of offspring. This will hamper the growth rate of the adult fish, as they will expend a lot of energy defending their territory, and compete for food with fry and fingerlings. The three following methods are commonly utilized to prevent this from happening:

1. Harvesting the mix-sexed culture before they reach sexual maturity or soon afterwards.
2. Raising the mix-sexed culture in cages or tanks that disrupts preproduction.
3. Raising a mono-sex culture consisting of males only.

Growth Rate in Mixed-Sex Culture

In a mixed-sex tilapia culture, fish are typically harvested before they reach sexual maturity or soon afterwards. This restricted culture period makes it even more important than normal to facilitate the fish growing as quickly as possible since they have to reach their proper size within a limited time frame. It is therefore common to avoid dense stocking of mixed-sex tilapia cultures. It is also important to avoid using stunted fish since such fish will reach sexual maturity while they are still too small for the food market.

Blue Tilapia (*Oreochromis aureus*), Nile Tilapia (*Oreochromis* **niloticus**), and their hybrids are common in mixed-sex cultures since they will attain a marketable size before they commence to spawning. Species such as Mozambique Tilapia (*Oreochromis mossambicus*) and Wami Tilapia (*Oreochromis urolepis hornorum*) are avoided by most operators since they will be too small when they reach sexual maturity.

By choosing the right strain of tilapia, and providing the fish with a suitable environment and proper nutrition, it is possible to achieve a growth rate fast enough to allow fry produced in the spring to reach a marketable size by autumn in temperate regions. For a four to five month long culture period, it is common to stock one month-old fry in grow out tanks. The average weight at harvest can then be expected to be around 0.5 pounds (220 grams), when supplemental feedings with protein rich food is carried out. As stated previously, the recommended stocking density is one pound of fish per five to seven gallons of tank water (.5 kg per 20-26 liters). Therefore, for the most part, the quantity that can be raised is largely dependent upon the tank size.

Tilapia Growth Rate for All-Male Fingerlings

All male fish are grown by operators using a mono-sex cultures method, since the male tilapia grows faster

and reaches a larger size than the female. All male batches can be obtained through hybridization, hormonal treatment, or manual sexing and separation. It is important to note that none of these methods can guarantee 100 percent males in every batch. If you desire large tilapia, the amount of females in the growing unit should not exceed 4 percent. Many operators use more than one method to ensure a low degree of females in the growing unit. Predator fish of a suitable size can also be added to the growing tank to devour any offspring.

All-male tilapia cultures are often densely stocked. This decreases the individual growth rate of each fish, but it normally results in a higher yield-per-unit area. Densely stocked cultures are more susceptible to ill-health, so careful water management is critical since poor health can have a devastating effect on growth rate and lead to massive losses.

In a suitable environment with an adequate supply of nutrition, it is possible for 50-gram fingerlings to become 500-gram fishes within six months. This means an average growth rate of 2.5 grams per day. You can expect the average weight gain to be 1.5-2.0 grams/day. The culture period needs to be at least 200 days, often more, if you want to produce fish that weighs almost 500 grams. Keep in mind, that maintaining water quality at higher densities becomes more challenging.

Table 32 Below: Average production values for male mono-sex Nile and Red Tilapia in an aquaponic system. Nile Tilapia are stocked at 0.29 fish/gallon (77 fish/m3) and Red Tilapia are stocked at 0.58 fish/gallon (154 fish/m3).

TABLE 32. *Average production values for male mono-sex Nile and Red Tilapia in an aquaponic system*

HARVEST WEIGHT PER TANK (lbs)	HARVEST WEIGHT PER UNIT VOLUME ((lb/gal)	INITIAL WEIGHT (g/fish)	FINAL WEIGHT (g/fish)	SURVIVAL (%)
1,056 (480 kg)	0.51 (61.5 kg/m3)	79.2	813.8	98.3
1,212 (551 kg)	0.59 (70.7 kg/m3)	58.8	512.5	89.9

TILAPIA FARMING

HOBBYIST TO COMMERCIAL AQUACULTURE

EVERYTHING YOU NEED TO KNOW

- Different and Best Tilapia Species to Grow
- Breeding Tilapia
- Growing Tilapia
- Harvesting Tilapia
- Tilapia Characteristics
- Water Quality Parameters
- How to Maintain Water Quality
- Fish Feed Options and Recommendations
- Potential Problems and Solutions
- Water Filtration
- Tanks (Options and Recommendations)
- Ponds (Options and Recommendations)
- Tank and Pond Construction

- Tilapia Industry (America and Globally)
- Food Industry and Tilapia
- Water Testing Equipment
- Tilapia Automation Options
- Water Pumps Simplified
- Plumbing
- Waste Removal
- Growing Your Own Tilapia Feed (Duckweed, etc.)
- Tank and Pond Liners
- Tank and Pond Location Considerations
- Aquaculture Resources
- Marketing, Bartering, and Selling your Tilapia Harvest for Profit

PART VIII

Appendix

Helpful Resources

FarmYourSpace.com *Website Topics*

	"FARMYOURSPACE" WEBSITE CATEGORIES		"FARMYOURSPACE" WEBSITE CATEGORIES
1	6 Easy Bread Recipes Healthy & Homemade	25	Human Urine as Fertilizer
2	7 Reasons to Begin Aquaponics	26	Hydroponics
3	8 Reasons Why to Grow Your Own Food	27	Importance of Supporting Decentralized, Small-Scale Farming
4	8 Ways How to Make Healthy Organic Soil	28	Make your own bell siphon
5	10 loans or grants you can use to obtain property	29	Maximizing Your Space Tips
6	Animals / Poultry / Livestock	30	Money Making Ideas
7	Aquaponic Business Plans	31	Money Saving Tips
8	Aquaponic Design Plans	32	Mothballs to Keep Snakes Away
9	Backyard Aquaculture	33	Non-toxic Cleaning
10	Backyard chicken coops for different climates and budgets	34	Nutrition, Health, Organics
11	Beekeeping	35	Off-grid Living
12	Canning	36	Raised Bed Gardening Tricks
13	Clever Gardening Ideas	37	Root Cellars
14	Composting	38	SUPERFOODS You Can Grow
15	Cooking	39	Survival
16	Couple earns six figure Income	40	Surviving Big Brother & Gov't Regulations
17	Do-It-Yourself Drawings & Instructions	41	Sustainable Farming
18	Fruit & Nut Trees	42	The Many Health Benefits of Gardening
19	Gallery of Gardens (submit page)	43	Time to Reclaim our Food Independence is Now
20	Grow 25 pounds of Sweet Potatoes in a Bucket	44	Tips for starting your own Organic Garden
21	Homesteading 101	45	Traditional Gardening (New Ideas!!!)
22	How A Home Garden Produce Enough Food To Live On	46	Vertical Gardening
23	How to make your own DIY fertilizer	47	Water Conservation & Water Quality
24	How to Quickly Pickle Veggies	48	Worms (Vermiculture)

FARM YOUR SPACE

The author is creating a website **www.FarmYourSpace.com** that will have a great deal of helpful information on it, a Q&A feature where you can get your questions answered, many articles, pics and videos related to aquaponics, vertical gardening, and other helpful ideas to maximize your space; as well as improving the effectiveness and efficiency of your farming operation. I encourage you to check it out. The table above lists some of the topics FarmYourSpace.com will cover:

NOTE: Some popular aquaponic resources commonly found on the Internet are not included within the following list of resources, as the author has found that they either do not provide sound advice, lack integrity, or are not reliable enough to recommend.

THE AQUACULTURE NETWORK INFORMATION CENTER

The Aquaculture Network Information Center (AquaNIC) is gateway to the world's electronic resources in aquaculture AquaNIC is maintained at Purdue University in West Lafayette Indiana, and is supported by the Illinois-Indiana Sea Grant Program and Purdue University's Department of Animal Sciences. The AquaNIC site contains links to aquaculture sit at other state Land Grant universities, USDA sites devoted aquaculture, professional organizations, and other sites with aquaculture information. **AquaNIC can be accessed via: WWW: http://ag.ansc.purdue.edu/aquanic/**

CROPKING, INC.

CropKing, Inc., has been specializing in the business of controlled environment agriculture and hydroponics since 1982 and manufactures greenhouse structures at their facility in Lodi, OH. The company sells to both hobby and commercial growers throughout the United States as well as internationally, emphasizing quality, competitive pricing, and a full range of services to its customers. For more information visit: www.cropking.com; email: cropking@cropking.com; or call 330-302-4203; 134 West Drive, Lodi, OH 44254

PROFESSIONAL AQUACULTURE SERVICES

559 Cimarron Drive
Chico, CA 95926
PAC is operated by Tony Vaught, with over 30 years experience in production aquaculture. PAC offers a *source of fish* in their Aquaponics System Starter

Package for those establishing a new aquaponics system, consulting services and trouble-shooting consultation for system design, feeding and fish health.
Phone: (530) 343-0405
Cell: (530)-519-1051
Fax: (530) 343-0405
tvaught@proaqua.com
http://www.proaqua.com/
http://www.aquaculturedirect.com/

Aquaponics Business Plans

Two real world aquaponic business plans,
in which you can edit, are available at:

www.FarmYourSpace.com

USEFUL INTERNET WEB LINKS FOR MORE INFORMATION

- www.iasproducts.com/Main.html
(Has good prices for some aquaculture components, including auto feeders)
- www.caaquaculture.org/
(The California Aquaculture Association site)
- www.dfg.ca.gov/Aquaculture/
(California Dept. of Fish & Game site for aquaculture, permit included on disk)
- www.fish.washington.edu/wrac/
Western Regional Aquaculture Center website
- http://aqua.ucdavis.edu/index.htm
(The UC Davis Aquaculture website has a lot of publications and links)

GREENHOUSES

- *How to Build Your Own Greenhouse,* Roger Marshall, ISBN: 13-978-1-58017-587-6

SARE LEARNING CENTER

The USDA's Sustainable Agriculture Research and Education (SARE) program has funded the publication of many fine books over the years and now offers some of them as free downloadable PDFs. For example, *Building a Sustainable Business* is $17 in print but free as a download. SARE also publishes bulletins, grant project reports, and much other useful information. www.sare.org/publications/.

Note to Reader

Please visit the website **"FarmYourSpace.com"** to obtain other helpful information and post your project to help others in the community.

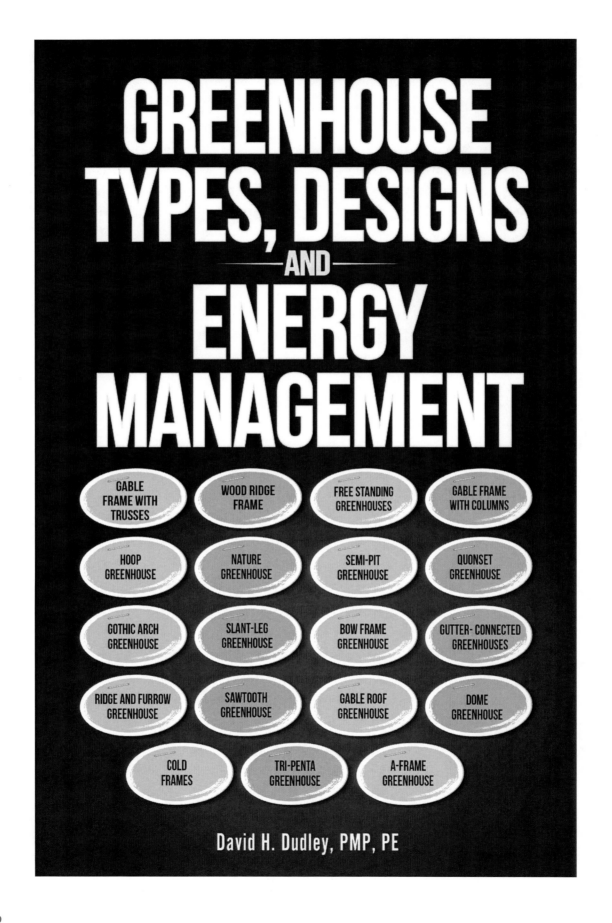

EVERYTHING YOU NEED TO KNOW ABOUT GREENHOUSES

✓ What you need to know before building a greenhouse.

✓ Things to consider before you buy a greenhouse.

✓ How to earn extra money with your greenhouse

✓ Tips for owning a hobby greenhouse.

✓ Easy plants for greenhouse starters.

✓ Watering considerations for your greenhouse.

✓ How to minimize energy cost.

✓ Things to include in your greenhouse (ergonomic tables, specialty lighting, designated spaces, etc.).

✓ Greenhouse shading.

✓ Fans, heaters, ventilation systems.

✓ Automation systems for your greenhouse.

✓ Different types of greenhouses and greenhouse materials.

Greenhouse types, construction, heating, and cooling; shading, seeds & seedlings, environmental control systems, permitting, greenhouse uses, reducing operational costs, and much more is covered in this valuable book, providing you with everything you need to know about greenhouses and achieving optimal success with your greenhouse.

AQUAPONICS

Build and Operation Manual

STEP-BY-STEP INSTRUCTIONS
400+ Pages, 200+ Helpful Images

2nd Edition

| Media/ Grow Bed Systems | NFT Systems | Raft Systems | Hybrid Systems |

David H Dudley, PMP, PE

GROW AN ABUNDANCE OF ORGANIC FOOD AND SAVE MONEY

EASY TO FOLLOW BUILD DRAWINGS

USER-FRIENDLY INSTRUCTIONS

FUN, REWARDING, AND INTERESTING TO ALL

FRESH ORGANIC PRODUCE AND PLENTIFUL HEALTHY FISH

ABUNDANCE OF FISH AND VEGETABLES THROUGHOUT THE YEAR

LOWER FOOD COST FINANCIAL REWARDS

This 400+ page user-friendly book (how-to-guide) includes:

✓ **Everything You Need to Know About Aquaponics**

✓ **How to Set-Up & Operate an Aquaponic System of Any Size**

The author, David H Dudley, PMP, PE, is a professional aquaponics consultant who has helped many individuals and organizations develop aquaponic systems. His accomplished career in aquaponics and aquaculture includes serving as the Construction Manager of the Oklahoma Aquarium, Engineering Manager of the nation's largest caviar producing company, overseeing life support systems of four large aquaculture facilities, designing a $5M aquaculture operation for white sturgeon, and Project Manager of a large fishing clinic facility for the U.S. Department of Wildlife. David also holds advanced degrees in civil engineering and nutrition/dietetics, owned a commercial nursery, and has several decades of experience in vegetable gardening. David understands every facet of aquaponics and clearly communicates aquaponics in a way that truly helps others.

www.FarmYourSpace.com

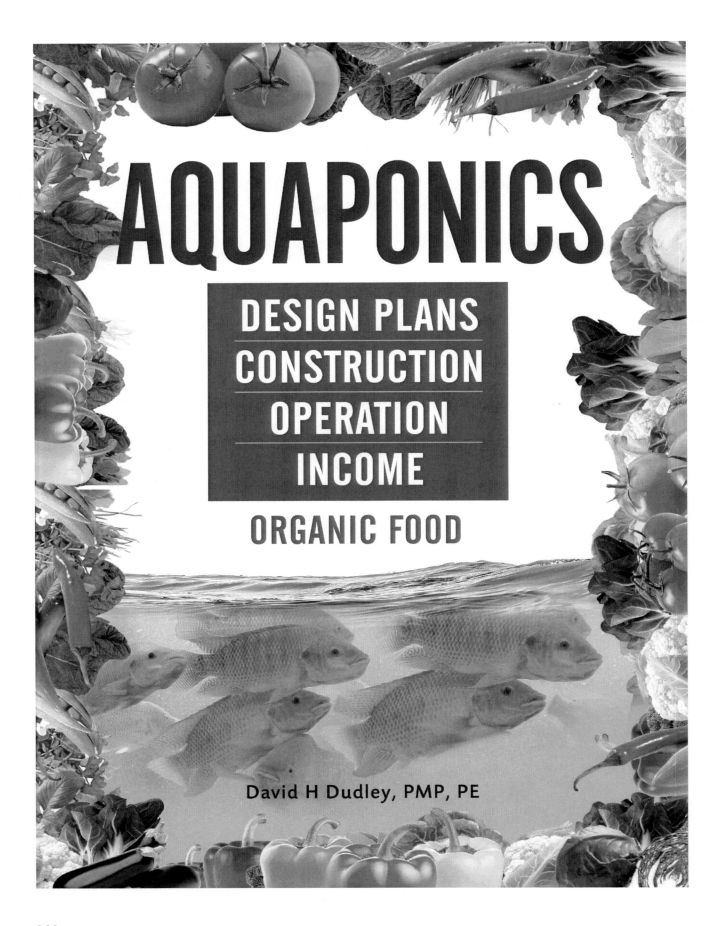

AQUAPONICS

DESIGN PLANS

CONSTRUCTION

OPERATION

INCOME

ORGANIC FOOD

David H Dudley, PMP, PE

AQUAPONICS for PROFIT

2nd Edition

EARN **EXTRA MONEY, BARTER** SURPLUS HARVEST, **PROFITABLE BUSINESS**

David H Dudley, PMP, PE

AQUAPONICS
HOW TO DO EVERYTHING
3rd Edition

FROM BACKYARD TO
PROFITABLE BUSINESS

David H Dudley, PMP, PE

Aquaponic Design Plans
Everything You Need to Know
from
Backyard to Profitable Business
4th EDITION

David H Dudley, PMP, PE

Aquaponic Design Plans, Instructions & All You Need to Know
Fresh Organic Produce and Plentiful Healthy Fish
Feed Your Family Healthy Food + Barter and/or Sell Surplus
Everything from Beginner Basics to Operating a Profitable Aquaponic Business

Easy-to-follow step-by-step instructions show you exactly how to build and successfully operate your own aquaponics system. Included is everything you need to know about Aquaponics: How to build a system, successfully maintain your system, selecting and raising the best fish species, the best way to grow lots of organic food, construction drawings, material costs, build tools needed, how you can automate your system, how you can operate off the grid, how to expand your system, breeding your own fish, most profitable plants to grow, best methods for feeding fish while reducing waste and cost, managing water quality, and so much more. Whether you are interested in aquaponics as a hobby, to grow your own healthy food, reduce your food costs, earn extra income or all of the above, this is the resource that will help you achieve those goals.

Aquaponic Design Plans
Everything You Need to Know from
Backyard to Profitable Business
4th Edition

This 600+ page book provides detailed directions to create and maintain different types of aquaponic systems of all sizes so you can consistently feed your family environmentally friendly healthy organic food and earn extra income. This valuable how-to resource consists of three important sections:

- Design Plans, Instructions & Everything You Need to Know About Aquaponics
- How to Set up & Operate different types of Aquaponic Systems of any Size
- How to Turn Aquaponics into a Profitable Venture

The author, David H Dudley, PMP, PE, is a professional aquaponics consultant who has helped many individuals and organizations develop aquaponic systems. His accomplished career in aquaponics and aquaculture includes serving as the Construction Manager of the Oklahoma Aquarium, Engineering Manager of the nation's largest caviar producing company, overseeing life support systems of four large aquaculture facilities, designing a $5M aquaculture operation for white sturgeon, and Project Manager of a large fishing clinic facility for the U.S. Department of Wildlife. David also holds advanced degrees in civil engineering and nutrition/dietetics, owned a commercial nursery, and has several decades of experience in vegetable gardening. David understands every facet of aquaponics and clearly communicates aquaponics in a way that truly helps others.

www.FarmYourSpace.com

ISBN 978-1-68489-026-2

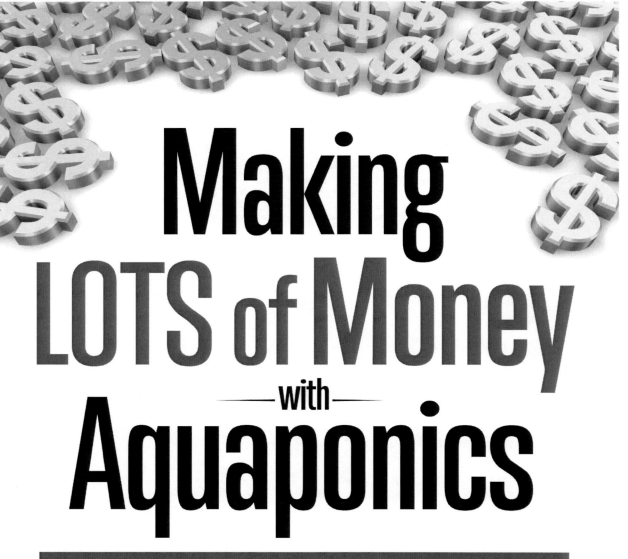

Making LOTS of Money
with
Aquaponics

Profiting *and* Bartering

David H Dudley, PMP, PE

Making LOTS of Money with Aquaponics
Profiting and Bartering

Making lots of money with an aquaponic system is easily achievable, as a side business or as full-time endeavor. This valuable resource will show you how to barter your harvest surplus and make extra money with your aquaponic system. Everything you need to create a profitable aquaponic business is also included. Lastly, this book provides you with real-world aquaponic operation economic, budget, costs, and revenue data you will need to be successful. You will learn:

- ✓ Fish species that generate the most revenue per pound.
- ✓ Vegetables that provide the highest profit margin.
- ✓ Fish species and vegetables that are in the highest demand by consumers.
- ✓ Non-vegetable plants which provide greater revenue than vegetable plants.
- ✓ Other aquatic species that can be grown in aquaponics which can generate more revenue than the commonly grown aquaponic fish species.
- ✓ Costs involved in setting-up and operating an aquaponic system.
- ✓ How to minimize your costs.
- ✓ Best places and methods for selling your fish and plant harvest.
- ✓ Regulations and legalities involved in setting-up and operating an aquaponic business.
- ✓ Best ways and places to barter your aquaponic surplus.
- ✓ How to legally label your harvest as 'organic'.
- ✓ Best approaches to having a successful aquaponics business.
- ✓ Benefit-Cost Analysis of an aquaponic operation.
- ✓ How to generate the largest profit margin.
- ✓ Which aquaponic systems — Media-Bed/Flood-and-Drain, Nutrient Film Technique (NFT), Raft System / Deep Water Culture (DWC) — are the most profitable. Pros and cons to each of these types of aquaponic systems.
- ✓ Numerous other ways in which you can earn additional revenue from your aquaponic system, beyond selling your fish and harvest.
- ✓ Time management strategies, how to obtain free labor, and much more.

WWW.FarmYourSpace.com

A portion of proceeds from the sale of this book are donated to benefit the special needs community at Country Breeze Farm. Thank you for your help.

COUNTRY BREEZE FARM

Overview

Country Breeze Farm is a holistic community with a heart that empowers persons with intellectual disabilities to live to their fullest potential with dignity and purpose. We provide exceptional housing, life-enriching programs, and loving, comprehensive care in a safe, vibrant, inclusive farm-style community.

Our residents and day clients, called Farmers, are valued as individuals. Each is important, personally known by caregivers and staff, and nurtured to live a happy and full life. Farmers live, work and socialize with their peers on the farm, and also have lots of opportunities to interact with the local community, and participate in a wide variety of activities.

Country Breeze Farm is anchored in the core values of faith, hope, love, compassion, and all care is delivered by the principles of the Golden Rule. These values become part of each Farmer, caregiver and employee and are manifest in a friendly community that is filled with remarkable and authentic joy and growth. New milestones, miracles, and expanded capabilities of the Farmers are witnessed every day; and are often celebrated in one way or another so as to provide positive reinforcement and further embolden a community team atmosphere. It's a place where residents and day clients become family with each other and staff, and a place where Country Breeze Farm becomes home.

Mission

Country Breeze Farm is a vibrant not-for-profit community for adults with cognitive disabilities, and often, other challenges. We are dedicated to enabling our residents, and day clients, to achieve their full potential, providing them and their families a future of hope. Country Breeze Farm encompasses a safe and comfortable rural environment with programs and services that enables our special farmers to be blessed with a good quality life with purpose, love, and nurturing companionship.

www.CountryBreezeFarm.org

Country Breeze Farm

Secure Campus & Facilities

Country Breeze Farm has a wide variety of facilities and infrastructure to support our special ladies and gentlemen, called Farmers. First, consider that the farm has a completely secure campus featuring a security station at the entrance and a secure perimeter fence. The security station has full gate control and provides video monitoring for anyone entering or leaving the premises.

24-Hour Video Monitoring by Staff and Loved Ones

In addition to stringent protocol and well-trained staff, video monitoring is provided at various places around the farm, which are accessible to management at all times. Some of the live video feeds can be viewed by families online.

Residential Housing with Community Areas

The living arrangements feature individualized bedrooms custom furnished for each resident according to their special needs. The open community room has tables, couches, and recliners where residents can hang out, relax, share meals or snacks, socialize, watch a show on the screen or play games. The facility is staffed 24/7, features specialized bathrooms, and safety glass throughout.

Community Building

Country Breeze Farm features a unique multi-use building with a stage that allows for worship services, cafeteria dining, indoor recreational activities, and entertainment events such as plays and musicals. The building also has a fitness center, classrooms for arts and education, administrative offices, a kitchen, a reception area, bathrooms, and maintenance and storage facilities.

Recreation & Events

Country Breeze Farm features a campus designed and filled with peaceful places, outdoor lunch & picnic areas, and more. The outdoor recreation areas include places for bocce ball, basketball, volleyball, frisbee, soccer, walking paths, fishing, paddleboats & canoeing, picnic outings, as well as places for music concerts and festivals. Indoor recreational events and activities are just as plentiful and include a fitness facility, music, as well as many other activities.

Indoor Riding Arena & Barn for Animals

Country Breeze Farms features the opportunity for Therapeutic Horseback Riding. This allows residents and day clients the opportunity to enjoy and bond with the animals. An outdoor fenced-in area is also available for riding horses and keeping goats.

Greenhouses & Aquaponics

Greenhouses and aquaponics on-site allow our special ladies and gentlemen to actively work at producing healthy food, raise fish, and grow flowers.

Outdoor Organic Farming

Healthy food production extends out to the fully functional outdoor organic gardening areas. Residents, day clients, and staff thoroughly enjoy eating the produce they grow, and the satisfaction of selling it at the Country Breeze Market.

Chicken House & Homing Pigeons

Chickens and homing pigeons provide further animal interaction. Fresh eggs and are available for our special ladies and gentlemen to eat and sell.

Environmentally Friendly Campus

Country Breeze Farms is an environmentally friendly campus. It features permeable driving and parking areas with natural filtration and buffers to mitigate stormwater runoff and pollution. Buildings are also energy efficient and contain appliances and equipment that reduce the impact on the environment. The facility emphasizes recycling, conservation, and the use of environmentally friendly products.

Programs

Country Breeze Farm encompasses a safe and comfortable environment with programs and services that enables our residents and day clients (called farmers) to be blessed with a good quality life with purpose, love, and nurturing companionship. Our around the clock qualified loving staff help our farmers discover and enjoy occupational projects, whether it be caring for the land and animals, cultivating and harvesting organic produce and flowers, helping in the office, or working in other ways on campus. Well-trained staff encourage and assist everyone so they can participate in many different activities, such as therapeutic horseback riding, exercising in the fitness facility, crafting, music program, indoor/outdoor recreational activities, excursions into town, speech/occupational therapy, and daily chores.

Country Breeze Farm

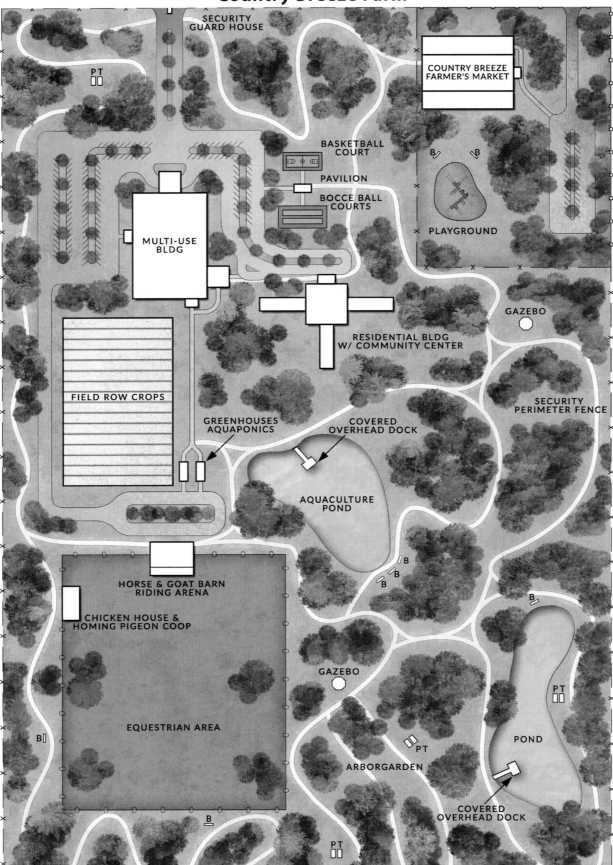

If you benefited from this book,
would you please leave me a positive
review on Amazon?
It only takes a moment.
Positive reviews are a tremendous help
to me and are greatly appreciated.

Thank you SO much!